Review of the earlier e-bool *You Believe In Magic* from S

"Unashamedly approaching its subject from the perspective of a fan, Simon Wordsworth's labour of love exudes the knowledge and enthusiasm of a lifelong aficionado but also comes with the critical distance of a specialist committed to documenting the story of its subject as comprehensively as possible.

John Sebastian's pre-Spoonful performing and recording career is presented as a prelude to the initial coming together of the band amid the lively Greenwich Village coffee house scene in 1965. From here on the two and a half year whirlwind ride that was the Spoonful's career is chronicled in detail, as are the growing tensions between Sebastian and Zalman Yanovsky and the notorious June '66 drugs bust that cost the band their hipster cred and which ultimately proved to be the beginning of the end for the outwardly fun-loving foursome.

Following Yanovsky's firing in June '67 and Sebastian's decision to walk away from the band the following year, the book focuses on the individual band members' various solo endeavours, attempted reunions and the Spoonful's official deification when they were inducted into The Rock & Roll Hall Of Fame, in 2000.

Alas, despite Wordsworth's even-handed approach for reasons best known to themselves the band have chosen to distance themselves from the book, meaning that what began life as a celebration of The Lovin' Spoonful concludes with more than a hint of frustration and a little disappointment." GRAHAME BENT.

First published in 2014 by Simon Wordsworth

Sw006j0924@blueyonder.co.uk

Do You Believe In Magic

the *almost* authorized biography of The Lovin' Spoonful

by Simon Wordsworth

TABLE OF CONTENTS

NEW FOREWORD 2014

This book should have come out 20 years ago. Political reasons, personal reasons and the fact that the entire band had issues with it are just some of the reasons why it didn't. Oh, and nobody wanted to publish it.

Rooting around my loft recently (looking for Fred Neil material for Peter Neff's upcoming biog – look out for it) I stumbled upon a box of Spoonful memories including a disc with this book on it. It got me thinking, "Hell, it's been all this time and still nobody has produced anything on The Lovin' Spoonful. Why not publish it as an e-book? No hassle"

Well I did that in January 2014 and was rather surprised at the response with almost a hundred takers at the time of writing. Then, of course, Steve Boone's memoirs were published and all of a sudden there was an actual choice to make on the Spoonful book front. Feeling that my effort was a bit slapdash and having a "moment" on seeing a picture of the group hung at The Royal Academy no less, I now have produced this second edition which brings the story up to date, with the addition of several pictures and some more research.

So here we are. Please remember that my interviews were recorded during a different era. I'm sure time has softened those hard edges but I have had no contact with any of the group for over a decade and a half so I can't be certain. Apologies to Karl Baker for not including his mammoth discography although a smaller version is online on the Spoonful's site.

Quotes from the group referring to one of the earlier drafts of this book:

"Verbose. Where are the jokes?" – ZALMAN YANOVSKY

"I thought you liked us" – JOE BUTLER

"I haven't read it yet" – JOHN SEBASTIAN

FOREWORD

Growing up in the southeast of England during the late '70s/early '80s was a frustrating and numb experience. Knowing there must be more to life and culture than what was happening around me, it was towards the past I found myself searching, in particular into the unreal world of The American Dream. The drama of Kennedy's thousand days interested me whereas I could only despise Margaret Thatcher (even then). Television like re-runs of *The Monkees* and *Saturday Night Live*, films like *One Flew Over The Cuckoo's Nest*, anything with Buster Keaton, even *Bob & Carol & Ted & Alice* seemed only to impress me and not those in and around my ever decreasing circle. Musically, while the other kids at school were into The Jam and the Two Tone stuff, I was overdosing on The Beatles. Not only their music, but the reasoning behind their ever changing appearance.

Then a guy came into my class who was a lot older but had been put down a few years. He was so articulate; it could only have been because of his attitude. He began to fascinate me with the music of The Beatles era from America; The Doors, Creedence Clearwater Revival and The Byrds. This was the stuff! In search for more of this elixir, I went into a local oldies store to discover something for *myself*. One of the first singles I picked up was solely because it looked good; The Lovin' Spoonful on *Kama Sutra* - very sixties and groovy. The "A" side, "Nashville Cats", failed to impress me but the flip, "Full Measure", excited me enough to want to discover more of this particular group's music. Finding the album *Everything Playing* was enough; their magic moved me like no music ever had. Seeing footage of the group perform "Do You Believe In Magic" thrilled me. I was hooked and, like a first love, I have never been able to let go.

Always wanting to know more, I found I couldn't uncover anything about the Spoonful (as *I* called them) without great difficulty. From the scraps on offer, I soon found out that the band had always received short shrift for their material and I couldn't believe that I was the only one who treated them with more respect than yer Herman's Hermits or Paul Revere & The Raiders. John Sebastian's songwriting during the Spoonful's brief tenure was up there with Lennon & McCartney, Brian Wilson and Ray Davies. The Spoonful were innovators and one of the first groups to retaliate to the third division acts England was sending over to America in the mid '60s.

Around the start of the nineties, older but less wiser, I started to gather material on this band that were at their peak whilst I was being born. This personal "*On The Road*" style adventure, into meeting these people to discover what went on around and within them, changed a little when I found that I was not the only one with an admiration for the Spoonful's work. It was just that I went further than most. I wasn't really committed to writing any book but what was essentially a bullshit excuse for spiritual growth became a reality through everyone around me asking, "So, when is the book coming out?" My New Year's resolution as far back as 1995 was to write what is in your hands now.

What follows is the closest you're going to get to the truth - for now. More often than not it was difficult to extract what really went on behind the scenes, and even then some of the information I did glean had to remain off the record. I realise there is a lot of "venting" from certain members of the group. This came about because nobody had ever asked the questions I wanted answered. Some of their replies I guess they regret; since the entire group saw an early draft of this book, I have had next to no contact with them bar Joe Butler. This book is *my* interpretation from the evidence I gathered. There is now a comparison for this book as in August 2014, Steve Boone released his memoirs *Hotter Than A Match Head* which is a joy to read and fills in the holes left by this book. Bravo Steve!

My hope is that this book - *Do You Believe In Magic* - becomes the bench-mark for a more studious attempt that would catapult the Spoonful into the hearts and minds of the students of this generation. My biggest wish has been for someone to take my research and turn it into a *No One Here Gets Out Alive* or *Timeless Flight* but this never happened. A while back, some people at the BBC needed help for a *Rock Family Tree* on the Greenwich Village scene and I was more than happy to pass on what I know, as I wanted to see the finished product. It is now almost fifty years since these guys first made an impression on the world. I for one would like to salute that.

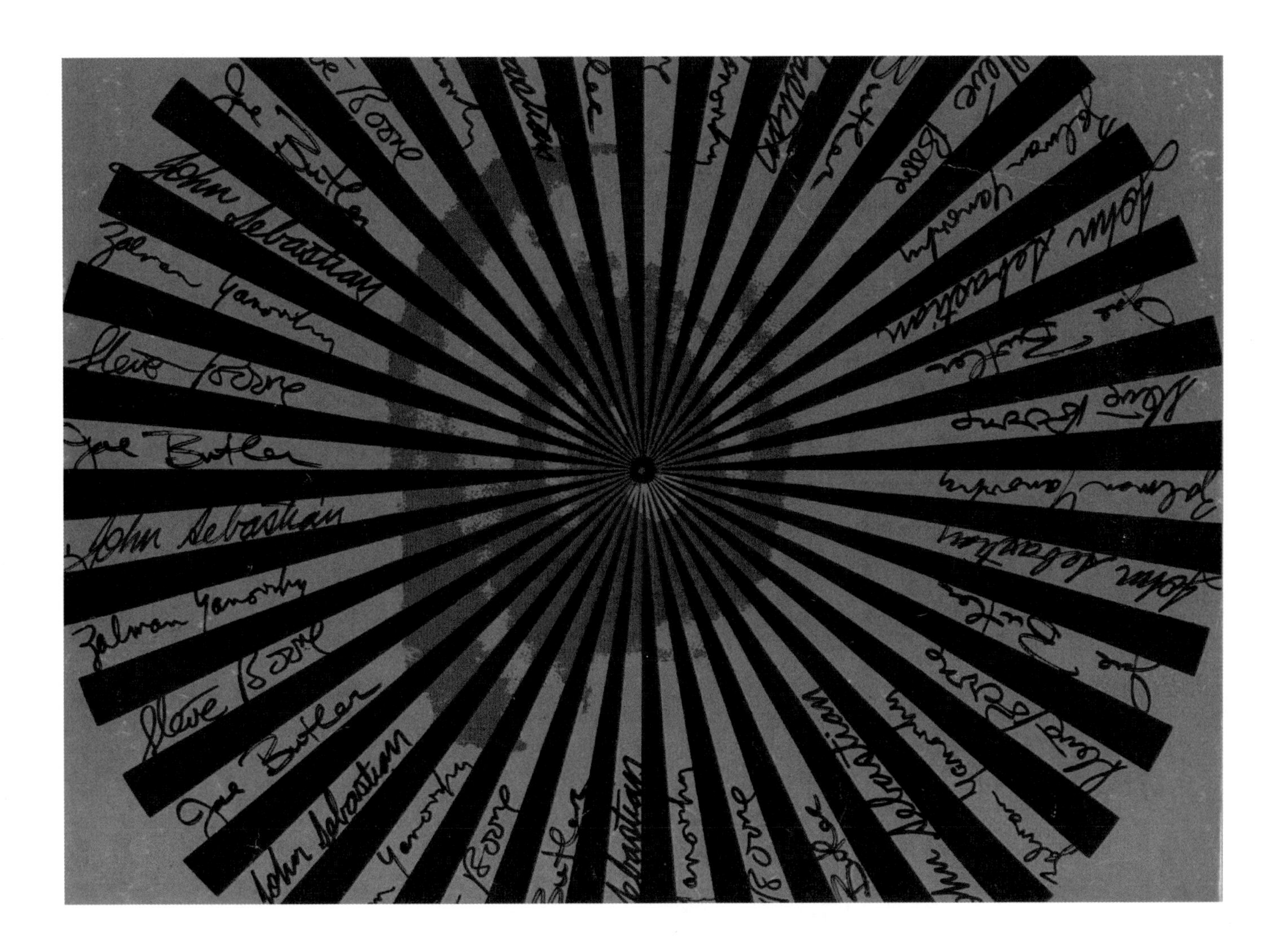

THE LOVIN' SPOONFUL

CHAPTER 1 – BLEECKER & MACDOUGAL

Clearly the inspiration for The Lovin' Spoonful came from the so called "British Invasion" of the United States in early 1964, and this cataclysmic event (in terms of the history of popular music) certainly sparked off their story. Even though the Spoonful were at their peak for only eighteen months in the mid-1960s, it would be wrong to dismiss them as a flash in the pan, as they all had extensive musical backgrounds prior to the formation of the group in early 1965.

Obviously the pivotal point for the group was its undoubted leader, John Sebastian. His individual pre-Spoonful history is far more substantial and interesting than the rest of the group put together, although it is important to chart all the Spoonful's musical roots, alongside those of their first producer: only these particular people could have created the sound of The Lovin' Spoonful.

John Benson Sebastian was born in New York City on March 17th, 1944. His father, John Sebastian Senior, was of Italian descent (his real name was Giovanni Puglese before he changed it in his twenties) and had several options for other careers, as he was a political science major, but found it impossible to ignore his first love, which was music. After studying at Haverford College, he spent two years at the Universities of Florence and Rome studying the music of Veracine, Sammartini and other early Italian composers. Sebastian Senior then went on to play the harmonica as a classical instrument, to some acclaim, in the concert halls of America and Europe.

Mark Sebastian, his second son from his wife Jane, and John's only brother, who is seven years John's junior, outlines his father's achievements: "He is widely accepted as the greatest harmonica player that ever lived, because of his ability in the classical realm. A critic described him as "The Paganini of the harmonica". He made records for several different labels including Columbia, Decca and Deutsche Grammophon, the most widely known of which is *John Sebastian Plays Bach*."

John Sebastian also appreciated and understood his father's talents: "I always call him a harmonica virtuoso, because there was really nobody that could touch him. He was a magnificent player and interpreter of classical music, but to my mind some of his real hits were things that he would write, like little four or five minute pieces." Sebastian Sr. never achieved anything like the fame of his first born, but he was a relatively modest man on the outside, as far as his namesake son remembers: "I'd say he was never really able to attain anywhere near the recognition that I, for one, always wished for him, but that never was his goal, he was a classical musician. He wanted to be a soloist, and he did that, which was the way he wanted it. Eventually, some of the great composers of the time wrote pieces for him to play. He transposed a lot of flute and violin sonatas by Bach, and he adapted a lot of classical works for the harmonica."

In a television interview, Sebastian Sr. tried to describe what particularly drew him to the harmonica, not an instrument generally recognised in the classical field: "I think that it's possibly the old thing of people who seem to have an artistic talent that they are not even aware of, that seems to just draw them towards it. I was drawn to this instrument when I was very young, and I began to hear in it a tenderness, and things that it could say, that no-one was saying with it, and I began to want to demonstrate what it could do."

For the first seven years of his life, John Sebastian lived with his parents in Greenwich Village, New York, in a musical environment; harmonicas were always lying about the house, and musical visitors included Woody Guthrie and Burl Ives. Thus it would be easy to assume that Sebastian would be keen to follow in his father's footsteps, but not so: "The harmonica was my first real instrument. I stopped playing when I was about five though, because I was frequently asked whether I was going to be like my daddy when I grew up, and that seemed like something to steer away from, even at that age."

After spending the next four years living in Italy, specifically in Rome, the family moved back to New York in the mid-1950s, to Washington Square, again in Greenwich Village. This relocation broadened Sebastian Jr.'s musical interest: "I became interested in rock 'n' roll the minute I came back from Rome at the age of 11. Alan Freed wasn't quite on the radio yet in New York, but you could hear Elvis Presley. I wouldn't say that was the full extent of my listening, because very often I was listening to four or five hours of my father practicing every day. Mom used to sing, and she was always playing Ella Fitzgerald and all those great ladies who sang in front of the big bands, and I also listened to chamber music."

The time spent away from home made the young Sebastian eager to catch up, to the extent that he absorbed all he could in a short time: "Being in Rome had thrown me out of whack with my contemporaries when I came back. I was really curious - I heard a record or two and went nuts! I was brought up a little differently from the others, since we were living in Europe. I was more of a child. Like, when I came back, there was the Brooklyn Fox (theatre). I wanted to catch up so badly; the result was I went further than anybody else." Sebastian's creative outbursts were not restricted to musical endeavours, but also to the written word. In 1954, in a copy of *Color TV Stars*, an article appeared headlined 'George Gobel Is Funny, by John Benson Sebastian, Age 10'. Alongside a passport-sized photograph of the author is a five-paragraphed testimonial to the merits of the comedian, published due to Sebastian's father being a friend of the publisher, Bill Duff.

By the time he was a teenager, Sebastian had started to play the guitar: "My first few chords were learned for some early folk song at about nine years of age, but I really didn't put it together until I was 12 or 13, when I started singing in an accapella rock 'n' roll group that we felt needed some musical accompaniment. We were called The Fearless Foursome Plus Two, and we were into Italian and Jewish rock 'n' roll, Dion & The Belmonts, The Diamonds, that sort of thing. I also began to learn Elvis Presley and Buddy Holly tunes." John Sebastian Sr. clearly recalled the change in his son's interest in music: "One day, he heard an Elvis Presley record, and one by Mississippi John Hurt, I believe. The next day, he said to me "You know dad, I really like the guitar". And I said "Well, it could be a passing phase, you're only fourteen and this might be another toy for you". I didn't want to invest too much money, so we walked down Third Avenue, where there were a lot of pawnshops, to see if we could find something for twenty or twenty five dollars. He bought that guitar, and that was the last I saw of him, studies went to blazes along with everything else. He was with that instrument all the time and he even played harmonica and I didn't know he was doing it. He'd been watching me for years, but I never taught him."

The reason that the young Sebastian felt it necessary to master this instrument away from his father was probably due to shyness. John Sebastian Sr. explained his son's behaviour thus: "I must say my son's done everything with the least amount of resistance. That means he's done everything quietly. He never came out and rather dramatically said "You know dad, whatever you say, I'm not gonna do it!" but he did what he wanted to do without my knowing it."

Sebastian's first instrument was a $12.50 Royalist which he once described as "A surprisingly good guitar, and at the time, just what I needed, because it had the really lousy sound that I was looking for!" It was soon exchanged for a more impressive Harmony Crusader, which the teenage Sebastian took to Blair Academy, where he contrived to acquire a spanking new Martin. There were many students at Blair whose parents had provided their offspring with expensive guitars, which they would subsequently lose interest in playing. This was apparently due to the scheming Sebastian, who would tune their guitars, then loosen some of the strings a little so that they would not sound as good as they had shortly before. Completely duped, one student was more than willing to sell the instrument to a beaming Sebastian. "But I was strictly amateur" he maintains. "My music was the same as every other school kid. It came out of the radio, and what I liked was essentially what was popular around 1957. Elvis was still on Sun Records and Carl Perkins, Buddy Knox and the others were coming out of Nashville with their swivel hips and guitars. Black musicians like Fats Domino and Clarence "Bullfrog" Henry were there, too, and Chuck Berry - who is the all-time heavy for the entire idiom, as far as I'm concerned."

Sebastian is almost certainly referring to 1956, by which time Presley had moved to RCA, although part of the deal which took him there was that everything he had released on Sun (plus some unreleased but completed tracks) would move with him to RCA. RCA certainly released much of this material in the mid-1950s. Carl Perkins enjoyed his only major hit, "Blue Suede Shoes", in 1956, and had minor hits in each of the next three years, although Buddy Knox enjoyed his purple period of less than nine months of fame in 1957, during which three of his singles reached the US Top 20. Fats Domino enjoyed six US hits in 1956, and eleven in 1957, and Clarence "Frogman" Henry - so called because his singing voice was said to resemble that of a bullfrog - achieved only one US pop hit in the 1950s, "Ain't Got No Home", which was released in late 1956 and was a hit in 1957. Finally Chuck Berry, who certainly was "the all-time heavy for the entire idiom" (by which Sebastian means vintage rock 'n 'roll), did marginally better chart-wise in 1957 than in 1956.

In a move that was to become familiar in his younger adult days, Sebastian began playing the guitar in earnest in an attempt to woo members of the opposite sex: "The first time I really got serious about the guitar was in pursuit of some young ladies who were interested in folk music; I guess I was about fifteen or sixteen at the time. During the course of one summer, I was busy cramming the first Joan Baez album, along with four or five others by real traditional artists such as Ma Rainey." Sebastian also started to play the blues harp when he became absorbed by the music and heard the instrument used in that style.

One Sunday morning, in mid-November, 1960, John Sebastian Sr. appeared on the TV show *Robert Herridge Presents*. His elder son had gone along with him to the rehearsals and was captivated by another guest on the show, Sam "Lightnin" Hopkins, one of the great Texas bluesmen. His style was country blues, and his playing was a mixture of free improvisation and inventiveness with an enchanting narrative style all of his own. "My father often said that was the day he saw me leave home", Sebastian recalls. "I was snowed by Lightnin' and started following him around the clubs. I had a wonderful time learning his licks, his life-style and his philosophy."

Sebastian's relationship with Hopkins was clearly the foundation on which his musical ability was built and during this period, he consumed all that he could: "I had already heard Lightnin' on record, but I was certainly not prepared for how great he was. My roommate from Blair Academy had an apartment where I lived part-time and Lightnin' ended up there because it was a place he could stay for free. I never played on stage with him, I carried his guitar and bought him gin, and that was about it. But the fact was that what Lightnin' delivered was something very exciting and very beautiful and had very little to do with me. As time went by, I was allowed to accompany him in living rooms now and then. He'd sort of nod and smile when I'd play a lick back at him, but ours was not a tight, tight relationship. He was very suspicious of most white club owners, but because I'd spent a little time with him, I think he'd gotten to know not to lump me with them, so I became somewhat his friend."

At one Village Gate gig, on the bill alongside Hopkins was a Negro baritone by the name of Valentine Pringle, a protégé of Harry Belafonte. Pringle had problems with his accompanist that night, so Sebastian, with the cockiness of youth, approached Pringle and told him his problems were over and that Sebastian himself would take over the job. Hopkins gave the nod, convincing Pringle that to hire Sebastian would be a good idea. However, Pringle was not, at the time, the be all and end all of the idiom, as Sebastian recalls: "Valentine Pringle was built like a football player, with this wonderful black baritone sound, an incredibly rich voice with a Paul Robeson-like quality. Unfortunately, it was simply a few years past the point when that kind of voice and presentation was going to make it." One of the first gigs that Sebastian played with Pringle was in Washington, DC, at a club called The Shadows. It was here that Sebastian met and befriended Cass Elliot ("There was no avoiding it, you had to love her") who was performing at the club alongside James Hendricks and Tim Rose under the name of The Big Three.

The first album on which John Sebastian appeared was Pringle's debut, *I Can Hear America Singing*, in 1963. The album also marked the recorded debut of trumpeter Hugh Masekela. The photograph of Pringle on the sleeve, alongside a testimonial from Harry Belafonte ("One of the great new voices of our generation"), shows that Sebastian's description is accurate, as it is of the voice: an incredible instrument that ranged from deep bass to high tenor. The material chosen suited this outstanding voice, as the sleeve notes confirmed; *"I Can Hear America Singing* includes a sweeping cross section of American railroad songs, folk songs, spirituals, work songs and a Pringle original, *Put Some Weight On That Line*." Although Sebastian cannot remember which songs he played on, a soon to be familiar sweet harmonica can be heard on both "Night Herding Song" and "Red Rosey Bush".

Greenwich Village in 1963 was a Mecca to any prospective folk singer. Away from the large blocks of New York, this labyrinth in downtown Manhattan symbolised the Bohemian culture with its various coffee-houses and smoke-filled basements. The Village, as it is known, enticed hundreds of would be musicians, writers and poets to its streets, in search of like-minded people to ignite their passions. For the musicians, the place to be was the park in Washington Square. Sebastian had one major advantage over his rivals and contemporaries - he already lived there: "That was a terrific advantage - I could go to get the tortellini for my mother and I'd run into all sorts of great music people."

With his liberal parents virtually allowing him to wander around locally, Sebastian had the playground to himself: "I was allowed to participate in the scene about two years before any of my contemporaries. The mere fact of going to The Village horrified most parents, but in my situation, there was no fear involved. I was there every night, five hours a night, walking those streets, walking into every single club and basket house that existed because I knew where everyone was, and that was crucial. I had the advantage of familiarity with that area: I knew which streets to go to, which clubs were just for tourists, which were reserved for jazz. There was no point in my going into them unless, of course, John Hurt was playing. It was such an ecstatic time. No doubt about it, I felt blessed." Mississippi John Hurt became a huge influence on Sebastian, and not only for his musical skills: "I would go down nightly to hear him when he was in town. I used to notice that John's audiences were always full of beautiful young college women, and here he'd be singing about oral sex, and these women would crowd around him saying "Oh isn't he cute!"

Born in 1894 in Toec, Mississippi, Hurt soon moved to Avalon in Carroll County, which remained his home for the rest of his life. A farmer (and sometimes railroad worker), Hurt was recorded in 1928. His three finger picking method and steady thumb beat gave his style of country blues a very distinctive sound. His gentle voice shone on "Stack O'Lee Blues" and the moderately erotic "Candy Man", but his recording career was brief until, in 1963, blues collector Tom Hoskins re-discovered Hurt, tracking him down using clues from Hurt's earlier song, "Avalon Blues". Although he was by then seventy years old, Hurt's voice had, if anything, improved, while his guitar playing was undiminished in its quality. He was invited to the Library Of Congress to record his repertoire, and an appearance at the Newport Folk Festival led to him playing the Greenwich Village clubs.

On his travels around The Village, Sebastian would always be seen with his guitar and wearing a holster full of harmonicas, which enabled him to play with many local musicians and eventually, with John Hurt: "I would go down nightly to hear him when he was in town. I'd been working on the same street for a while and coming in every night to play music with him backstage, then he asked me to come up on stage, and for the remaining two weeks of that engagement, I was playing every night. I was being exposed to Doc Watson, John Herald, John Hammond and many of the Village locals who were around at that time. I was getting Gary Davis licks second-and third-hand from my friends who were taking lessons from him, but I remained very focused on Mississippi John, who had this positive attitude in his music that was very important to me, as I wanted to become a songwriter."

Strange as it may seem to the outsider, this musical baptism was not enough for Sebastian and in the summer of 1963, wanderlust took over. Apparently disillusioned with his musical ability, according to close friend Fritz Richmond, Sebastian quit New York University after only a year and ventured to Marblehead, Massachusetts, to make his fortune as a sail maker. Unbeknown to Sebastian, however, was the fact that before he could get to the sail-loft, he would have to serve his apprenticeship by sanding down the bottoms of the boats. It was at this juncture that he discovered he was allergic to anti-rust paint: "It made me swell up like a balloon!" Hence a swift return to The Village.

Fate took Sebastian's hand at this point, because on the very same day that he returned home, he received a phone call from one of his folkie friends, Stefan Grossman, telling him that he was in a band and that rehearsals started that day! This was the illustrious Even Dozen Jug Band; Grossman and another group member, Peter Siegel, were collectors and performers of jug band music, which enabled an enthusiastic Sebastian to listen to a great deal of material of the genre in a short time. Blacks in the rural South developed jug band music during the Ragtime era in the early 1920s. The main instruments were guitar, banjo, washboard, mandolin, harmonica and kazoo. The genre was named after the use of an empty liquor jug, which was played by blowing air over its mouth. Notable groups and influences for Sebastian were The Memphis Jug Band and Gus Cannon & The Jug Stompers. The revival of the style during the '60s encouraged white musicians to emulate this music which had never been widely heard.

Other members of this large ensemble, not always an "even dozen" (sometimes more, sometimes less), included many soon to be celebrated folk artists such as Steve Katz (later of The Blues Project and Blood, Sweat & Tears), Joshua Rifkin (whose ragtime piano albums were highly influential in the 1970s), Maria Muldaur (then Maria D'Amato) and mandolin magician David Grisman. As most of the group were still in high school, their parents would drop them off at rehearsals and collect them later - hardly rock 'n 'roll!

Grisman told *Goldmine* magazine how it happened: "Stefan Grossman organised it. Basically, there were groups of musicians who were into different kinds of music - there was the bluegrass faction and the blues faction, and there was a label called Spivey Records, Victoria Spivey, and I guess she wanted Stefan to put together a jug band. He had friends in both camps, the bluegrass and the blues, and he organised this thing out of people that used to come to Washington Square Park and knew each other."

Maria D'Amato fell into neither of these camps. She remembered, also in *Goldmine*, why she was asked to join: "They wanted me because they said they needed some sex appeal! (Laughs). And believe me, they did. They were a bunch of pimply-faced high school kids." The self-titled album that was released turned out to be on Elektra Records due to a little artfulness, as Grisman explains: "Actually, we started rehearsing for the record, and then, in the folk world, all of a sudden the buzz was out that jug bands were going to be the next craze. Elektra Records had just hired Paul Rothchild as a producer, and he stole us from Spivey Records, basically."

Maria Muldaur hints that it could have been the lure of the dollar that turned the heads of the young group: "For making the record, we were each paid $65." Sebastian's contribution to the album was minimal, but even so, it was a foot in the door. He played harmonica (harp) on three cuts and kazoo on "Original Colossal Drag Rag". The album is very listenable and one that none of its contributors has ever regretted doing, although they all, as

Grisman put it, "had other pastures to pursue. The Even Dozen was a side thing that I got roped into. My main thing was bluegrass." The sleeve photograph portrayed the two ladies and the ten men all resplendent in their matching uniforms with blue shirts and dark waistcoats. Sitting atop the Elektra Records roof around two water tanks, the ensemble display all the instruments used to make their music. Sitting with his leg over a large metal beam is Sebastian, with his harmonicas on his hip belt, debuting the smile that would adorn many subsequent record sleeves.

The rear of the LP sleeve credits all the musicians and lists the songs on which they played, yet there is no mention of Sebastian, only one John Benson. Sebastian explained the reason for this to *Zig Zag*: "Well, that was my first ever recording on the harmonica and that was a very funny period in my life. I wasn't too sure of myself and in view of the fact that my father was a well-known harmonica player, I was scared, I suppose, because up until then, that was my first claim to fame. It's funny in retrospect but it was a weird and slightly worrying situation. I didn't want to blow it." As the group was so large, it was very hard for them to get bookings and in their entire time together, they only played four concerts, as Maria Muldaur remembers: "We played Carnegie Hall twice, the *Hootenanny* television show and some church. Those were our gigs, two of which were at Carnegie Hall!"

The only record of an Even Dozen Jug Band concert comes from the excellent sleeve notes to the album, written by Paul Nelson: "I was quite unprepared for the tremendous blend of musicianship and good fun that they presented in concert. Their daffy choreography, charming bashfulness and hilarious ad-libs on the size of their group displayed a fine sense of natural and rambunctious showmanship. Tuning presented a fantastic problem, and at one point there were thirteen musicians playing on the stage at the same time. Nobody seemed to know what was going to happen next. But the marvellous thing about all the confusion was that it worked, and worked beautifully; all the winsome bumbling and blushing produced exactly the right and genuine effect. And the music was fabulous. Whether barrelling through what is probably their best number, "The Original Colossal Drag Rag", or belting out another of their own compositions, "The Even Dozens", they had the audience (myself willingly included) in the palm of their hand."

The Even Dozen project apparently only lasted six months. The size of the group was problem enough, but when they became divided about whether to carry on as a serious or fun project, dissolution wasn't far away, and anyway, most of the band had to go back to college. A mutual familiarity with the language of the drug culture helped Sebastian to become friends with producer Paul Rothchild: "At some point in the session, he made a remark that had to do with reefer, which nobody else picked up. Afterwards I went over to him and very quietly asked him if maybe he had a little something, and we immediately started hanging out together. I was an absolute appendage of Paul's for about a year. He gave me all sorts of work as a harmonica player, and I learned a lot about making records from watching Paul work."

In that year (1963), Sebastian played on some of the best albums to emerge from the Greenwich Village folk boom. Elektra Records founder and President Jac Holzman fortunately had an ear for quality music with no apparent commercial value. By January 1964, when the Even Dozen album was released, Elektra had achieved some success and Holzman was picking what he liked from the clubs in the Village to record for his label. The first Elektra album on which Sebastian appeared as a session player was the supreme *Tear Down The Walls* by Vince Martin & Fred Neil. This came about due to a chance meeting on the streets of The Village, fondly recalled by Vince Martin: "Fred and I were going to work at The Gaslight one day and there was this young fellow walking down the street in a trench coat with a holster full of harmonicas. I recall that the dialogue went something like "Do you really play those harmonicas or do you just like to wear that?" The kid says "I play", so we told him we were working at The Gaslight and who we were and he said "Oh wow! Can I come down and play?" Well, he showed up that night and blew us off the stage! And that's how we met John Sebastian."

Sebastian joined Martin and Neil after that night, and along with Sebastian came his cohort at the time, Felix Pappalardi, who played the guitarron, a large Mexican bass guitar. Sebastian pointed Paul Rothchild in the direction of The Gaslight, as Martin recalls: "Paul Rothchild happened in and asked us if we'd like to do an album. Fred was much more truculent than me – "No, no, no, you don't need to do this, you don't need to do that", and I said "Yes, you do, we need the money!" This was 1964, and I had just got married for the first time." With all four musicians travelling down MacDougal Street to The Playhouse at night, they moved into Mastertone Recording Studios in the daytime to record what became *Tear Down The Walls*. The recording techniques may have been primitive but the end result sounded very clean, with every voice and instrument easily picked out, as Martin explains: "In those days, we're talking two track, and that's how come the music sounded so good. We had two 12-string guitars and Felix was playing guitarron and John was playing harp and it was just wonderful. It was the best singing I've ever heard, frankly, Fred and I together."

Sebastian proved more useful to Rothchild than simply as a musician: "I became somewhat of a second hand for Paul. When we were recording the Fred Neil sessions, he had the incredible editing skills and I had a really good sequential memory of the takes. He could play a take for me and I'd say "That was the third one, just before we did the good one, and it was right after the take where Freddy played the incredible guitar break, but everybody was too wiped out to actually play the tune at the end very well," and so we had to play it again. I was the guy who remembered everything, and I also learned a lot about editing from just watching Paul." Sebastian's success in the recording field brought out his self-confidence, something Joe Boyd (a friend of Rothchild's) found a little off putting, "When I first met him he was arrogant and a bit hard to take. He was justifiably confident of his abilities as a harmonica player and a bit of a show-off."

Overall, with its mixed bag of blues, folk and a special ingredient - honesty - *Tear Down The Walls* could have been the start of something but it wasn't to be. Howard Solomon, a future manager of both Martin and Neil, and at the time owner of the Cafe Au Go Go in The Village, suggests a reason why the combination only recorded the one album: "*Tear Down The Walls* was the leading edge of what the whole folk movement was about. It's just the most. Paul Rothchild produced that with Jac Holzman on Elektra, but there again, Fred never saw his royalties. He has a negative balance to this date with Elektra. He got a total of, if I remember right, $2100 for recording *Tear Down The Walls*. I mean, that's a national anthem for God's sake!" N.B. The music industry is full of such accusations, but it should be noted that not all such claims can be substantiated. It is, after all, easier for musicians to maintain that they have been ripped off than to admit that they stupidly frittered away their earnings, although undoubtedly there have also been instances where dishonesty has played a part in an artist's financial downfall.

It was during the stint at The Playhouse that Sebastian first became aware of The Beatles. "I remember walking into the Playhouse Cafe with Freddy Neil, and seeing a Beatles poster on the wall. It was a novelty - everybody was saying "Wow! What's this?" In fact, it was the lure of The Beatles that led to Sebastian meeting Zalman Yanovsky, as Sebastian recalls: "Cass Elliot introduced me to Zal Yanovsky, on the very night that The Beatles played the Ed Sullivan show for the first time (7th February, 1964). I was meeting Zal Yanovsky at Cass's house for the first time. We watched the show, then we sat down and played together for what must have been two or three hours, after which we both went to our separate corners and Cass, who was always a wonderful go-between, would keep saying to Zally "You know, he really wants to play with you", and coming back to me saying "You know, Zal loved the way you play, he really thinks you're great". I would say Cass is quite responsible for how fast our relationship grew in those early days."

Zalman Yanovsky was born in Toronto, Canada, on December 19th, 1944. Aged only eighteen months, he was kidnapped from a restaurant, only to be found five hours later down an alley. Born to Avrom, a "political cartoonist" and Dvora, both of the Jewish persuasion, Yanovsky spoke only Yiddish up to the age of five. Yanovsky, like Sebastian, grew up in a liberal, left wing household (with his sister Buba). His father was born in the Ukraine and his mother came to Canada from Poland as a child in the 1920s. Both sides of Yanovsky's family first settled in Winnipeg where Avrom's politically active parents had an involvement in the Winnipeg General Strike of 1919. In 1928 Avrom studied at the Winnipeg school of Art whilst drawing cartoons for union newspapers.

In the early 1930's Avrom moved to Toronto and studied at the Ontario College Of Art. A surviving cartoon by Avrom, that appeared in the Communist Party of Canada's newspaper, *The Worker* is a rather gruesome piece that promoted a boycott of the 1936 Olympic Games in Berlin. Titled "Winter Sports in Germany" it features an Ice hockey-playing Hitler beheading his opponent with an axe, whilst the Nazi crowd cheered. A comic-strip Avrom created was called "Major Domo", which featured an armless secret agent for the United Nations Police Force who would boot his enemies in the face! Avrom spoke it as he saw it.

Toronto had a large Jewish community and the Yanovsky house was a hub of theatre people, Communists, Socialists, religious Jews and non-religious Jews. Around 1953 young Zal was on the picket line outside the American Embassy in Toronto protesting the infamous Rosenburg case. The young Yanovsky studied at the Morris Vinchefsky School were his mother taught. His mother was also a member of Toronto's Yiddish Folk Choir, whilst his father was kept busy in Toronto's Yiddish Theatre as a set-builder and sometimes actor. When Zal was 11 his parents bought him a guitar and encouraged him to learn folk music along the lines of Woody Guthrie and Pete Seeger. Yanovsky's musical interests started with his family and blossomed around 1956/7; "My mother played the piano. I had a Roy Rogers guitar, which my parents bought for me, at one point. I never really played it - that went away. I had another guitar and took lessons for a very short period of time but I didn't practice and stopped taking the lessons. I think I started playing seriously when I was about fourteen. By and large I'm self-taught. Buddy Holly's "That'll Be The Day" was a very pivotal record, I do remember that, "Boy, is this different." I loved the guitar, it was very clean and simple, you know. I liked "Be Bop A Lula", "Suzie Q" that sort of country rockabilly stuff. I was never a big Elvis fan but I liked Scotty Moore's playing a lot."

Tragedy struck the boy not long after his coming of age, when he lost his mother to cancer, a tragic event he recalled in an early interview: "I knew she was going to die for months before she actually did. I'd see her there in her hospital bed and I'd try to be pleasant and cheerful when, inside, I knew that she was slowly slipping away and nothing could be done to help her. That was the worst part of it all - the sheer helplessness."

Obviously this traumatic loss affected Yanovsky deeply. "I was always the kid who didn't have a mother, to the other kids in school. I missed her a lot and my life seemed so empty for a long while. Something was missing from it, something that was very important - her love." Yanovsky's assumed inner torture led him to run away from home and live the life of a vagrant: "After high school, I was bumming around in various parts of Canada, sleeping on park benches, in Laundromats, and places like that. Cops would chase me away and if I gave them any lip, they'd throw me in jail for the night. Actually, I didn't mind - at least in jail I could get a good night's sleep." Yanovsky cut a pathetic figure in his two dollar Salvation Army trench coat, but he survived on the street using his initiative, a lot of cunning and some wit. He would steal the odd doughnut, but he got more joy by using his acting abilities, as he recalled: "I used to pretend I was a deaf mute, and had this card which I took around during lunchtime, when businessmen were out at the restaurants and in a good mood. They would feel sorry for me and give me a donation which I promptly used to buy food."

During Yanovsky's teens, his father sent him to Israel to work in a Kibbutz and to get a good Jewish education. Staying with his uncle, also named Zalman Yanovsky – a fervent Zionist who had emigrated from Canada to Palestine in 1931 – the young Zal studied half a day and worked half a day, six days a week. On his day off Yanovsky would busk on the streets earning: "a few sheckles playing Pete Seeger songs." The extended visit lasted around ten months before he returned to Toronto and the Laundromat where he started to give guitar lessons. As well as the Laundromat Yanovsky, "used to act as a funny kid who had a guitar around the clubs, the scene as it was" and it was through this window that he was offered a gig, playing lead guitar for a folk group called The Halifax Three, who were Richard Byrne, Pat La Croix and one Dennis Doherty. Doherty had started playing at the age of fifteen with a dance band called Peter Power; from there, he got the folk bug and joined a group called The Hepsters, then formed The Colonials with La Croix and Byrne before changing their name to The Halifax Three. When the group were playing a club on the East Coast of Canada, Doherty met Yanovsky. The latter recalled "I remember running into Denny at a bar when he was with The Colonials. Their accompanist left and I was catapulted from the dryer to the stage of the old Colonial Tavern in Toronto."

Pat La Croix remembers Yanovsky's appearance as quite disturbing: "Zal was in real bad shape, so we cut his hair and gave him a bath. This was before the dirty Rolling Stone image. Zally objected strongly, and I can see now that he was right." Yanovsky's antics also left an impression on La Croix, recalling a trip to New York: "When we played Carnegie Hall, he spent three minutes crawling over the stage looking for his guitar pick. After another concert, he climbed the roof of the Albert Hotel and began alerting the Jews of New York that the Nazis were coming: "People uf New York, the Nazis haf returned, ve are friendly people. Ze first order of the day - turn in your jewels!" Imagine that at 4 a.m...." With a little money and a few friends, Yanovsky became a very confident young man, but anyone who could live on the street must carry some scars. His sense of humour and his willingness to impress everyone was charming to an outsider, but he apparently did not switch off and could become an embarrassment.

The Halifax Three recorded three singles and two albums for Epic Records in 1963 before splitting up, when a plane in which the group was travelling crash-landed. Although nobody in the group was injured, they took this as a sign to quit, which led to Yanovsky and Doherty moving later that year to Washington, DC, where they were befriended by the owner of a club known as Max's Pipe And Drum. Max gave the pair jobs as bartenders and waiters, and allowed them to play a few interval sets, as a duo called The Noise, when other acts were headlining. This was where they met The Big Three just before they split with Tim Rose who subsequently ventured to New York to become a music publisher before enjoying some success as a solo artist. Elliott, Hendricks, Doherty and Yanovsky then started a new group, The Mugwumps, after it became clear that The Big Three, like The Halifax Three, had run its course. With new sounds coming from Merseyside, the four moved away from their folk repertoire and tried something new.

The Big Three had been managed by Roy Silver and Robert Cavallo - Cavallo owned The Shadows, a club that hired mainly folk groups and comedians, including the emerging Bill Cosby. This management duo took charge of The Mugwumps (one definition of which comes from a Native American word for someone who sits on the fence) and the group played The Shadows and various clubs in New York during its brief life. It was during one of their stays in New York that Sebastian met Yanovsky, although Yanovsky notes that the pair had previously met when Sebastian played at The Shadows with Valentine Pringle. When The Mugwumps returned to Washington, Sebastian was invited to join them, although there are suggestions that this was not entirely due to his musical skills as he had access to (according to Yanovsky), "the best grass in New York." However, Sebastian did not stay long with the Mugwumps, due to the fact that his musical bonding with Yanovsky was adversely affecting the quartet's material, and thus slowing their progress: "I was playing a blues lick at Zal, and he'd answer and play an Elmore James lick back at me, and we were having a jolly good time. But, of course, these arrangements, rather stiff that they were, were not coming off. Roy Silver will never get respect from me because he took me aside to tell me that I was fired, and I told him he was full of shit and making the big mistake. He said "Look man, I know where it's at", and I remember thinking "You'll have to realise you don't know where it's at in a few years". And sure enough...."

Sebastian returned to New York and continued with his recording sessions. Shortly afterwards, The Mugwumps followed him into town on the pretext of recording demos. They used studio musicians for the sessions, and Sebastian had to watch from the booth, infuriated that he was not allowed to join in, as the musicians hired were inadequate. In an interview recorded shortly before her death, Cass Elliot recalled the experience: "We'd played five sets the night before in a club, then driven two hundred miles to go make a demonstration tape, made the tape and then straight away turned around to get back to our gig. It wasn't really well done, we didn't get to double track it and do a lot of things we would have done."

The Mugwumps tapes were released when both The Lovin' Spoonful and The Mamas & The Papas were at their commercial peak. Cass Elliott's recollection - "That's the closest I ever got to rock 'n' roll" - was quite accurate, as the tapes give the impression of the group's transitional period. They only had enough time to put down nine tracks, a mixture of what are now rock 'n' roll/R&B standards ("Searchin'" and "You Can't Judge A Book By The Cover") and original material ("Everybody's Been Talkin'" and "Do You Know What I Mean"). The comedian Bill Cosby wrote the beautiful "Here It Is Another Day", yet the single released during The Mugwumps brief tenure, recorded for Warner Bros., paired a song by Chris "Yesterday Man" Andrews, "I'll Remember Tonight", with "I Don't Wanna Know", written by John Beecham and David Rowberry.

The top side had a taste of what was to follow with regards to its harmonies, but the voices are too far back in the mix, confronting the listener with the poor musicianship of the session players (although Yanovsky recalls that he performed all the guitar solos.) Yanovsky's totally unique vocals are first heard on these recordings where he growls through the cover versions. When all nine tracks are heard together, one can sense that The Mugwumps were a little ahead of their time. The embryo of the now familiar Mamas & Papas sound is almost audible, as is some of the wackiness that Yanovsky would contribute to the Spoonful.

After the single flopped, bookings were thin on the ground for The Mugwumps and they took what work they could, as Sebastian explains: "Roy Silver had realised that part of their audience was under-aged kids sneaking in and trying to hear the band, so he suggested that we do a show on Wednesday afternoons! It was a very forgiving audience; they were not street kids who would go "Ya, yer mothers!" That was the show that led Cass Elliot to coin the term teenyboppers - she was responsible for inventing the word." Her recollection, that "We were together nearly ten months", seems accurate, and for their final gigs, they ventured into New York City for one last time. Sebastian recalls; "The Mugwumps were all staying in the Albert Hotel and they came into town to play the Peppermint Lounge. It was the last gig, the swan song. They played a real rock 'n' roll club and went over like a lead weight. They opened up for Joey Dee & The Starliters, and here were The Mugwumps, who had been politely received by the children of the diplomats who had allowed their kids to go out, but in New York, the audience would go "Get off the stage!". They were essentially a folk group; they didn't really have the roots. Anyway, The Mugwumps died. We all sat around the Albert Hotel for six months, Denny combed his hair and Cass decided she was going off on a solo career. Zally and I were staring at each other saying "We've blown up a band, what's going to happen to Cass and Denny?", but, of course, fifteen minutes later everything was fine with Cass and Denny."

Sebastian continued to do session work throughout '64 for several Elektra acts including The Irish Ramblers, Tom Paxton and Judy Collins (on her version of Eric Andersen's "Thirsty Boots"). Another interesting album in which Sebastian became involved through his Elektra connection was similar to the Even Dozen project, with white artists covering black material. The one-off LP was called *The Blues Project* and featured musicians such as Geoff Muldaur from The Jim Kweskin Jug Band, Dave Van Ronk, Danny Kalb and Eric Von Schmidt. Sebastian was credited as one of the assisting musicians alongside Fritz Richmond and one Bob Landy - actually Bob Dylan under a fairly obvious pseudonym. Sebastian already knew Dylan: "I had become friends with him playing in basements in Greenwich Village. He and I were never on stage together or anything, but we used to run into each other and play in the back room at Gerde's" (Folk City). Dylan played piano on only one track, "Downtown Blues", with Sebastian on harp. Sebastian looks back on the album as another milestone in his career: "One of the great records from that time was the *Blues Project* album. I was there for every minute of that one. The cut I did with Eric Von Schmidt ("Blow Whistle Blow") was just wonderful right away. The whole record went that way. The minute you got into the studio, everybody was so stoked to be there that it all worked. It was real, but I wasn't too nervous. You could smoke pot in the bathroom or drink rum in the control room - take your pick." These sessions were useful for Sebastian as he was well paid, but it took a letter from his father to put him in his place. "Soon I was making $53 for a three hour session. I remember writing to my father about it. "Gee, this is great; this is what I want to do. I'm a studio musician". And he wrote me back a great letter that I remember to this day, saying "You be careful. You'll be selling it note by note, and you'll lose your soul."

Another member of the circle of musicians living in Greenwich Village in 1964 was Erik Jacobsen. He had become burned out as a performer, and had started to produce and write songs for other artists to record, as he felt this would provide him with better prospects. He was born in Chicago, on May 19th, 1940; all four of his grandparents were from Norway and both his parents had managed to find a way to get to America. Growing up the young Jacobsen had taken piano lessons, before moving to the tuba before playing the sousaphone in a concert orchestra.

His attraction to folk music was formed during his school days: "The school I was going to, I guess, was responsible for kindling and generating my interest in folk music, as, during the fifties, they held one of the first ever folk music festivals. They had Pete Seeger there, and after hearing him, I just had to get a banjo. Spurred on by that banjo plunking away on those early Kingston Trio albums, I joined a local group called The Plum Creek Boys, and when I graduated school, I took them to New York City, to see if we could make it in the big-time." The group could have been on a wild goose chase, but in true Hollywood fashion, they went to see an impresario of the burgeoning folk scene for him to assess the group's abilities, as Jacobsen recalls. "It was my intention to look up Albert Grossman. He'd come from Chicago; same as me, and he was now a big wheel in New York folk circles. Everybody said I should go and see him, because if he liked us, then we were in with a chance. Well, Al Grossman signed us up and became our manager, said that we were going to be great, and we began to tour around the country. By this time we'd renamed ourselves The Knob Lick Upper Ten Thousand - the other guys in the group were Dwain Story and Peter Childs, and we were playing country/pop bluegrass music - a rare old combination."

The unfortunately named Knob Lick Upper Ten Thousand would enjoy a fairly successful career compared with most acts of the time. They recorded two albums for Mercury Records, however, future Dylan manager Grossman got the group a $5,000 advance, then pocketed $3,500, so they only had a little time in the studio. They performed at Carnegie Hall as well as a fortnight's engagement opening for Muddy Waters in Chicago. Jacobsen's group also endured a country-wide tour called the "Hootenanny Hoot" alongside a group called The Modern Folk Quartet where he first got turned on to marijuana.

In early 1964, Jacobsen first heard The Beatles, and within an hour of first being exposed to "I Want To Hold Your Hand", he saw the writing on the wall and abandoned folk music for good. The Knob Lick Upper Ten Thousand had enjoyed some success among the college campus set, and had released a couple of albums on Mercury Records, with a third one ready to go, yet Jacobsen was prepared to leave all this as the sound of The Beatles opened his ears to what could be done: "Until then, it hadn't occurred to me to use bass and drums. Hearing The Beatles not only put loads of ideas into my head, it made me start thinking about electric folk music - it suddenly seemed so simple! Certain that my new role in music should be as a producer, arranger, discoverer, middleman and maybe publisher, I quit the group and began to look around."

The first person Jacobsen stumbled upon was none other than Tim Hardin. Needing a blues harp player to accompany Hardin, Jacobsen was introduced to Sebastian, who explained "Jacobsen and I began work when he came to me with a series of acetates of Tim Hardin (including the song "You Say You Love Me") and said "What do you think?". They were terrific, and I thought the guy was a genius. Jacobsen said "I can't get any interest from anybody, I've taken this record around to so many labels, and nobody will talk to me, they don't get it". Erik then said to me "Would you go as far as to speculate a little with me and make a record with this guy? I can shoot you a couple of bucks, but I can't pay you session fees." Remembering the words of his father, Sebastian agreed to play for Hardin and looks back on the sessions as another important event in his musical upbringing: "The Tim Hardin session was about my third or fourth session in my lifetime, and it really felt like a point of departure for me, somehow. Tim was a marvellous composer, lyricist and stylist and I learned a lot from him." Hardin had been in the Marines in the late '50s, where he had become addicted to heroin. When he first met Jacobsen, he had asked for marijuana as well as wanting to know where to score the killer drug. Drugs were not the social norm at this time in the sixties, and obtaining them involved delving into the seedier parts of The Village, as Jacobsen remembers: "Tim Hardin, John Sebastian and I were the only music business guys, in what was then the alternative world coming up, who used drugs. I mean we had to go to junkies to buy pot, there was nobody else taking it."

Jacobsen maintained Hardin's interest in songwriting by paying him $50 for every song that had two verses and a chorus. In typical cunning junkie style, Hardin would plagiarise blues material, swapping lines and verses around whilst adding some of his own ideas to make a song of his own. Hardin's vocal sound was unique, with hints of jazz, country and blues making a delightful blend that gave him an edge over most other folk artists. After an earlier attempt at signing for Columbia Records had failed due to Hardin's habits, Jacobsen planned to give him another chance, and arranged the session with Sebastian, which was recorded in November, 1964, with Felix Pappalardi assisting on bass.

Sebastian's interjections on harmonica and his rhythm guitar work impressed Jacobsen, and the sessions went well enough for them to join forces. Sebastian and Jacobsen started working together with the intention of producing hit singles, as Sebastian explains: "We were just at the beginning stages as far as rock was concerned, and we were just experimenting with material and writing. We became a duo for a while, with him on one side of the glass and me playing all the instruments on the other." Jacobsen: "Sebastian and I would sit around with the specific intention of making hits together. We'd work out a song on paper, make sure we knew exactly what we wanted, and we'd hire the cheapest studio we could, to cut a demo. He'd multi-track the guitars and sing back up, and I'd play drums maybe, then I'd try to produce, with the limited means at our disposal, a tape which would be good enough to impress an established recording artist." These tapes had an unconventional sound, as Sebastian was one of the first folk artists to try and electrify his instruments. Jacobsen claims "He was the guy, the folk musician that got the electric guitar first." However, this did not go down too well with his contemporaries, and Sebastian recalls the shocked reaction of his folkie friends, which pre-dated the Dylan uproar at the 1965 Newport Folk Festival: "This sounds really weird, but there was a point in time when me and about four other guys I knew were playing electric guitars and thumbing our noses at the folkies. There were real camps of music in those days which didn't interact, and I fell into this electric camp."

After one session with a duo called Two Guys From Boston, Jacobsen decided to call in a two musicians he had met during his days on the college campus circuit, Jerry Yester and Henry Diltz, from The Modern Folk Quartet. Jerome Alan Yester was born in Birmingham, Alabama, on January 9th, 1943, but he was raised in Joshua Tree, California. Like Sebastian, his father was a musician, and Yester, also like Sebastian, remembers that music was never forced upon him: "I used to go to gigs with him and anytime I'd talk about playing music, he would never encourage me. He never discouraged me either, but he knew it was a rough life." One Christmas, the eager young Yester was given a plastic ukulele that he promptly wore out. This was then upgraded to a guitar, and Yester was hooked: "When it came around for my time for getting out of high school, I didn't know anything else!"

Yester would go on to play in numerous groups. He started off playing guitar in dance bands at Junior High School dances, then he joined The Squires (not the group in which Neil Young played), who were the Notre Dame high school band, performing standards like "Night And Day" and "Cherry Pink And Apple Blossom White". From there he joined The Chessmen, a group comprising two saxophones, trumpet, piano and guitar, which had cardboard music stands on which a knight (from the game of chess) was stencilled. His first recordings were with a group called Tom Driscoll & The Tom Cats, and took place at Sound Enterprises in Hollywood: as Yester recalls, "It was a song called "Jungle Blues" that we did ourselves after "Tequila" came out. In the break, instead of saying 'Tequila!', our sax player stepped up and yelled 'Umgawa Bwana!'." In 1960, following the obvious failure of his first recording, Yester caught the folk bug. "Once I got into folk music, there was no more rock 'n 'roll, because it was really a change of philosophy, a change of outlook, and acoustic music became my love." The first folk group in which he played was with his older brother, Jim Yester, who was born on the 24th November 1939. Unoriginally, they called themselves either the Yester Brothers or Jim and Jerry; they sang around the Southland in local coffee houses until Jim joined the US Army, whereupon Jerry formed The Inn Group with girl singer Karol Dugan, who also played guitar, John Forsha (6 and 12 string guitar) and Yester himself on banjo. Yester missed the boat, financially, on a few occasions in his musical life, the first time as a member of The Inn Group.

Folk singer Randy Sparks had the idea of combining several folk groups into a large ensemble, and roped in The Inn Group, as Yester recalled in an interview with *Goldmine*: "We rehearsed at Randy's house in Tarzana every day for a couple of weeks, then went to Columbia Studios and made an album in the traditional two three-hour sessions." Then, as John Forsha told *Omaha Rainbow*, "We went ahead and recorded the first New Christy Minstrels album and made a wonderful deal - we got one twelfth of one per cent. Delightful! We had to sue Columbia for the royalties, which turned out to be $500 a year, which wasn't too bad." The New Christy Minstrels were intended only as a studio aggregation, but while The Inn Group were on tour, the album shot up the charts. Sparks phoned Yester, telling him to cancel everything, as Andy Williams wanted the Minstrels for his national TV show. "I told him we couldn't do that," said Yester. "We had commitments. He would have to count us out. So we ceased to be Minstrels, and they went on to sell millions of albums, and The Inn Group did nothing and broke up after about six months."

Now things get confusing. The Inn Group had been part of The New Christy Minstrels, which was a group consisting of groups as well as a few solo performers. Yester played on the first album by the Minstrels (*Presenting: The New Christy Minstrels*) although he only appears on early printings of the cover. However, someone who was on the later covers, but did not play on the record, was Larry Ramos, who joined one of the final line-ups of The Easy Riders with Frank Miller and Doug Myers. Back in 1957, when they were fronted by

Terry Gilkyson, The Easy Riders had a US Top 5 hit with "Marianne", but by 1962, Miller was the only remaining original member. Ramos left The Easy Riders to join The New Christy Minstrels and Yester took his place. Phew!

Yester regards the album, *Easy Riders*, recorded in August/September, 1962, for Epic Records, very highly. "It was produced by Don Law, who was prominent in Nashville and had produced Flatt & Scruggs. It sounded so good, and these Nashville guys knew how to record a group with two guitars, a banjo and a stand-up bass. The arrangements were a little naive in places, but ambitious - I still like it a lot." Yester then went on to join a New Christy Minstrels clone band, Les Baxter's Balladeers, who recorded a self-titled album for Reprise; Yester's voice can be clearly heard on "Sail Away Ladies". His next group was what he had been rehearsing for all his life.

The Modern Folk Quartet had stemmed from a coffee bar in Honolulu called Greensleeves, which was owned by Teheran-born Cyrus Faryar, and it was at that coffee bar that Faryar first met the other members of the MFQ, Chip Douglas (real name Douglas Farthing Hatlelid) and Henry Diltz. Yester replaced one Stan White, who had blown the group's chances of signing with Albert Grossman in 1963 by launching into a tirade about agents sucking the life-blood out of their clients. The next manager with whom they tried to sign, Herb Cohen, refused to listen to White's abuse and promptly threw him out onto the street. The group needed a replacement fast, and Yester answered the call.

The MFQ's first gig was at the 1963 Monterey Folk Festival, on the same bill as Bob Dylan. Cohen then signed them to Warner Bros., and their eponymous debut LP was released towards the end of the year. The album showed off the quartet's remarkable powerful harmonic blend and passion on a range of folk material they had adapted. As the press release stated, "There is a wide range of music here, from the vigorous to the pacific, the sober to the rollicking to the reflective." It continues, in classic press release style, "These songs are mostly unknown as this is being written. But wait a few weeks..." The group then appeared briefly in a Warner Bros. movie, *Palm Springs Weekend* starring Troy Donahue and Stephanie Powers, and with this initial boost, the quartet went on a 'Hootenanny' tour alongside Erik Jacobsen's Knob Lick Upper Ten Thousand; during which a lasting friendship was forged amid the hardships of such a tour. As the Modern Folk Quartet posed alongside Albert Grossman's Rolls Royce for the sleeve photo of their second LP, aptly titled *Changes*, in February 1964, Yester first became aware of The Beatles. As he recalls, "Three little girls, in Catholic high school uniforms, came up to us and said "Are you The Beatles?". We'd heard they were going to be on *The Ed Sullivan Show*, and we rented a motel room and after that no one got haircuts! Within a couple of months, Chip had got an electric bass, and a couple of weeks later I got an acoustic electric guitar."

After a tour of New England alongside Judy Henske, who had previously sung in The Whiskeyhill Singers with Faryar & Dave Guard, and whom Yester subsequently married, the MFQ were playing in Greenwich Village when Erik Jacobsen asked them to sing on a session, for the demo he was putting together with John Sebastian. Jacobsen had written a song called "Lady Godiva" as an imitation surfing number, as that was in vogue in the latter stages of 1964. He wanted the MFQ to sing on it, but Faryar and Douglas could not make the session, so Jacobsen put it to Sebastian that he should sing. Sebastian took some persuading, as Jacobsen recalls: "I told Sebastian, "You've got a great voice, why don't you sing on some records?", and he said "Who, me? You've got to be kidding!" You see, he was a harmonica player, an instrumentalist, and he hadn't really thought about singing. I remember him being surprised at first that I would even suggest such a thing, but I convinced him, and I got him to start writing more songs too."

Sebastian recalled the song and its lyrics to *Zig Zag*: ""Lady Godiva" had lyrics like this; 'Lady Godiva, got a '38 Ford now, Powered by a Chrysler that's stroked and bored now, She and her brother put it together, It's Omaha orange, and done in red leather'. Those were the days - we were trying to be surf types at the time. In fact, we were trying to be anything and everything." Yester remembers the session well, and also the inspiration for the song: "Everybody got into The Beach Boys when "I Get Around" came out, so it was like, "let's make a madrigal kind of sound in a rock 'n 'roll record". I guess Felix and Erik got this idea to make this hot rod record, as Erik wrote the song and Felix did the arrangement. Felix played bass, and singing in on it was me, John and Henry Diltz and an unknown bass singer." It was the bass singer who stuck in the memories of both the Yesters as Jim, now back from the army, attended the sessions and confirms what his brother remembers. "The guy was a black classical bass singer." (Yester then went on to impersonate the man's pompous manner: 'Put 'em down Laaaady Gee') "And we said, "Can you loosen it up a little, maybe sound a little more black?." Nobody can remember the name of this mystery bass singer - as Yester says, "I saw him that afternoon and I never saw him again."

Sebastian said of "Lady Godiva", "It was released somehow, but not very visibly." In fact, nobody admits to either releasing the song on Laurie Records or, not surprisingly enough, to the name of this group - Pooh & The Heffalumphs! This historic recording is impossibly difficult to find, but fortunately exists in Jerry Yester's archives, and is hilarious. The song's kitsch lyrics made it resemble "G.T.O." by Ronny & The Daytonas, and after all the fuss in getting Sebastian to sing lead, he is drowned out by Yester's voice, which is much more prominent. However, the single's B-side, "Rooty Toot", is a Sebastian original, sung by its writer in a "cutesy" style. Of this song, obviously written in the style of a Jan and Dean/Beach Boys composition, Sebastian recalled, rather disinterestedly, "I wrote that with my cousin when I was sixteen. Actually, my cousin wrote all of it", he added, in a vain attempt to disassociate himself from the song. It is easy to see why, with lyrics like 'She's my baby and I don't mean maybe.' The single provides no clue as to what was to follow, though a song that was also recorded at these sessions, yet never released, was "Warm Baby", which did not reappear until the Spoonful's second album but did show that Sebastian had the talent to write cosy love songs even at this early stage in his songwriting. Six rough mixes of the song remain in Erik Jacobsen's archive.

After the session Jacobsen saw the light: "It soon became apparent that the best vehicle for the songs and the ideas we had buzzing around our heads would be a group, and it was decided that John would develop his guitar playing and singing and we'd try to find suitable guys to play the other instruments. Ever since *A Hard Day's Night* had hit the village, everybody wanted to be in a group, so all we did was find the right people. First of all, Zal Yanovsky arrived. He was in The Mugwumps, and that's how I became involved with Bob Cavallo. With the other Mugwumps wanting to get into other scenes, we struck up a mutually satisfactory deal. So, Cavallo became the manager." The story goes that on dissolving their management deal, Cavallo took The Mugwumps and Roy Silver took Bill Cosby. Needing a rhythm section, Jacobsen pointed Sebastian and Yanovsky in the right direction: "It so happened that another of my concurrent projects - I had my fingers in a lot of pies during this stage of my career, hoping that at least one would be successful - was producing, together with Herb Cohen, New York's first Beatle

JOE BUTLER

imitators, a group called The Sellouts. Most other groups were still stuck on "Green Onions" and that sort of stuff, but these guys were into doing rank cops of Beatle tunes, and drumming with them was a guy called Joe Butler."

Joseph Campbell Butler was born in Great Neck, Long Island, New York on September 16th, 1941. His father, Joseph Sr., was the classic Irish cop who did his best, but having three daughters as well, times were hard. Butler grew up to become a tough street wise kid: "By the time I got out of grammar school, I was pretty well developed. I was physically stronger than most kids my age, because when I was five or six, my friends were eight and nine and I always kept up with them." This aggression extended to Butler becoming the school tough guy, as he told an early interviewer: "I didn't have to fight much because I had a reputation. But that's the way I was. Everything I've ever gone into has been attempted with an intense aggression to succeed - I scared the hell out of a lot of people." Butler worked throughout his high school days, taking jobs ranging from a paperboy or running a delicatessen through to being an undertaker - this job did not last too long after Butler had to help with the embalming.

Butler started his musical education quite early on in his life, as he reveals here; "My mother's claim to fame was that she had sung in a talent contest in New York and come second to Frank Sinatra. She was always singing around the house and that's where I got the taste for it. My first experience of being in a band was at grade school. I used to get three or four guys together and sing these songs, play imaginary instruments or bang on cans. It wasn't really a band just an approximation of what a band could be.

"At about twelve or thirteen, I started getting interested in guitar and drums. Eventually my father bought me a guitar from a record store but I don't think Segovia could have played it. So I gravitated towards the drums and got a set and set them up in my basement and I would play along to records for hours. I was really captivated, hypnotised and possessed by music; it was never out of my mind. Little Richard, Chuck Berry, Fats Domino, Elvis Presley, Bill Haley, Buddy Knox - these guys were in my blood and bones. I was fired in that crucible; it was not a decision that was hard to make. It's hard to understand if you've always grown up with rock 'n 'roll but I was totally possessed by music from the time I was thirteen or fourteen, so much so that my friends thought I was crazy.

"I formed a group when I was about fourteen and we used to do weddings. Part of the attraction was that we were little kids that were a band - it was a freak act! (laughs) People thought that it was neat that we were able to play these songs like "Lady Of Spain". That band progressed even up to high school where I played at the senior prom. I sang a Fabian hit of the time, "Turn Me Loose", and a couple of other songs. We were really popular. Great Neck was an interesting cultural place to grow up in, very diverse, because at one point the UN had been there. We played in black bars, Polish weddings and even garden parties.

"When I was in high school, I used to sneak into New York City and go to the Palladium on a Wednesday night to learn all the Latin dances. There you could see people like Harry Belafonte and Tito Puente. The reason I wanted to be a drummer, and the kind of drummer that I wanted to be, was down to that experience because

THE KINGSMEN
NEW DIMENSION IN
CONTEMPORARY DANCE MUSIC
VOCAL AND INSTRUMENTAL GROUP

AUDITION BY
APPOINTMENT ONLY

TELEPHONE
WESTHAMPTON 4-2358

Tito Puente would be standing up there with the girl, Abby Laine or whoever. He was that guy at the front but he also played drums. I learnt all the Latin dances there, the Mambo, the cha-cha but I couldn't tell any of my friends, it was like studying ballet, you know! However, my musical pursuits were interrupted by two rough years in the Air Force. Man, I'll tell you, that kind of life really did change me, it conditioned me to control myself."

While fulfilling his military obligations as a weather technician in Texas, Butler took up boxing. In the Butler scrapbook is a picture of a proud Butler standing over a fallen fighter. Maybe the fact that the other boxer got up to knock Butler down had something to do with his change of heart, but he managed to divert his aggression: "Between college and the Air Force, I learned to add up and to kill people, but I decided I didn't want to do either, so I played the drums a lot... and played them loud." In 1961, on official leave, Butler formed The Kingsmen, an eight piece twist band, with school or Air Force friends Sonny Botari (guitar), Seth Conners (vocals), Clay Sonia (bass), King Charles (saxophone), Jan Buchner (drums), and with Skip Boone and his younger brother, Steve, on guitars.

John Stephen Boone, apparently a relation to Daniel Boone, was born in Camp Lejeune, North Carolina on September 23rd, 1943. During his youth, Boone's parents, Emmett and Mary, owned a resort in the wilds of Pennsylvania and this restricted the young Steve from forming lasting friendships: "Outside of the little community, it was like a wilderness, so I didn't have too many good friends. All my friendships lasted two days." After a six-month period in Florida, where Boone first took an interest in sailing and speedboats, the family settled in Long Island. He wanted to become a naval aviator for his military service, but his dreams were shattered on June 20th, 1960, as he distinctly remembers: "I remember what happened very clearly. My friend, Bob Shank, and I were out at the bowling alley in East Hampton. It was the last night of school and we were celebrating getting out of the eleventh grade. It was about midnight and one of our classmates, Jim Harkness, came up in his car and said, "I'll take you home". He had a reputation for being a drinker, but we went ahead anyway. His parents had bought him a big Tri-Powered Chevy, a very fast car. We dropped Bob at his house and headed into town, down a long road that was well known to be dangerous, and he went very fast, even though it was foggy. We never made the corner and hit a tree head on at about sixty miles an hour. The only thing I remember is a white flash." Typically, the driver was barely injured, with just a scratch to his head, but Boone came off a lot worse: "When the ambulance got to the accident, they thought I was dead and treated Jim. Then one of them saw me moving and said, "Hey! He's still alive". They took me to the hospital - I broke my right leg in the calf area and the lower fore leg, broke my hip, pelvis, and my shoulder, dislocated my arm and got concussion."

Boone left the hospital in late August 1960, to go home, yet he was in a cast and had to use crutches for over a year. During this period of convalescence, Steve's older brother, Skip, put a guitar in his sibling's hands and taught him a few chords. In the spring of 1961, Steve and Skip met up with Butler and joined The Kingsmen (not to be confused with the "Louie, Louie" group), who were a loose ensemble as Boone explains: "The Kingsmen varied in numbers from four to about seven or eight. It varied depending on the jobs we had. They had two drummers in some incarnations and sometimes Joe would be singing in front, and then play a couple of numbers on drums."

Boone was still at school and had to be smuggled onto the Air Force base on Long Island when the group played gigs there. However, his stay in the group was short-lived, and after he graduated, he left The Kingsmen, probably after a fight with his brother. Boone then switched to bass and formed The Steve Boone Blues Band, which included Ricky Pearsol (nobody can recall any other members), which "wasn't the world's greatest band." The group was only together through the summer of 1962, but it was all experience: "We only played one or two jobs. One of them was at Eastport, in the basement of an ice cream stand, and we also played a couple of nights at Gene's Famous Sandwiches, which was a Long Island institution. It was very popular with Broadway stars vacating in the Hamptons, they would always stop at Gene's Sandwiches."

Boone returned to The Kingsmen in the summer of 1963. They were playing mainly at the Palm Terrace between Riverhead and East Hampton at this time, still on Long Island. The group was the first to put dances on in Springs, the arty colony where Jackson Pollock lived, and other gigs included The Surfing Sand in Montauk and The Cottage Inn in East Hampton. Having a black saxophonist in 1963 in America was a brave move by The Kingsmen, and they used King Charles's colour to their advantage, as Boone recalls: "He could get us work, he knew all these people. The Cottage Inn was a black nightclub and it was most famous because a lot of big R&B stars would play out there. It was a very small place, but James Brown, Ike & Tina Turner and Bo Diddley all played there. Even in those days, the black acts could only work for black audiences. We were a white band (almost), and the reason we were popular (with the black owners) was that we could attract these white socialites with money to come into their night clubs, so they liked us - they thought we were the greatest."

As the demand for gigs increased, music became full-time for The Kingsmen and they travelled to New York, to 720 7th Avenue, as Steve Boone vaguely remembers: "In 1963 or early '64, we cut four songs at Dick Charles's Studios on 7th Avenue. Two of them were originals and two were covers." Details of these recordings are very sketchy and from piecing together recollection from three of the Kingsmen, the two covers were "You Belong To Me" (a 1962 hit for The Duprees) and "Unchained Melody" (recorded by Al Hibbler in 1955). One of the originals, which were both written by Skip Boone, was "Second Time I Fell In Love", but no one can recall the other title. These first recordings of Butler and Boone exist only on acetate in Joe Butler's collection - somewhere. "Unchained Melody" includes contributions from a session singer, as Butler recalls: "Don Johnson was a friend of mine from the Air Force - he happened to be African-American and sang very occasionally with us for fun."

The idea behind the recording sessions was an attempt to get signed to a label, but when this didn't happen, the group split up. The nucleus of The Kingsmen (Skip Boone, Jerry Angus, Marshall O'Connell and Butler) became The Sellouts, with Herb Cohen as their manager, and moved to Greenwich Village, as Butler recalls: "We came to New York and played in these places - I slept on the stages, and my pillow was in my bass drum. Then you'd try to find somebody to take you home. It was hippy dippy time - not to go out and sleep with somebody - but you'd meet somebody you want to go to bed with. In those days, you could do things like that and we did, just very casually. I didn't have a great trauma; I could have run back to Great Neck, so it was not a big Kiplingesque adventure, by any means." The Sellouts played Fred Neil and Beatles tunes in clubs in The Village to tourists, who took their chances, as Butler remembers: "The Sellouts worked in a place called The Playhouse that could seat twenty to thirty people. The owners would feed them Coke and rum extract and get their cover charge for the drinks. We would then leave the stage for forty five minutes, while they cajoled and bullied the people who had paid their $10 cover and forced them to leave, even at knife-point. Then we would go on again. There were other

The
$ELLO

places where we would play forty minutes on and twenty off, six and seven sets a night." Joe Marra, who owned the Night Owl Cafe in The Village recalls another trick the club owners would employ: "One of the funniest things these little clubs did, was they had a $5 cover charge on the menu in red ink. Now they all had red lights, so you'd be in this club and you'd have a coffee and the guy would say, "That's five bucks", and they'd take you outside, under a normal light, and sure enough it would be $5. Of course, you didn't see it inside the club!"

During one of their marathon stints in The Village, The Sellouts managed to impress one man, Erik Jacobsen: "That was the first group that actually showed up as a little rock group in Greenwich Village, they were the first rock group. They were unabashedly imitating The Beatles, and I made a little deal with them and Herbie Cohen, and we rehearsed some numbers." One track from these sessions still exists on tape in Jerry Yester's archives, with Jacobsen counting in the take for a mono mix. Written and sung by Joe Butler, "I'll Tell You Who I Love" is a superb slice of '60s pop. The lyrics may be a bit insipid, but the excellent guitar sound of Skip Boone's Les Paul is reminiscent of The Searchers in their prime, while Butler's confident vocals are an indication of how good The Sellouts must have been. The unavailability of the second track, "Laugh Of A Clown", remains a frustration.

The now classic line-up of drums, bass, lead and rhythm guitars was new to Jacobsen, who soon took Sebastian and Yanovsky to check out The Sellouts, an occasion which Butler laughingly remembers: "Yes, they used to come up and steal all my secrets - it's true!" Sebastian also remembers that initial meeting: "We were cruising round The Village and we went to see a band called The Sellouts, who had an echo machine, which we thought was really hip. Nobody had heard of slap echo at this point in time, or any other kind of processing. It was cool, and I fell in love with Skip's guitar. Skip and I got talking, and I told him what a great guitar it was, and we said we were looking for a bass player. Skip said, "My brother plays bass, but he's riding around Europe on a motorcycle right now", and I remember Zally and I going off to one side and saying, "That sounds right, here's a guy that's trying to find out a bit about the world, this could be the right kinda guy", so we rented out a place where we could have an audition."

Boone's adventurous trek round Europe began when he turned twenty one and received a settlement from his car accident of some $10,000. With his best friend, Peter Davey ("We were like brothers"), an heir to a fortune which enabled him to match Boone's spending power, the pair flew to England in September 1964. They bought motorcycles, were ripped off in the strip clubs of Soho, then ventured to France, where they began a memorable two months in mainland Europe, visiting almost every major city. Highlights of the trip included seeing a fantastic group in Copenhagen, Denmark, who played American rock 'n' roll, but could not speak the language, riding on the banking of the Monza racing circuit in Italy while Phil Hill, Roy Salvadori, Bruce McLaren and the Ford team were testing Ford GT40s, a trip to the Ferrari factory in Maranello, where Boone chatted to Michael Parkes, the works driver for Ferrari, and bumping into Boone's high school girlfriend at the US embassy in Rome, on the night of Lyndon Johnson's election victory on November 3rd. The money ran out in Barcelona, Spain, where the pair shipped their bikes home and got back to Long Island for Christmas 1964.

After visiting his brother on his return, Boone revealed what The Sellouts were up to at this time: "When I came back from Europe, they had already moved to Greenwich Village, and I went to visit them at Trudy Heller's on 9th

Street. They did songs like "Shout" and a lot of twist stuff, like "Peppermint Twist" by Joey Dee & The Starliters, who were one of the hottest bands around. What The Sellouts had done was gone from being a twist band to playing English stuff, Beatles, Rolling Stones and early Moody Blues, and they might even have had some originals." Butler remembers The Sellouts' stage presentation: "The drums were set up high, and behind them was this big rotating polarised wheel and this animated thing appeared to show what looked like fireworks constantly going off from my head with these little dots of light, and Jerry Angus could do back flips while playing bass, it was amazing."

Boone was told that Sebastian and Yanovsky were interested in meeting him, and went to his audition, but before he even played a note, he was already in the group. According to Sebastian, "When he walked in, Zally and I were standing at the far end of the hall, and when we saw this guy - real tall, red hair and just bones - he looked like Mr. America, so we knew right away that he was our guy." Sebastian had already turned down another potential group member - Stephen Stills. "I really wanted to play bass in Sebastian's rock 'n 'roll band", Stills told Sounds in 1971, "But, alas, they passed me up." Neil Young also, as Young told John Einarson, "I desperately wanted to be in The Lovin' Spoonful. I was living in a hovel on the Lower East Side and I was watching this group getting together. They didn't know I could play electric guitar, bass and drums. I wanted to be their bass player but they wouldn't give me the time of day. To them, I was just a kid wandering around the village."

Boone remembers the audition that changed his life: "I played for them in a little club called the Music Room, where we jammed. When John, Zally and I got together, we instantly clicked, we got along fine and it was great. Then they asked me, "Do you know any drummers?" Jan Buchner, who had been in the Kingsmen at one point, was out on Long Island. I knew him and could work with him, so I said, "Let's go out and rehearse with him". We went out to Bridgehampton and rented this place called the Bull's Head Inn Hotel, that was closed for the season, and rehearsed in it for the month of January (1965). We worked up three or four originals of John's songs and about five or six of Chuck Berry's, that kind of stuff." During this period of rehearsal, Sebastian received a call from Bob Dylan that almost finished the group before it had started, as he explains: "I picked up the telephone and the voice on the end says "Hi John, this is Bob. Listen, I'm going out on the road pretty soon and I was wondering if you wanted to be in the band". I had to put my hand over the phone and just stand in the phone booth for a minute and say "What is happening?" You have to remember that at this point in time there was no more important writer in the United States than Bob Dylan and he was asking me to come and play with him, and I'm there rehearsing a completely unknown, unproven band. I watched incredulously as my mouth said "Gee, I'm really sorry, I can't do it. I've committed to playing in this band and we're working up tunes and I can't just walk out on rehearsals now". And so that's how I never went to work with Bob Dylan."

What Sebastian did agree to, however, was to play on the sessions for Dylan's new LP, which would turn out to be the seminal *Bringing It All Back Home*. The only snag was that Dylan wanted an electric bass player, and this was an instrument with which Sebastian was hardly familiar: "Well, I wasn't about to tell anybody that I didn't play much bass. He'd probably seen me play bass once because nobody else did. It was basically, "Play bass until the bass player gets here". I still don't know to this day which tunes, if any, actually remain of the stuff I played on. I suspect it all was overdubbed by Harvey Brooks, as it probably should have been."

In reality, Steve Boone also played on the album; it transpires that Sebastian needed a lift to the sessions and that Boone obliged. Boone went in with Sebastian and recalls "John couldn't cut the parts, so Bob said, "Well, you're a bass player, why don't you try it?" and I played on four songs - "Maggie's Farm", "Love Minus Zero", "On The Road Again" and one other." To confirm Boone's claims, a photo is included in Daniel Kramer's book, *Bob Dylan*, showing Boone, albeit from the rear, with bass guitar in hand, taking instructions from Dylan. To confuse things even more, the book also includes two photographs of Sebastian alongside Dylan - playing bass!

Previously, on his way home from the 1963 Philadelphia Folk Festival, where Sebastian had backed up Mississippi John Hurt, the idea of the name Lovin' Spoonful came into being. It was suggested to Sebastian by Fritz Richmond from The Jim Kweskin Jug Band while the pair had been discussing both a name for a band and Mississippi John Hurt. Richmond's idea stemmed from a line from a Hurt song, "Coffee Blues". Sebastian clicked to the idea: "I immediately liked the name because it had a little mystery, and it also had this kind of fly in your face warm, fuzzy feeling that was so unfashionable that it was going to work." A journalist once put it to Sebastian what exactly it referred to and he replied "Okay, it is a reference to cunnilingus. It comes from a song by Mississippi John Hurt called "Coffee Blues". And that's it." Sebastian did elaborate further, later in the same interview, when asked if "Coffee Blues" was one of Hurt's more famous songs. "Yes, it was a big crowd-pleaser because of his particularly innocent delivery and his guileless way of presenting it. His audience was frequently filled with beautiful college women - he always had appeal for the women in the audience. He would usually start by taking a sip from a coffee cup and say "I always have my cup of Maxwell House coffee, 'cause it's good to the very last drop." And then he'd drink, and you knew instantly it was Scotch. Then he'd resume playing, and with great innocence, play this song that went 'I love my baby by the lovin' spoonful', and everybody would know what he was referring to. It was a set piece for him, and that's why it was memorable."

The name was run by Steve Boone on the first meeting; he thought it was fine, so it stuck from then on. After a small rehearsal period, The Lovin' Spoonful played their first gigs, as recalled by Boone: "We did a couple of mini-gigs that were not in a club or anything. I can't remember where they were but they didn't work out all good and Jan (Buchner) was obviously not fitting in."

With Buchner still in the group, the management team went to West 3rd Street in the Village to see Joe Marra, who was the owner of the Night Owl Cafe, as named by Fred Neil, to try to get a gig for their unknown band. Marra remembers this day well: "When Cavallo and Jacobsen came to me, we decided we were going to have this big experiment with rock' n' roll music. In preparation for the show, we moved the stage to a different place and rewired the lights. Music was just starting to change from folk to rock and the first rock band I hired was the Spoonful. The only act I had used before that, that played electrically, was Fred Neil. People would fight to play with him: you'd only hire one but you'd end up with a dozen. He played for me in '64, but up until that time, basically, everybody had been folk. Now I had known John - John had played (with Hardin and Neil), but John hadn't sung. The Spoonful at the Night Owl was the first time he had gotten on-stage and sung with a band."

The story continues in an article from a *16 Magazine* feature titled "The Desperate Days Of The Lovin' Spoonful", written by Marra in the '60s, that exudes his larger than life character and playfulness: "Opening night the word was out, and everybody in the Village came to the Night Owl to see The Lovin' Spoonful. There was a high moment of excitement when the boys began to tune up. Finally, they broke into their first number and when I say 'broke', I mean it. They broke glasses, windowpanes and eardrums. Like they were so impossibly loud that there wasn't enough room for their sound and the audience in my tiny little club. So, guess what? The audience left. Man, they weren't even polite. John Sebastian sang incredibly softly. As much as you COULD hear the band was as much as you COULDN'T hear John. They did a six number set and by the time they finished, they'd cleared the place out! Listen, even I ran out. But my mother liked them. Yes, she did - and she sat there grinning and clapping through the whole ordeal."

For this first show Marra had hired a folk singer, Gil Silver, and compere Al Mamlet, as well as five waitresses for his tiny coffee-house that had a legal capacity, somehow, of 135. Erik Jacobsen owns a tape of this very gig: "It's so interesting - you hear Joe Marra, who says, "Ladies and gentlemen, it is the very great pleasure of the Night Owl Cafe to present, on bass, Steve Boone, on guitar, Zal Yanovsky, lead vocals John Sebastian and Jan such and such on drums - let's hear it for The Lovin' Spoonful!" And you hear like literally three people clapping. (On the tape) there's all their first songs, they stop in the middle, Zal trying to tune between each one is just total agony, you hear him strum the guitar and it will be kind of in tune and then he'll start tuning and it gets worse and worse and worse. There's some funny things on there, the electricity went out in the middle of the set and John never did have a voice that projected that far, it's kinda funny."

After two weeks Marra could take no more. "The last night, we were there on a Sunday on a winter night in February and we took seven dollars and fifteen cents for a three act show" (The *16 Magazine* feature claims seven dollars and eighty five cents, a figure Marra refutes!) "At the time I told Bob, "These guys don't make it", and we let them go." Marra to this day is upset by his necessary duty: "You know, it was a tough New York winter with snow on the ground and it was hard but the night club business is real tough. But the band - at the end, even their girlfriends weren't there! They really didn't make it, they didn't have what they needed, they needed Joe Butler." Buchner was fired and went into the Pete Best file. Boone recalls that it was not solely musical reasons that necessitated the drummer's departure: "At some point, everybody saw that Jan was not working out. He had blonde hair and it was real short. He didn't have the long hair and he didn't fit in. His style was totally old '50s style; he wasn't a hippy at all. I mean, he didn't even care for The Beatles!"

The Sellouts had acquired a contract with Mercury Records, thanks to Herb Cohen, but this was not enough to enable them to hold onto Butler who had been following Sebastian's work ever since he had heard his first demos: "One day I was in Herbie Cohen's office when Erik brought up a single. One side was "Rooty Toot" and the other was a surfing thing that Jerry had worked on, "Lady Godiva". After hearing both of them Herbie asked me which one I liked and I said, "I really like this "Rooty Toot" thing," and Jake said, "Well that's not the one we're pushing and I know something about that." So I said to Erik, "We all have our opinions, I mean you say something but I may know something too. I like "Rooty Toot"; I like the guy who sings it. I think it's cute but the other one is just another surfing song and it sounds like a rip-off of a surfing song too." Erik was pissed."

Butler was drawn to this new group, yet he still tried to ensure the continuation of The Sellouts: "Well, it was a down time and I was really attracted to the star quality of Zally, his tremendous charisma. I was not as impressed with John as I was with Zally, but I knew the writing was good and interesting and I'd always liked Stephen. I knew our cover band was really doomed - I wasn't able to produce the writing then, I wasn't sure how to go about it. I could play guitar but I didn't really learn enough to be able to write songs for a couple of years after that. So it was a sad time, although I got The Sellouts a guy who I had worked with, Seth Weinberger (aka Conners, from The Kingsmen) and he made a couple of tapes with them."

Butler had to endure an audition of sorts, before he could join The Lovin' Spoonful, one which everybody who was present remembers. Sebastian sets the scene: "Immediately preceding us, in the only room large enough to rehearse in, was The Paul Butterfield Blues Band, complete with Sam Lay, who was one of the most devastating drummers in the world. So, just to begin with, the sound coming out of the room, as we all stood around waiting to try Joe out, was so devastating. I can't imagine him being anything but horrified. I don't know how good I could have been as a drummer at that time, but no matter how good I was, I know it would have scared me to hear Sam Lay!" Jacobsen takes up the story: "I remember when they tried him out, they played "Johnny B. Goode", and about a quarter of the way through, he broke a stick - but he was so enthusiastic to join that he carried on, beating the shit out of his crash cymbal with his bare hand, which was getting increasingly cut up by the rivets. He kept going till the end of the song, by which time his hand was pouring blood all over the kit, but they said he could join...I guess he must have impressed them." Sebastian agrees: "And so, at that point we decided, "Well, that's as much heart as we could ask for, so the guy's got the job."

Boone claims that this was hardly an audition: "It was a rehearsal that he sat in on. I guess you could call it an audition, but he already had the job if he wanted it. Everybody liked him and we'd seen him before." Butler confirms "Well, this deal was kinda made; I don't know if it was so much an audition or just a confirmation. I mean, if we had really hated each other, it would have fallen apart. The die was cast with the manager, Bob Cavallo, and the producer, Erik Jacobsen, and I really wanted to be a part of it." The positive feelings of everyone involved made it a hard offer to turn down. Boone can boast that he could see what was ahead: "I did have the vision. John, Zally, Erik and Bob Cavallo sounded so positive when I talked to them." A small transfer deal was made with Herb Cohen and Butler was free to be join The Lovin' Spoonful.

With the rejection of the Night Owl ringing in their ears, the group holed up in the notorious Albert Hotel on the corner of University Place and East 10th Street in Greenwich Village for a month of intense rehearsal. Jacobsen recalls the period: "We scraped together the minimum essentials of equipment and they began rehearsals in the basement of the Albert Hotel, which has to be the worst rehearsal hall you could ever imagine. It was just incredible! Cockroaches everywhere, rivulets flowing across the floor into big pools, slime all over the place, mushrooms and fungi growing in the corners, plaster and old flaking paint falling off the ceiling, and over on the far side, this giant furnace, throbbing and thundering away incessantly. It was just awful, but they practised there day in and day out for weeks and weeks, while we tried to get them some gigs and a recording contract."

Boone and Butler then moved into the Albert, into a poky little room made all the more cramped by the fact that it was stuffed full of the Spoonful's equipment. Cass Elliot and Denny Doherty were still living in the Albert. Since The Mugwumps had split, they had not found any work and Butler recalls what they were up to: "They whiled away the hours hurling firecrackers onto the roof and, occasionally, whole chickens which exploded loudly on landing." The owner of the hotel didn't mind - Butler adds: "Denny would sleep with the woman at the Albert Hotel and pay our rent. Whenever we got pestered, we sent Denny, she loved Denny and Denny would appease her."

The exuberance and willingness to impress each other soon meant that running down corridors shouting and hollering became the norm and the Albert became infested with the young. However, it was meant only as a stepping stone; nobody wanted to stay there too long, as Butler explains: "It inspired us because it made us frightened of poverty." Over the years, the Albert Hotel has attained a reputation similar to the nearby Chelsea Hotel. Any hotel would have stories to tell but this place housed several of the major rock personalities of the 1960s. Mike Bloomfield would: "Recommend it as an absolutely essential part of the experience of living", and Tim Buckley, who wrote *Goodbye And Hello* in the Albert, described the hotel once as "Expensive, but the best place I ever lived."

Early January in New York, 1965, with zero income, drew the quartet together as a unit. Butler: "We sold bottles, the things I did as a kid, the whole Spoonful, we went out that whole winter and sold bottles for just a nickel apiece, and made money for food." Eventually, around March. 1965, Jacobsen and Cavallo managed to secure the group a residency at the Cafe Bizarre - for $185 a week and plenty of tuna fish sandwiches!

Concurrently, members of the Spoonful were still helping out Erik Jacobsen on his next bunch of demos. One of these featured Dwain Story from Jacobsen's Knob Lick Upper Ten Thousand on lead vocals with Yanovsky on guitar and the rest of the Spoonful on handclaps! The record, prophetically titled "A Little Lovin'", would come out on the Stallion label (run by Charles Koppelman and Don Rubin) but was not to be the start of anything big, as Jacobsen recalls: "Dwain was not able to continue. I don't know how you say it in a nice way - he lost his mental focus. There was a period there where he went a little emotionally unstable. Actually, he was hospitalised, kind of disappeared." Another demo that paired Yanovsky with Denny Doherty under the alias D&Z, was part of a new craze Jacobsen was trying to start as Yanovsky recalls, "Erik wanted to create a dance craze. I don't know what was out there at that moment - maybe the Hucklebuck. Dwain Story wrote "The Slurp" so Erik had all these Slurp tunes. A big black guy named Caesar sung a kind of a solo Slurp that was unbelievably embarrassing. Needless to say nothing happened. The lyrics were good though, 'The slurp's been around since way back when little babies do it all over their chin.' (laughs)" Two songs from these sessions still exist in Jacobsen's tape archive.

Joe Marra recalls the Spoonful's time at the Cafe Bizarre: "When they worked at the Bizarre, they don't want to admit it but they went into purgatory and that was their purgatory (laughs). The Cafe Bizarre had these poor guys doing six shows a night, five or six times a week. They got $185 a week doing that." In a latter group interview, with *Hit Parader* magazine, Sebastian recalled what had occurred at the Bizarre, after the mere mention of the place brought a loud "Boo!" from his colleagues: "The mikes didn't work, and we started one tune and did it about eight times faster than we've ever done it since because we were all very uptight. Joe was very uptight because he had never played anything with us before and he didn't even know how we sounded." But through hard work, things started to happen, as Butler points out: "But we got to eat there and we got to rehearse there and we lived on ice cream and tuna fish, which was good - it wasn't death. It was funny, some nights, maybe at the weekend, you'd get people out on the dance floor - thirty couples and it would be packed - but certain days, there'd be nobody. Then all of a sudden two of The Kingston Trio would walk in and watch and come back for a few shows, and told us we were great and nothing was gonna stop us. Then all The Byrds came in from The Ed Sullivan Show and just sat there and said "You guys are fucking great." The encouragement of The Byrds, and in particular drummer Michael Clarke, made the Spoonful feel more confident, as The Byrds were filling the niche the Spoonful wanted to explore, as Sebastian recounts: "The drummer from The Byrds came up to us and said, "Gee, you guys are so great, I wish I was with your band". We were shocked! In New York, if you belonged to a band there was real chauvinism, you'd never admit to admiring another group. If this was not true of the heaviest band out there, with all this publicity, let us out there!"

Even with the money the group was now earning, there wasn't enough to keep the team of six afloat, as Jacobsen remembers: "I was totally bankrupt, despite my various ventures which included a publishing company (Faithful Virtue) with Tim Hardin and John Sebastian signed to it, and I was even evicted from my apartment. I had to move in with Bob Cavallo, who was now my partner - 50/50 straight down the middle - but he was broke too! So it was desperation point, touch and go whether we'd get a record deal before lack of money forced us to abandon the whole thing. I was toting around this single we'd cut with my last $790 - two of John's tunes, "Do You Believe In Magic" and "On The Road Again" - but wherever I went and played it, the answer was the same. Warners, Capitol, Columbia, and one by one they all passed it up." The money the group were earning at the Bizarre was not enough and the sandwiches were not all that great either, so Cavallo went back to see Joe Marra at the Night Owl: "Bob came in and he says, "I've got the band," and he wants to bring them back into the Night Owl. I asked him how much they were making at the Bizarre and he told me and I says, "Well, bring them, and we'll give them what they were getting before," which was $300 plus their food. When they came back, the energy had changed, the club, the band, everything."

For their return, Marra booked support acts for the Spoonful: The Tad Trousdale Trio (!), The Blues Project and The MFQ, but under the moniker The Fat City Four, as they were trying out a new rock approach. With the addition of (Fast) Eddie Hoh on drums, the group had a new bite to their sound and were soon to move to the more receptive west coast. In the same way that the dismal conditions of the Albert were akin to The Beatles' digs in Hamburg, the Night Owl became the Spoonful's Cavern Club. They started to draw crowds, which delighted Marra: "When the Spoonful came back, I owed about $25,000 to $30,000, a lot of money, so I would do anything for publicity. I took this 8 by 10 photograph of the Spoonful and blew it up to six feet by for feet and placed it in the front window, and people thought that they were stars - they would have to be stars to have such a big photograph!"

Cass Elliot's "teenyboppers" were now fixing their eyes on the Spoonful. With Butler's charm, Yanovsky's antics, Sebastian's sensitivity and Boone's air of mystique, there was plenty of choice. The personalities of New York started making a beeline for the Night Owl, which started the chain of events that led to the group acquiring a

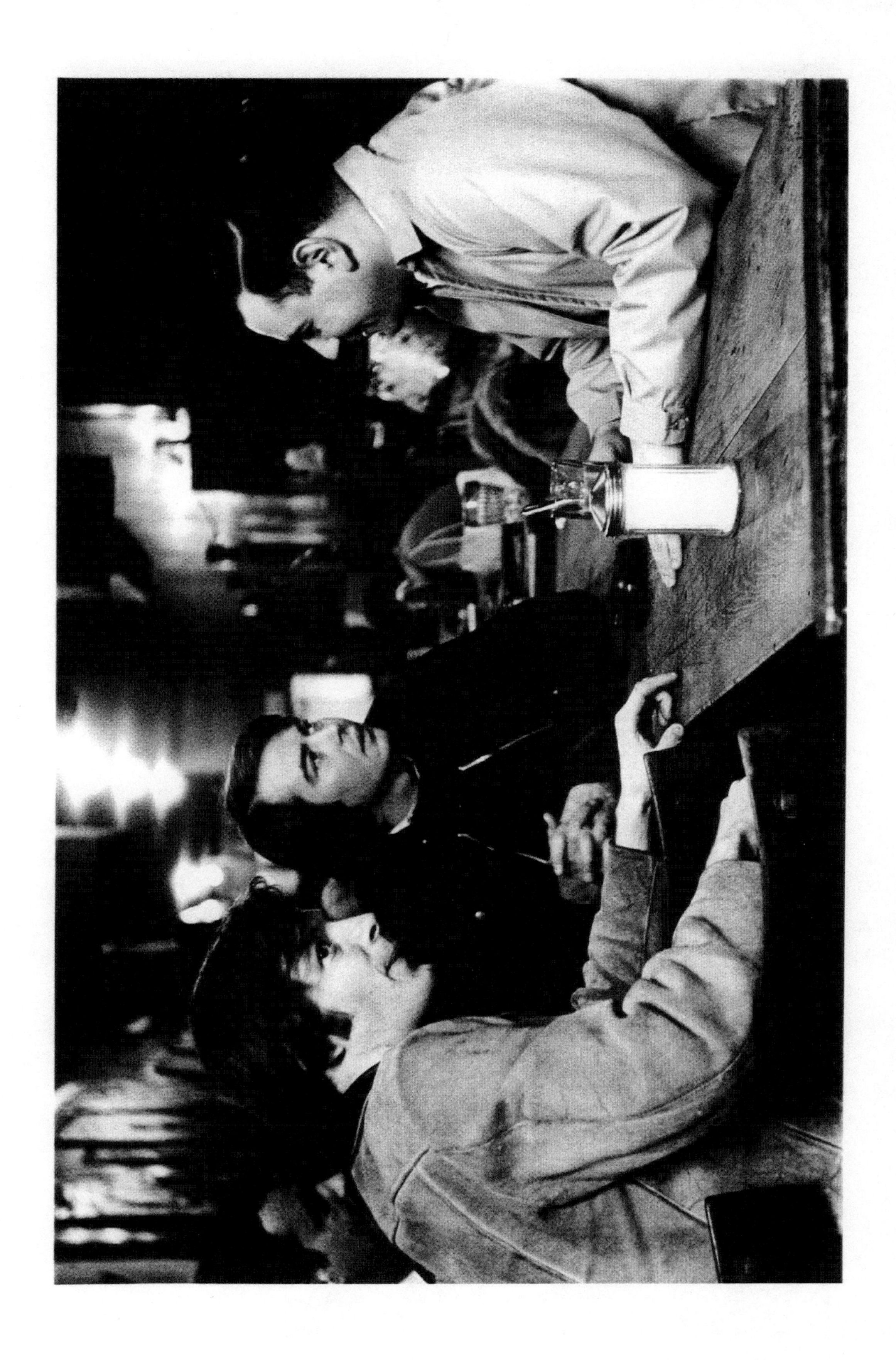

record contract, as Sebastian recalls: "What started the ball rolling was that Phil Spector came down with a couple of people and just sat there the whole evening, mostly with his ear against the wall, listening to us play. In fact, I found out recently from an American drummer by the name of Charlie Drayton that it had been his father who had gone to Phil Spector and said, "Hey, there's some bad white boys playing blues down in the village and you ought to catch this." The way it worked in those days was that Spector was such an influential producer that the minute he showed interest, the entire Brill Building had filled up the place by the next couple of nights."

After they had cockily turned down Spector's offer of a recording contract, the next person to offer the group a deal was the president of Elektra. Jacobsen: "The Spoonful was just wiping everybody out at the Night Owl - there was a real buzz going round about how great they were, and one night, Jac Holzman dropped by and, on the strength of what he saw and the potential of what he envisaged, he offered us a deal involving $10,000" (a debatable figure). "That wasn't much in terms of big money, but it sounded great to us at the time and it would have prevented us from going under, so we told Jac we'd do it."

Unlike almost any other record company president of the time, except maybe Ahmet Ertegun of Atlantic, Jac Holzman was genuinely involved in the music side of the business. This deal seemed a sure thing to him; Paul Rothchild was still working at the time with Sebastian, who had recently played on Fred Neil's sublime *Bleecker & MacDougal* and Tom Rush's first two Elektra albums, and Sebastian was also an acquaintance of Holzman's. Everything was going according to plan, until at the last moment Jacobsen and Cavallo dropped out - they had had a better offer. To this day, it is not entirely clear why the Spoonful did not sign for Elektra and some of the group claim they never even knew such a deal was offered.

Paul Rothchild once supplied a financial reason: "First of all, Elektra did not even give The Doors $10,000 to sign. Jac Holzman never gave anybody more than $3,000 to sign, no matter who they were. When the Spoonful were up for grabs, Jac offered them $3,000, they wanted $5,000, and after weeks of negotiation, he lost them over that $2,000 difference. He loved the material and the act. They were local, easy to keep tabs on and dedicated to me, they were a natural and it still didn't happen." Rothchild's comments could be correct, as years later Holzman told *Goldmine* "I thought The Byrds were wonderful, but they wanted $5,000, and in those days, that was ridiculous money. The other group I desperately wanted to sign and I thought I had, but ended up losing, was The Lovin' Spoonful." Boone reckons that the Spoonful would not have wanted to be associated with what was essentially a folk label, yet the group actually did record for Elektra, albeit not very much.

As some sort of apology to Holzman, an agreement was made for the Spoonful to cut five tracks, not their best, which Elektra could release if or when the group struck gold. As with The Mugwumps, Spoonful fans were able to hear a time capsule of their favourites before anybody outside New York knew anything of them. The songs were included on a composite album alongside modern day white blues interpretations (a progression from *The Blues Project* album), by the likes of The Paul Butterfield Blues Band, Tom Rush, Al Kooper (prior to forming The Blues Project group) and a one-off combo, Powerhouse, headed by Eric Clapton and (under an alias) Steve Winwood.

The Spoonful tracks have a sort of garage-y, demo feel to them, which is part of their charm. The feeling of potential greatness is evident, similar to the sensation when listening to *Pre-Flyte*, the early recordings by the nucleus of The Byrds. Unimaginative bass lines and only adequate drumming can be ignored when listening to The Lovin' Spoonful on *What's Shakin'*. From the Spoonful cover repertoire came a retread of "Searchin'", which stuck heavily to the previous Pappalardi/Mugwumps arrangement. It is doubtful that the Spoonful knew that The Beatles had also chosen to cover this song on their Decca demo, but both versions manage to display a certain confidence. Chuck Berry's "Almost Grown" has some energy, exhibiting the Spoonful's rough edges, and was probably the first take. The other cover was an apparently hilarious version of The Hollywood Argyles' "Alley Oop", with Yanovsky yelling out the lyrics. Unfortunately, Elektra sat on this track and it has never been released.

The two Sebastian originals show the potential in his songwriting, alongside a more mediocre level. "Good Time Music", which was to become a trademark of the Spoonful's sound, tells the story of why the group came into existence. The singer, Sebastian, tells us that he has been disillusioned by the music that he has been listening to for the last couple of years on his radio until 'them kids come over from the Mersey river' brought him around mentally to 'think about the blues and start all over again.' The rhythm to "Good Time Music" is stolen from "Doctor Feelgood" by Dr. Feelgood & The Interns, which the Spoonful included in their set list at the time. Sebastian readily admits to this, although he maintains that the intention was to copy a different song: "What it's really based on is "Hi-Heel Sneakers" (by Tommy Tucker). "That was the tune we'd heard and gone nuts about. Actually, that pre-dates the Spoonful, that was me and Felix Pappalardi, not that we'd written it together, but we were all listening to the radio when we were playing at night on MacDougal Street. For several weeks, that was the tune we all wanted to play, so I eventually wrote my own "Hi-Heel Sneakers'." "Good Time Music" is the first Sebastian composition in which he really expresses himself and makes a great song out of his thoughts. The same cannot be said of "Don't Bank On It Baby", a failed attempt to demonstrate his aloofness that pales in comparison. The blend of influences and the originality of The Lovin' Spoonful is evident from these cuts; the next step was to use them as a vehicle for hit records.

During their successful stint at the Night Owl, in a rare foray outside The Village, the Spoonful played the Club 47 in Cambridge, Massachusetts. The gig came through the recommendation of Fritz Richmond, and they were the subject of a review by Paul Williams for the paper *Folkin' Around*, which was probably their first ever review. Williams describes the group's repertoire at the time (June 1965) and their impact on stage, both individually and as a whole: "The most exciting act to hit Club 47 in a long time is a group of noisy rhythm and blues players who call themselves The Loving (sic) Spoonful. In fact, from my way of seeing it, far and away the most exciting thing to happen to music in years is the electrified revival of real down home rhythm and blues. The Loving Spoonful consists of two electric guitars, one amplified bass, various amplified drums and cymbals, an amplified harmonica and an electric autoharp. All this may sound a bit out of its element in Club 47 (a folkies paradise), and it is. The balance was so bad on the first number, first night, that it was necessary to go across the street to hear anything at all. By the second set, the balance was as good as it could possibly be in such close quarters. It was still almost impossible to hear the vocals, but what you could hear sounded great."

The reason for all the over amplification was explained by Sebastian in a 1980s TV interview: "The Spoonful where booked to play the Club 47, which was a bastion of this traditional music cult, and boy, did we want to kill in that room. I remember the sheer joy on Zally's face as we began to play and a young woman in the audience with ironed hair, suddenly reached for her ears with her fingers. Zally gave her a beautiful benevolent smile and turned his amp up to ten!" Butler recalls the venue more for procreative reasons than one of how musically ground-breaking it all was: "My memories of Club 47 are out in the backyard between sets making love in the grass with a girl and after the set trying to scrub the green off my knees so my then girlfriend wouldn't notice it. So, we have different memories of different things."

Continuing with the review, Williams went on to note: "Sebastian is a good but unexceptional singer; he is the group's best guitarist and one of the best mouth harpists around, something the Spoonful should take more advantage of. Butler is a fabulous character; he devotes himself wholeheartedly to his music and comes across on stage like nobody since Little Richard. He goes absolutely wild, and watching him you can't help wanting to do the same. He is an excellent drummer; the group's spokesman for rhythm as Sebastian is for blues. I'm not sure just how to judge the bass; I wasn't very impressed with him, but that doesn't mean he's no good. As for Yanofsky" (not the last time his name would be incorrectly spelt) "he is a quite good guitarist, though he suffers a bit in comparison with Sebastian. The group has a solid rhythm and blues approach: down home music with an overpowering beat, differing from much mainline rock and roll in its purity." Boone addresses Williams' comment about R&B: "The reason the Spoonful did so well as opposed to the other folkies - and I don't say this to blow my own horn - was that Joe and I had played in a rock band. Except for The Sellouts, we were the first (act of this type) who knew how to play with a beat and John and Zally had these folky guitar styles which we brought the beat to."

Williams mentions that the group's repertoire also included Chuck Berry's "Thirty Days" and "Wild About My Lovin'" (adapted from an old ragtime song) in addition to the songs performed on *What's Shakin'*. He also reveals the strength in depth of Sebastian's original songwriting, even at this early time claiming "The Spoonful did a number of what they call ballads, slow rock 'n' roll with a lot of R&B approach mixed in. My personal favourites in this style were "Didn't Want To Have To Do It" and "Younger Girl". The latter is particularly evocative, and shows very well how a song can be sensitive without the saccharine sweetness of most pop-standard tunes. The group has quite a bit of good, unfamiliar material. I should certainly mention "On The Road Again", "Magic", which they've reportedly just recorded as a single, and "Good Time Music", a fabulous song. All the songs I've mentioned have, in my opinion, strong potential in the pop market. The Loving Spoonful is doing the sort of thing that teenagers and other pop-music addicts want nowadays - their sound is different from what's on radio today."

Returning to the Village, the management duo had still not signed the Spoonful's recording contract when they were recommended to see a couple of guys just starting out in the business on their own, as Jacobsen recalls: "We'd entered a verbal deal with Holzman and were waiting for him to prepare the necessary documentation when someone suggested that we go and see these guys called Koppelman & Rubin Associates, so we felt we had nothing to lose by going to play them our master. "It's a smash!" they shouted, "This is the new group: we want to be in on it, we'll start a publishing company, we know everybody, we used to be in the Brill Building with Don Kirshner." They just snowed us with their enthusiasm, but they appeared to be really genuine about the tune - and they had a winning way about them, whereas Jac Holzman was much more methodical and business-like, talking in terms of insuring the lives of the group members and things like that."

The deal was made after Charles Koppelman and Don Rubin went to see the Spoonful in person at the Night Owl, a day Koppelman looks back on smugly: "The first song, "Do You Believe In Magic", was incredible. The first thing I did was kick my partner Don Rubin, who told me not to be too enthusiastic as it would make the price higher." After this meeting, Cavallo and Jacobsen signed up with Koppelman and Rubin, a decision that would haunt them and The Lovin' Spoonful to the present day.

Charles Koppelman was born in 1940 in Brooklyn, New York. After majoring in physical education at Adelphi College in Garden City, Long Island, in 1959, he formed a trio with Artie Berk (Berkowitz) and Don Rubin (Norman Rubinstein). Koppelman used the surname Cane when working in the trio, who decided to call themselves The Ivy Three, as their college was ivy-covered. In 1960, The Ivy Three signed a record contract with Shell Records and recorded a dreadful song about the cartoon character Yogi Bear, "Yogi", that Koppelman had written with producers Lou Stallman and Sid Jacobsen. Unbelievably the song became a US Top 10 hit in July 1960. The trio recorded three other singles before calling it a day.

Koppelman had previously played basketball with one Don Kirshner, and in 1961, when Kirshner was running Aldon Music, a music publishing company; Koppelman renewed their contact, which led to Koppelman and Rubin getting a job writing songs for $25 a week. When Columbia Pictures bought Aldon Music in 1963, the 24-year-old Koppelman rose from the ranks, becoming the managing director of Screen Gems/Columbia Music, with Rubin securing an executive role. The pair then briefly worked for Big Seven Music, a subsidiary of Roulette Records under the reputedly Mafia-linked Morris Levy, before a headline in the April 24th, 1965, edition of Billboard, the music industry weekly, announced: "Koppelman, Rubin Form Company." Charlie's aunt, Sarah Koppelman, recalls that this company, Koppelman-Rubin Associates, would never have started without a loan of some $80,000 from her husband, Leon Koppelman. With this cash boost, the pair formed a record production company in their own name, as well as a music publishing division, Chardon Music, named in homage to Kirshner's Aldon (which was a partnership with Al Nevins).

When Koppelman and Rubin signed the Spoonful in July, 1965, the contract also took in Jacobsen's Faithful Virtue publishing company and more, as the latter recalls: "Koppelman and Rubin bought themselves in as partners on the publishing and production, and the record company they selected would be presented with the finished masters ready for release." After toying with the idea of releasing the single on their Stallion label, all Charlie and Don did was to simply walk down their corridor to the office of Kama Sutra Records, with the acetate of "Do You Believe In Magic", and signed a deal within a week.

Kama Sutra was the baby of Hy Mizrahi, Phil Steinberg and Artie Ripp (of whom it has been said that his name inspired the term "rip-off.") Ripp's guru in the record business had been George Goldner, an entrepreneur who had more record labels to his name than most. From the late '40s to the early '60s, Goldner had started up, and then sold, labels such as Tico, Rama and Gee and had discovered Frankie Lymon & The Teenagers, The Flamingos, Little Anthony & The Imperials, and many more. His reason for selling was an addictive gambling habit, and the buyer was always Morris Levy.

Under Goldner, Ripp learnt about the music business first hand (he once put up a down-on-his luck Alan Freed) with payola scandals, providing prostitutes for disc jockeys and the like. When Goldner started Red Bird Records alongside Lieber & Stoller in 1964, Ripp joined the recently formed Kama Sutra. Philip Steinberg had a rich musical pedigree of his own as well: "I grew up in Brooklyn, attending Lincoln High School, graduating in '57. At this time Neil Sedaka, The Tokens, Neil Diamond, Barbara Streisand, Mort Shuman and many others, including Jay & The Americans, were schoolmates and/or friends. They were all in various stages of their careers and would often have sessions at our houses, working up their current music. At the time, rock 'n' roll was new - there were doo-wop singers on every corner, and I became one making a record for Irv Spice on his Mohawk record label. My brothers, Robert and Mark, were a songwriting team, and that would be at the centre of the Kama Sutra story."

Steinberg recalls the origins of Kama Sutra: "It was the summer of '61, and I was friendly with a man by the name of Eric Nathanson. He and his twin brother, Steve, would be in and out of the record business for years. Eric was over at my house rehearsing and heard some of the tunes my brothers had written, or were working on. He thought they would be perfect to build a publishing company around and we started talking about copyrights, lead sheets and getting rich. Later that week, Eric was on the beach (Brighton Beach), where he met a guy by the name of Hy Mizrahi. Eric talked to Hy, who at that time was in the retail business. Hy came over to the house with Eric, listened to my brothers' play their tunes, and knew he wanted in. I was reading The Kama Sutra, and we decided to form a company. Eric, Hy and myself divided the company 1/3, 1/3, 1/3 and called it Kama Sutra Productions, with a publishing arm called Tender Tunes. Hy's retail store caught fire" (rumour has it that a fire sale was appropriate, reckons Ripp) "and with the insurance money ($60,000) we opened up a suite of offices in 1650 Broadway. A gorgeous secretary and some furniture - shazam, we were in the record business!"

For Ripp to join, somebody had to bail out. The one to miss out on the rich pickings would be Nathanson, as Steinberg reveals: "Very few people know about this. About a month or two into the start of this company, Hy and Eric were starting to have a hassle, this would be a harbinger of things to come, and they started not getting on together. Hy arranged to buy Eric out for $100, and he took it." Steinberg comments on the background to Ripp's takeover of Nathanson's shares: "Artie had been in the business for quite some time, he had cut a hit with Doris Troy off a demo, "Just One Look". Most of all, he had worked closely with George Goldner. Artie could not stay away from the Kama Sutra offices because of a beautiful creature named Sandy, who would go on to perform as a writer/singer under the name Sandy Kane. Anyway, Artie and I became really good friends, and I came to be very fond of his wife, Phyllis.

Artie was living in Queens and it was at a party at his apartment that I talked to him about going into business together. I had discussed it with Hy, who wasn't wildly keen on the idea, but didn't stop me from pursuing it. Artie was fired from his job soon after our conversation and found it impossible to find a similar position, so we invited him in as our partner and he accepted it. Hy never really wanted this and there would be friction and bad blood right up to the very end - and past it. So the company and the faces were now complete, for good or bad. Hy, Artie and Phil - Kama Sutra, entwined forever."

Kama Sutra was soon up and running, as Steinberg confirms: "Kama Sutra, very quickly, was cutting demos of my brothers' work. I had hired J.J. Jackson, who would go on to make his own hit records. The office attracted many aspiring writers and producers, one of whom, Tony Michaels, would bring us the Shadow Morton, Tony Michaels, Joe DeAngelis group, The Shangri-Las. We were doing our recording out of Allegro Studios, which was in the basement of 1650 Broadway." Starting off as a production company, Kama Sutra achieved hits with The Shangri-Las and Jay & The Americans. With this success, in June 1965, Kama Sutra became a record label and secured a distribution deal with Metro-Goldwyn-Mayer (MGM) in a three-year deal. An incident that no doubt helped secure the interest of MGM is recalled by Howard Solomon, the owner of the Cafe Au Go-Go in the Village: "The first time the Spoonful played formally in a different place - previous to that they had been playing at the Bizarre - they were introduced at the Cafe Au Go-Go. I had a promo party for MGM with The Animals booked upstairs but The Animals couldn't get in, the place was so packed. Three hundred people for my place was a lot of people, it was quite an event."

Phil Steinberg remembers first hearing "Do You Believe In Magic" and seeing the Spoonful perform for the first time; this would lead to the group securing a long time contract with Kama Sutra, which was somewhat unusual in the days when the 45 ruled: "One night, early in the evening, I got a call from Charlie (Koppelman*)* to come over to his office and listen to something he had. He played me an acetate of "Do You Believe In Magic", and I told him it was a hit record, and wished him good luck. He told me they had taken it to all the majors and probably all the minors, but no one was interested. I was. I loved the sound and told him to do nothing with it unless it was with me and asked what it would cost. I believe it was either $5,000 or $10,000 they wanted to get for it, or had sunk into it. I left them and ran into my office, played the disc for Artie and Hy. All three of us looked like we had swallowed the cream. One of the wonderful things of those years was how well our ears were working - the three of us could hear a hit.

"A day or two after the Koppelman meeting, we went to the Night Owl Cafe in Greenwich Village, to see this group that made that "Good Time Music". I was stunned - there was John with his glasses and autoharp or harmonica or guitar, Joe Butler laughing on the drums, Steve Boone on the bass and a maniacal Zal Yanovsky on guitar. They played a long set and I thought I was losing it. Everything they played sounded like a hit. Not just a hit, but a Top 5 record! I stepped outside to get my balance. Was I losing it? Was I really hearing what I was hearing? I was. They all did go Top 5."

In the Summer of 1965, Koppelman & Rubin Associates and Kama Sutra Records, both newly formed companies, took control of the Spoonful's output, with MGM distributing the material and overseeing the whole operation. The contract signed had the Spoonful agreeing to deliver three albums plus a "Best Of" per year. According to Jacobsen, Koppelman & Rubin Associates were receiving 9% from Kama Sutra, who were in turn receiving 11% from MGM. As to what slice of the pie the members of The Lovin' Spoonful received - Phil Steinberg offers: "We are around the time frame when an artist would get 3% of 90% of records sold and paid for. That would go up over the contract life to 4% and hold at 5%. Producers were getting 1½ - 3% of 90% of records sold and paid for. We had been working on a record label deal with MGM that would allow us a greater share of the profits from records sold and would also allow us the ownership of the tapes."

CHAPTER 2 – MAGIC TIMES

Even with full-page adverts in the trades, the first single on the Kama Sutra label in June of 1965, "You're My Baby" by The Vacels, failed to make a significant impression on the charts. Their next release, however, would help make the label an international corporation by the year's end. 'Do You Believe In Magic", Sebastian's "pop anthem" was a combination of rock 'n' roll, rhythm and blues and just pure excitement. With Sebastian's idea to electrify the autoharp, an instrument he had seen Maybelle Carter from The Carter Family play, the song also had an identifiable sound.

The song is about the power in music, its ability to release all restrictions and take over a person as well as producing a warm feeling that can satisfy. It also contained the classic, oft repeated line; 'I'll tell you about the magic and a free your soul, but it's like trying to tell a stranger about rock and roll.' As Steve Boone states, "Rock and roll was something that got into you, it wasn't a fad. It consumed you."

Sebastian claims that the song was based on some of the Motown chord progressions, notably Martha & The Vandellas' "Heat Wave" and that "Do You Believe In Magic" was, "only the fifth or sixth song I'd ever written. It came in a flash, and it was the first tune to give me any degree of recognition. There was joyousness in it, and while I wasn't an active participant in the full-out hippy mentality, success allowed me to subscribe to the theory that "everything is possible now."

Released on the 20th of July (the same day as Dylan's "Like A Rolling Stone") and described by *Cashbox* as, "a rollicking teen-angled romancer with an infectious danceable riff," "Do You Believe In Magic" went from number 96 to 79 to 64 to 42, and then reached the top twenty, before peaking at number 9 in the middle of October, 1965. The success of the single was supported by trade adverts and appearances on TV shows including the Lloyd Thaxton Show and a couple with Merv Griffin. Other TV appearances, that still exist, include Hullabaloo, Shindig (where Yanovsky met, then dated the actress Teri Garr) and an American Bandstand performance of the song from August, filmed the day after Dylan's concert at Forest Hills, New York, where he was starting to win his audience over and open the door for his disciples.

All these performances show four exuberant young fellows, resplendent in their striped T-shirts and smart waistcoats topped by Beatlesque haircuts. No matching attire here, yet you could see there existed a common bond among the individual nuances, from the perceived John Entwistle-like calmness of the bassist, the exuberance of the drummer, the manic clowning of the guitarist and the musical professionalism of the guy with the granny glasses playing autoharp. In fact, Sebastian was very fond of his autoharp which he kept in a crush proof case. One day Yanovsky saw an old battered up autoharp in a junk store, promptly bought it, smashed it some more then replaced it in Sebastian's case – just to see the look of horror on his partner's face.

The Lovin' Spoonful almost always received favourable press after "Do You Believe In Magic" became a hit, but one journalist/photographer sussed out early that the Spoonful were going to be massive and made the "exclusive" deal in return for a cover story. Don Paulsen, the then co-editor of *Hit Parader*, who took the first picture of The Doors, recalls when his attention was first grabbed by the Spoonful, "I first saw the Spoonful at the

Night Owl and was blown away by their music and their talent. We did an interview with them in Koppelman and Rubin's office and we were impressed by their personalities, they were so vibrant. In fact, it was like four brightly coloured rubber balls, you throw them into a room and they're bouncing off the walls and off each other. They had such spirit, energy, enthusiasm, humour and wonderful ideas.

"After the interview they said, "Hey, come on; let's go down to the Village. We'll take some more pictures," because they wanted to show me where they had written, 'Tim Hardin Is A Bad Boy' on a wall. Then we put them on the cover of *Song Hits* (a lyric magazine who had the same publishers as Hit Parader) before their record even came out." From then on, *Hit Parader* was on the spot when anything interesting occurred in the Spoonful camp. The major press also started to take note, the August edition of *Billboard* ran the prophetic headline, "Folk + Rock = Profits".

With chart success the Spoonful were now hot property, but staying loyal to the man who showed faith in them, they played a week engagement at the Night Owl, towards the end of July, where they were filmed for a prestigious documentary as Butler recalls, "Suddenly we were important because somebody thought we were important - even anthropologically. The Canadian Film Board decided they had their finger on the pulse of something when they came down, looking for this scene. They blocked the street for two days, setting up cameras. I remember them putting transparent skins on my drums so they could shoot through and that was interfaced with an African tribe playing drums and in the shot a guy's face blends into mine in the same motion.

"The film wound up at the World's Fair in Montreal (in 1967) on a screen that was like 120 feet high by 80 feet wide - it was an amazing documentary, I wish I had the footage." Richie Havens was also filmed but failed to appear in the final cut. Joe Marra recalls this week residency, "Literally, when I had the Spoonful you had people sitting on top of people, I mean we are talking about turning away hundreds of people every night. One of my ideas was not to let them be on the stage too long, it was short boom, boom shows. If people want to see them, they'll pay again –"Don't let them assholes stay on the stage!"

"It wasn't like when Bob Dylan made his legendary performance at Folk City, because nobody knew that he was there! When the Spoonful were at the Night Owl Cafe, the police would have to come on the sidewalk with horses and chase them off." Butler agrees; "People could look through the window, so it would just start stacking up and pretty soon the police would come down just to let the cars go down the street - even sometimes at rehearsals!"

Mark Sebastian recalls seeing the group around this time; "On-stage the Spoonful was a study in chaos. Zal would be cavorting around the stage, often with rubber toys hanging from the peg-head of his guitar, a Guild Thunderbird, known as "The Shark". A lit cigarette was usually impaled on one of his string ends, sometimes issuing a shower of sparks as he brushed into things around him. He would jump about, provoking and breaking

THE BEATLES, OUR SPECIAL FRIENDS
PATTY DUKE'S HARD RISE TO FAME
DECEMBER
25c
CDC
Song Hits
MAGAZINE
ORRECT LYRICS BY PERMISSION OF COPYRIGHT OWNERS
SONG HITS of Today
THE LOVIN' SPOONFUL WILL BE AMERICA'S NEW IDOLS
SONG HITS of Tomorrow
MOHAIR SAM
JUST YOU
ELP! ALL 7 SONGS
JUST A LITTLE BIT BETTER
I'M YOURS
RIDE AWAY
LAUGH AT ME
HOME OF THE BRAVE
DO YOU BELIEVE IN MAGIC
CATCH US IF YOU CAN
SUMMER NIGHTS
COLOURS
THE SINS OF A FAMILY
HEARTACHES BY THE NUMBER
HANG ON SLOOPY
ANNIE FANNIE
HEART FULL OF SOUL
SAD SAD GIRL
NOTHING BUT HEARTACHES
EVE OF DESTRUCTION
WE GOTTA GET OUT OF THIS PLACE
ACTION
THE LETTERMEN · THE MOODY BLUES · JODY MILLER
DONNA LOREN · THEM · SAM THE SHAM · CHRIS CONNELLY

up the audience and his bandmates. John, trying to remember recently written lyrics, attempting to achieve some semblance of projection to the audience, would end up drawn into the havoc wrought by Yanovsky.

"The overall effect was of four people having a lot of fun on-stage. Steve Boone would thump on the bass, weaving and leaning to the music like a long sea anemone. Joe Butler also handled some lead vocals and held down the beat. His cover boy good looks were no hindrance in interesting the "teenyboppers", young female fans that invaded Greenwich Village on weekends from outlying communities like the Bronx and Brooklyn. Their music was a bit rough at first, but became very good with the many nightly sets demanded of them."

For what could have been his last time with the group, Marra pulled out all the stops, "In July, I really wanted to make a big to-do but Bob (Cavallo) wouldn't let me do it. I wanted to get a big spotlight in the street, block the traffic and bust everybody's balls. You're looking to promote and without money it's a little hard. The Spoonful had a young appeal so we got thousands of helium balloons with "I Love The Lovin' Spoonful" on them. We made the waitresses wear them and we gave them out to people on the streets, nobody had done a promotion like that. We had people coming back for years wanting them and the night the Spoonful left for California, after the release of their first single, we let all the balloons go."

Butler happily recalls this last show, "That was the night when John was playing the last solo and Zally took some wire cutters and cut the strings off his guitar. John looked away for a second and Zally had just gone "snip" and cut every string off his guitar! (laughs)" Butler can recall what happened next, on one of the first occasions where Yanovsky's over exuberance would fray the nerves of the other members in the group, "Zally started a food fight and he was like a caveman, he had an ability to turn primitive but he's never been the master of it...never been able to survive it in some ways."

Fuelled by their acceptance from the New York scene, it was decided by the management duo that the Spoonful should venture out of their niche and try some uncharted waters. Long hair was still not welcomed in most parts of the United States, so it was agreed that the group should travel the length of the country to San Francisco. Erik Jacobsen; "If we went out to, say, Long Island for a gig, we took our lives in our hands because people had a savage hatred for long hair. The suburbs were just hotbeds of animosity and hostility. Our first trip out of town was to San Francisco and though we were aware of the Byrds' "Mr. Tambourine Man", we had no idea how many similar musical trips to our own were happening on the coast. Folk Rock really seemed to have taken a hold, particularly in L.A., where the commercial aspects were really being pushed forward."

In late 1965, San Francisco was blossoming into the counterculture capitol of the United States. A revolution was starting on the streets of Haight and Ashbury with gay pride parades and the Indian invasion of Alcatraz Island making headlines. The San Francisco Police Department dealt heavy handedly with most demonstrations and with Barry McGuire's anti-establishment rant "Eve Of Destruction" reaching number one in September, the divided nature of the young and the establishment, that said yes to Vietnam, was akin to a pot boiling with the lid ready to explode. The seeds of the now famous music scene had only been sown for a few weeks when The Lovin' Spoonful arrived in mid-August.

LOVIN' SPOONFUL

SUITE 306
200 W. 57th STREET
NEW YORK NY 10019

First stop was DJ Tom Donahue's club as Sebastian recalls, "We played a strip club but it was a very visible strip club called Mothers. Things could happen in those days, which just wouldn't happen now. I mean, here we would go out and we would play for half an hour and then out would come "Topless Maria" the go-go dancer. She would dance bare breasted and we would play blues or whatever we could play, then she would leave and we would resume. It was the club trying to adjust to these different forces that were on that street at that time. Carol Doda, who was famous for having the first silicon breasts, was down the street."

Supporting the Spoonful were the local group The Vejtables whose drummer, Jan Errico recalls, "I remember they had to use my drums that week because theirs hadn't shown up when the equipment was shipped. Joe Butler pushed aside my floor tom and said, "I don't need this because I can't play it anyway." It was funny when we had to play behind Topless Maria in between our sets, because her top kept getting bigger every week because of silicone injections!" Even though the Spoonful were in the charts, they still had second billing to Maria.

On the plus side, Ralph Gleason, the music critic for the *San Francisco Chronicle* saw the Spoonful at Mothers and gave them a glowing review, stating that they were, "The best group in the U.S! I'm glad to be alive at a time when I can hear them." This critical rave, by a well-respected writer, enabled the group's week-long residency to be a sell-out - and Butler got to "meet" Carol Doda! The group then moved on to meet a new circle of friends who would prove to have a significant impact on The Lovin Spoonful's tenure.

Larry Hankin, from the theatre-comedy troupe The Committee remembers his first innocent meeting with the Spoonful; "They were playing at The Peppermint Tree, a new Rock dancehall up the street about five or six doors away from the Committee's theatre. We would rehearse in the afternoon in the lobby which had porthole windows to the street outside. We'd use the lobby because it was big and we could do warming up Yoga and exercises on a big expanse of floor. One day we were exercising and playing "Improvisation Group Games" when we looked at the porthole windows and saw four faces peering in.

"They all started to mock us and imitate us through the windows and made us break up in laughter. They were as good as us and had an incredible sense of play. We opened the doors to see who they were and the four Spoonfuls' ran in and started a finger shoot-out. We took cover and a finger-gun battle broke out in the Committee lobby. The Spoonful against The Committee – four against seven. Snipers behind the bars, overturned table for defence – finally, our director stopped it, grudgingly, so we could get back to the serious job of comedy. And that was the bond right there."

Having been a wow in San Francisco, the group went on to Los Angeles as Boone remembers, "We played The Crescendo (where they were described as "A rollicking, romping, rakish folk-rocking foursome" by *Variety*) and the Trip that was in the basement of the Playboy Club and it was right across the street from Ben Franks, the famous all-night restaurant. That's where I met Crosby (David, of The Byrds). Of course, John and Zally knew him from earlier, I didn't. I hung out with Crosby and we went out and popped some - you know whatever."

In fact, the carefree drug scene on the west coast was quite different to the secretive nature adopted by the Spoonful at home as Jacobsen explains, "I remember going to a gig that the Spoonful did out there and I couldn't believe it because I was invited to smoke pot...out there in the open, on the dance floor. My God, back in New York, paranoia struck deep, and I mean it! It was a case of locked doors, towels stuffed into the crack underneath it, incense sticks to hide the smell... oh boy, those clandestine little gatherings!"

The Spoonful then took a lucrative gig at the Rose Bowl in Pasadena supporting Herman's Hermits, where their first confrontation with pandemonium occurred as Sebastian recalls, "We drove to that in a convertible with no accompaniment, no police. We did the show, got back in our convertible, they opened the door at the exit to get our car out and we got mobbed. It was the first time, we were completely unprepared. I remember Joe got a big red mark around his neck as they were pulling some chain that he had on, somebody was trying to pull my shirt off and of course you know how a collar resists tearing and so I was being literally strangled at one point... and somebody was cutting hair, it was terrible. What it was, was the United States experiencing Beatlemania and now any four young men with long hair who played music meant something different than it had a month before."

With the group returning to New York in September, the New York Post sent Susan Szekely, for her column *Teen Talk*, to review the Spoonful (who were back at the Night Owl) and interview them afterwards in Googies, a bar round the corner where they hung out between shows. Totally missing out on the humour and vivacity of the Spoonful, Szekely gave them a haughty review, which the kids must have seen through. On the 20th of September, *Newsweek* ran a feature titled, "The Folk and the Rock" commenting on Dylan's recent turnaround and putting the Spoonful in the league of his followers, alongside The Byrds and Sonny & Cher.

The *Newsweek* article mentioned that they had witnessed the Spoonful's show at the Fox Theatre in Brooklyn, a series of shows Boone lists as his number one musical milestone, "The Murray The K, Brooklyn Fox shows with the Motown Review were terrific. The only two white acts on the show were us and The McCoys who had "Hang On Sloopy". It was a ten-day run, two shows a day, matinee and evening, and it was the most entertaining musical experience I've ever had. The line-up was The Four Tops, The Temptations, Martha and The Vandellas, The Marvelettes, Stevie Wonder and Patti Labelle. I mean, this was as hot a show that you could possibly hope to be part of and at the end, every night; everybody would come out on stage and sing together.

"To hear Patti Labelle, and at this time she was only about 18 years old with long straight hair, wearing a gingham dress, come out and sing "You'll Never Walk Alone", well the audience would not breathe a breath for about four minutes - she was earth-stopping. She was so good a singer and just the whole Motown Review, all these great musicians, bass players from my dreams; it was just the best, the biggest musical experience of my life." The Spoonful also performed skits with the groups as well as surprise guest Marvin Gaye.

In the second week in September an advert appeared in the *Daily Variety* announcing auditions for what was to become The Monkees. It could have been, 'Hey, hey, we're the Spoonful' as Steve Boone explains, "We were offered the script before they put out the casting call. We'd had our first hit out, come back from our first tour and they took us into an office. We turned it down because we'd already established ourselves with the hit." Sebastian agrees; "They approached us through our agent. We just laughed him out of the room. It wasn't the kind of thing we'd even consider. We had priorities other than money." David Jones, whom The Monkees was built around, recalls, "I saw them (the Spoonful) many times, there were many other groups tried out at the time

The Monkees were being put together, Jan & Dean were trying to put a show together, The Beach Boys were trying to put a show together!"

Another almost Monkee, alongside many including Stephen Stills, Danny Hutton and Paul Williams, was Jerry Yester, "I was picked as a Monkee, in fact, when The MFQ were at the Action. Bert Schneider and Davy Jones came in to see me and then talked to me after and said, "You wanna come down (to) Colgems and read through some stuff?" I said, "Sure, sounds interesting." I went up to audition for Bob Rafelson, just some impromptu stuff and then they called me back and said, "Yeah, we want you to be a Monkee." I said, "Wow!"

"But the thing that bothered me about The Monkees, was that it was manufactured, it wasn't real. I tried to talk them into making The MFQ, The Monkees, I said, "We're a real group and that kind of stuff happens to us." Yester bailed out of the project just as it was about to explode onto the market, just like he did with The New Christy Minstrels. On being asked if he regretted not being a Monkee, he replied, "Oh, sometimes when I don't have the rent!"

As well as playing The Action, The MFQ played The Trip on Sunset Boulevard (opening for The Velvet Underground and Donovan) and as Yester recalls, "We did one gig at The Mecca, in Downey, way out near the L.A. Airport and Phil Spector came out in his limo', and that's where he first heard us." After being rebuffed by the Spoonful, Spector was keen to record a folk rock single with The MFQ. He had a song in mind; "This Could Be The Night" written by Harry Nilsson, with the arranger being Jack Nitzsche. Why hardly anybody has ever heard of this potentially massive song is down to one person - Phil Spector.

Yester recalls Spector's bizarre behaviour, "With Spector, it seemed like six months at his house, eight hours a day, seven of which would be taken up with him telling stories and having his bodyguards give karate demonstrations, sending the limo out to Pinks for hot dogs, working a little bit on the song and going home. I was real good friends with Jack Nitzsche at the time and he would show up at the house to work on our arrangement, and Spector would say, "Wait a minute, I've got to change my shoes," and he would go upstairs and never come down again."

Spector was also interested in producing Yester's wife, Judy Henske. Her guitarist, John Forsha, was present at these sessions: "We hung out in Spector's mansion in Hollywood. He had three black belt karate experts as bodyguards and electric fences and gates. We'd go to parties there and he'd go upstairs to change his shoes every half an hour. During that period we got involved with some interesting people through Jack Nicholson's ex-wife. We went to a party at her place one night with Sharon Tate and Roman Polanski and all the rest. I was standing in the kitchen and some guy in a suit comes in smoking a joint. I turn round and he passes it to me and it's James Mason who was there with his daughter, Portland. All these folks were there and we didn't know them. We just hung around trying to look unobtrusive and take notes."

The MFQ did not waste too much time, however, as while they waited for Spector to put something on his feet; they did session work with The Ronettes', "Paradise", Bob Lind's, "Elusive Butterfly" and The Righteous Brothers', "Ebb Tide". Also from this period is a wonderful first take unreleased rendition of the song "Long Way To Be

SUNDAY OCT. 24th
8 till 12 P.M.
THE FAMILY DOG PRESENTS
A TRIBUTE TO
SPARKLE PLENTY
THE LOVIN' SPOONFUL
AND
THE CHARLATANS
LARRY HANKIN
WITH
RUSS THE MOOSE SYRACUSE
LONGSHOREMEN'S HALL = FISHERMAN'S WHARF
AT THE DOOR

Unhappy", sung by Spector, which was made as a demo for Judy Henske. Finally, with about thirty eight people providing the Wall Of Sound, The MFQ put down their vocals, in front of Brian Wilson who wore a bathrobe and slippers! Like Wilson, Spector was on his way to disappearing from normality, and with him he took the finished tape of "This Could Be The Night". The MFQ were crushed.

Meanwhile, on the 16th of October, The Family Dog, a concert organising troupe headed by Luria Castell, Al Kelly, Ellen Harmon and Jack Towle, presented its first show at the Longshoreman's Hall, in San Francisco, with featured acts The Jefferson Airplane, The Great Society and The Charlatans. Being held on the same day as a huge Vietnam Day peace march, where Allen Ginsberg and Ken Kesey and The Merry Pranksters had held court, and helped by a well thought out poster campaign, the hall was near to being full. The show exceeded expectations and goes down in history as the beginning of the Haight-Ashbury scene. A lot of little puddles had started running together and The Family Dog booked the hall again, hoping to repeat the first gigs success.

Luria Castell had been to Mothers, where she claimed at the time, "Dancing is the thing - when I heard The Lovin' Spoonful I couldn't stop. It was such an enveloping thing." Here she met Jacobsen as he recalls, "I prided myself on my image at that time; I had adopted this old-time look with waistcoats and watch-chains and stuff and I imagined I was pretty unique - so imagine my surprise when Luria showed me a photo of The Charlatans, who were all dressed like it!" Castell made arrangements for Jacobsen to meet The Charlatans and for the Spoonful to headline The Family Dog's second venture at the same modernistic, dome shaped union hall near Fisherman's Wharf.

The concert, titled "A Tribute to Sparkle Plenty" named after Dick Tracy's curly-locked waif, was held on October 24th with support from The Charlatans and co-emceed by Russ "The Moose" Syracuse, a local disc jockey and Larry Hankin. Jerry Garcia had his first LSD trip at the concert (LSD was six months away from being declared illegal), also attended by the Beat poet Michael McClure and Ken Kesey's crew. The concert was even more of a hit than the first, with people on the same wavelength finding each other - The Lovin' Spoonful left San Francisco wanting more.

With the group in L.A., Kama Sutra released the similar in style follow up to "Do You Believe In Magic", "You Didn't Have To Be So Nice". Again there was the distinctive sound of the autoharp and the shuffle speed, but the repetitiveness did not seem to matter, as the song followed its predecessor into the American top ten. The song also found a niche for Jacobsen's cascading bells sound that he had used on "Lady Godiva". The muse of the song was a good choice for the second single; it was not anthemic but just a simple boy/girl piece.

Sebastian recalls his version of the origins of "You Didn't Have To Be So Nice": "That came out of a little piano piece Steve Boone would play at any rehearsal where there was a piano around. I said, "That's a hit; what is it?" He said, "How about if we called it "You Didn't Have To Be So Nice"?" That was the key. I got all the lyrics in half an hour after he said that title line." Boone disagrees with Sebastian's version of how the song came into being, "Well John's memory is totally bogus about that. I wrote the melody and the first two verses and John helped me finish the last verse and the chorus, 'Today said the time was right for me...,' he helped me write that. When you hear John's story of it, John, I don't mind you hearing this! (Boone shouts into the tape recorder). He made it like Steve had some noodling part on the piano and he wrote the whole song and that's bullshit! It's not the way it was and I don't mind telling him that!"

You Didn't Have To Be So Nic

Words and Music by JOHN SEBASTIAN and STEVE BOONE

THE GOOD TIME MUSIC OF THE LOVIN' SPOONFUL

a product of Koppelman-Rubin Associates, Inc.

on KAMA SUTRA Record KA-205

Distr

FAITHFUL VIRTUE
MUSIC CO., INC.

With the influential *16 Magazine* now discovering the Spoonful, MGM signed up Koppelman-Rubin Associates as independent record producers on a non-exclusive basis. Their agreement called for thirty two sides in the next twelve months. With this expansion, Koppelman and Rubin took on Gary Klein as the professional manager for Chardon Music and Faithful Virtue. Only days after releasing the Spoonful's second single the time was ripe for Kama Sutra to release theirs and the Spoonful's first album, recorded at Bell Sounds Studios, at 237 West 54th Street, New York.

Unimaginatively, the label copied the formula of the time and titled the album after the Spoonful's first hit single. The cover for *Do You Believe In Magic* bore all the visual trademarks of the Spoonful, with the striped T shirts, the granny glasses and the laughing faces. Their look was soon to be adopted by the Californian surfer - how cool could you get? The portrayal was not completely all it seemed, as in a contemporary interview Yanovsky claimed, "The re-touchers took the pimples off my face and the tartar off my teeth, but they couldn't get the bedbug bites off my arms. There were too many, if you look you can see them - that's realism!"

The album contains twelve tracks out of which only four can be claimed as Sebastian originals. Apart from two fairly new at the time tunes that the group chose to cover, the remainder were, as Sebastian says, "old songs from the thirties, which we could re-write and electrify." After commencing with the title cut, the next three songs on the album were all attributed to the group, under the title, "Traditional. Adapted and arranged by;"

The first of these, "Blues In The Bottle", sung by Yanovsky, is memorable for its fuzzy guitar introduction and particular good-time feel. The song was a result of an earlier jug band influenced album as Sebastian explains; "There was definitely a source for "Blues In The Bottle" and that came from Stampfel and Weber - The Holy Modal Rounders." These two surnames were actually tagged onto those of the Spoonful's, making this a song with six credits. Sebastian remembers The Holy Modal Rounders fondly in a '90s interview; "They were wonderfully crazy, especially on their first albums. They were a wacky duo and I consider them a tremendous influence on the Spoonful. When I say the Spoonful, I'm talking in many cases Zally and I, during the first six months or so when we were putting the band together. I think that even in their present incarnation, Steve and Joe would be the first to admit that they sort of had to learn that aspect of things from us." Butler agrees: "Steve and I really had to ride herd for a while. I didn't really get a lot of the jug band stuff."

The source for "Blues In The Bottle" is explained on the liner notes of The Holy Modal Rounders self-titled debut album, written in 1964 by Peter Stampfel; "This goody was learned from a tape sent to Luke Faust and us by Bill Barth of Takoma Records. It was originally recorded by Prince Albert Hunt's Texas Ramblers around 1930. I made up new words to it because it was easier than listening to the tape and writing words down." From the Rounders effort, the Spoonful added some new verses and changed the instruments substituting fiddle and banjo for electric guitar and bass, making their "Blues In The Bottle" a grandchild of the original. After a suggestion that Sebastian plagiarised the Rounders interpretation he pondered, then said, "I don't know if we ever denied that they came up with (the new arrangement). The fact is that most of those, that were in the public domain, I didn't take them all for myself, I split them up four ways with the other members of the group."

Maybe - but whilst reading through the credits to the album in 1992, an angry Joe Butler bellowed, ""Blues In The Bottle", "Sportin' Life", I never get paid on these fucking things! They send all the money to John...I haven't got any payment on these in twenty years!" Even though Spoonful friend Phil Ochs had desperately wanted to pen the notes for the Spoonful's debut, the job went to Stampfel, probably in recognition of his pioneering work. Stampfel, who later went on to run the Spoonful's fan club with his girlfriend Antonia, later complained that the published version of the liner notes were slightly different to his original. By changing the punctuation the notes read that Butler had played in gay (as in happy) clubs on Long Island instead of gay (as in gay) clubs.

This was not the only falsehood about the notes as Stampfel told the magazine Comstock Lode, "We interviewed the band and we were shocked. We asked them how old they were - in 1965 you had to include things like that. They paused and decided how old they ought to be. I thought that was phoney but I didn't say anything. They just wanted to be as popular with teenage girls as possible." Butler took two years off his life in all the fan magazine articles stating later that his time spent in the air force hadn't counted.

The origins of *Sportin' Life* were explained by Sebastian in the publicity material for *Tarzana Kid*, for which he re-recorded the song in the seventies, "Willie Nelson wrote a song called *It's My Life* and it's almost the same tune. It's one of the folk process tunes that has really been smirched around over the years."

My Gal, the B side to *You Didn't Have To Be So Nice*, stems from a version of the song that had appeared on the album Jim Kweskin & The Jug Band as does *Wild About My Lovin'*, although Sebastian claims to have first heard the latter on a composite ragtime album. The Spoonful's version is almost identical to the Kweskin Jug Band's, with only a couple of different lines. This tune was also re-recorded by Sebastian for *Tarzana Kid*, where the notes claim: "Wild About My Lovin'" (Traditional, stolen by John)."

The only totally new, previously unreleased John Sebastian song on the album, "Did You Ever Have To Make Up Your Mind", is a lyrical highlight and one of Sebastian's more appreciated works. Presented in a jaunty, whimsical mood, the song tells of Sebastian's youth; "During my summers I was a camp counsellor and I think the inspiration for "Make Up Your Mind" comes from falling in love in rapid succession with three or four different sets of beautiful sisters, that were also councillors at the summer camp. As a result of the quandary of who to try and attach myself to, I managed to get a couple of songs."

The song is Sebastian at his story-telling best and its cuteness and coyness even allows room for a spoken cameo from the girl's father warning, "You better go home son and make up your mind." The style of the song was an attempt to copy another of Sebastian and Yanovsky's favourite groups of the time, although this did not work out as intended as Sebastian recalls, "We wanted to do a record that sounded like Huey "Piano" Smith and The Clowns because they were a piano based band. What came out of us never sounded like them, you know?" Sebastian also recalls the musical process for the track; "The intro is me and Zally finger-picking on two guitars, there's also some ragtime picking in there. At one point Zally is playing his electric guild with all the treble turned off."

THE GOOD TIME MUSIC OF THE

LOVIN' SPOONFUL

KLP/KLPS-8050

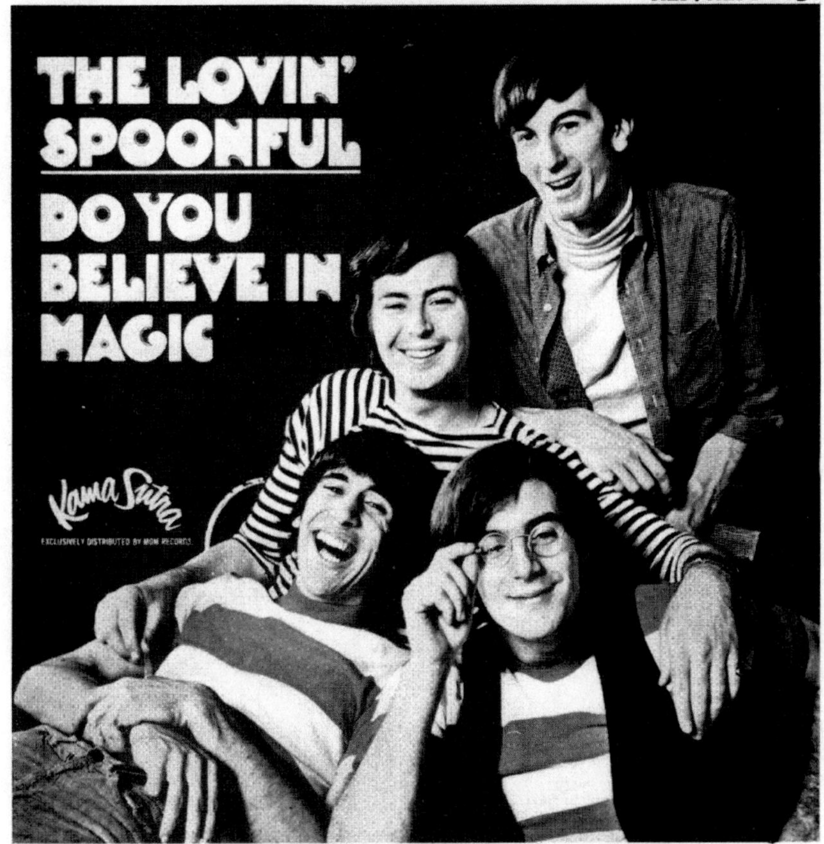

There are plenty of imitators around but imitators don't make news! Innovators do – and THE LOVIN' SPOONFUL are innovators! They're also outta sight!

IS ONLY ON KAMA SUTRA KAMA SUTRA

EXCLUSIVELY DISTRIBUTED BY MGM RECORDS

A PRODUCT OF KOPPELMAN-RUBIN ASSOCIATES/PRODUCED BY ERIK JACOBSEN

"You Baby" is the first song where Butler is allowed the lead vocal ("We were always looking for a song for Butler to sing," recalls Yanovsky). Although Butler was regarded as the second vocalist in the group, "You Baby" shows his casual assurance and that he could easily shine against the rest of the group in the singing department. The song is presented in a relaxed style that is refreshing in comparison with the rest of the album. Nobody in the group can remember the circumstances of exactly how the song appeared but they should be pleased that it did. From the successful partnership of Barry Mann and Cynthia Weil, with assistance from Phil Spector, the song stems from one of Sebastian's favourite records from the sixties, *Presenting The Ronettes*.

In a 1966 interview, Sebastian claimed that The Ronettes album was, "the most ingenious symphonic rock and roll. Veronica's (Ronnie Spector) voice and Phil Spector's music are young and fully aware of the excitement beat music can generate." Jerry Yester can recall Sebastian's stirring on first hearing the record, "The first time I heard The Ronettes was when John came pounding on my door at ten o'clock in the morning, shouting, "You've gotta hear this, you've gotta hear this!"

In fact, Yester had already become involved with the Spoonful whilst The MFQ were still in New York. He had played piano on "Do You Believe In Magic" and helped out on the album also, "I was asked to come over and help during the Spoonful rehearsals and do vocal arrangements and stuff like that. I did "Fishin' Blues" - it wasn't a case of writing stuff down because they didn't read music. We just sat around a piano, I said, "You sing this note and you sing this." They were just real basic singers, I mean they weren't into doing real tricky parts - they didn't want to do real tricky parts, so we just did simple stuff. It wasn't a lot of work on my part; I just guided them, basically."

The song "Fishin' Blues" can be traced back to Henry Thomas to whom the Spoonful would later dedicate a song. Thomas, born in Texas in 1874, is noted as being the oldest songster on disc. His style was varied - blues, ragtime and spiritual songs were all handled impressively. The significantly identifiable sound of Henry Thomas is his playing of the panpipes or "quills", as they were known. With similar lyrics, Thomas's recording of "Fishin' Blues" is delightful with a pennywhistle solo that Yanovsky translated onto guitar.

From Fred Neil's first solo album, *Bleecker & MacDougal* that Sebastian had played harmonica on, the Spoonful chose "Other Side To This Life" for Joe Butler to sing. Neil was present at the session but this did not seem to daunt Butler as he puts down another impressive performance. This is the Spoonful's interpretation of Folk Rock although they hated the term. Compared with the latter-day versions of the song by The Jefferson Airplane and The Youngbloods, among many, the Spoonful's effort is enhanced even more. The song evokes Neil's poignant need to escape the city into the more open spaces - in his case Coconut Grove, in Florida.

Musically taken from the song "Prison Wall Blues" by Gus Cannon's Jug Stompers, although entirely credited to Sebastian, "Younger Girl" is a lyrical delight about the temptations an adolescent can bring, that has stood the test of time with ease; 'Should I hang around, Acting like her brother, In a few more years, They'll call us right for each other.' These are lines that are so true to all men. Like every young rock 'n' roll group, the Spoonful had its legions of female fans, but males bought their records also, probably relating to the experiences Sebastian expressed so well in song.

Whether or not an experience Butler went through relates to this song is not known, but around the time the album was being released there was a matter of a delicate unwanted distraction to be taken care of as Butler leads into here, "She was dancing topless in a night-club for chrissakes, so I presumed she was eighteen - it was like Jack Nicholson in *One Flew Over The Cuckoo's Nest*. You know, I really didn't care that much but I remember being with her father in the car, "Do you want to marry my daughter?" "No sir, we made a big mistake." I played the part where I'm younger than I really am and Cavallo played the father. The girl I got pregnant got $1500 to send her and her whole family to Puerto Rico. Jesus Christ! It was funny, but it wasn't funny as that's where the first Spoonful money we got went."

"On The Road Again", performed at rip-roaring speed with Yanovsky hoarsely belting out the vocals, is on the far end of the scale away from the version that appeared on the Even Dozen's album, from only a year earlier. Yanovsky enters the guitarist's hall of fame with an exhilarating solo, which proved his years in oblivion were not wasted. The last cut on the album shows the entire group's musical prowess and in particular Sebastian's spectacular blues harp ability. With a reference to Joe Marra's club, "Night Owl Blues", the first in a series of instrumentals by the group, made people turn the record over and start all over again - it was as good a blues piece as any.

On the released version there is an annoying fade during a blistering Yanovsky solo, which has always been frustrating to the listener. Why this occurred was first answered by Sebastian who replied, "Okay, well now here is an interesting little piece of trivia. In fact there isn't much more of "Night Owl Blues" as it ends abruptly a few seconds afterwards because Stephen stops. As a matter of fact, it was quite an amazing thing cause I remember we were all... the other guys were like fairly transfixed with the take. We were really enjoying playing it and all of a sudden Stephen stops playing and on the tape you hear Zally say, "Stephen, you stopped!" Stephen had thought the take was bad or something, I don't know, but it made him stop. We listened back to it and said, "Aww, this is the good one, we'll just have to fade it in the middle of the guitar break."

The real story of why he stopped playing and the reason for Sebastian's pause, is recounted by Boone, "What happened really was - it was an all night long session and also, me and I think Zal, had been doing Black Beauties, amphetamines, to stay awake. Every time it would come to the place where I'd do the bass solo, right after Zally, I would always get my bass solo right but somebody else would then make a mistake, so it wouldn't count as a take. Finally, four hours into doing this thing, and doing speed, we get to the part and Zally does his solo perfectly and I get to my bass solo and I just can't do it, my fingers just froze, so I stopped. Erik goes, "Steve, I can't believe you just did that!" and I go, "Oh fuck," or something like that. So you hear "Night Owl Blues" and it fades on Zally's solo. That's why it ended abruptly - you heard it from the horse's mouth!" (Well, Black Beauty's).

Don Paulsen attended this particular recording; "I remember there was an all-night recording session that I did an article on in *Hit Parader* when they were finishing up their first album - five or six songs overnight. I remember every once in a while they would take a break from recording while Erik Jacobsen would do some remixes or a microphone set up or something and they would say, "We're going up to the roof, don't bother us, we'll be down in ten or fifteen minutes," and they would all come down giggling. It was the sixties, drugs were around but they were pretty discreet about it. I'd say in all the time I was with them there was never any kind of the typical Hollywood wild party, orgy drug scenes, or anything like that. They were really not that kind of a group."

Overall the album is a delight. It's the best one the group were to do according to their lead guitarist, "I think relatively speaking as the albums progressed they became a little less interesting. Acoustically I think it's a great record, the first record. It's pretty basic, there was not a lot of overdubbing - it's almost live." The blend of the Spoonful's influences was transferred to the modern day perfectly on *Do You Believe In Magic* and the original material was above anything coming out of America at the time, excluding Gene Clark's material with The Byrds which was on a par with Sebastian's. These two groups led the counter-attack to the British Invasion, spearheaded by The Beatles and jumped on by many lesser acts. The reverse would now happen, with a US invasion of the UK imminent.

Do You Believe In Magic was reviewed in *Billboard* who said, "The phenomenal success of their initial hit single skyrocketed the off-beat group in national prominence and is the foundation for this exciting folk-rock-blues album which will meet with equal success in the LP market." In reality the timeless masterpiece only slipped into the top 40 in the US charts, peaking at number 32 - not bad for a debut album.

When San Francisco's Fillmore Auditorium opened its doors for the first time on November 6th; back in New York Bob Dylan jammed the night away with Brian Jones, and Don Paulsen used his contacts to take a rare photo of the pair together. Also that memorable night in New York, Jacobsen was discovering just with whom he had signed on the dotted line; "When the great blackout hit New York City, I was in the Kama Sutra office talking business with them and right away they opened up the closet with the special key and got out a bunch of guns - big rifles and shotguns - and said, "Let the motherfuckers come, we're ready for them!" (laughs) Phil Steinberg, he was the main wild guy, Hy Mizrahi was a nice, good looking guy who must have put in money and then of course there was hard driving, crazy Artie Ripp."

Boone seconds Jacobsen's recollection about the firepower available to the heads of the Spoonful's record label, "They were just crazy kids from Brooklyn. All I can remember about Phil Steinberg was he used to have a machine gun and he would go up on the roof of the Brill Building and fire it off!" Steinberg readily admits to his wild behaviour; "I did fire off my gun on the roof of my office. I also shot out the television set on a quick draw. That's when I beat Hugh O'Brian."

The one of the three Kama Sutra partners the Spoonful dealt with most was Ripp as Sebastian recalls, "He was and still is a very compelling man. I mean he's been the prototype for a lot of 'rip off' characterisations but the fact is he was very involved with the music and the excitement of it all. He helped out a lot, in his own way as a kind of cheerleader for the Spoonful. They were all pretty crazy there as time went on, absorbing the sixties as we all were, and things were pretty nuts over there."

Insiders in the record industry have always considered Kama Sutra as a Mafia company. According to Ripp, he once shamed his partners into telling him that Kama Sutra was 10% Mafia owned ("That's like being a little pregnant," quipped Ripp) as Steinberg and Mizrahi had allegedly borrowed $10,000 and then some from local mobsters to set up the company. These gangsters started to haunt the offices of Kama Sutra and upset the secretaries. Their leader was Sonny Franzese, a caporegime (a capo is a lieutenant) in the Colombo crime family and also a silent partner in the Kama Sutra, as testified by his stepson, Michael Franzese.

According to Ripp, aware that the FBI and the IRS were watching Kama Sutra's every move; he made a straightforward appeal for mercy in an attempt to get Franzese to disappear out of his life. This involved getting drunk with the Mafioso and putting some money in a brown paper bag in return for some freedom. On hearing what Ripp had to say on this matter, a furious Phil Steinberg retorted, "To think of Artie Ripp confronting me is laughable. To say he shamed me is dishonourable and untrue. Men like Sonny Franzese I knew all my life, they were all over the entertainment business. His son Michael was nearly raised in my office. Ripp appealing for mercy from Sonny is a comedy and a farce. The Mafia is a real benevolent group - please."

Steinberg does admit to getting some heat from the gangsters; "Morris Levy made a move. He tried to infer that he somehow had a piece of the Shangri-Las. He spoke to me about it. I said, "Fuck off." We were never the victims of a Mob take-over. Investigations, long investigations, by the Manhattan DA, the FBI and the IRS bear this out. There was never any money borrowed from the Mob, so there was never any money to return. Artie lavished in running to be seen with Mafia guys. I grew up with these people all my life. I know the street and I know its rules. I am known and have always been known as a 'stand up guy.' A brown paper bag with money and that was that bull-a-shit!"

The gossip among the industry had some positive sides, however, as Steinberg explains, "We had become known as a Mafia company. There was good and bad in that, because perception of what is going on can be more important than what really is going on. It worked for all parties concerned. That doesn't mean everything everyday went lovey dovey. Again, nobody had to loan any money - a favour is enough to become involved. The permutations are endless. The people around my office were hard men and these things would come up - you just had to have the balls to deal with it."

After the enjoyment of playing alongside the Motown Review in New York, the Spoonful jumped at the chance of joining The Supremes on a bus tour of the American south. Sebastian, looking back, saw the tour as an attempt to be appreciated by a black audience, "At that time black groups were finding, maybe, that their major audience was in young white teenagers and we were anxious to be accepted by the black community because we felt we drew so much from R&B. In some ways you have to remember that racism had a little break there in the sixties. There was not nearly the categorisation that existed, "Now well, you're this style of music, so you'll be on this station and you'll play these markets." At the time of the tour, however, Sebastian was not keen to have two weeks away from New York, as he had just met young Lorey Kaye and fallen in love.

In America - and the south especially - racism was still rife and segregation was still predominant as a disconcerted Sebastian recalls, "Certainly we were seeing the south first hand. We were, you know, a bunch of New York kids and I don't know...the real segregation, I mean separate toilets seemed like a distant bad dream. It didn't really seem real and for us to actually tour the south with The Supremes and their band was an unpleasant revelation." It wasn't long before the racial tensions affected the Spoonful and Boone can hardly forget the events of one evening during the tour, "We'd done a show in Louisiana and after the show was over we all got back on the bus and drove to an all-night restaurant where blacks were not allowed in. So the Spoonful went in to order some breakfast and the blacks were going to get carryout. As we were ordering, John Sebastian was on the phone calling Lorey and these big rednecks across the bar started taunting him, giving John shit like, "Hey, look at the faggot with the peppermint striped shirt, let's go over and kick this little faggot's ass cause he's talking on the telephone and he won't even look at us."

ADMISSION:
U.S.L. Students $1.50
All Others $2.50
Tickets on Sale at:
"Prof" Erny's, Staggs,
Wa Wa's Grocery and at
U.S.L. Student Center

EARL VAN DYKE & ORCH

BLACKHAM COLISEUM

Wednesday, November 10 — 8:15 P.M.

SPONSORED BY U.S.L. STUDENT COUNCIL

"Fortunately, a lot of the other customers were college kids who'd seen our show. It was starting to get real ugly and right about the time they were getting ready to come over to take John and cram him into the drain, a couple of the bigger college kids stood up and said, "Wait a minute, you can't do that, these guys are entertainers, we just saw them." At the same time, Diana Ross had seen what was happening and she went back and got the whole band off the bus, some of them were pretty big dudes and they were going to come in a rescue our ass. "They all came off the bus and come marching into this restaurant, so we got the hell out of there and Zally jumped right into the arms of the band leader, it was really funny! It was also close. I've lived in the south, man it could have been real ugly, we could have got our hair cut off and our teeth knocked out - we were lucky."

Relieved when the tour of the south was over, the Spoonful went to a friendlier Hollywood to film an appearance for the movie *The Big TNT Show*. The musical co-ordinator for the film was Phil Spector, who had assembled some of his current favourite performers for this concert film. Filmed on November 29th, the Spoonful's performance of their two hit singles provides an extremely rare glimpse into how the group played live alongside immaculate performances by their R&B heroes like Ike & Tina Turner, Bo Diddley, Ray Charles and The Ronettes. The excitable raw performance by the Spoonful starts off with Butler getting the beat all wrong and "Do You Believe In Magic" comes to an abrupt halt after a few bars, to a loud, "Joe's fault!" from Yanovsky. This error was kept in the final cut of the film. Once they get going, the song is twice the speed of the record but this only enhances the performance. The version of "You Didn't Have To Be So Nice" is nearer the record and is a spine tingling moment also. Everything that Paul Williams mentioned is proved right by this footage; the personalities, the overpowering beat and the pleasing amateurism is all there to behold. To watch this hedonistic performance exudes a natural high and when partially shown on UK television in the '80s, it brought about a whole new audience to the Spoonful's music. A truly classic performance.

Sebastian reflects on the group's on-stage animation, "A lot of that was Zally when you get down to our stage performance. I was good as a kind of foil for Zally, my main thing was keeping the beat, cause when you get right down to it, Stephen's real steady, Joe would rush and Zally would rush. So the trick was just to keep the main thing. Zally had this marvellous stage manner and so whatever explosiveness we had was gonna come from him." It was put to Sebastian that in *The Big TNT Show*, Butler showed an iron will and a formidable store of pent-up energy, to which he replied, "Joe had a good and very consistent energy but his strength as a drummer was sort of like an athlete's strength. They say some athletes would be good in the 400 or they'll be good in the sprint but they can't do the other thing. It was just difficult for him, Joe's background was not really as a drummer, it was more as a performer." Sebastian's comments on Butler's ability are a fair assessment with regards to what live Spoonful material exists from the beginnings of the group, but their overall aberrant performance endeared them to a lot more people through this performance. The Spoonful's showing in *The Big TNT Show* makes it easy to judge them against The Byrds, as they also appeared in the film performing their first two hits. Both bands were on a par with each other as both displayed an exciting presence, although Michael Clarke's military style drumming alongside their visible moodiness towards each other mars the performance of "Mr. Tambourine Man".

Also heard in the movie, filmed a couple of days after The Merry Pranksters' first "acid test" at the Longshoreman's Hall, but not seen, were The MFQ. Spector had promised the group a slot in the film – Yester

The BIG T★N★T SHOW
EXECUTIVE PRODUCERS: JAMES H. NICHOLSON, SAMUEL Z. ARKOFF & HENRY SAPERSTEIN · PRODUCER & MUSIC CO-ORDINATOR: PHIL SPECTOR · DIRECTOR: LARRY PEERCE

recalls playing in-between the acts - but he reneged and only included their song "This Could Be The Night" in the opening scenes, over footage that showed the bands arriving for the show. The Spoonful are spotted larking about on the street and end up knocking over a giant replica of their first album cover.

Mentioned by *Newsweek* as one of the Spoonfuls' contemporaries, Sonny & Cher were making a follow up to their number one smash from August, "I Got You Babe", when Sonny Bono thought of using the Spoonful to help with the publicity for the follow up, "But You're Mine". Bono was not as fresh as the pair's image suggested and had already had a history in the music business, writing, producing and performing under different aliases, waiting for one to ignite in the eyes of the record buying public.

Steve Boone; "After "Magic" came out, we were like the darlings of the critics and everybody loved us. Sonny Bono came to a concert and said, "Will you guys come and do a session for us up at Atlantic Records?" I thought Cher was cute anyway, so I'd be glad to do it. We get up there and there's already a whole session going on, like twenty people. There's two bass players in the studio already and I'm standing there and I go to Zally, "Like what do they want us here for? They won't notice us on this record." We didn't want to be part of it just for the publicity value; we were against all that kind of stuff."

The Spoonful are nowhere to be heard on this track. The reason for going ahead with the session was due to the attendance of one of the top brass in the music business as Boone points out, "We really respected Ahmet Ertegun, who was the head of Atlantic and he was there. Then Sonny came out and he said, "We have parts ready," cause he did Phil Spector kind of sessions where they had five guitars, three bass players and six drummers - that's how Phil did his sessions with like forty people in the studio playing all this shit at once. It was sort of like gratuitous, they exploited us and it got in the trades."

Through Sebastian's girlfriend, the fortunate photographer at this session was Don Paulsen who recalls, "Lorey was a woman who was on the scene quite a lot. She met me and we talked a few times. At the time she was a waitress at The Bitter End and she had told me that the Spoonful were doing a session with Sonny & Cher. I walk into this studio and Sonny is still rehearsing the band. I recognised the whole Spoonful and a couple of New York session players and they are all going, 'chung, chung, chung' - this one note!" The end result was not too great. The song stiffed and almost managed to knock Sonny & Cher from the public eye, until an old recording was found and rush released.

The session provided Paulsen with a little nest egg as he happily points out, "I went out into the hall and Bob Dylan was there with Sonny and Cher, so I snapped a picture. I've sold that a few times, a rare smiling picture. Al Kooper mentioned to me that Dylan had the hots for Cher so that's why he was happy!" Butler also used the occasion to make a pass at the young singer.

The tip that Lorey Kaye gave Paulsen led to her being employed by *Hit Parader* as Paulsen remembers, "Lorey was a social butterfly in a way, she loved to know what was going on - who was doing what. She got a job on *Hit Parader* and it worked out very well, she was ambitious and used her connections. It was her idea to do a gossip column, so it started out with her writing it herself, calling it 'Granny's Gossip'."

With the Spoonful coming out of New York and making a name for themselves, it wasn't long before other bands tried to emulate their success. First out of the blocks were The Young Rascals with the single "I Ain't Gonna Eat Out My Heart Anymore". Other bands were being booked into The Night Owl including The Magicians, The Blues Magoos and The Strangers. The Spoonful needed to assert their authority and gain even more appeal. Their next single would keep their heads above the water for a good year.

During the bus tour with The Supremes, Sebastian found the muse to write his most popular song ever, as he recalled to Don Paulsen in 1966, "On a horrible day, going from Baltimore to South Carolina on a bus in the pouring rain, I got the idea for "Daydream". It was really the lowest, a terrible day. I was feeling very depressed because I had just visited with Lorey and I was going away again for another stretch. I was musing about it and took out my guitar and started plucking - that was about the only thing I could do to keep from flipping out. Then I just thought of 'what a day for a daydream.' I wrote the song in about twenty minutes, the whole thing presented itself very clearly."

Everybody over thirty knows "Daydream", whether from the Spoonful or of the many cover versions - albeit with nobody ever successfully managing to duplicate the soothing emotions produced by the Spoonful's instantly loveable, laid back tribute to tranquillity. The antiquated shuffle, with Boone's bar room tinkling piano at its core, motivated the masses into accepting The Lovin' Spoonful into their hearts and minds. Other musicians were to take note too, either thematically or stylistically; The Kinks with "Sunny Afternoon", The Young Rascals with "Groovin'" and a big feather in Sebastian's cap, The Beatles with "Good Day Sunshine".

This association would not seem likely until Paul McCartney admitted, to *Playboy* in 1984, that his influence for "Good Day Sunshine" was in fact "Daydream". Sebastian explains the evolution of "Daydream", with a reference to another Beatles connection, "The primary motivation was, strangely enough, "Baby Love" (by The Supremes) because we were trying to come up with something that had a beat like "Baby Love" and I figured that that straight eight feel was going to be the next big thing. I found out both from reference material and directly from John and Paul from The Beatles that they were doing the same thing. It wasn't so much tunes, as to try and cop an interesting beat and that was very much part of the Spoonful's evolution. Once it got filtered through the four of us, it didn't really sound like "Baby Love" anymore, but it still had that Motown groove to it."

So Sebastian's interpretation of *Baby Love*, written in the company of Diana Ross and Co., turned into one of The Beatles' more popular album tracks. This was news, even to Sebastian when he read McCartney's recollection in 1984, although Sebastian added in 1991 that the song "Deep Purple" by Nino Tempo and April Stevens was another influence for "Daydream", "Well the chords are the same, I loved "Deep Purple" and I'm sure that I was influenced by it." To record the song, Jacobsen spliced together a loop that went round and round, overdubbing the bass to keep everything tight. The Spoonful rarely recorded live and vocals were always overdubs.

DAYDREAM

Words and Music by John Sebastian

RECORDED BY
The Lovin' Spoonful
ON PYE

ROBBINS MUSIC CORPORATION LTD. 3/-

35, Soho Square, London, W.1.

Selling Agents: Francis, Day & Hunter Ltd., 138/140, Charing Cross Rd., London, W.C.2.

Another group, who's first single's mood was similar to that of "Daydream", were The Mamas & The Papas, who had formed when Cass Elliot and Denny Doherty joined with husband and wife John and Michelle Phillips. The call to join the group came at a good time for Elliot and Doherty as they were on the verge of being kicked out of the Albert Hotel for not paying their bill. The single, "California Dreamin'" (released in November '65) was a top five hit in the States and led the way to a successful few years for the two ex-Mugwumps. The two songs charted around the same time with "Daydream" just missing out on a number one by one place. With the success of this single, Koppelman and Rubin, hungry for product to fill their agreement with MGM ordered the group into the studio for another album. The only snag was that their repertoire had yet to be replenished since the first album.

The album *Daydream* was released no less than four months after its predecessor. With two of the tracks already out on singles, it was surprising that out of the remaining ten, only one was a cover. Apart from the occasional nod to another member of the group, Sebastian showed that he could produce quantity as well as quality in his songwriting. Quite a roll as it was put to him, "Well it's not so much of a roll as a draw, there's something pulling and when you have a situation like that...remember, the band started around jug band tunes, recycled Chuck Berry tunes. I'm not talking about albums now I'm talking about what we played when we played live and we had been playing live for six months before *Daydream*.

"I had written three tunes before the Spoonful, "Good Time Music", "Don't Bank On It Baby" and "Didn't Want To Have To Do It", so really it was the fact that the band's output had (dried up). We needed new material and I was simply writing to fill a void. I was not writing with any idea of accumulating a publishing catalogue or anything, I was just writing out of desperation!" Sebastian thrived on the challenge to come up with near to an album's worth of material. The fact that his songwriting was in demand, alongside the tardiness of his fellow members, stimulated him into composing at a rate never achieved before or after this album.

Pretty much a throwaway, "There She Is" was given to Butler to sing though Yanovsky's guitar solo is the highlight of this song, alongside Sebastian's charming hint at sex; 'I have found rolling around, somewhere very private, How her touch can mean so much, but I can't describe it!' There is some hilarious film of the group performing the song on Hullabaloo, showing the Spoonful surrounded by several fitful dancers with Butler struggling to sing into a microphone placed badly at his side whilst drumming simultaneously. The reason for the poorly placed microphone was due to this being one performance that Butler nearly didn't make, "I remember the *Hullabaloo* show was filmed in the big NBC Studios in Brooklyn, not far from Coney Island. Just before we went on, we found our way upstairs onto the roof so we could smoke some marijuana. We walked through this exit door, turned on the light switch and there was this cement ramp and on either side of the ramp, sunken down maybe eighteen inches was all these machines that ran the elevators and generators.

"So we went out on the roof, smoking the joint and we had a few minutes so I stayed to finish it. On their way out somebody deliberately, or by accident, had shut the light switch off. There was bright light on the roof but when I came in the room the door slammed behind me and it was pitch black except for the sparks coming from these machines. I wasn't sure where this ramp was - I was petrified and stoned out of my mind - so I started throwing coins so could hear where they fell. Eventually I found the ramp and made it down to the other door, got it open and was relieved to find a stab of light. I finally got downstairs within moments of us being on stage."

A much deeper song about relationships, "It's Not Time Now", proves just how introspective Sebastian was becoming and how well he could interpret his thoughts into songs. The song deals with his thought process during arguments; that it would be better to stop and think before hurting somebody's feelings and destroying what has been built between the couple.

The songwriting credits list Yanovsky alongside Sebastian's name and the pair harmonise well throughout this country and western tinged tune, where Sebastian plays lead guitar (with sponge under his guitar strings to produce a different sound) on a rare occasion. From the sessions that spawned "Lady Godiva", "Warm Baby" has ska overtones, with Butler's gunshot-like echoing drums and Sebastian's high falsetto backgrounds memorable features. Yanovsky's vocal approach on "Day Blues", deep, low and moody, is his best on record - his superb phrasing shows that he could really sing the blues well and here he is far better than on any of his other recordings. The song is a rare Sebastian/Butler composition though the latter admits, ""Day Blues" was my idea primarily but most of the writing was done by John."

Apart from the spoken opening being a direct steal from John Lee Hooker's "Walkin' The Boogie", "Let The Boy Rock And Roll" is a complete Chuck Berry rip-off, though co-writer Butler remembers the beginning as something else, "I wrote some of "Let The Boy Rock And Roll" and it was my idea for the song. The beginning was mine from some old jazz record. I said that I wanted to do a song with 'let that boy rock and roll' in it and John started writing. Then we needed a first verse (so I wrote one) and John said, "Did you do this yourself?" He was shocked that the song was so good."

Butler's first attempt at songwriting was a little unaccomplished but so were a lot of early rock 'n' roll lyrics. However, apart from Yanovsky's superb Chuck Berry guitar, the song has few redeeming features and is the only weak track in the collection. "Jug Band Music" with Sebastian on lead vocals alongside Yanovsky's "yakety throw-up guitar" is Sebastian's salute to the music he loves, although the song sounds nothing like it. A highlight of the group's set, "Jug Band Music" tells of various ailments ranging from a cowboy with a headache or being wiped out by a beach boy with the only cure being Jug Band Music! With the singalong coming to an end, a sharp Sebastian subtly inserts, 'And everybody knows that the very last line is the doctor said, 'Give him jug band music, it seems to make him feel just fine!'

"Didn't Want To Have To Do It" has been described by one writer as, "As heart-breakingly accurate as they come" and that is seconded here. With the "It" referring to breaking up a relationship, the song was only ever a B side, yet fits neatly on any of the hundreds of Spoonful "Hits" packages that have been released over the years. As a hint, Sebastian offered in *The Lovin' Spoonful Guitar Book*, which came out in 1967, that on the opening Fmaj.7 one should, "Play the bass note with your thumb (Lightnin' Hopkins' style)." In the introduction to the book, Sebastian puts forward his fondness for strong chord use, "The easy positions of some chords sound thin to my ears. I like full sounding chords that give the sound of an orchestra."

The only cover on the *Daydream* album comes from the same obscure source as the rhythm from "Good Time Music" - Doctor Feelgood & The Interns. William Lee Perryman born in Atlanta, Georgia in 1911, a.k.a. Piano Red a.k.a. Doctor Feelgood, an albino, was a shouter of good time songs who accompanied himself on piano. His style was a mixture of boogie woogie, honky tonk and steam hammer! He added The Interns when he rediscovered himself as Doctor Feelgood (get it?) in the early sixties, after recording for several labels. One of his songs from

1961, "Mr. Moonlight", struck a chord with The Beatles when they were out in Hamburg and they eventually recorded the song on the *Beatles For Sale* album in 1964.

The song the Spoonful took was "Bald Headed Lena" written by Perryman and one C. Smith (not Edgar Sneed as stated on the album,) takes Yanovsky to the opposite end of the scale from his interpretation of "Day Blues" to a uproarious singalong. He laughs his way throughout one verse but this is only a prelude to a chorus of Yanovsky gargling. This must be a first on record - a gargling solo - but it only adds to the enjoyment of the craziness that is going on here, although the song loses its edge after repeated plays. Apparently "Bald Headed Lena" became a number one hit in Sweden.

Often credited to Sebastian, probably due to a printer's error, it is not certain, is Steve Boone's "Butchie's Tune". The song is about a "groupie-mother", Jeannie Chow, who had toured with The Byrds and The Beatles and had lived in the Albert Hotel while the Spoonful had played there. Butler recalls the lady fondly, "Butchie was a good old girl - interesting woman, she was kind of like an older sister/mother. She put us all up at separate times and slept with several of us or none of us. I'm not sure if I ever slept with Butchie. Anyway, she's a neat gal and would fill me with these stories about The Beatles about how the best thing Paul liked to do was play a little boogie woogie and things like that. She filled us with excitement - she had touched the stars and slept with half of them."

Boone acknowledges Butler's comments and admits to having had a relationship with Butchie, "She was this really great gal and I mean tremendous person and we kind of became an item but I didn't want to have her as my girlfriend. She was older than I was and she was like one of those smothering types. I didn't want any of that, so I wrote the song." The song is about Boone wanting out, but trying to put it gently. It has a country style and was sung in concert by Boone in his Southern drawl, but handled on the record, admirably, by Butler.

Butchie was more than a passing phase for the Spoonful, however, as just like Cass Elliot had married James Hendricks in the Mugwumps days, Butchie became the first Mrs. Sebastian (just like she had done a short time earlier with Chris Hillman of The Byrds.) Butler informs; "I'm going to tell you something now. John was being threatened with the draft so we married John to Butchie, the girl from "Butchie's Tune", as she had two kids, right? So he wouldn't have to serve. I'd already served four years, Steve was exempt - he had hurt his leg and Zal was Canadian. So we did that, then lo and behold Lorey, who was motivated somewhat by finances, found out somehow that her boyfriend was married and went totally bananas!" Butler admits to his own selfishness, but he could see what was going to happen; "Erik and me, we get them together. Lorey wants to marry John and says he's getting a divorce and I said, "Lorey, if he gets a divorce, his name goes into the computer again." "I don't give a fuck, this can't happen," whatever it was she said. So John went ahead and did it on his own." This decision would cause sour repercussions further along the line. Butchie went on to marry the actor Bob Denver but that was legitimate.

Sebastian remembered it a little differently to Rat magazine, "I was about to have to really do a freak show...I went down and really put on a show for the draft board – did a few numbers and I left but they still had me 1-A. They're very hard to impress down there. Actually, my father had a very convenient heart attack at that very moment – which we now refer to quite laughingly as his friendly, lucky heart attack. At the time it was very grim but suddenly I had this enormous file of cardiograms to explain why my father was on his death bed, when actually he was recuperating quite nicely." Unless Sebastian had just seen *Alice's Restaurant* or not, some files were allegedly thrown behind a cabinet in this matter.

The last track on *Daydream* continued the series of instrumentals. "Big Noise From Speonk" is a reference to Butler's origins on Long Island, "I had a friend, Bobby Haggard. His father played with Bob Crosby and he wrote a song called "Big Noise From Winnetka" and that was a take on that." Sebastian's harmonica parts on this instrumental are reminiscent of the work he did on "Candy Man" on Fred Neil's *Bleecker & MacDougal* album a few months earlier. The instrumental is not as raw and exciting as "Night Owl Blues" and suffers in comparison although it had a very hard act to follow. Also like its predecessor, it contains a frustrating premature fade. Not to say it is a poor instrumental as "Big Noise From Speonk" has an competent style of its own.

In fact the whole album is far more polished than *Do You Believe In Magic* and although the group have always bemoaned the lack of time they had in the studio, *Daydream*, track for track, proved that the group, and Erik Jacobsen in particular, had found their groove. There is not a common thread on this second album but there is a steady, comfortable presence towards their music which enabled them to go from the raucous ("Bald Headed Lena") to the serene ("Didn't Want To Have To Do It") and connect it all to an ideal of their own identity. As was tagged on the record labels - "The Good Time Music Of The Lovin' Spoonful" - and it really was.

CHAPTER 3 – IN A DAYDREAM

The first few months of 1966 were taken up with a heavy concert schedule and promotional interviews. One such discussion appeared in the "gentlemen's magazine" *Cavalier*, that highlighted the group's humour and sardonic contempt for fools. Obviously encouraged by the nature of the magazine they were being interviewed for, Butler noted that, "You press guys don't catch on very quickly," before the group set on the nonentity reporter mercilessly;

Q: Which is the best group in rock and roll music today?

ZAL: I think that the best group now playing music that is roughly called rock and roll is a brilliant young quartet called The Lovin' Spoonful.

Q: When are you fellows going to write a good protest song?

JOE: We have one. It's called "Bald Headed Lena". It's about atomic fallout.

Q: Your sound is hard to define. You've mixed all the sources for popular music.

JOHN: I had spent a couple of months buying gin for Lightnin' Hopkins. I learned a lot - got to play exactly like him, right down to the mistakes.

Q: Let's do the name thing. Where'd you get "Lovin' Spoonful"?

JOE: There's been a lot of crap about it, but we got it from a Mississippi John Hurt song, 'I love my baby by the loving spoonful'.

Q: Come on. You're putting us on. There's something sinister about the name.

ZAL: You mean something to do with drugs?

STEVE: Or was it something about sex and perversion you had in mind?

ZAL: Remember, Sir, as you wend your way on many paths and delve into other's minds, smut is in the eye of the beholder.

With that scathing attack ringing in the ears of the *Cavalier* journalist, the interview was terminated. Clearly the group had tired of the usual favourite colour type questions and gave as good as they got in interviews. They may have been getting to blasé around this time, or just plain forgetful, but in March the group appeared on a TV show (*Hullabaloo*) with Sammy Davis Junior, Sonny & Cher and The Supremes, an appearance which only Butler can recall. "Sammy helped me with my steps," he remembered in 1996.

Negotiations to get the group to Europe had taken a positive step on the 1st February when The Beatles' manager Brian Epstein's company, NEMS Enterprises, merged with the Vic Lewis Organisation. The deal made Epstein, through Lewis, the British representative of America's General Artists Corporation one of whose acts were The Lovin' Spoonful.

Following the success of the "Daydream" single, its follow up, taken from the first album, "Did You Ever Have To Make Up Your Mind" was released in April '66. The group was on such a roll, that this far inferior record would copy its predecessor and end up at number two in America. While it rocketed up the charts the Spoonful spent time in the studio creating a soundtrack for an underground movie.

With the Spoonful's continued success, Cavallo deemed that he needed a bigger office. The new premises Cavallo chose were being vacated by the entertainment management company of Jack Rollins and Charles Joffe. In the interim of both parties moving, they got to know each other's business and this led to a deal being struck where the Spoonful would score and appear in a movie by a client of the management duo. Among the list of clients in the Rollins-Joffe stable were Harry Belafonte, Mike Nichols and Elaine May but the one chosen for the film was an up and coming night-club comedian, who had been delighting his audiences in Greenwich Village, Woody Allen. For this mutual project, Allen had been approached by film producer Henry Saperstein, who had also produced *The Big TNT Show*, to help him out with a duff film he had acquired on the cheap from Japan.

Saperstein worked for American International Films, noted for the subsequent low budget gems *The Trip* and *The Wild Angels*. In Saperstein's travels to Japan (he would usually return with the latest *Godzilla* monster movie) he struck upon one Kagi No Kagi (roughly translated as *Key Is The Key*). The Japanese company who owned the film, Toho Productions, had already dubbed the film into English, with the hardly inspiring new title, *A Keg Of Powder*. When Saperstein showed this film to his fellow A.I.F. executives back in America, instead of being absorbed by the film's suspense and action sequences, they fell about laughing uncontrollably and shouted back comical retorts towards the nonsense on the screen. This event gave Saperstein the novel idea of dubbing a new soundtrack over the original in a way that there were Japanese actors following one story line, with American voices concocting a comical dialogue to another. It was either this or trashing the film he had just bought, so Saperstein called Woody Allen and after viewing the film with the sound turned off, Allen agreed to work on the project and the concept of *What's Up, Tiger Lily* was born.

Allen's intention was for a brief one-hour film, as it was clearly a one-gag scenario, but the producer wanted more. Even though they were one of the hottest groups of the time, the Spoonful's visual contribution was basically only to pad out the thing. So little care and attention went into the Spoonful's two segments, that only a bass player's hand is visible - even though Boone was actually present for the filming! The finished work, which included filmed Allen segments wrapped around the piece, does have some comical moments, but Allen was correct, at eighty minutes the film is far too long. Boone disagrees, "I think it's terrifically funny myself, once you get into the mood as to what's going on. If you don't know what's going on and you think you're going to see a Woody Allen movie, it's like, "What the fuck is this?"

Boone speaks for the group as he puts forward their reasoning for being involved in the project, "The idea appealed to us as about as hip as you could get. Think about it. You take a Japanese James Bond movie, which was a serious movie, take all the soundtrack away and then have Woody Allen come in and overdub this search for an egg salad sandwich recipe story; I mean it's a real hoot when you think about it. For us it was a very hip comedian wants to hire us to come in and put on this very hip soundtrack and we could just play anything, pull the strings, throw things on the ground, fart on a microphone - whatever we wanted. We did everything."

With the new comic dialogue added to the film, the project was switched to the recording studios at National Sound Recorders for the Spoonful to add the musical soundtrack. Fortunately Don Paulsen and the other co-editor for *Hit Parader*, Jim Delehant, attended the sessions and wrote an article titled, "Makin' Movie Music". Referring to how a group on top of their fame would seemingly waste time actually taking time off away from the limelight to score a B movie Paulsen happily recalls, "It was part of the times, the sixties were an anything goes kind of time." Another major factor was that Yanovsky had an enthusiasm for the project as Sebastian recalls, "Zally was always a big fan of Japanese spy and horror movies, so he loved the idea."

As this was a complete departure for the group, a musical producer, experienced in the field, was called in, with Jacobsen away looking at new groups including The Charlatans whom he subsequently signed to Kama Sutra, although the material he recorded with them was never released until 1996. Sebastian was more than impressed with the man sent in to show the Spoonful the ropes, "The music supervisor was Jack Lewis, and he really knew what he was doing where we didn't. He gave us a crash course in movie scoring. We had a really spontaneous feel working on the movie - we did the whole thing in ten days, really fast." Jacobsen recalls that it was Lorey Sebastian who helped bring in Jack Lewis hence he was on the side-lines. Jacobsen, in hindsight quite rightly, wanted to create the third Spoonful album instead.

Lewis was the right man for the job according to Don Paulsen; "Jack had experience and the technical expertise for the particular qualities you might need to make the music work in a movie context, as opposed to just being a record producer." Jack Lewis (who according to Yanovsky, "had a steel plate in his head") had already produced music for *Lawrence Of Arabia* and *The Victors*, yet at the time of his sessions with the Spoonful he said, "This is the most difficult score I've ever done. Last night I did a thing for Atlantic with twenty four pieces - it went off like a snap, but this is the most unique, original thing I have ever done. The Spoonful are fantastic to work with, some of the most creative guys I've ever met."

Looking back, Paulsen agrees, "The level of creativity they showed in doing this gave me an enormous admiration for their ability to just improvise on the spot and come up with some clever and unusual and yet entirely appropriate music. There was one scene where a man was in a bar and underneath the bar he had a chicken in a little cage. One guy says, "Hey Won Fat, why does your chicken look so happy?" And the barman says, in a mock Peter Lorre voice, "My chicken is getting married tonight - to a cobra ha, ha!" John Sebastian hears this and he took a bass string and scraped out the tune of "Here Comes The Bride" and it sounded like a funeral dirge - what an inventive mind." Originally the idea was different, as Jack Lewis said at the time, "We had a koto player for this scene but he got a better job at a Japanese restaurant!"

The film itself opens up enjoyably with Allen describing what was to follow. He promises, "Lots of raping, looting and killing," then goes on to make an extravagant claim regarding the history of overdubbing Japanese films, "It was done in *Gone With The Wind*, not many people know that. It was Japanese people actually and we dubbed in Southern voices!" The first few gags prove that the idea could have worked (After making love, a man thanks the woman for, "clearing his sinuses") but after a promising first twenty minutes the jokes come thin and slow until the whole idea becomes strained and peters out.

The Spoonful appear in *What's Up, Tiger Lily* against a black backdrop, supposedly situated in a night club with some wild shots of people supposedly dancing along to them, edited into their two segments where they perform

"Fishin' Blues", from the first album and a splendid new track, "Respoken". The Spoonful were paid union scale for their toil, as they were supposed to collect 2% of the films' profits, which needless to say they never saw a penny of. In fact Allen sued the production company, due to the addition of the Spoonful, claiming that the producers had tampered with his work. The soundtrack album fared no better than the movie, which sunk without a trace until Allen's later success, peaking at a pitiful number 126 in the US. It did not appear in the UK until the nineties. This is sad because a brave effort such as this deserved a far better fate.

Needing a few songs to insert into the movie, Sebastian went into overdrive, "Whatever irons were on the fire at that time went into the movie. In fact, most of it was written in that week." Alongside a majority of instrumentals, culled and extended from the film, the album included rays of light such as "Pow" (the working title for Allen's version of the film). Sebastian remembers the original idea for the beginning of the song, "For the intro, Zally had an idea to record a piano as it was pushed from a building. They wouldn't let us do that, but the idea was typical of Zally's sense of humour."

One of the co-writers of "Pow" was Skip Boone, who was friends with most of the group, "Zally came over one day," Skip recalls. "We were just fooling around on guitars and we got some kind of a thing going. I think it was a sort of throw-me-a-bone situation, because later on Zally called me up and said, "You know that thing we played the other day, we've made it into a song and John has written some lyrics." For me back then it was great - I actually got $2,800!"

Sebastian was in delightful form for "Pow", that runs along the film's opening titles, which includes some of his funniest lyrics. Taking the theme of misfortune, he produces a scenario of petty comical mishaps from the opening; 'I've always been the guy with his finger in his nose when the passport picture gets taken.' To the ingenuity of; 'I was standing in an artsy fartsy restaurant a few frozen dinners ago, when I stumbled on a waiter full of crepe Suzettes and I ran out the door flambeau.'

The other track on the soundtrack, with new vocals, ("End Title" has a verse from "Fishin' Blues" in it) is the aforementioned "Respoken" that the rhythm section believe should have been released as a single. This is one of Sebastian's undiscovered treasures, short, genuine, and dealing with what was becoming a common subject; the difficulty in verbally communicating with one another. The final line of the song; 'Let's call every word barrier broken,' shows his dependence on conversation being the great rift healer. After their appearance in *What's Up, Tiger Lily* the group were offered several film scripts although as Boone recalls, "It never got beyond talk. There were never any offers made." While the group waited for the soundtrack to be pressed, they went abroad for the first time.

The Spoonful had not really set England on fire. "Do You Believe In Magic" had gone relatively unnoticed (NME described it as, "an undistinguished bouncer") with the Spoonful's version being outsold by a Mickie Most produced effort by an unknown group called The Pack, which just missed out on the top 50. With the potential of "Daydream" and the obvious PR they could attract with a personal appearance, they had to go. The Byrds had already done a small tour in August '65 that had been ravaged by the British press due to poor stage performances and their attitude towards the media in general. The change of climate had knocked the stuffing out of most of The Byrds, however, they did manage to make contact with John Lennon and George Harrison and after a warm up gig in Blaises in London they had met Brian Jones on a social level and got high.

On the eve of their biggest ever concert; at Shea Stadium on August 15th, 1965, The Beatles noticed the Spoonful too as Butler explains, "Zally and I got into their drum kit that they were sending to the stadium. It was at Manny's Music. Zally got out a felt tip marker and put our logo, which was a spoon with a heart in it, all over every drum head and also put 'Welcome To Amerikka'. Also we rolled a couple of joints and taped them to the snare drum."

Some of The Beatles knew and admired the Spoonful's music (Lennon had mentioned he thought they were "nice" in a press conference) and after Yanovsky's and Butler's antics, they were looking to reciprocate. Down the line from Harrison to David Crosby, Crosby to Cass Elliot, Elliot to Jacobsen, the Spoonful had heard that The Beatles were looking forward to meeting them. So, leaving the US with "Daydream" at Number two, the group boarded the BOAC VC-10 jetliner - destination: Heathrow Airport, England. Cavallo was already in London, sorting out the itinerary for the group; they were to reside at the Mayfair Hotel in Piccadilly Square, where Dylan had stayed and were to play at Blaises, where The Byrds had performed. The highlight of the trip was a special invitation only gig at the Marquee on Wardour Street in Soho, home to The Who and the up and coming British blues scene.

The entourage consisted of the band, Jacobsen, publicity man Daniel Moriaty, road manager Rich "Toad" Chiarro (thus named by Yanovsky) and Don Paulsen who went with a dual purpose, "The magazine paid for my airfare over to England and the Spoonful paid for my hotel, so both would get a share of my photographs." Yanovsky was on form for the trip, being himself he boarded the plane in New York with sandals and no socks wearing dark sunglasses, only to be met with a typical British April shower on landing. Immediately on debarking, the group were besieged on the tarmac by the press, ready to record the event and bombard the group with questions.

Knowing the importance of the trip, the group were all darlings and, unlike The Byrds, were up to the inquisition without applying the moody Dylanesque sarcasm of Crosby, McGuinn and Co. With the typical "Build them up before you knock them down" attitude of the British media to anything exciting and new, the press of the time is totally upbeat and full of admiration. Even Boone's ignorant display of the Iron Cross around his neck failed to upset, although this was probably due to the Champagne reception given to the press, laid out at the Spoonful's expense, unknown to them. As was a 1932 Rolls Royce that had been hired to take the group from the reception to their hotel.

The first night in England was spent being thrown out of various public houses, due to their long hair being unpopular with the local landlords. After settling into a less restrictive pub, they discovered Britain's archaic licensing laws and found themselves on the street at 11pm. At the press reception, someone had thrust a party invitation into Butler's hand. The host turned out to be a cousin of the millionaire Guinness clan chief Lord Iveagh, Tara Browne, who bore a striking resemblance to Steve Boone at the time.

Browne's small house was situated down a picturesque cobblestoned street in Belgravia and was frequented by several pop stars, actors and rich young sophisticates on a regular basis. On this particular night actor Ben Carruthers was at the house where marijuana was on offer, as was cocaine and LSD. Boone remembers the entire group being given blocks of hash at the party. The following morning the group hit Carnaby Street and as Sebastian related to *Zig Zag*, it was quite a day, "Oh man, that visit was a bit of a vacuum packed trip but it was one of the most amazing days I've ever had. I spent the whole morning walking around London with this large lump of hash, which I was just breaking off into pea-sized bits and leaving them in my mouth to dissolve and get swallowed in my coffee and so on. By the afternoon, I had sort of reached the opiate stage of hashish, when you can't see anymore and I finally fell asleep in a dressing room. Next thing I remember was Zally shaking me and shouting, "Hey man, you've got to sing "Daydream"." Well I felt okay when I woke up and I managed to sing it all right."

This performance was for a TV show called *Top Of The Pops* where they shared the bill with The Rolling Stones. Backstage pictures of their meeting, taken by Paulsen, seem harmonious but as Boone explains this was not the case, "Hell no, we wanted top-billing and we were arguing with Jagger to sort out who went on first!"

Another TV performance, this time live, for *Ready, Steady Go*, alongside Manfred Mann, Dusty Springfield and genius comedian Peter Cook, where the group took the mickey out of the show's nervous presenter Cathy McGowan, endeared the Spoonful to the British public. Next on the agenda was a trip up north to play a couple of ballrooms in Birmingham that were non-events, as they played to an old-aged crowd, who hadn't a clue who the Spoonful were.

Returning to London on April 18th, the group played their one night at the Marquee, for which they were paid 50% of the door. Peter Eden, a record producer who had been Donovan's first manager until the previous November, managed to get a ticket for the concert, "When the Spoonful came over here I was doing some work for Pye (the Spoonful's record label in the UK) at the time. They were to do this one promotional thing at the Marquee, to get the media along. They came on just like they were dressed on their first album cover, the striped T-shirts and all that. They were a cartoony group and it really worked, Zal was dancing all over the place - they were fun. When I saw them they were not that good, but there was a magic about them, it was Sebastian holding them together quite a lot of the time. To the side of me were John Lennon and I think George Harrison and they loved it, everybody loved them and they got such a good reception. It was nice - it was like a party."

Eden recalls the performance clearly, as they made a favourable impression on him, as did an incident during the performance recalled by Paulsen, "Shortly after they started their set, it may have been after the first song, there was a power failure. They didn't feel like they needed electricity, Joe Butler kept the rhythm going, John played his harmonica and they started an impromptu jam so the audience wouldn't feel bummed out." The power failure came during "Fishin' Blues" and after the little jam and a short break where Butler said, "I'd tell a joke right now but I don't know any that aren't dirty," the group came back on and went straight back into "Fishin' Blues" at the exact point of the original halt. The audience responded to this piece of Spoonful humour and Paulsen recounts that this helped to win over the heavy musicians in the audience, "I think their grace under pressure put them in good stead with the audience and in particular with John Lennon, George Harrison, Spencer Davis and a number of other musicians who were there."

marquee artists

Artistes representation and management
~~Licensed annually by the L.C.C.~~

18 Carlisle Street Soho Square London west
telephone GERrard 6601/2

An Agreement

made the 22nd day of March 19 66

Between Marquee Club. hereinafter referred to as the "Management" of the one part and THE LOVIN SPOONFUL hereinafter referred to as the "Artiste" of the other part.

Witnesseth that the Management hereby engages the Artiste and the Artiste accepts an engagement to present The Loving Spoonful
appear as

(or in his usual entertainment) at the Dance Hall/Theatre or other Venue and from the dates and for the periods and at the salary stated in the Schedule hereto.

SCHEDULE

The Artiste agrees to appear at one Evening and .... Matinee performances

at a salary of £ ....
50 % of the gross advance and door takings. The Management guarantees a minimum of £ ....

one day(s) at Marquee Club, 90, Wardour Street, W.1. on April 18th 1966
.... day(s) at .... on ....
.... day(s) at .... on ....

SPECIAL STIPULATIONS

1. The Artiste shall not, without the written consent of the Management, appear at any public place of entertainment within a radius of 4 miles of the venue during a period of 4 weeks immediately prior to and 4 weeks immediately following the engagement.

2. The Management shall, at their own expense, provide (*a*) first-class Amplification and Microphone equipment (*b*) Grand Piano and (c) (at dances only) Relief Band or music.
The Management agrees that any other bands performing the engagement(s) shall be composed of members of the Musicians' Union, and in the event of Musicians' Union action arising from the engagement of non-Unionists, the Management will be responsible for payment of the full fees as stated in the agreement; also that the playing of Recorded music shall not exceed Twenty minutes during the performance.

3. The price of admission to be not less than .... per person in advance and .... at the door.

4. The Orchestra/Band shall play for a maximum of 1½ hours in separate sessions. Dance to commence at 7.00 and terminate at 11.00 Approximate playing times for Artiste, ... to .... and .... to ....

5. Salary payable by cash to group
on/~~within~~ night of engagement.

6. The Artiste shall supply, without charge, photographs, wording for publicity and programme details (when required) to .... for receipt not later than .... days before the commencement of the engagement.

7. .... shall appear personally throughout the performance.

8. Group to arrive and set up by 7p.m.

This Agency is not responsible for any non-fulfilment of Contracts by Proprietors, Managers or Artistes but every reasonable safeguard is assured.

Signature Robert J. Cavallo P/A
Address ....

Licensed annually by the Westminster City Council.

Also in attendance that night was Tom McGuinness from Manfred Mann, Steve Winwood, Jonathan King and according to Harrison (who years later was interviewed on Sebastian's radio show where he informed the host) the Spoonful's Marquee gig was the fateful night of his first meeting with Eric Clapton. Harrison seems to remember this more than the Spoonful gig, "When the Spoonful were at The Marquee, John and I went down and sort of hung about backstage with them. We were going down to their hotel, I can remember just seeing Eric; "I know him, I'm sure I know this guy and he seems like, you know, really lonely." I remember we went out and got in the car and went off to Sebastian's hotel and I remembered thinking, "We should have invited that guy 'cause I'm sure we knew him from somewhere and he seemed, like, lonely."

Harrison and Lennon had just finished recording the rhythm track for what was to be "Doctor Robert" and were tired and groggy, but still stayed at the hotel until about 2 am. Butler remembers Harrison returning the compliment from his and Yanovsky's Shea Stadium offering, "George said, "We wanted to pay you back and give you a present," cause at that time nobody was really carrying, certainly not intercontinental and he said, "but I rolled a joint and Patti and I smoked it and I forgot." So about an hour later a chauffeur comes to the door with a little package. It was nice, you know, kind of a gift."

Jacobsen happily recalls the night, "We were in a hotel room together, drinking and smoking hash. Zally got totally soused and was throwing liquor bottles out of the open window, four stories up onto the street below! Steve, of course, didn't have much to say, Joe I don't know what, but John Sebastian could only talk about his movie project. They had just done *Help!* I think, and John was going on and on about *What's Up, Tiger Lily*. I mean it was something to hear John going on and on and on and people's eyes were just glazing over in boredom and because everybody was so stoned.

"The only person in the room that I could see that had anywhere near their wits about them, because George was kind of boring, was Lennon who was sitting there uncomfortably and I said, "Hey John, how are you doing? Do you want to smoke some hash?" He said, "Sure, let's go" and we went into another room and I sat with the guy for two and a half-hours. He just struck me as the greatest, I mean, he was just so interested in things, a great sense of humility for somebody who was such a huge star. We talked about English TV, English press, what he thought of America and just had an absolutely wonderful time talking to him. At the end of the evening he just said, "I'm going now" and I went to the door with him and he said, "Good evening, Sir." I kinda monopolised on John Lennon that night."

Paulsen remembers the evening well and recalls the complaints from the night-manager regarding Yanovsky's behaviour and the talk being mainly musician chat and American and English differences. "It was a very mellow low key kind of happening," Paulsen recalls. "There was maybe a dozen people in the room and during a lull in the conversation the manager of The Yardbirds, Georgio Gomelsky, turns to John Lennon and says, "So tell me John, what is the meaning of life?" Completely out of the blue. Where did this question come from? John Lennon gave this guy a sleepy, "Who are you?" look through half lidded eyes and didn't know quite what to say so Erik Jacobsen jumped in and said, "I think that's a question best answered in the morning!"

After the gig at Blaises, Brian Jones turned up backstage and took Sebastian away and invited the rest of the group to a party at his house. In his article "They Conquer England" Don Paulsen wrote, on entering the Rolling Stone's house, "Inside, Brian sits on the floor playing a large Indian sitar, occasionally sipping milk right out of the bottle. John Sebastian, on the sofa, plays an acoustic guitar. Someone seated behind Brian is playing a dulcimer. The three musicians improvise and John takes the lead with a Fred Neil blues song. Zal examines the sitar with great delight. More guests arrive and the musicians go upstairs to play in private."

Today Paulsen says, a little less politically correct, "The musicians went upstairs and were not heard from for quite a while, goodness knows what was going on there!" (laughs). Erik Jacobsen offers, "They were hanging out over at Brian Jones's house, I was over there too and saw the big African lesbians. Oh baby, what a place he had going over there!"

At ten o'clock the next morning the Spoonful were woken and were on the move again as they had to fly off to Sweden, where they performed on a TV show which also featured The Hep Stars, a forerunner of what was to become Abba. Returning to London for another performance on *Ready Steady Go*, during a break in rehearsal, Sebastian and Paulsen both discussed their homesickness as Paulsen had recently met the woman who was to be his wife too.

The group were soon on their travels again. This time they went to a private function in Ireland, where they played at, according to the invitation, "A party in honour of the honourable Tara Browne on his 21st birthday at Lugalla in County Wicklow (outside of Dublin), the country residence of his parents, Lord Oranmore and Browne, and Oonagh (Guinness) Lady Oranmore and Browne."

Browne was host to more than 500 guests including Mick Jagger, Keith Richards, Brian Jones, Anita Pallenberg, model Chrissie Shrimpton, Beatle brother Mike McCartney and John Paul Getty. The former did not make much of an impression on Erik Jacobsen, "Mick Jagger was there and that was the first and only time I had seen behind the scenes with Mick Jagger - total asshole, a blazing asshole of the highest kind. I mean, they've done great work and it's the only rock band that matters, but boy, what an arrogant little prick!" Although, according to Marianne Faithful, Browne's party was the first occasion where Jagger and Shrimpton first took acid together, with the result being apparently disastrous.

Jacobsen mysteriously adds some more information about the day, "I remember quite a bit about it, the incredible birthday in Ireland, which was unbelievable. All the people across the courtyard with the huge chunks of hash that the guy Martin, who'd had his third eye opened, brought over." This was quite an occasion, Yanovsky's party piece of squirting a soda siphon across a room exploded into a mass food fight among the Spoonful. This was very stressful to Moriaty, an Irishman, as to him he was visiting with royalty.

HIT PARADER
BEATLES' U.S. SCHEDULE
THE "INNER" CYRKLE
WBBF/ROCHESTER, WCOL/COLUMBUS, WCBQ/SAN DIEGO, WKDA/NASHVILLE.
35CENTS·CDC
SEPT.
ZALLY AND THE BOYS
SPECIAL SPOONFUL SECTION
MEET the BEATLES
JOHN SEBASTIAN EXPLAINS "HOW I WRITE MY SONGS"
"WATCH US MAKE MOVIE MUSIC"
STEVE
TOP TUNES song lyrics
TURN DOWN THE DAY
I SAW HER AGAIN LAST NIGHT
DAY FOR DECISION
MUDDY WATER
ALONG COMES MARY
LITTLE GIRL
MY LOVERS PRAYER
OVER, UNDER, SIDEWAYS, DOWN
SOMEWHERE MY LOVE
CAN'T LIVE WITH YOU CAN'T LIVE WITHOUT YOU
HERMITS! This Door Swings Both Ways
Plus ALL the songs from the Spoonful "DAYDREAM" album
COME WHAT MAY
5-D ★ RAIN
PAPERBACK WRITER
HAVE I STAYED TOO LONG
LAND OF MILK & HONEY
I PUT A SPELL ON YOU
RICHARD CORY
YOU CAN'T ROLLER SKATE IN A BUFFALO HERD
TOP TUNES song lyrics
PLEASE TELL ME WHY
EVEN IF I COULD
WHOLE LOT OF SHAKING IN MY HEART
LI'L RED RIDING HOOD
EVERYBODY LOVES A NUT
SWEET PEA
DON'T BRING ME DOWN
PACK UP YOUR SORROWS
WILD THING
LOVE LETTERS
the gal with the cat named Dog Norma Tanega
PRIVATE LIFE OF BEACHBOY DENNIS WILSON
BOB LIND "I DON'T CARE WHAT PEOPLE CALL ME!"
BYRD BY BYRD
JOE TELLS ALL ABOUT ROCK and ROLL DRUMMERS

The next day Boone, Butler and Yanovsky returned to the scene of the party for a day of horseback riding in the Wicklow mountains while Sebastian went shopping, where he found an enormous old Irish harp in an antique shop. Sebastian then left a day before the rest of the group, as he was anxious to connect with Lorey Kaye. The airline people were not too happy when he arrived at the airport with his precious treasure and asked if he could carry it on board! The next day, before he boarded an Aer Lingus jet-liner heading for New York Boone told *Beat Instrumental*, "There's no doubt about it, England's a great place and we'll definitely come back." They never did.

Not too long after his 21st birthday party Browne was killed at the wheel of his car on December 18th, 1966. His death was immortalised in The Beatles song "A Day In The Life" from *Sgt. Pepper's Lonely Hearts Club Band* where Lennon mentions a man blowing his mind out in a car, not noticing that the traffic lights had changed. This was only partly true as Browne swerved to avoid a Volkswagen that had pulled out from a side street into his path. His Lotus Élan then hit a stationary van - Browne was pronounced dead on arrival. One witness said, "I saw the driver pinned like a doll in the wreck, the steering wheel was bent like a flower stem." His passenger, model Suki Potier escaped with bruises. Browne was buried at the foot of the Wicklow Mountains, near the sight of his extravagant 21st birthday. He was due to have inherited £1,000,000 when he reached the age of twenty five.

The Spoonful returned to New York having successfully launched their British publicity machine. The single "Daydream" was to peak at number 2 in the UK charts and become their biggest hit there. Returning to the United States in May, the Spoonful were supposed to go to San Francisco area for a giant "Peace Rock" dance at the Harmon Gym in Berkeley, to play alongside The Grateful Dead. Their appearance was cancelled as Sebastian married Lorey Kaye. Lorey was a Jewish girl, so at the wedding, with the Jewish guests on one side of the chapel and Sebastian's Italian relatives on the other, Yanovsky decided to throw spaghetti at the couple as they left the church.

In the end the Spoonful only played one concert in the Bay area, at the Greek Theatre in Berkeley on Saturday, May 21st 1966. The date is important as it led to the eventual disintegration of The Lovin' Spoonful. Erik Jacobsen; "Basically, we had been hanging out with The Committee, which was an improvisational group in North Beach. We'd come out several times before, then the guys were headlining at the Greek Theatre. We had befriended these guys, Larry Hankin, Carl Gottlieb, Howard Hesseman, Don Sturdy, Gary Goodrow and they were all there. I was hanging out there mainly because the pot smoking and LSD taking world was pretty small then and that was like a haven for that and this small time guy was selling drugs over there."

Roy Loney who at the time was in a local group called Lost and Found which would later turn into The Flamin' Groovies, (the Flamin' being their salute to the Lovin' in the Spoonful's moniker) attended the notorious concert, "The only time I saw The Syndicate Of Sound was opening for The Lovin' Spoonful at the Greek Theatre in Berkeley with The Charlatans. The Charlatans stole the show. They had just signed with Kama Sutra and were working up new material, and that was the tightest I'd ever seen them. The Spoonful was really ragged, really pathetic. It was horrible actually, and we'd been so excited about seeing them." In a forerunner of what was to come, Butler has a clear memory of the concert, "The cops were guarding the stage and the trickiest thing happened, I almost got a black eye. I was hit by a block of hash and I had to keep playing my bass drum, managing to hide it under my foot. People threw drugs on stage where they would throw jellybeans for The Beatles.

THE GOOD TIME MUSIC OF THE

LOVIN' SPOONFUL

Saturday, May 21 — 8:30 P.M.

— ONLY BAY AREA APPEARANCE —

Presented by the ASUC FRESHMAN CLASS — Univ. of Calif. HEARST

GREEK THEATRE • BERKELEY

PLUS SPECIAL ADDED ATTRACTION

Tickets: **BELOW DIAZOMA** — General Admission $4.25 All Students, $3.50
ABOVE DIAZOMA — General Admission $3.25 All Students, $2.50
TERRACE GREEN — General Admission $2.25 All Students, $1.75

Agencies: **ASUC Box Office**, Bancroft and Telegraph, Berkeley — 848-4800
ASUC Box Office — Enclose Stamped Envelope)
wntown Center Box Office, 325 Mason
n Clay Box Office, 2137 Broadway

By then they were throwing rolled joints and blocks of hash and the trick was not to have the cops confiscate it before you could smoke it."

It was quite a usual experience after gigs away from home that Yanovsky and Boone would pair off, hire a car and revel the night away. On a previous occasion, Boone had put his foot down a little too hard on the accelerator and crashed one car, returning it to the shop in a sorry state, only minutes after taking the keys. These excursions were not special events as Boone points out, "He might have been closer with John and longer friends, but on the road, Zally and I were the two together. We were always really tight." What started off as a, "Zally and Stephen go off for a good time evening," to quote Sebastian, turned into the complete nightmare.

The events of this week in May, 1966 have become blurred in the minds of the participants and their friends. Some of the events of the nightmare are "off the record" and on a couple of occasions band members have insisted that their recollections are not recorded; once forcefully. No two stories agree regarding the Spoonful bust. From records from the time one can definitely say that after the concert, Boone and Yanovsky picked up their rental car and drove to the Pacific Heights home of The Committee's manager, Bill Love, whose real name was William Loughborough. The two Spoonfuls had wanted to score some pot and Love sold them some. Leaving the scene, Boone and Yanovsky's car was stopped by the police, who promptly found the drugs under Yanovsky's seat, prompting the arrest of the pair. The reason of how they became noticed by the police is just part of the mystery. One report said Boone had, "executed a high-speed U- turn" which Boone denies.

The first question put to Boone on the matter was what the facts of that night were; "Well the facts were that Zally and I were arrested. The facts were that the cops found some pot under the seat, under Zal's seat. The facts are that the cops never saw the pot on either my or Zally's body and the facts are that it was a rent-a-car, that we had just picked up that evening and could have had pot under the seat from anybody." According to Yanovsky, in a rare interview from a 1972 film produced by the National Film Board Of Canada called *Rock-A-Bye*, it was more than just pot, "Stephen and I were riding in a car and the police stopped us and they found about four ounces of dope, that is grass, about two ounces of hashish, cocaine, a lot of uppers and some downers, right?"

Butler is adamant that the whole scenario was a set-up, "This is for Steve and Zally, but I must tell you something. First of all, the cop was waiting for them when they walked out of the house. When the cops got them in the car, one of them recognised and knew who they were and on the spot said, "This guy set you up, we knew you were coming." You see they set up the thing where, "He set you up, why don't you double back on him? He's the one we've been trying to get." To make matters more confusing, Sebastian claims the policemen were only, "answering a screaming woman call," and stopped when they happened upon two longhaired guys.

The patrolmen later claimed that they saw Yanovsky, "making motions". The drugs were soon located and the pair were on their way to the cells downtown at the Bryant Street Hall Of Justice. In a desperate but foolish bid to avoid prosecution, Boone tried to bribe one of the officers; "Classic mistakes were made and I will take the responsibility for making the biggest mistake, and that was appealing directly to the police officer to accommodate some sort of a deal and that was a mistake. If I could ever correct one thing in my entire life, I'd never do that again."

Thrown in a cell, stripped naked, Boone and Yanovsky were paraded in front of the chief of police for the area. Their phone call was used to summon Cavallo who arrived shortly thereafter with an anxious Charles Koppelman hot on his heels. Word of the arrest soon travelled down the Spoonful grapevine as Phil Steinberg confirms, "The minute they were busted we knew about it. I was flying out to see them to see if we could do some damage control but Charlie and Don (in reality it was only Koppelman) got on the plane and went out and we stayed."

The crux of the matter was to avoid a certain deportation of their lead guitarist due to his Canadian citizenship as Erik Jacobsen explains, "They (the police) found out he was here on a visa that had been turned down in all these places cause his dad was a communist. He had been denied (a visa extension) and San Francisco was the last place that we were trying to get his visa extended to stay in the U.S. So it was an awful pressure they had on us by simply saying, "Listen, we'll see to it that he's charged with this crime and that he doesn't get a visa." They had us by the short hairs, like they say."

Boone confirms the situation, "They dragged us into this office and they said there was no equivocation, he's out of here tomorrow morning on the first plane back to Toronto, unless you do the deal. It was that cut and dried." The police wanted names. Yanovsky gave them names. From the same 1972 interview, where swearwords were bleeped out, Yanovsky said, "So I was going to be deported and they said, "Well you don't want to be deported, who sold you the ****?" And I said, "He sold me the ****!" and I told them at the drop of a hat and that's what happened."

John Sebastian sums up the scene; "In the course of one evening, they went from being members of the hottest group worth talking about, except maybe for The Beatles, to being threatened with that group's demise - that's all in one hour. They'd been taken out of their car, the police sat them down, and in one hour (he angrily snaps his fingers) they had to make a decision: would they co-operate with the police?"

Influenced by the people around them who had invested in their future, Yanovsky and Boone squealed. The other part of the supposed deal was that the police wanted the pair to introduce an undercover police officer into the world of The Committee, so they could arrest the kingpin of the operation, allegedly Chip Monck (who later found fame as one of the organisers of Woodstock). This was a farcical attempt as Yanovsky recalled, "I introduced an undercover agent into the hip life of San Francisco! (laughs) And I went around, (laughs) with this guy for like three days. This guy had, like, very short hair and the guy looked like a cop." Yanovsky then sarcastically acts out what happened when he introduced the agent, "He's my cousin, hey he's a nice guy, wanna sell him some ****?"

Boone disagrees with the length of time spent with the agent, "They (the police) agreed that they would not bust anybody, that they wanted somebody just to be introduced to the circle, not even directly to the person responsible for it. We never did introduce him directly, we just went to a party and he came in the door with us and they all said, "Hi Steve, hi Zal and who's that?" "This is our buddy," or whatever we called him, I forget, and we left. That was it, we did no more than that." Ironically, Boone was handed his hash back by a policeman who didn't know what it was. Boone told the fool it was resin for his bass.

The people behind the decision to help with the authorities were the ones with everything to lose and nothing to gain, Bob Cavallo and Charles Koppelman, as Boone says, "This is the way he (Koppelman) does business today, from what I can see. He'll do anything to keep his artists working out there, Bob Cavallo too. You know I'm never going to let him off the hook. He was a buddy of mine; Charles Koppelman was not a buddy. Cavallo, you know, hung with us, we went out drinking together in the early days, and we'd all sleep on his floor some nights and everything. It was a real disappointment to me because he was older and he'd graduated from college and he knew better. He knew we could've at least found out what our options were before we just agreed to this."

So, sometime shortly after their arrest, Yanovsky, Boone, Cavallo and a not so undercover officer once again went to score some pot from Love. On this occasion Love had none to sell, but still smoked a couple of joints with what he thought were his friends. The next day the police went to Love's home, armed with warrants to arrest him with possession of marijuana. Love was at work at a medical laboratory, however his wife was arrested and she had to leave her baby with a downstairs neighbour on her way to the cells. Later the police arrived at Love's place of work and led him off in handcuffs. His wife was eventually released and Love was charged.

Larry Hankin knew Love well and offers some background on the fall-guy; "Bill Love (Loughborough) managed The Committee Theatre. He was a friend of Alan Myerson, the owner/director of The Committee. He was older – about 45-50 to our 30ish ages. He was a research scientist in real life and is actually the inventor of the circular, grooved "flat magnifying glass" (made of clear plastic) that's sold in stationary stores all over the world. His contribution was a keen mind and sense of humour and a skewed paradigm of the world that was really cool to us. He was hip, knew a lot – loved Jazz - a regular father-figure.

"No one was as "far-out" as Bill Love in the sixties. He had many brilliant and interesting "hip" musician and scientist friends. Bill Love was a heavyset, cool Buddha with a long scraggily beard, a crooked front tooth; long, thin white hair tied in a messy ponytail and always wore overalls. His favourite thing to do was to make sets of tuned drums out of the round Quaker Oats cereal containers. Over the years as our theatre manager, he made thousands and gave them away. He had a set of eight fastened together in a straight line and played them in Jazz bands all over San Francisco. He was great on them.

"So, Bill was our theatre manager and all around father figure. He and his wife were "family". His wife, Sandy Love was a pretty, sensitive, delicate and pure soul who prided herself on being an artist and a poet. She was whisked away half-naked by the police and thrown in jail that night several months pregnant. She was surprised, terrified and handled roughly by the police ("A Hippy") and spent several days alone in a cell and two months later spontaneously aborted her child. This was directly blamed on the police and Zal and Steve. Hence the local anger turned to pure outrage.

"And that is why The Committee was so angered at Zal and me when the bust went down – we totally and immediately had embraced them as family – so when their bust came down The Committee company were doubly hurt – it was as if brothers had turned in brothers and sisters. A crime and an insult."

After repeated attempts, this author was unable to persuade neither Koppelman, Rubin or Cavallo to an interview, though as Jacobsen said of the latter, "He doesn't drink anymore, so he can't reminisce. I'm sure he feels very fondly about the whole thing but guilty because he....feels guilty about the way it turned out, that thing."

The significance of the bust could be lost on today's generation but one has to remember the times. Hatred was rising between the camps of the police and the emerging Hippie cult. The Ronald Reagan style of conservatism was rearing its ugly head; the then Governor of California clamped a lid on any protest in the Berkeley community. One only has to listen to the Canned Heat song "Sic 'Em Pigs" to realise that everything was not rosy. If the counterculture discovered the story of the bust, hasty judgments could easily be made.

John Sebastian; "You have to remember the framework of the period, people's perception of the police was changing radically. In the Village before 1967 policemen were still people who looked after you. Frank Serpico (policeman in the Village, immortalised by Al Pacino in the masterpiece *Serpico*) took friends of mine home and put ice on their balls so they would make it through a bad shot of heroin. But after 1967 this whole pig thing had started and you were dealing with a very different flavour of the police department." Serpico shared many a joint with Joe Butler, who was shocked to find out that he was a policeman.

With their friends co-operating with the police, the other half of the Spoonful were completely oblivious to what was occurring on the other side of town, "We didn't even tell John or Joe," Boone recalls. "We did a concert the next night at Berkeley (the poster for the Greek Theatre show does say, "Only Bay Area Appearance", the concert was probably at Cow Palace) then they went down to L.A. the very next morning. We said we were staying behind to do record promotions."

Apparently, in the car on the way to L.A., Cavallo told Butler and Sebastian what was really going on. Butler was frantic, yet Sebastian seemed unconcerned, as Boone says, "That's the point where Joe said, "I cannot believe John has no interest in this at all." Well you know something; John had started to distance himself from the rest of the group prior to that, even almost to the day this whole thing happened. John and I have never talked about it over the years, so I don't know what John thinks, but apparently John showed no interest in trying to get things worked out."

Sebastian, by all accounts, was completely infatuated with his new wife up to the point of the rest of the group dreading her presence. This obscured his thinking on group matters, yet in hindsight Sebastian reveals what he thinks should have happened, "You know, in retrospect, I wish that it all hadn't been kept from me at the time because...I think the reason it was kept from me was that I would have said, "Take the bust. You know, let's be pot smokers, not finks." Sebastian's offhand remark ties in with his image more than his inner thoughts.

The story of the bust was allowed to lie low for a while but through word of mouth throughout the underground culture of the west coast, the nails were slowly being hammered into the coffin of The Lovin' Spoonful.

At only fourteen years of age, seeing his seven year elder brother finding fame and fortune, Mark Sebastian did the natural thing and tried to emulate John's success. Mark wrote a song, "Summer In The City", and left a tape of it with his brother before leaving for Italy to spend some time with their father. Brother John, not short of songs himself, dutifully played the tape and discovered a potential use for the song; "I said to Mark, "Gee, I really don't like the beginning of it, it doesn't get exciting but then the chorus is this wonderful release. So let me try and write a more tense, gritty beginning and then when this chorus comes, it will be a big pay off."

Mark Sebastian recalls his original effort and what made it into the finished song, "I had different verses which talked about stickball games and feeling trapped in the city - a kid who normally goes to camp and gets away but this is the first summer he actually stays in the city. The part that remained is, 'But at night it's a different world...' That all existed in my original tune, with the same music that appears on the record. John said that he thought the verses needed to be more energetic and he had that great powerful verse that he came up with and Stephen contributed to the instrumental break."

During the *What's Up, Tiger Lily* sessions, a friend of Jack Lewis', Artie Schroeck, had come up with a piano riff that had left an impression on John Sebastian. One night a few weeks later, as Sebastian was about to go to sleep, Mark's chorus, the piano figure and some new lyrics all fell into place. Taking it into the studio and adding a piano interlude Boone had been looking to fit into something, the song came together. With Butler claiming to have contributed to the lyrics, "Summer In The City" became quite an ensemble piece, with the nucleus coming from outside the group. It was also The Lovin' Spoonful's only number one hit record.

"Summer In The City" showed another side of the Spoonful unclear till now. A miniature symphony of urban heat noises mixed with superb production qualities, the song includes an emotional bungee jump away from the heat until it goes as far as it can, then the listener is snatched back into the turmoil of the boiling cauldron that is the city. No mean feat for a three minute pop song.

The lyrics build different textures in the minds of the listener. John Sebastian's "powerful" opening verse is a familiar scenario, one that everyone can relate to with; 'Back o' my neck gettin' dirt and gritty. Walkin' on the sidewalk hotter than a match head.' This is followed by Mark Sebastian's tantalising release; 'But at night it's a different world, Go out and find a girl, Come on, come on, and dance all night, Despite the heat it'll be all right.'

John Sebastian's last verse includes a hint of the surreal (supplied by Butler with the wheezin' bus stops) which is a contrast to the first verse and takes the lead from his brother's line of thought. The recording of the song, on the eve of the Spoonful's return from the UK, was a triumph of production endeavour. Utilising atmospheric noises of the city with new developments in recording techniques, albeit cheaply, "Summer In The City" stands alone as the group's most atypical sounding effort in their short history. With money to spend on such activities, they secured the talents of Columbia staff producer Roy Halee, who was as keen as the rest of the group to experiment.

It had all started so quietly as Don Paulsen remembers, "The Spoonful did several sessions for "Summer In The City" and I was there when they were doing some of the basic track, the rhythm track at the very beginning. The one thing I remember most about that session is that in the studio they had these large waste baskets made out of compressed cardboard and Zal Yanovsky saw one of these and decided to hit it with a drumstick to see what sound he could get."

This effort failed to produce the desired effect, so Butler took his snare drum and situated it at the bottom of the large stairwell at Columbia Recording Studios. "It was so funny," Butler recalls. "On the tape every now and then you would hear a door slamming and the sound of someone coming down the stairs!" The particular sound was only attained after some trickery by Halee as Sebastian explains, "It's actually him wowing the volume on a speaker that was mounted on top of the stairwell and picking it up on a microphone at the very bottom. Pretty much all the twos and fours were wowed that way. That is, the volume is goosed at the moment that the drum is hit and then cut off so that you don't get the rest of the kit. Roy Halee perfected that and went on and used it on "The Boxer" for Simon and Garfunkel - it's the same sound."

As the song was developing, the group would run what they had over and over in the control room. At one point Jacobsen would switch the playback from the recording studios' loud speakers to a tiny car radio speaker, to get an idea of what it would sound like to the masses. To Sebastian, the song was starting to resemble George Gershwin's "An American In Paris", where Gershwin represents the traffic in the thematic part at the beginning and end of the piece. The radical idea of overdubbing actual sounds of traffic appealed primarily to Yanovsky and his exuberance for the idea insured that an expert in the field would be called in, whom Sebastian remembers fondly, "We hired this funny old soundman, obviously from the radio era and he had old acetates of car collisions, traffic jams and car horns. We listened for hours and selected the horns that we wanted."

It was not that easy to add these effects to the existing tracks as Jacobsen recalls, "We could only punch the sounds in on one track, so at a given signal, he would have to slip-start his records." The memory of being woken by the sound of a pneumatic drill and the obvious choice of one wimpy sounding car horn starting off a barrage of horns, was used to great effect in "Summer In The City" and added to the atmosphere of the record. How they managed to fade the sound of a pneumatic hammer into a delightful piano piece and make it all sound so sweet is a mystery. Separate the stereo and more wonders can be heard; a little touch of autoharp, a bright snare drum passage, demonic bass runs, as well as layer upon layer of quality harmony vocals.

Some of this harmony work was down to Mark Sebastian; "I was very excited as I had a little input on the background vocals. I remember it all very clearly and in fact I even have a picture of me at the session. Joe Butler was doing some backgrounds on an overdub basis with my brother and I was able to suggest some harmony directions, which were very simple. It was just where I thought the harmony voices should be seated, relative to the vocal. Some of my suggestions stuck and when you're fourteen years old, well, I was agog!"

One idea that was vetoed was the suggestion to end the song abruptly as Jacobsen explains, "Originally it was going to end with a big explosion that was supposed to be the end of the world, but that was too hookie. So we made a copy of the second half of the song and then did some overdubbing." With the help of a promotional film of the group filmed by Judd Yalkut, that shows the Spoonful playing about in the recording studio and Central Park, in the manner soon to be utilised by The Monkees (by way of The Beatles' *A Hard Day's Night*), "Summer In The City" became a sizeable hit world-wide and is the group's shining moment.

The only problem with the song was that the vocalist on the record, Sebastian, could not repeat the feat in a live situation, as Yanovsky said at the time, "It turns out that while Steve is playing organ, poor John has to play piano, which he can only do by concentrating and not singing. So Joe sings lead when we do it live." Butler managed to perform a few vocals live, a feat only a few other drummers have accomplished successfully. Even lip-synching the song on a TV show called *Hollywood Palace* had its problems but they turned a possible embarrassment to their advantage in true Spoonful style, as they feigned confusion as to where the car-horns were coming from.

It comes as no surprise that the Spoonful's most popular, and easily most timeless song, should be a collaborative effort. Out of all the people involved in "Summer In The City", no individual has ever alone reached such a height of creativity. Throughout the middle period of 1966 the Spoonful toured relentlessly. The day "Did You Ever Have To Make Up Your Mind" peaked at number 2 in the US charts found the group at the Santa Clara Fairground, being supported by The Chocolate Watchband. A couple of weeks later the Spoonful performed in an illustrious line-up that included The Byrds, The Beach Boys, Love and Percy Sledge at the Summer Spectacular concert at the Hollywood Bowl.

Come August and the Spoonful were on top of the tree, "Summer In The City" was number one in the US and was on the verge of being in the top ten world-wide. Don Paulsen noticed the intimate reactions between a group at their peak, "Every time I saw them, particularly in later concerts, they would usually close the set with "Do You Believe In Magic". Every time I've seen them do that song, John and Zal would share a look. They would look at each other at some point and just smile, like they had remembered that this was the one that got it all started. This was where we began and it was a joy to still do this song and we can still share this stage together making this music. That look was a special moment, there was a history in a glance."

The Spoonful were now deemed popular and wholesome enough for Coca Cola to make an approach, offering thousands of dollars for the Spoonful to appear in a commercial for their product. "It was another Spoonful first," Boone remembers. "And John and Joe were the assholes of all time and refused to do it." Boone is still riled at his cohorts' refusal to claim some of the prize he thought was due, "It was $150,000 which was a lot in those days, a lot. The story was (Boone shouts into his microphone) Joe and John turned it down for aesthetic reasons. They didn't want to do commercials for a product they didn't believe in - bullshit! It was bullshit. We should have taken the money and ran, we would have been better off and besides all of us drank Coca Cola!"

Sebastian, who claims the fee was $100,000 (Butler's figure is $75,000), says of the incident, "It was just the times. We were anxious to separate ourselves from the marketplace." Boone has a different reason for Sebastian's refusal; "It was probably Lorey. She probably said, "John, you can't do a commercial for Coca Cola, that's so uncool." Butler regrets his decision to oppose the idea today, "John and I didn't want to do it and Zally and Steve did. We thought it would have cheapened us and frankly Cavallo was right. He said it wouldn't have meant anything, people would have given us that." Boone agrees, "This would never have killed us. Well, Coca Cola is considered as American as apple pie, it's like the biggest commercial on TV!"

In reality, Sebastian used the offer to assert his place of authority within the band. Even though he thinks he was a little harsh himself, Sebastian's severe moralistic way of letting the others know who was behind the band's success, was a good decision. John Sebastian; "What I had really selfishly neglected to notice about that, which I think is a valid point that the other guys I'm sure would make to you, was that the other guys weren't writing songs and here at last was an opportunity for all members to benefit in the same way. I figured that I didn't want to rub my nose in it yet but I know the other guys did but then they didn't write the songs that got us to this point. It was one of the first times where I very coldly had to keep the standard that I felt the band had, in a puritanical way."

Butler recalls Sebastian's grandiose attitude towards the commercial, "John said, "Well who's going to write it? I'll have to write it." He was just very...he just didn't think anybody's work was as good as his and in some ways he was right. But this time he wasn't. I could have written more with John and it would have helped him. He needed other influences, like mine and Zally's ideas, things we told him directly, by the way, even phrases in his songs and stuff. When he just shut himself off, that's when his work turned to shit."

Usually on split group decisions, Cavallo and Jacobsen would have the casting votes as Butler recalls, "Sometimes we had three and three but usually with six people you get a four to two more often than a three and three. I don't know what we would have done in that case, whoever had the most forceful argument would sway." The Coke offer was turned down at the time the Spoonful were recording material for their third album and arguments had already started over what was going to be the next single. Also, a track written by Boone and Yanovsky had been openly ridiculed by the rest of the band and Erik Jacobsen. The single the group were split on, this time Butler and Yanovsky were against and Sebastian and Boone for, was called "Rain On The Roof".

Sebastian once introduced the song as being, "considered by the group as our "Candy Ass Tune." "He was being kind to himself," spits Butler on being told this. "It was worse than that, mawkish and insipid, it was horrible. It was not good that we had anarchy and it was certainly not good that the anarchy was fuelled by John's presence and when that happened people were musically not wanting to do it anymore and were holding back. "Rain On The Roof", I almost didn't play drums on, I hated it that much. I said, "If it's that fucking good, you do it!"

Butler is correct. The Spoonful had just opened a new door with "Summer In The City" and its power and drive could have been the turning point into a more adult approach, but "Rain On The Roof" dragged them back down into a chart fodder realm. At the time of its recording, Sebastian told Don Paulsen about the basis for the song; "Another song I wrote recently came about when Lorey and I just had an evening in the house with the rain coming down on the roof. We had been talking about rain on the roof for a long time and last night I wrote a song about it."

While the group all had steady girlfriends apart from Boone (Yanovsky with actress Jackie Burroughs and Butler with Leslie Vega (cousin to Peter Yarrow from Peter, Paul and Mary), with both couples subsequently getting married) Sebastian's relationship was an intense one and public displays of affection became nauseating for the people working around the Sebastians. A family friend, Don Paulsen sticks up for the couple, "The apartment that John and Lorey had, had a back porch with a metal roof. They would sit there and listen to the rain pitter-patter on the roof, so a lot of the songs were just the joy of love. I know what it's like, the joy of a man whose found a woman that he thinks is going to be his mate for life and they are sharing and doing things for each other. I began

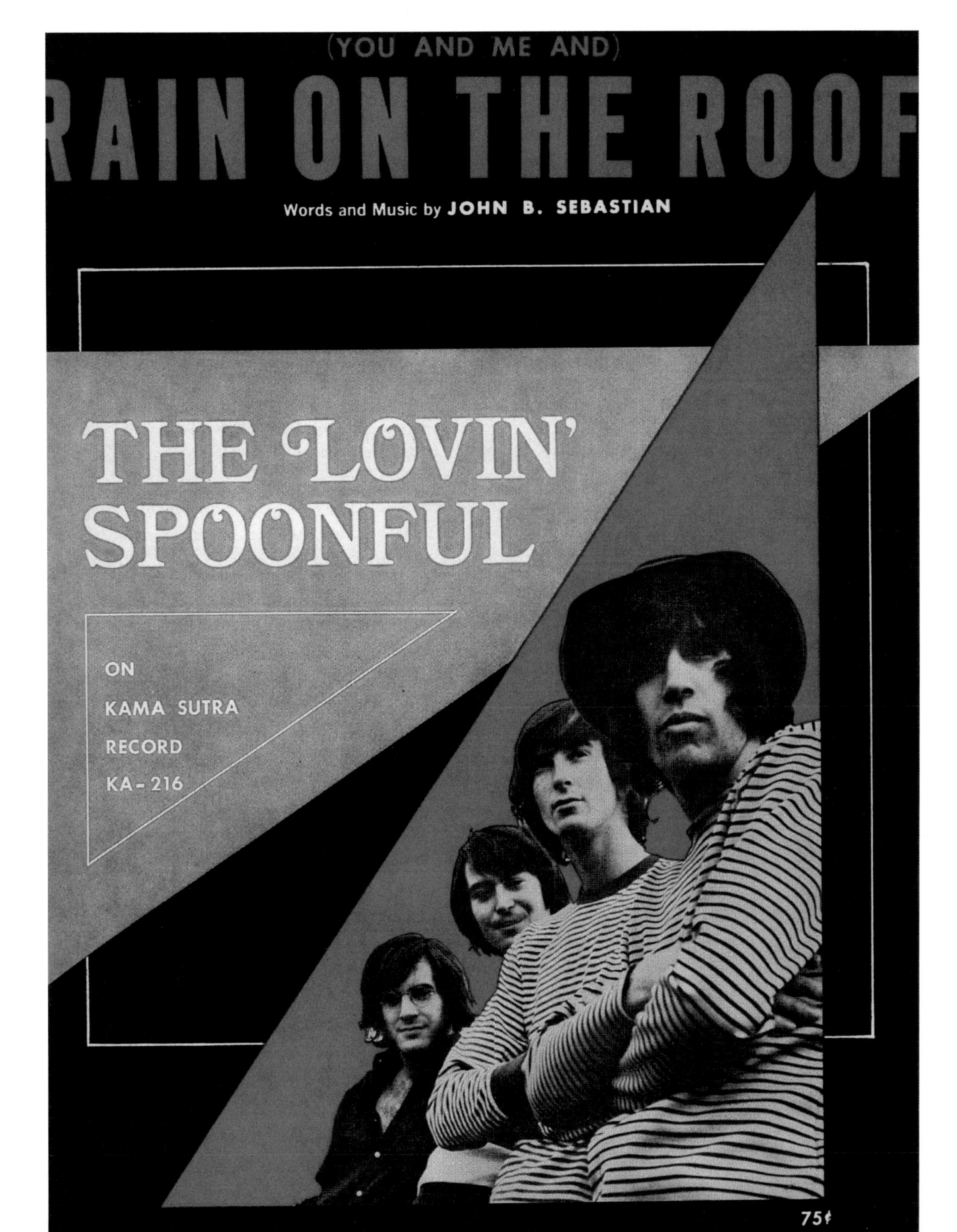
(YOU AND ME AND)
RAIN ON THE ROOF
Words and Music by JOHN B. SEBASTIAN
THE LOVIN' SPOONFUL
ON
KAMA SUTRA
RECORD
KA-216
75¢
FAITHFUL VIRTUE
MUSIC CO., INC.
Distributed by

ROBBINS
The Big
3
FEIST
MILLER

one article with trying to capture some of that joy. I walked into their apartment and they are saying, "Hey Don, do you know how to make blueberry pancakes, we're making them."

"It was like he's got this full time woman living with him now who had such enthusiasm, joy, curiosity and ambition and they were very happy together. Some friend of theirs had taken a picture of them together on a windswept hill in California and they were so happy about that picture. They hung it on the wall in a prominent place in their apartment, which expressed the love that they had for each other. I don't know if other people have spoken about that but that's what I saw. I saw a great deal of love between John and Lorey. It may have turned his focus away from the group's activities, however."

Before Butler knew it "Rain On The Roof was out, "It was not worked on the way it should have been: we'd put in five or six hours at the studio and the next day, God damn it, they would be handing them out to disc jockeys. You couldn't stop them. We didn't even have a chance to listen the next day to make changes because they were so hungry for product." But the businessmen knew what would sell and sure enough "Rain On The Roof" kept up the run of top ten singles, possibly helped by a delightful film made by Stephen Verona to publicise the single. The simple idea of a large white blank canvas, some paint and the Spoonful produced a little gem. With Yanovsky prancing around in what looks like Buster Keaton's swimsuit, the Spoonful draw a picture to symbolise the song, with the obvious result that they get covered in paint -Butler suffering the worst of it.

As it climbed the charts, the Spoonful returned to New York on August 24th, for a concert at the Wollman Rink in Central Park. The day before, the Spoonful had all attended what was to be The Beatles' last concert appearance at Shea Stadium as Butler recalls, "When they did the second Shea Stadium appearance, we went to sit in the audience. We had, at that time, "Summer In The City" at number one. We were told by a couple of people, "Well the Stones went last year and there was no trouble, nobody bothered them." This was the time, maybe it was a Beatles spin off, that girls were really chasing you and cutting your hair and ripping your clothes off. It was expected probably more than warranted! (laughs).

"But what happened was, this time, because of security, they left the lights on. Zally was dressed as a Monk. John, Steve and I were just there. So a couple of girls recognised Stephen and I and within five minutes there were fifty or sixty girls and we were under the seats. Soon the seats were buckling and we were scared - we thought we were going to die. Somehow the cops got them off us and Brian (Epstein), their manager found out that we were there and got us into the locker room and we were there with The Beatles you know. We smoked a joint with them. Ringo was there and he looked miserable, little bit of a guy, Paul was very glad hands, Steve said that he liked his Hofner bass and Paul said, "I'll get you one, here try it out."

Sebastian recalls the chatter between the two groups; "John Lennon began to dress like me at a certain point. In fact, that was the main subject of the conversation when I went backstage at Shea. I remember the rest of the band teasing John about his new thing, which was to look like me, because he had funny round glasses and big sideburns." Joe Butler; "They all got dressed and we're all high, you know, and right before they went out into the hallway they put their arms around each other like The Rockettes and did a little kick thing. It was like, "Here it is now, we've got to face the civilians." We walked out to the dugout with them and sitting there in the dugout were The Rascals. They had obviously wrangled some special thing, we were in the seats we didn't know anyone, and here we were hanging out with The Beatles. The Rascals gave us looks that could kill, talk about those dagger looks. They were pissed, it was very competitive, and we thought we were the cat's ass indeed!"

Unknown to the Spoonful, the concert they gave the next day helped begin the demise of the Night Owl Cafe. Joe Marra; "The city started putting on these concerts in the Park for one dollar, now how can you compete with that? You can't. Dollar for dollar advertising money, no way. So what they did was syphon off the business from the Village. It was a deliberate attempt to spoil the scene and to knock out the clubs, which eventually they did do."

The concert in Central Park was written about in the *New York Times* where Robert Shelton gave them a great write up. Before long, the influential *Time* magazine discovered the Spoonful, listing them as one of "The New Troubadours" and Look magazine wrote a lengthy piece on the group. Sharing the headlines on the cover with the bitter competition over the Governorship of California between Republican Ronald Reagan and Democrat Pat Brown, the Spoonful article included humorous snippets about the group's rise. Significantly, a picture of the Sebastians made its way into the piece, with Mrs. Sebastian dressed rather disconcertingly as Granny, taking her role from *Hit Parader* to the extreme.

Around this time, Lorey Sebastian convinced her husband to try to help support another rock magazine, the emerging *Crawdaddy*. The editor, Paul Williams, recalls her ambitious manner, "John and Lorey were considering investing in the magazine which was sweet, but it didn't really happen. She certainly had a strong personality, very much made herself part of the scene around the importance of John and the Spoonful - forced herself."

Kama Sutra became more eager and released another new single less than a month after its predecessor and Elektra released *What's Shakin'*, with a Don Paulsen colour picture of the group on the cover, as their attempt to cash-in. In the special Spoonful edition of *Hit Parader*, a proposed world tour was announced including a concert in Rome on September 18th followed by ten days in England, supported by Dusty Springfield. In the end the Spoonful were replaced by Los Bravos on this tour, probably because of the fear of Yanovsky not being allowed back into America.

The new single was so good, that Kama Sutra didn't know what song to use as the A side. "Nashville Cats"/ "Full Measure" showed the diversifying styles of the Spoonful. On the one hand the whimsical Sebastian and on the other the realistic Boone. On the more intelligent West Coast, Boone's "Full Measure" was a sizeable hit and even made the top 100 on the strength of its sales there, however, Sebastian's "Nashville Cats" was the more widely played and pushed the single into the top ten.

" Nashville Cats" is Sebastian's paean to the unsung heroes of country music - the session players, with the guitar lick at the beginning admittedly stolen from Johnny Cash's guitarist of the time, Luther Perkins. This was Sebastian's first effort in the C&W field and he had just met a pedal steel guitar for the first time at the recording session for the song, "I had forty five minutes experience on a Fender pedal steel when we cut that. The trick is, Zally got a sound on his guitar kind of like a pedal steel. He played a bunch of hot licks and all I did was add the slides you do with your feet at the end. We would cheat any way we could, but we did play the instruments ourselves." Saying that Butler reckons that the pedal steel was played by a musician from a country band playing down the street.

In the song, where Sebastian incorrectly claims that Sun Records came from Nashville and not Memphis, an error Yanovsky would not let him forget. He also predicted that; "There's 1,352 guitar pickers in Nashville," casually in the song. When Sebastian went to Nashville in the '80s to do a TV show, he was knocked out to hear that he was within fifty of the actual number of session guitarists at the time! The song inspired a spoof version called "Noshville Katz" by The Lovin' Cohens, which is liberally filled with Jewish humour. It was only a novelty but it did show Sebastian's music was being recognised and imitation is some form of flattery.

Boone's superb Phil Spectorish *Full Measure*, is far and away the highlight of his career. The song, about giving and taking, included Sebastian's name in the credits as a trade-off due to Boone's name appearing on *Summer In The City.* Sebastian added little to the song, of which Boone recalls, "It wasn't about anybody, it was just a riff that I did on the piano and I wrote the words to the riff."

With a heavy piano and organ introduction "Full Measure" has a complex but beautiful arrangement, with Butler's lead vocals and group harmony work only adding to the splendour. At the half way point, the song fades, only to be re-introduced with a sharp snare drum snap. Jingle bells are then heard, on the mentioning in the song of Christmas and "Full Measure" ends with Yanovsky screaming, showing his exuberance for this upbeat song. The song is a goose bump moment for this writer and the one track that never fails to raise the spirits and the initial inspiration for further investigation into the group. The single was their only double-sided hit in America and was the Spoonful's last UK top 30 hit, without touring they would fade from the British consciousness.

November 1966 started off on a sad note, with the death of Mississippi John Hurt, at the age of seventy three. The Spoonful were on such a hectic touring schedule, that they probably did not have time to notice the death of the man that gave them their name. Two days later the group were in St. Louis and three days after that they played at the Hunter College Auditorium in New York City, where they were reviewed by Robert Salmaggi in a local paper. Under the headline "The Folk Rock", No.1 Spoonful, Salmaggi claimed of the Spoonful, "They're in and they're the action that is what's happening."

With all 2,320 seats full, plus around 300 other people squeezed onto the sides of the stage, the show was a success, although no mania here as, "at least you could hear and see, no one stood on his seat." But this was an exception, at one concert during this period, Sebastian reacted badly to yet another stage invasion, "I swung my guitar at some young girls who had decided to swarm the stage and it was terrible because after the show I found out that one of the girls had actually gotten struck. She was wearing glasses and I had struck her glasses, they hadn't cut her but they had made a definite mark. It just made me realise what a desperate guy I had become. It really made me feel very changed. It had been so difficult to get the music across and not to be swarmed as a music idol."

NASHVILLE CATS

by JOHN B. SEBASTIAN

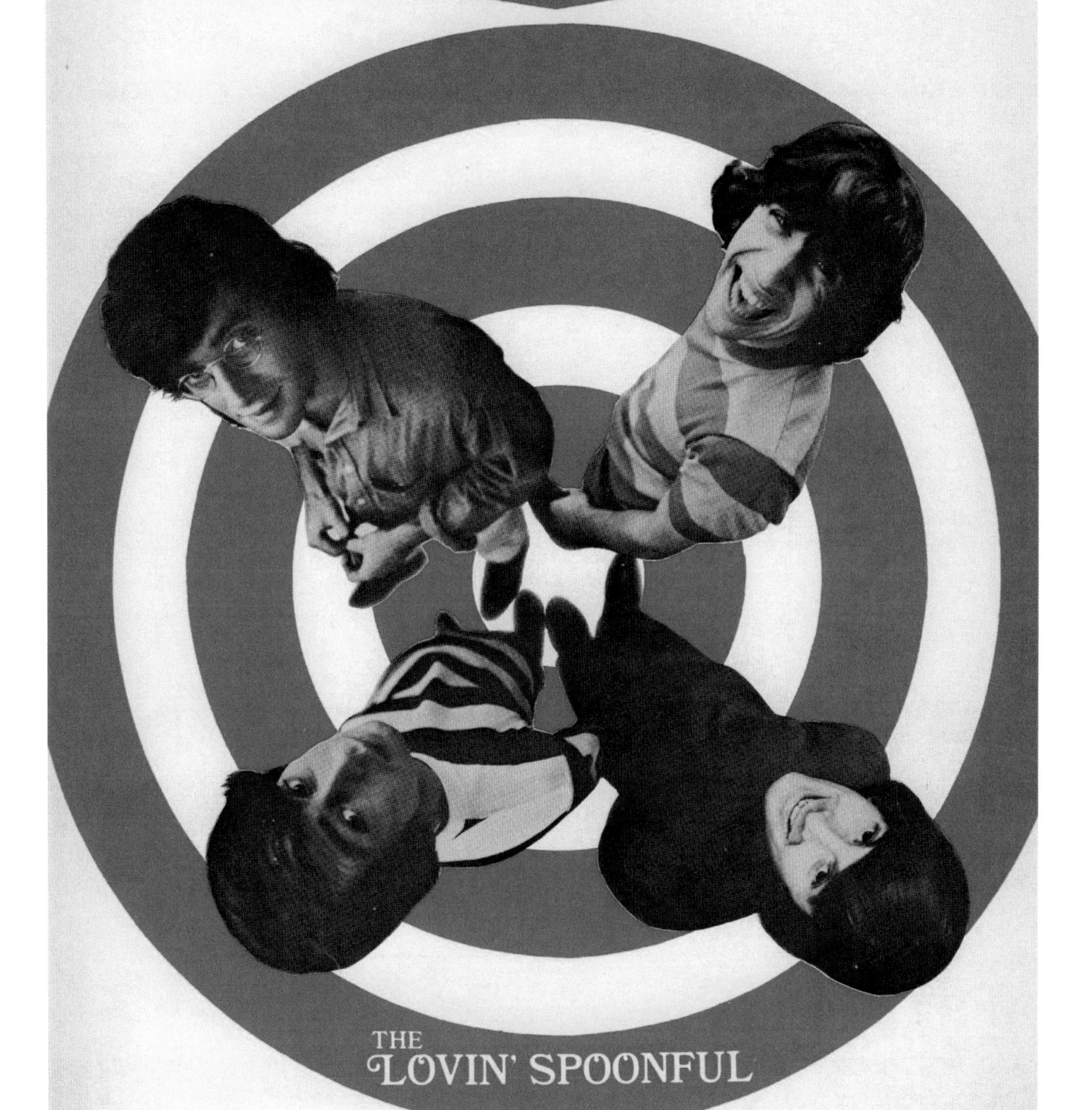

ON KAMA SUTRA RECORD KA-219

FAITHFUL VIRTUE
MUSIC CO., INC.
a product of Koppelman-Rubin Associates, Inc.

75¢

Distributed by

In the *Village Voice* of December 15th, 1966, Richard Goldstein reported on a Spoonful one-nighter in Chicago, where it was clear that the touring schedule was becoming a frustration to the group. Sebastian snapped at inane questions from the local disc jockeys, Yanovsky openly mocked Butler's weight and Boone was distant. Indeed most Spoonful observers noted Boone as being a passenger and Butler recalls Yanovsky spinning a coin in an effort to end the ridicule he was unfairly receiving from Yanovsky. If it fell heads, Yanovsky would keep calling Butler "Fatty", if it fell tails, Butler got five hundred dollars from Yanovsky. As the coin landed, Yanovsky announced, "That's heads, fatty!" Yanovsky's nickname for Cavallo was BFB – "Big Fat Bob"

The last concert on the tour was a homecoming for Yanovsky as the Spoonful played at the Maple Leaf Gardens in Toronto, Canada. The first time the Spoonful played Toronto, at Massey Hall in May '66, the show was a sell-out. At this gig a Canadian TV pop show interviewed the group backstage. The interviewer knew Yanovsky from his early days in Toronto and thought he was going to get back some money he'd lent Yanovsky. What he did get was a middle finger right in front of his camera. This footage is priceless as it includes a brief interview with a visiting Avrom Yanovsky. Butler semi-seriously bemoans his treatment from Yanovsky: "We get along very well except he steals vegetables when we're eating." "He throws food," Boone explains. "And says vile and vulgar things which offend our sensibilities because Steve and I are so shy."

In fact Henry Diltz always mentions that most of his photos of the group were ruined by chiefly Yanovsky's and Boone's insistence on "flippin' the bird." For this Toronto concert only 3,000 fans barely formed a sound cushion in the cavernous Gardens. A local magazine made Yanovsky the cover star for this second return and sent Sylvia Fraser to follow the concert and its aftermath. Describing the concert she wrote, "In a series of supersonic booms, the Spoonful empty their "bag". Steve, the Shy One, edges away from the spotlight. Zal, the Funny One, grabs it. He makes grotesque faces to the audience. He is all mouth. A mouth bracketed by hair. A mouth leaping out to teenyboppers. "Oh Zal, you are so beautiful!" shrieks a pink-cheeked groupie on the knife-edge of hysteria.

"A violinist buries his ears in despair. Union rules require that twenty six local musicians be hired along with the pop groups on the program. Tonight, sitting in tuxedos at ear-level to the stage, they are earning their money. A John cultist, hair flying, tears sliding, breaks free and kisses John. Expressionless he hits her in the stomach with his guitar and then the police take over." Interviewed afterwards Yanovsky spoke on the mania surrounding the tour, "We've been mobbed a few times and once a guy came after me with a gun. He thought I'd run off with his daughter. I've hit a couple of chicks. John punches, gives black eyes. That's the lowest." Musically the group failed to impress the reporter and a colleague, Ralph Thomas of The *Toronto Daily Star* said, "Last night they sounded sloppy." For this three week pre-Christmas tour the management had hired a luxurious DC-7 at a cost of some $10,000 - they grossed $180,000, according to one report.

Fraser followed Yanovsky to his home in the Village to secure an interview for her paper, in an attempt to write a rare overview of the young man. On arriving she described the scene thus, "A stereo set blasted folk-rock through the basement living room. On a kitchen counter was an enormous tomato juice can personally autographed by Andy Warhol. Framed on the wall of the colonial, brown-tone living room was a blackhead with a sentimental history. We went through the kitchen where a rubber frog dangled from the ceiling, a frog that made *The Ed Sullivan Show* on the end of Zalman's guitar, into the main bedroom, Zalman was mixing himself a Cubra Libre. He turned off the stereo, eyed me semi-hostilely through a fog of smoke and challenged: "OK, interview me."

Fraser's attempt at portraying a picture of Yanovsky failed when she interviewed the man himself. During the interview an Iguana arrived from a fan in Texas which stole his attention. A few days later, like a child with a new toy, he gave the animal to actor Jack Gilford's son. It was only when she spoke to the people closest to Yanovsky that Fraser secured an accurate portrait.

Jackie Burroughs told Fraser; "He's a very magnetic person. When he's in a room, everyone watches him and, if he's down, he drags everyone down." This line of thought was echoed by Rich Chiaro, "Zal's completely undisciplined. When he's up, he's one of the finest people but when he's not being funny, he's terrible. He used to be awful about wrecking hotel rooms, and he has a thing about room service. He'll order up a hundred sandwiches just to look at them." Dan Moriarty remarked; "Zal generates madness in people. Once he said in an interview that he liked girls with an overbite and honest-to-God, THOUSANDS wrote in."

Years later Joe Butler painted a similar picture, highlighting Yanovsky's mischievousness, "Zal Yanovsky is one of the most fascinating, amazing people that I have ever met. I joined the Spoonful because of Zally. He truly was the most naturally charismatic person, without uttering a word he was just there. Some of the things Zally did were just too outrageous that when I think about them...I'll give you a for instance. And this was a kind of guy now that when he did something it wasn't just once in a while it was truly unrelenting. Every time we got on a plane we almost wet our pants. We would be suppressing laughter because we knew what was going to happen because it always happened. When Zally would get on the plane he would round up all the magazines he could, hide them, and one by one go through the magazines from the cover to the end drawing penises with balls going into the mouths, ears and between the legs of every man, woman, child and animal in the magazine. As soon as he got half a dozen or so done he'd sneak them back into the magazine racks on the top. So we knew what was coming.

"Halfway through the flight there would be gasps of horror or outrage followed by someone gasping, "My God!". The bell would ring and the stewardess would be summoned and she would have to round up all the magazines. This was not one flight. There was a period when this went down for about six months - every flight. This was the kind of thing Zally would do. He would decide when to stop. It was the same with the food fights, over ordering food, and Zally would always start a food fight. It was his way of relieving the boredom and the stress of being on the road."

For this book, another person on the periphery, Don Paulsen, painted the most authentic picture of all four of the dissimilar characters that made up The Lovin' Spoonful; "Zal was like the class clown. He was very, "Look at me, wow, yuka, yuka," you couldn't miss him. He had this out-going humour. John was a little more contained but he also had a sharp wit about him and he was very perceptive, very precise. Steve was sort of the quiet one. Almost every group has a quite one but still waters run deep, there's a dimension under that too.

"Joe Butler would chime in with things from time to time. He was like the Paul McCartney of the group, in that he was the one that was good at public relations. He was the easiest guy to get along with and just a wonderful sweet guy to be with." Mark Sebastian adds, "Joe Butler was often the motivator and organiser to the others, helping arrange set lists and generally keeping the others moving forward."

For Christmas 1966, needing a rest from one another, Yanovsky returned to Toronto, Butler to the Canary Islands, Boone went home to the Hamptons and the Sebastians pulled their crackers in New Hampshire, near the summer camp of his youth. Cavallo, for whom the group had bought a tractor for the property he had acquired from their talents, "watched the store" as the Spoonful had just released their third album.

CHAPTER 4 – RUSH TO JUDGEMENT

Hums Of The Lovin' Spoonful failed to progress the group's essence any further than their last proper album. Whereas before, one could define the blended jug band music that developed into the folk rock tinged sound, *Hums* appears to be just a collection of songs. Around the Spoonful, The Beatles were releasing *Revolver*, The Beach Boys *Pet Sounds* and the Stones *Aftermath* - established bands creating new sounds. That is to say nothing of all the new bands, catching up the Spoonful in terms of popularity and creativity.

Not that there is anything drastically wrong with *Hums*. It became a fairly successful album, but it would be their best shot to escape from their familiar laid back themes and delivery. The Spoonful never said that they were on this planet for the revolution, but when the time came and they realised what was happening around them, they were caught totally on the back foot and their attempts at psychedelia were somewhat artificial and embarrassing. Sebastian has a hand in all the songs on *Hums* (although he had little to do with "Full Measure") and left to his own resources, he mainly continued to follow the path of songs about his new love.

Yanovsky resented Sebastian's move away from the "Do You Believe In Magic" approach. This became clear to the people who knew him after seeing the Spoonful's first appearance on the important *Ed Sullivan Show* in January of 1967, as Jerry Yester recalls, "John was getting softer and softer and Zally was getting more and more bored. That isn't why Zally got into the Spoonful, I mean Zally was going crazy cause he was playing a lot of the guitar when they got together and by the end he was not playing guitar at all. I saw the *Ed Sullivan* "Nashville Cats" performance, and I saw Zally playing and I don't know the story, but I do know from looking at Zally's face. I'll bet you a hundred bucks that he wasn't happy with the session. He didn't get to play what he wanted to; he ended up playing what John wanted him to. A steel guitar ended up doing the solo, Zally didn't even do the solo and when Zally gets unhappy he gets real crazy and he could get destructive back in those days. So his way of answering the problem was turning up and being really obnoxious. He was just a pain in the butt and he knew it - it was his intention. You know it's sad too, because they were really wonderful together."

Butler remembers the Spoonful's first appearance on the significant show for a completely different reason, "*Ed Sullivan* was the pinnacle. You did that show and boy you were considered hot stuff. The first *Ed Sullivan Show* we did had Johnny Mathis and I went up to Johnny Mathis and told him how much I enjoyed his voice and recordings. Then for the whole week, once a day, I would get a bouquet of flowers inviting me to lunch and of course you can imagine what grist this was for Zally's and John's mill. It was merciless so I finally had to say to Johnny, "Don't send me anymore flowers or notes inviting me to dinner. I respect you but I'm not gay and have no inclination to be gay and I have a feeling that's what this is about."

Brooks Arthur had been the studio engineer on the Spoonful's first two albums. For *Hums*, however, a new studio was chosen, hence a new engineer was brought in who was an immense talent in the field as Boone recalls, "In some ways *Hums* is my favourite album because we had Roy Halee as the engineer. He got a lot of the sounds on the record that we never had before, it was more imaginative sounding." Erik Jacobsen was more than happy to have Halee on the board, "We decided to go over and record at Columbia, so we did a lot of our great shit with Roy. He was a fabulous engineer to have on your side. He went on to make a great producer, so you can imagine what he was like to work with as an engineer."

Boone recalls the relaxed time spent recording the album at Columbia, "It was a very free spirited album, it wasn't structured. We were not trying to sound like "Magic", we were not trying to sound like "Daydream". Whatever the consciousness, it was, "Here's the song, let's go in there and do it." I had got very comfortable with the group and the other guys did too. We were at the peak of our career and we were given unlimited freedom by our record company to go in to the studio and do what we wanted to do. The budget was there, there wasn't executives breathing down our necks."

The first track on *Hums*, "Lovin' You", typifies Sebastian's direction of the time. A pleasing track but nothing special, the tweeness is akin to "Rain On The Roof", as Sebastian explained once, "I just woke up in the middle of the night in California with this feeling." Sebastian does add a twist and the lyrics are a touch more complex than they at first seem to be. Bobby Darin, a close friend of Charles Koppelman, covered the song and had a hit with it. Another song of Sebastian's, "Younger Girl", had been recorded by another of Koppelman's acts, The Critters, which reached number 42 in May '66.

Sebastian told Don Paulsen about "Lovin' You" in the *Hit Parader* article, 'A Listener's Guide To *Hums Of The Lovin' Spoonful*', "We did this with a twelve-string guitar, the fairly common acoustic and electric band and on the end Zally played a phallon, which sounds like a bagpipe." Paulsen then asked what a phallon was to which Sebastian replied; "It's a Swedish instrument imported by Guild. It's a long tube with a keyboard on it and variable pitch and volume. It's like a hand-held portable organ." Paulsen discloses the real title given to this instrument, away from the restrictions of his magazine, "It was a tubular device that one wore strapped over one's neck and it could resemble a phallic symbol if one held it in one way and it was probably Zally with his sense of humour who called it the "Fabulous Phallus!" Actually, it was a tubon."

"Bes' Friends" tells of "the paradox of friend and lover," to quote Sebastian and is delivered in Dixieland style, with friend Henry Diltz playing the clarinet and Butler on an old style drum kit with high crowned cymbals. The song also has evident banjo and tuba with Sebastian's over the top side of the mouth delivery supporting the theme. Sebastian was once asked to perform "Voodoo In My Basement" at a concert in the '80s, to which he retorted, "I don't do obscure shit!" This is a fair statement to make regarding this song. Another totally unique sound from the Spoonful though, with tribal drumming and eerie falsetto background singing; add to that Yanovsky's growling lead vocal and the song becomes distinct, but it is too silly for repeated plays. It has the hallmark of being left out of the group's first album.

It was put to Boone, that with the inclusion of this and other weak songs, that it was surprising that the rest of the band did not contribute to the album. Boone and Yanovsky had written a song called "The Dance Of Pain And Pleasure" which was left off the finished album, and left a bitter taste in the mouths of the writers as Boone explains, "John, Joe and Erik hated the song. It wasn't a whole song, it was a verse and a chorus, and we wanted to see if they were interested in doing it. It was a very simple thing but I'll tell you right now, if we had made that record it would have been a classic because it addressed something that today is very contemporary."

Asked to explain, Boone said, "Well, "The Dance Of Pain And Pleasure" is kind of like life. It's like everything that appears to be great also has a bad side to it and conversely everything that appears to be bad could have a good side to it and that was what the message of the song was. But I guess to John, Joe and Erik it sounded so simple, so naive that they couldn't get it." Indeed this might be the case. Existing lyrics do not agree with Boone's thinking that this would have turned into a classic; 'Old folks, young folks, Measure by measure, Talk about the dance of pain and pleasure.'

Reminded of the song, Erik Jacobsen chuckled then said, "I couldn't take it seriously. Possibly I was short sighted but it's too late. I cannot recall it, I hope I'm not making fun of something that's going to turn out to be one of the great works of the twentieth century. I remember they were very serious, but every time you work with a group that has one major songwriter, everybody wants to have their song looked at so you do the best you can. I remember not being impressed at the time."

Sebastian's thoughts on the song agree with Jacobsen's, "What it was, was the democratic phase of the Spoonful, that terrible moment that happened with every sixties group (laughs) where their political consciousness' began to get in the way of the way that the band worked. In many cases the band were not really a total democracy, you know. We tried to fabricate one song and the results were that everybody was trying to write songs and very often they were less than wonderful (laughs)."

On a more positive note, Sebastian continues, "At the same time I was encouraging Zally and Stephen to write because they weren't writing with me at that point. That was frustrating but at the same time I did want them to kick in because there was a lot of stuff that was demanded of us. The more material we had the better, in my mind but it was to get it good enough to go on the record. Of course Erik is a little less democratic than I am and he would go, "Hey this is the most horrible thing I ever heard in the last year, maybe two years, what do you think John?" And, you know, we'd all be in this embarrassing position - but that was Jacobsen. Thank God he was not a glad-hander. That's why our records were good, that he demanded a degree of just natural musicality and lyrical interest and the thing worked."

Butler realised the importance of the rest of the group contributing to the Spoonful catalogue, but he was not going to let their name be ruined by substandard material either. On being reminded of "The Dance Of Pain And Pleasure" he said, "It was crazy and bullshit and it had no basis of fucking anything. It was like daring somebody to accept it as a piece of music, so you would actually have to do the work on it. It didn't have a beginning or an end. It may have been what we should have been doing, which was writing a song."

On being told that Boone still had faith in the song, Butler stormed, "Oh, Jesus Christ! I'll listen to it again, I haven't heard it in a long time, maybe it was ahead of its time, but I have a feeling it's a piece of crap! None of us were mature enough to really use the creative juices. When we linked up it was fine but everybody had their own petty ways, kid's stuff, you know? John became selfish and cut himself off and Zally, I guess, through excesses of life-style and excessive demands on relationships and I ... each of us in our own way failed the others. You know, we were kids, we were just God damned kids!"

Yanovsky uses the song as part of his list of reasons why he was unhappy being a part of the successful group, "It was not that close to being finished. It was a bit of a kibbutz, you know, but that's okay. I felt personally that I was always fighting my hand but I liked that anyway." The criticism stuck to Boone and Yanovsky as the former remembers, "It was a turning point for Zally and me. For Zally it was more of a turning point, he was like, "Well fuck them. If they don't want to do my song and we've got to do "Bes' Friends" and things like that..." And that's where he started to get pretty rebellious and this is after the bust, too. Zally and I were like these two (insignificants) and everybody else was picking on us and we were the ones that kept to ourselves."

It is easy to understand their mood as one of the tracks on the album is about Sebastian's dog! "Henry Thomas" is the title of the song, yet the subject reference is not the blues performer but Kahuna, a Golden Retriever bought during an earlier tour in California. The reason for the title is that the music for "Henry Thomas" is a direct copy of one of Thomas' tunes, "The Fox And The Hounds". Larry Hankin, by now a close friend of Yanovsky, supplied the Jew's harp on this nonsense song, with Sebastian playing the slidewhistle. Yanovsky would extract a little revenge by calling the dog a different name so it would only respond to the name Yanovsky gave it. At one party chez Sebastian, Yanovsky got the dog drunk on Champagne.

Larry Hankin explains how he got his only ever session work; "As far as *Hums*, I played Jews Harp just as a hobby around the house. When they needed a Jews Harp player, their producer (that tall, skinny perfectionist with the long hair and granny glasses) and Zally suggested yours truly. So two days before I went into the studio with them, Zal's wife made me a tiny leather Jew's Harp case for the occasion. It looked like a miniature guitar case – approximately three inches long (she sewed the brown leather together herself) and I marched in carrying it like all the other guys who carried in regulation sized guitar cases. The visual was very funny. They played and then I did the overdub. We got it in three takes. I never did another gig. I thanked them for the mention on the album cover. The Jew's Harp in its case was stolen years later in San Francisco."

"Darlin' Companion", probably most famous for Johnny Cash's version that appeared a few years later on his superb *Live At San Quentin*, includes one of Sebastian's delightful verses which ended; 'As long as I've got legs to stand on, I'm gonna run to you.' The excellent guitar solo was actually a duo between Yanovsky and Sebastian. Again the subject matter is his wife and the song is admirable but lacks any substance. On this theme, writing about these last two songs that appear on the first side of *Hums* in *Crawdaddy*, Paul Nelson wrote, "Artistically, they are probably the most fully-realised songs on side one, a fact which raises no optimism from this corner."

Out of the only two new songs on side two, the first, is an all-time Spoonful unrecognised classic - an overused word but suitable here. "Coconut Grove" just oozes tranquillity from the opening note to the last. The music had already been heard, as it was one of the instrumentals from *What's Up, Tiger Lily*, "Lookin' To Spy", but here it was turned into a triumph. In the Paulsen interview, Sebastian recalled the inspiration for the song, "I started writing this song with Freddy Neil and some other people and I went out on a small boat. I was lying under the sail boom, on my back, feeling the motion of the waves. I wrote the first two verses but I never had a bridge. The bridge I wrote recently, which completed the song as a singing thing. I finished it after a weekend Lorey and I spent on Long Island. The original verses were written three years ago."

Yanovsky contributed the music for the "bridge" hence his inclusion in the songwriting credits, although "Lookin' To Spy" was listed as a group effort. The tempo of the song matches the experience of the boat rocking from side to side and exudes a pleasant relaxing feel. Whether the influence of dope helped Sebastian find the right words is open to question, but drugs were regularly consumed on the boat.

On a later, separate occasion on Neil's celebrated boat, his producer Nik Venet recalled a confrontation with the President of the day, "One time we had drifted too close to Nixon's compound and we were all snoozing, cause everybody had done enormous quantities of drugs. The next thing we know, they had these huge coast guard helicopters above us and I said to myself, "Oh this is great, here I am vacationing, totally straight, with two stoned creatures and we're going to be busted by an international squad of coast guards!" They really came down on us but it was just another day in the life of Fred Neil."

In Sebastian's way, he pulls off an intimate mood of isolation from the outside world and all its troubles. Boone recalls Coconut Grove - the place, "It's a beautiful part, it was the folkie section back then in the sixties, like the Greenwich Village of Miami. We went there for a gig in early '66 and that's where Fred Neil lived and John used to go on vacation and visit there." The calmness of the place was the reason Fred Neil lived there. A lot of musicians in Greenwich Village looked up to Neil as a role model but sometimes it would all become too much for him and, without telling a soul, he would leave the Village and head for Coconut Grove. Today, Sebastian says, "I owe so much to Fred Neil and Vince Martin."

The last new song on *Hums* is a middle finger to all those who taunted the young Sebastian for having to wear glasses. "Four Eyes", a sour to all the previous sweet, shows that Sebastian is not all lovey-dovey and that there is another side to his persona. The song includes a delightful appeal to the mothers and fathers of this world, on how to prevent their kin from the unnecessary playground banter; 'And please recall that after all, He wears them on his face.'

Hums Of The Lovin' Spoonful ends with the tour de force, "Summer In The City". In his review of the album, Paul Nelson relates the strength of this song comparing it to the rest of the album, "For once, both the lyrics and the arrangement are brilliant at the same time, and the song stands as a genuine classic of the New Music. Such is not the case with *Hums Of The Lovin' Spoonful*. In retrospect, only second-echelon adjectives, "good," "pleasant," "nice" etc. will do. If one can't object very strenuously to the warmth and fun of *Hums*, one can't get very enthusiastic about it either. And one should be able to get very enthusiastic about the Lovin' Spoonful."

Sebastian is on record saying that *Hums* is his favourite Spoonful album claiming its "overall diversity" as his reason, yet this is its biggest downfall. The eclectic mixture of country, skiffle, rock 'n' roll and even voodoo rhythms alongside the choice of using bizarre and esoteric instrumentation is too much in one go. You can over do a good thing and one gets the feeling that the Spoonful were trying too hard to diversify. Eventually they gave an impression of a band attempting to show themselves overtly proficient at the arranging process, managing to take away most of their earlier "pleasing amateurism," which was part of their charm.

It may have reached number 14 in the US charts, but with the inclusion of the three hit singles it should have done a lot better. But as 1967 began there was a hell of a lot else going on, The Jimi Hendrix Experience's first record had just been released and The Monkees' first album was at number one at the time of the release of *Hums Of The Lovin' Spoonful*. The band were to be lost somewhere between these two acts, with one headline of the time asking, 'How Did The Spoonful Become Left Out?' The Spoonful had not taken advantage of their foothold over the new American groups and left the door wide open. An exit door into obscurity that was to be held wide open by their contemporaries and the counterculture.

As 1967 commenced it was becoming clear that rock 'n' roll music was not merely just entertainment or a mouthpiece for the younger generation, but something to use as an anti-establishment tool. The generation gap was widening with the constant flow of folk singers speaking out about Vietnam and groups like The Doors and The Jefferson Airplane coming from the west coast, speaking about tripping out and wanting to kill their parents.

The music was a flag to wave and the musicians were deemed to be above the law. Joan Baez would be arrested for her campaigning against the Vietnam War and The Beatles would sign a petition urging for the legalisation of marijuana in this year. So, when it became clear that two members of The Lovin' Spoonful had turned in their drug source, the process reversed and the audience campaigned against the musicians.

As there was no recognised Rock Press at the time, the story emerged through the counterculture. Don Paulsen explains the background of the underground press, "Part of the explosion of the media was the rise of what was called the underground newspaper like the *LA Free Press*, *The East Village Other* or *The Oracle*. Anybody who had access to a printing press could put together some sort of magazine with some R. Crumb cartoons, pro-drug articles, feminist issues or some photographs of police beating up people at a demonstration. There was a huge flowering of the underground press and this was one of the arenas where the Spoonful were being put down, because these people were pro-drug."

Boone confirms Paulsen's last comment, "It was a political move that was starting to gather force. The anti-war movement was all linking up with the pot smokers and the hippies. So we were actually the first targets after the military and the government. We became the first people that they could paint as finks or co-operators, whatever you want to call it, that helped the authorities suppress the emerging revolution. There were these magazines called *The Berkeley Free Press* and *The Berkeley Barb*, newspapers for the counterculture, this is before *Rolling Stone*, and these two newspapers took it upon themselves to label us as traitors to the movement."

John Sebastian; "There was a polarity beginning between people of our age and hair length and the police. Zally and Stephen had no idea when they got into this how ugly it was to become." The union of this pressure against the group was somewhat unfair when one considers that the group never purported themselves part of any movement, they were just musicians who liked to smoke pot as Sebastian puts forward, "Look, we felt that we were ahead of our time. That's why we didn't embrace the growing hippie mentality; we had already been through that freedom thing at fifteen. So when we went out to California, and saw all of these people that were blissed out, I mean, it was only more encouraging to us."

Sebastian cannot speak for the entire group, however, as Butler embraced this "hippie mentality" to some extent. It was put to Butler whether he was aware of the hippie's somewhat fake camaraderie, to which he replied, "I don't know, in some ways there was a camaraderie and some of it was phoney and some of it was real. There were some people in the '60s that really believed in peace, love and understanding and god bless Elvis Costello for pointing it out."

BEAT THE HEAT

Here are a few very simple rules to help keep busts to a neat minimum.

1) Don't tell a stranger anything you wouldn't tell a cop.

2) Don't do anything with a stranger you wouldn't do with a cop.

3) A stranger is anyone, no matter how friendly, that you don't know very much about.

(The State admits to having 78 undercover agents concealed among us, and God knows how many the City has. Most of the people busted in the Haight recently have been done in by an agent they thought was a friend. As more & more newcomers arrive, such busts will become more & more common. Beware of spies. Beware of "perfect imitations." Make sure you really know the people you associate with. Remember: the City has declared war on hippies. Be advised.)

4) Be careful with people who have been busted recently. The case of the two Finking Spoonfuls should remind us that the heat has been known to make deals.

5) Avoid people & places that are not cool. Don't get caught in someone else's bust. Don't get busted by accident.

6) Make The Man work for his arrests. It's too late to protect your liberty when you've lost it. Be cool NOW.

gestetnered in the interests of Constitutional Liberty by the communication company, a member of the underground press syndicate, 3/24/67.

In reality it was not totally the *Free Press* that was behind the spreading of the word but a small group of local writers in San Francisco who came under the title "The Communication Company". These people produced leaflets that pulled the strings that forced the papers to act. The leader of The Communication Company was Chester Anderson, a good friend of Paul Williams who gives a brief history of ComCo; "These handbills were mimeographed sheets passed out (or left in strategic drop boxes) in the Haight-Ashbury district in San Francisco, starting just after the Human Be-In in Jan '67 and ending during the "Summer Of Love," in Aug '67.

"Chester wrote much of the material he and his partner Claude Hayward printed and passed out, but others such as Richard Brautigan, Emmett Grogan, Lenore Kandel, contributed. Because the Haight Ashbury was the nerve centre of the growing "Hippie" or "Counterculture" movement in 1967, the ComCo handbills were quite influential. Some of them - particularly "rants" written by Chester Anderson, who also wrote a science fiction novel called *The Butterfly Kid*, and who was described in Ramparts, 3/67, as "the unofficial historian of the psychedelic movement" - were widely reprinted in the Underground Press, i.e. weekly and very influential papers like the *Los Angeles Free Press*, *The East Village Other* (NYC), *The Berkeley Barb*, etc."

Bill Love was the manager of The Committee Theatre in San Francisco, which specialised in anti-establishment satire, hence he also knew of Chester Anderson. With local resentment growing fairly strong against the Spoonful as a whole, with some people throwing away their records, none went as far as Anderson did. He printed a leaflet describing each crime perpetrated by the Spoonful. In the piece he urged everyone with a conscience to never listen to their music again, advised friends of the group never to speak to them again and even suggested groupies not to "ball them." The essay was sent out to all the underground media in America.

When only one paper, *The Berkeley Barb*, ran the article in full, a furious Anderson and Hayward issued a second statement: "TO THE ERSTWHILE UNDERGROUND PRESS, GREETING: It comes as quite a shock to us that so far only one of the UPS papers has had much to say about the Lovin' Spoonful problem. We refer, of course, to the actions of Steve Boone & Zal Yasinski (sic) in helping the San Francisco Police bust Bill Loughborough on pot charges. In plainer talk they are <u>finks</u>. FINKS

"In case there are some of you who don't know, Bill Loughborough is the manager of the Committee in San Francisco. Due to the nature of the satire the Committee is engaged in, it is obvious why the SFPD wanted him busted. Bill Loughborough (Bill Love) stands trial on April 24. He will probably go to jail. Anyone who cares enough to spend thirty minutes reading the court transcript of the preliminary hearing, which we have in hand, would immediately know why Bill Love is about to go to jail. He was consciously and maliciously set up, turned in and sold by his friends (he thought), Steve Boone and Zal Yasinski. WHY? So that the Spoonful could continue to play and make money. As far as we know, the Spoonful is still merrily playing on to those poor people who still believe in magic, and still selling records on the Kama Sutra label. And Bill Love will go to jail.

"THE COMMUNICATION COMPANY DEMANDS TO KNOW WHAT IS THIS FUCKING BULLSHIT SILENCE THAT COMES FROM THE UNDERGROUND PRESS! Why haven't you spread this story as far as you can? We notice that some of you carry advertising from the Spoonful and Kama Sutra. We hope you choke on the money, baby. In San Francisco, we spit on the ground when Lovin' Spoonful is mentioned. The Spoonful doesn't play gigs in San Francisco anymore, and never will again.

TO THE ERSTWHILE UNDERGROUND PRESS, GREETING:

It comes as quite a shock to us that so far only one of the UPS papers (the BARB, not present at the recent Stinson Beach Love-Out) has had much to say about the Lovin' Spoonful problem. We refer, of course, to the actions of Steve Boone & Zal Yasinski in helping the San Frandisco Police bust Bill Loughborough on pot charges. In plainer talk, they are finks. FINKS.

In case there are some of you who don't know, Bill Loughborough is the manager of the Committee in San Francisco. Due to the nature of the satire the Committee is engaged in, it is obvious why the SFPD wanted him busted.

Bill Loughborough (Bill Love) stands trial on April 24. He will probably go to jail. Anyone who cares enough to spend 30 minutes reading the court transcript of the preliminary hearing, which we have in hand (copies on request c/o 901 Cole St., SF), would immediately know why Bill Love is about to go to jail. He was consciously and malisciously set up, turned in and sold by his friends (he thought), Steve Boone and Zal Yasinski. WHY? So that the Spoonful could continue to pley and make money.

As far as we know, the Spoonful is still merrily playing on to those poor people who still believe in magic, and still selling records on the Kama Sutra label. And Bill Love will go to jail.

THE COMMUNICATION COMPANY DEMANDS TO KNOW WHAT IS THIS FUCKING BULL-SHIT SILENCE THAT COMES FROM THE UNDERGROUND PRESS!

Why haven't you spread this story as far as you can? We notice that some of you carry advertising from the Spoonful and Kama Sutra. We hope you choke on the money, baby. In San Francisco, we spit on the ground when Lovin' Spoonful is mentioned. The Spoonful doesn't play gigs in San Francisco anymore, and never will again.

As long as the Spoonful continues to play and make money, as long as you pretend it didn't happen, or whatever else copout you care to make for the Spoonful, you are all shit. Either the Underground Press Syndicate means something, in which case we expect to see full coverage of this hypocricy, or else the Underground Press Syndicate is nothing more than the same old America shit in a bright new polyethylene extruded psychedelic wrapper.

THE COMMUNICATION COMPANY

Claude Hayward
Chester Anderson

Chester Anderson
Claude Hayward

"As long as the Spoonful continues to play and make money, as long as you pretend it didn't happen, or whatever else cop-out you care to make of the Spoonful, you are all shit. Either the Underground Press Syndicate means something, in which case we expect to see full coverage of this hypocrisy, or else the Underground Press Syndicate is nothing more than the same old America shit in a bright new polyethylene extruded psychedelic wrapper. Claude Hayward and Chester Anderson – THE COMMUNICATION COMPANY." A couple of other papers, including *The East Village Other*, reacted to this second statement but in reality, not a great deal of attention was given to it. "Most of our fans didn't even read the underground papers," notes Yanovsky.

The Spoonful had already lost too much ground to the West Coast groups. In the scramble of emerging groups, the Spoonful were being ignored by their hip audience, a fact addressed by Don Paulsen, "I do remember going into the Night Owl around the time "Rain On The Roof" was a single and the people there were complaining, "I don't know, John's getting kind of soft. All he does now is write love songs to his wife." Nobody can say how much Chester Anderson was responsible for the eventual disintegration of The Lovin' Spoonful but it is certain that he was a leading contributing factor.

As Greg Shaw said of Anderson in *Starling Magazine* in October, 1970; "The summer of '67 was a very heavy experience for everyone in the Haight, especially for Chester, who had taken upon himself the responsibility of being the conscience of the entire hip movement in San Francisco. He really wasn't doing much other than composing bitter, angry essays and putting them out on the street, but it was still more than most people were doing."

Boone is annoyed that he became a pawn in someone else's game, "We weren't even in a movement. We all smoked pot, but I wasn't like in the movement. I didn't advertise pot or carry signs, you know, I did it because it was something I enjoyed doing. So they effectively embarrassed the group by coming to concerts with placards that would say, "Don't Fuck The Band". Well they called it "don't ball the band," "don't buy their records." Some stores in L.A. and San Francisco put our albums in the front window with a big black sash across it, stuff like that."

Butler remembers that the whole thing could have been buried but for the intervention of Love's attorney, "We tried to hire this guy a lawyer and we would have got him off. But at some point he got this Goddamned civil rights lawyer that was going to challenge the pot issue. He would have got off with probation otherwise and we would have paid him for the bust."

Boone then, and now, thinks that marijuana should be legalised, "I'm sympathetic to that view, and I don't necessarily think you should accommodate the authorities when you don't believe marijuana should be outlawed or illegal." Saying that, Butler does admit that the group were quite prepared for somebody to serve time for the bust, "It was the choice we made at the time, we really felt we had to make it but we were going to throw this guy to the dogs."

In an interview with Yanovsky from the middle of March, it became clear that there was another side to the animated character the fans thought they knew. Coming from a session where he and Boone had produced some songs for Skip Boone's new group, Northern Lights, Yanovsky was visibly drained and depressed. After getting little response from their subject, the reporter turned off her tape recorder and the cameraman stopped clicking.

The reporter, Ellen Sander, wrote as her end piece an informed evaluation of Yanovsky's temperament, until now hidden from the media, "So exuberant, exhibitionist, funny, homely Zally has his moments of fatigue, depression and sulky petulance. It reminded us that he's a real live boy, a very special one, young and enormously talented. He's peculiar and moody at times, and this was one of them. A real live boy, not a musical automaton. Yes, a star, a celebrity, a success. But most of all a real live boy who's tired of putting on a freak show fourteen hours a day."

Kama Sutra reacted swiftly to the unhappiness in the Spoonful camp and rush released a greatest hits (*Best Of*) package to the world. Basically the resulting album was a compilation of the first two albums with "Summer In The City" tagged on at the close. In an attempt to make the fans buy the same material twice, the album was attractively packaged in a gatefold sleeve and included individual colour photographs of the Spoonful. More noticeable was the distinct faceless drawing of the group on the cover that would become synonymous with the Spoonful. The artist was a fan, Chrystal Russell, who had sent it to the group. She remembers only that, "It was just an attempt to get to meet the group - and it worked!"

To promote the album, the Spoonful appeared on *The Ed Sullivan Show* again, a couple of days after Yanovsky's sullen interview on March 19th, where they mimed to "Do You Believe In Magic" and played poor live versions of "Daydream" and "Bald Headed Lena". The first song had been filmed earlier in the day and featured the group disappearing and reappearing in different clothes and places - quite innovative for the day. One time Yanovsky disappears and a puppy from the ever-growing menagerie of the Sebastians' (which included a monkey) appeared in his place. For the filming Yanovsky wore a large police badge on his chest in a misguided attempt to make light of his situation.

The Best Of The Lovin' Spoonful was a big success and became the first and last gold album awarded to the group. Today, John Sebastian's gold disc is proudly displayed on his living room wall whereas Charles Koppelman's was sold at Sotheby's. Also released in March was the single "Six O'clock". This song is the painfully obvious successor to "Summer In The City". This tense, bold piece was an affectionate look to bygone days as Sebastian remembers, "For the first time, I was starting to yearn a little bit for my past. It's a song of recollection about my early romantic situations. Very often, in the early years, I'd end up in Washington Square in that kind of early morning after, and "Six O'clock" is about that."

Surprisingly for such a strong record, it only just crept into the top twenty in America. The reasons for the relative failure of the song could have been down to the bust becoming common knowledge but not so as Erik Jacobsen told *The Beat* magazine at the time, "Some hippies have dropped The Lovin' Spoonful and some have not, depending on how well they know the boys and what they are ready to believe about them. On the East Coast where the concentration of hippies is far less than on the West Coast their latest record, "Six O'clock" hasn't had nearly the success it had in the West. Of course, losing some friends has hurt them psychologically." In a busy month (the adverts read 'The Spoonful Runneth Over!'), a second soundtrack featuring the Spoonful appeared.

SIX·O·CLOCK
Words and Music by JOHN B. SEBASTIAN
12
1
2
3
4
5
6
7
8
9
10
11
Recorded by
THE LOVIN' SPOONFU
on
KAMA SUTRA KA-22
Distributed
by
FAITHFUL VIRTUE MUSIC CO., INC.
JBS'67

In 1963 *You're A Big Boy Now* became the second novel to be published for the young writer David Benidictus. Written in his early twenties, its style and bizarre content caught the attention of filmmaker Francis Ford Coppola. Coppola was working as a writer for Seven Arts and had worked on several scripts before being allowed a chance in the director's chair. In 1965 he bought the screen rights to Benidictus' novel with a six-month option, which he renewed twice before filming began. The screenplay is about as far away from the novel as possible, with the setting crossing the Atlantic from England and some characters going and new ones entering, with only the basic outline of the novel remaining.

The film tells the then fairly unfamiliar story of a young man's sexual awakenings. Bernard Chanticleer is given a free reign in New York City, away from his overbearing mother, (played by the excellent Geraldine Page, who was nominated for an Oscar in this role). Here he becomes infatuated with a go-go dancer-come-actress, ignoring the unsubtle advances of Amy, (an early part for Karen Black). After learning a painful lesson from the vain actress Barbara Darling, Bernard falls into the arms of Amy and the two run off into the sunset, well, a bagel factory, actually.

You're A Big Boy Now was submitted as Coppola's master thesis and does have the look of a student film, rather like Brian De Palma's *Greetings*, with cheaply shot scenes in Central Park and the Public Library. The difference here though, is the superb acting by the entire ensemble, with what is essentially a poor script. The movie flopped, yet Benidictus purports the blame, outrageously, at the door of The Lovin' Spoonful, "I got five thousand dollars for the rights and was supposed to pick up one and a half percent of the producer's profits. But it flopped terribly in the States and managed to lose twice what it cost to make. It occurs to me that *The Graduate* came out just at the same time. We had music by The Lovin' Spoonful. If we'd had Simon and Garfunkel it might have been a smash." This bitter statement is completely unfair.

The Graduate has a similar theme to *You're A Big Boy Now*, but passes itself off so much clearer than the confused and unbelievable story from Benidictus. Admittedly, the music for *The Graduate* is superb and goes with the times but the Spoonful's music is for 1967, whereas the novel is still stuck in the early sixties, a fact that Coppola tries to hide. *The Graduate* soundtrack may have had "Mrs. Robinson" (the only new song specifically written for the film), "April Come She Will" and "The Big Bright Green Pleasure Machine" but *You're A Big Boy Now* has "Darling Be Home Soon", the title track and "Wash Her Away" - more than adequate equals. Also, the Spoonful were doing what they were asked to do, instead of just popping songs into gaps in the movie.

Coppola knew of the Spoonful's talents. Although from beginning to end this was to be Sebastian's baby, with the rest of the group tagging on as onlookers. Sebastian recalls working with Coppola to be a pleasure, "Francis had heard some of my writing and decided that the Spoonful was the perfect group to do that project. It was a lot of fun working with him and he was wonderfully communicative. He would show me a mood for the song he was looking for in a given scene. He's a man that works very closely with his creative people, he doesn't delegate that kind of authority and so it was very exciting to work for him."

The group were given a month to come up with the completed soundtrack. Sebastian took three weeks to write the music, which made the recording of it rather hurried. Jack Lewis was again on hand, having bonded with Sebastian during the *What's Up, Tiger Lily* ten day thrash. This was to be completely different, however, as lush orchestral arrangements had been written. Sebastian did not know how to put his ideas across into an orchestral context, so Arthur Schroeck was again hired.

Jack Lewis, about twenty years older than Sebastian, told Hit Parader at the time of the sessions, "Between *What's Up Tiger Lily* and *You're A Big Boy Now* John grew six years, musically. John and Artie both have the same feelings about music so I thought it would be a good idea for the two of them to get together. They're musically matched like two identical pearls." The ever in attendance Don Paulsen was there for a session and remembers the recording process for the soundtrack, "Basically Erik Jacobsen was the one who sat at the control board and more or less monitored the sound levels, the mixes and things like that. Artie Schroeck took some of John's ideas and worked out a score that the orchestra could play. He could translate John's ideas into concrete form and Jack Lewis oversaw that. Jack was a definite asset to the project."

At the time Jack Lewis made it clear what he wanted out of the sessions, "We're trying to do two things at the same time - make a soundtrack and make a record. We want music that will fit the movie and will also be acceptable to Spoonful fans who'll buy the soundtrack album. Our primary concern is the relationship to the picture, since that's what we were hired to do." With Sebastian at the helm, the rest of the group spent most of the time away from the action. Photographs from the sessions show Sebastian hard at work, while Yanovsky played with Kahuna (or whatever he called it) and Boone read the paper. Despite this fact, Steve Boone still recalls that, "The second soundtrack was out of our hands. John wrote the songs but he had very little to do with it, I don't care what he says, the arrangers came in. It was really a turn off, all we did was we went in there and they stuck charts in front of us. It was like we might as well have need not have gone in, they could have hired studio players to do it. We just came into the session and played parts with charts, I was surprised, there was "Steve" on top of the sheet."

The producers of the film became upset with the proceedings due to the studio costs. The sessions would begin at around nine o'clock in the evening and go on till six o'clock in the morning, or whenever the engineer would start to doze. In the sixties, a soundtrack orchestra got paid three times more than the average session player. For one session, Lewis could not get the players he wanted until midnight, when the cost doubled. On some songs, a forty-piece orchestra was employed, only for their work to be wiped off the tape to be replaced by a different orchestra.

Tempers rose during these recordings, which eventually led to Jacobsen's departure from the Spoonful's set up. At the end of what had been an arduous session, Sebastian attempted a first lead vocal take on the single that preceded the album, "Darling Be Home Soon". The song was another homage to Lorey as Paulsen remembers, "He wrote "Darling Be Home Soon" waiting for Lorey to come home from her job working with me. So that was my unsung part in that song!" All the Spoonful women would attend recording sessions from time to time and on this occasion both Jackie Burroughs and Lorey were there. As he began the song, Sebastian looked lovingly into his wife's eyes and by the time he was half way through the take he began to cry and emotionally let himself go.

Satisfied that he had recorded the killer take, Sebastian left the studio hand-in-hand with Lorey. The next day the vocal take had disappeared off the tape and Sebastian blew his top, "It was a good take and yes, I was mad about that. You get in a studio and emotions run hot because you are giving yourself, you know, you're explosive." At the time Butler tried to reassure Sebastian, "I tried to explain to John that it's not you that cries, it's the audience.

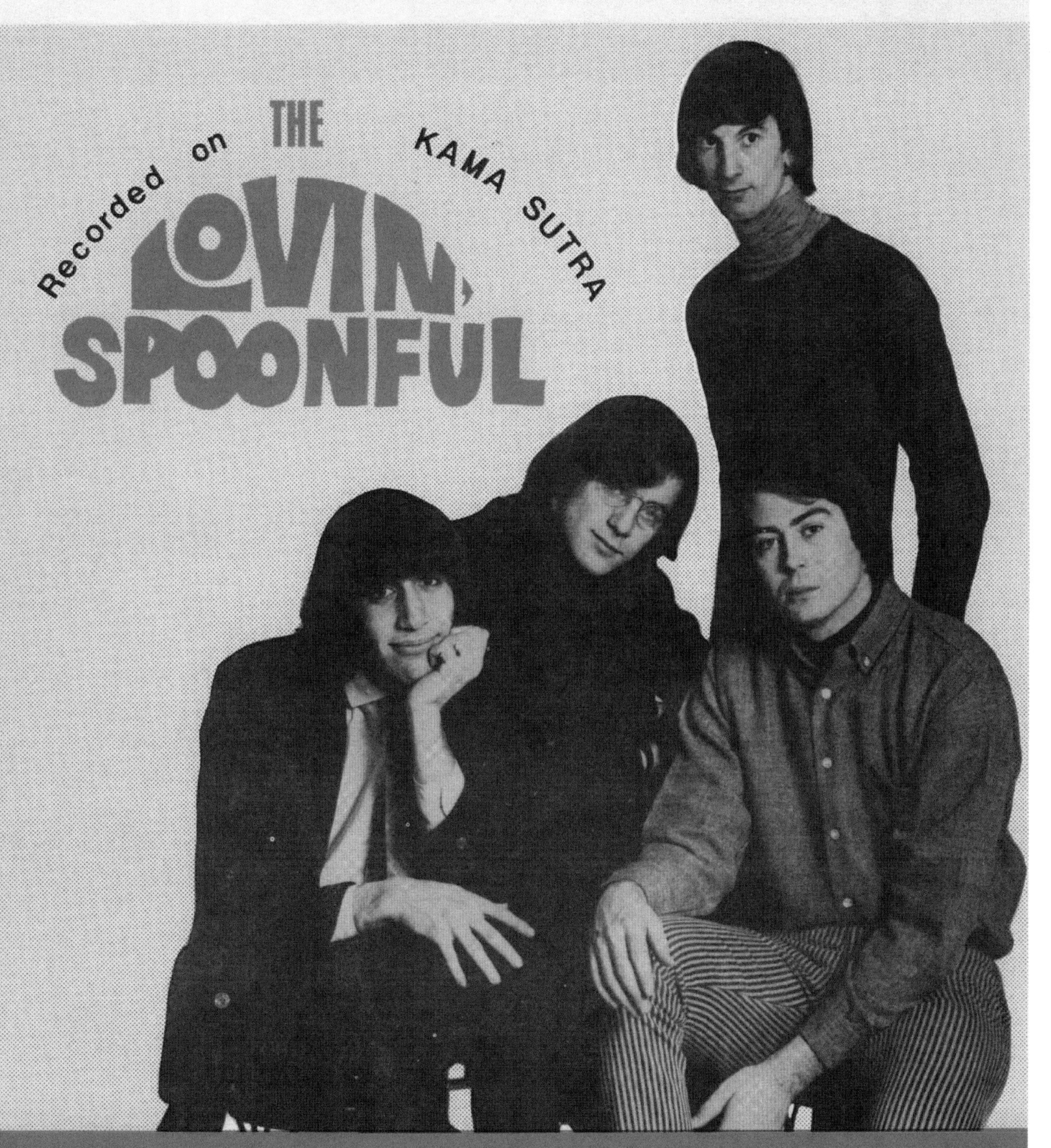
DARLING BE HOME SOON
WORDS & MUSIC BY JOHN B. SEBASTIAN
Recorded on THE KAMA SUTRA
LOVIN' SPOONFUL
Robbins Music Corporation, Ltd. London.
Selling Agents: Francis, Day & Hunter, Ltd. 138-140, Charing Cross Rd. London, W.C.2.
3/.

Holding back your tears allows the audience to cry for you, any good actor knows this. It would have been completely ridiculous to put it out and Jake was right and John was wrong. Yet John wanted that to be the take and he was incensed that Erik had recorded over it."

Erik Jacobsen puts forward the reason why he recorded over the vocal; "I wiped the vocal because it was three track recording. Bear in mind you couldn't proceed with a bad vocal and we wiped the vocal cause it sucked. It was flat the whole way. Well, he remembered how he felt, being totally stoned and looking at Lorey in the other room and her saying, "That was wonderful darling," and them going away. Then I had to come and clean up the tracks and I listened with the engineer, Brooks Arthur, and I said to him, "Listen, this is flat the whole way, isn't it?" He said, "Yes, it is." Johnny had a tendency to sing flat, I was the producer, I was making those decisions and you've got to trust that your artist has faith in your decisions.

"I mean it was one of a lot of tunes we were working on. He came in and said, "Oh God, that was fabulous," and I said, "No, it wasn't." That was one of those things where you wished you had more tracks because I could have just played that for him. Once something's gone it's, "Oh that was great, you know." Some of the group allege that Jacobsen deliberately wiped the vocal just to aggravate Sebastian, which Sebastian responds to by saying, "That's further than I'd go. I think it was an accident."

For Paulsen's article, Jack Lewis was the spin-doctor for the incident; "John was unhappy but he didn't dwell on it. Two days later he told me he'd been thinking about it and he'd come to the conclusion that it was such a fantastic performance it was destined never to be heard." The existing vocal take is good enough as Jacobsen says, "I don't think it held the record back, it did pretty well, I thought." This is the case. Nobody has ever said that Sebastian's vocal performance is poor on this song and anyway as Butler says, "You can't replicate it as if this is a once in a lifetime performance. How are you going to do it night after night?"

The puzzling thing is that Sebastian claims he always hated this type of song, "I had always heard so many songs about, "Gee honey, I'm going out on the road and it's gonna be so sad and aren't you sorry for me?" Now, the Spoonful had played in one place for a whole year, so the road was heaven for us. I was cynical about these guys who were writing road songs and I swore I'd never write one. Then I was out on the road for a while and I started to write one. I sort of pulled back and changed it so that it was written in the voice of the person who has to stay home. That's when I knew I had a song."

"Darling Be Home Soon" is a moving work and this was the mood Sebastian and the producers of *The Ed Sullivan Show* were trying to achieve, when the Spoonful performed the song on live television. What they all hadn't bargained for was Yanovsky who was hell bent on spoiling the moment everybody had worked so hard to set up. With spotlights hitting the string and horn sections of the orchestra as their portions of the song come up, Yanovsky continuously thrusts a rubber toad he had tied to the end of his guitar deliberately between the camera and Sebastian's face. Sebastian would then send out a mean stare in the direction of Yanovsky, who was getting through to a raw nerve effortlessly.

Butler recalls the incident as being the tip of the iceberg as at least Yanovsky's antics were restricted by television, "Well you look at him and it's really funny but John was furious. It was really destructive of the feeling of the song. It would be different if the song was a giant hit and it was being done years later or maybe it wouldn't, it did make a difference. That was only *The Ed Sullivan Show*, can you imagine what he did live when it didn't matter? I mean, he was just so miserable to be around at that point."

Friction between Yanovsky and Sebastian came to the fore during the sessions for *You're A Big Boy Now* also as Don Paulsen recalls, "Zal's sense of freedom was very hard to restrain at times. I remember at the time of the *You're A Big Boy Now* sessions and John was in the studio recording a harmonica solo and Zal was in the control room with Jacobsen. That was the time the movie and TV actor, Darren McGavin, who was a friend of Jack Lewis's, came in to watch the session. So Zally was playing to the crowd and I remember him on the intercom saying, "Okay leader, play "Ring Of Fire" with your harmonica, man." Or at one point he stopped the take and said, "If I might interject, are you putting us on?" He just kept egging John on and I felt, a few little comments fine, but Zal didn't know when to stop." Jacobsen concurs, "Zal was very hard to take. They were at each other's throats all the time, mostly Zal at his throat. Zal was a very fast thinking guy; he was the guy with the intellect and the wit. He could rip Johnny up and down anytime he wanted. And he did!"

With all the internal disputes, the music still manages to blend in with the movie exceptionally well and is not too obvious. Boone disregards the whole project, however, by saying, "The only good thing on the album is "Amy's Theme" (that Boone once said Sebastian stole from an Italian folk song) the rest was a bunch of John Sebastian bullshit." Recalling the origins of the instrumental that wasn't "bullshit", Sebastian says, "It was conceived at a urinal as I took a break from recording. However, the next day I forgot it. My father told me not to worry, that if the song was good enough, I would remember it. Sure enough, two weeks later, when it was time to record that segment, I did."

Only four vocals appear in the movie and the score is woven in and out by one Robert Prince. These are clearly written with the film in mind. "Girl, Beautiful Girl" is the theme for Barbara Darling, the callous young lady who toys with Bernard's emotions. In the song Sebastian is Bernard, who in the film leaves a note backstage asking to meet the woman of his passion to, 'come on up and see me sometime'. In a way, Sebastian's use of Mae West's catchphrase is what the character Barbara Darling is based upon. The woman that has "been there" and can humiliate and disregard the men she chooses. The song is an enquiry from a man that can see her "outsides" but really wants to know about her "insides" which in effect brings along the character of Amy who, not as beautiful, has much more of a personality and is a comfort to be with.

The theme song, "You're A Big Boy Now", runs along the lines of Bernard's "awkward stage" of puberty and includes Sebastian's delightfully subtle line; 'You know the girls are taking notice of you, They say your hair is getting curly too.' The song also describes Bernard's new freedom, away from his mother and the restrictions of school; 'You're run by you and not a classroom bell.' Here he is finding out about women. In the movie this means visiting the seedy part of town to view the flickering old *What The Butler Saw* type of film.

"Wash Her Away" is a throwaway romp, designed to fill the noisy discotheque scene. To achieve the hollow dance-hall sound, four microphones were placed one to a corner in the recording studio. The group then played as loudly as they could, with Butler's drums filling out the sound, with only Yanovsky's superb solo and Butler's screaming rising above.

The soundtrack would be the last completed work that the original quartet would work on. Yanovsky's behaviour had become too much for the people in and around the group, something that even Phil Steinberg couldn't fail to notice, "The real crux of what happened was Zal was acting very strange for about a year or so. He was really acting peculiar and he was causing tremendous hassles within the group. This had been coming, the bust only brought it on a little bit, and sort of made it all happen. Then it really became unglued, because at that point they were going to try and keep it all together and then they couldn't keep it together." Yanovsky once admitted that he kicked Butler's drums off the stage after an altercation.

Noticing that the group were on the verge of splitting up, Koppelman and Rubin cleverly renegotiated with MGM and put forward a lucrative new seven album deal for The Lovin' Spoonful. There was a catch, however, as Boone explains, "It was called a key man contract. When we signed the seven album deal, it was like the group can be anybody as long as John Sebastian is in it. Now I wish if I could ever go back and change anything, I would refuse to sign that contract. I should have said, "Oh yeah, well Steve Boone's not going to be in it." I should have done that. That key man contract ruined the band."

Steinberg thought the deal was a good one for all parties, "That was just a money gig. That was a way of guaranteeing product for guaranteed income and John Sebastian was the key man, so MGM couldn't get hurt. Also we couldn't get hurt, the Spoonful couldn't get hurt and the new deal was able to get through and everybody got what they wanted." Butler's only reason for signing the contract was simple, "For the money! We hadn't got any fucking money. Till that we hadn't got a penny. We wanted something; we wanted to get some money in the kitty. It was always being computed, being figured out, so we wanted a deal to make sure."

The fact that Sebastian was the key man in this contract did not bother the other members at the time. Butler could see the sly manoeuvre of Cavallo, who was wise to the inevitable split, in getting this contract how he wanted it, "The people in the label wanted Sebastian. They wanted his writing so they could get the publishing, they wanted the control. He was pulling out so where he'd approached people he was speaking for himself and it was really not doing us any good."

It was put to Boone that this should have been the case, as Sebastian was the central figure of The Lovin' Spoonful to which Boone had this to say, "There's no denying that, but the fact that he can come to us then and say, "Look, either do what I want or I'm outta here." What are you going to do? Your contract is then invalid and everybody's gone. He signed as a free, you know it's like an athlete who is the star of the team, "Well you know, you don't do what I want, I'm quitting, I won't throw the baseball anymore."

Boone struggles for words to describe Sebastian's subsequent self-indulgent behaviour after the contract had been signed, "So John, really in his own mind doesn't realise, because John is not, like, he's not a deep thinker. I'm sorry, he's not. He thinks about his immediate needs, his selfish needs and he's a...you know, I'll never take away from John's talent, his songs live on as classics of the twentieth century but he doesn't really think about the problems deeply and then he didn't think about this."

Sebastian's first decision, with this new power behind him, was to suggest the sacking of Jacobsen and even worse Yanovsky. Today, Sebastian regrets these awful decisions and on a good day he might admit to this, but the evidence points to his bloody-mindedness at the time, although he was supported by Butler on both decisions and by Boone on only one.

Sebastian reckons that the change in Yanovsky came after the bust, "The uproar affected our interaction, our spontaneity. We were simply different people after this happened. I didn't know what was going to happen to us. Zal became very difficult, very cynical about what we were doing, and, eventually, I went to him and said, "Zally, you've been trying to break the group up, it's not going to work, we're kicking you out." He was dumbfounded, but I had to do it. He was ruining what the Spoonful had done, our chemistry was disintegrating. Talking to Zally that way was the hardest thing I ever had to do in my life. I always felt I made the right decision, even Zal agrees that I did. But I wasn't quite prepared to play the heavy, to do the Michael Corleone thing."

As to who did the actual firing face to face, Sebastian once said, "Zally was threatening to leave for quite a while and eventually it became a real bore and I fired him." Boone sets the scene for Yanovsky's sacking, putting forward a completely different scenario. "Well let me tell you what really happened. I'm very clear on this because it pissed me off. John called a meeting at his house; Zally and John lived across the street from each other. Nobody had an agenda; it was just a meeting. I knew what it was about, Joe knew what it was about, John knew what it was about but Zally didn't know what it was all about. We had agreed the night before in a meeting between the three of us. I had not agreed but I had been out voted."

Butler puts forward some of his reasons for siding with Sebastian, even though to Butler, it was Sebastian who was the more unbearable, "Well Zally had made everybody miserable for a year. I mean just everyone; calling them names all the time and in front of friends, it was just so unpleasant. He was very disruptive, childish and even sometimes adult, miserable, really vengeful, foul-mouthed and generally mean. Not always, but just a lot. We couldn't have it musically, he could not be mocking the songs we were doing, and we couldn't have that. I don't give a shit how much I don't like John, I'll look over and smile at him if it completes the story, you know. I mean that's what it's about. I'll find something in him to like to make me smile."

Erik Jacobsen proposes the more likely reason for Yanovsky's dismissal; "Johnny was a sucker. He was naive and I guess he didn't really trust his instincts about where things were coming from. It's that old saying, once a guy gets success he forgets everybody that was there. He could forget about me, and that had an effect, but forgetting about Zal Yanovsky? I worked with him on all the songs, we had a good thing going and he withdrew from all of that and stayed at home with Lorey. I mean, she was a kid, like seventeen years old or something. I don't want to get myself in trouble, but she had a romance with Zal Yanovsky see? That was it, she had had a romance with Zal Yanovsky and Zal Yanovsky, brilliant provocateur that he was, a psychological gorilla with a no holds barred attack mode, he ripped into Johnny pretty good on that one!" In fact, Boone classifies himself as the only Spoonful member not to have had "a romance" with Lorey Sebastian although when asked about this Yanovsky only offered, "Not to my knowledge."

Another reason for Sebastian wanting Yanovsky to leave stemmed from an incident on a flight recalled by Butler, "Zally at one time got us in a plane, I wrote a song about it, and he broke down and cried. He said, "I can't stand you anymore John, you've become someone that I just, I just wanna kill you. I just hate you; I hate being near you. I hate the way you talk, I hate the way you smile, I hate the way you whistle, I hate the way you sing, I hate the way you play, I hate the way you think." You know he couldn't stand it."

Butler sees this event as a turning point and rues his error of not capitalising on the door opened by Yanovsky with this outburst, "That's when we should have rallied round Zally and said, "It's true John, you've got your head up your ass so when you look around all you see is yourself and it's really boring! For Christ's sake, we're your brothers, we've gone through more with you than you have with anybody else in the whole world and since when was it so bad hanging around with us." That's what I felt like saying. "When did you ever have a bad karma hanging out with me?"

On a separate occasion, a calmer Butler puts a little more background to the incident, "Well, there was a moment when Zally gathered us together and for him to do such a formal thing, because his whole thing was anybody who tried to do anything structured or formal Zally would try to go crazy with it, especially when he was very depressed. He wanted to blow everything apart but he had his reasons. John had become so full of himself, he was so fucking impossible, just his attitude, you know, it was a general disrespect in the way he treated all of us."

Looking back Yanovsky puts forward his reasons for his temperament at the time, "So far as the demise goes: I always tell people who really want to know that the whole thing was a mismatch from day one. We had a shitty record deal, personality wise we didn't all get along, we were destined not to. I never really fitted in with the band anyhow because I kind of go my own way. Charlie Koppelman and Don Rubin were thieves, Cavallo at best ignorant and Jacobsen, I think, was not a great record producer. I think all the best cuts never got on the record, quite often, certainly not the best performances. Erik was a real perfectionist and this band was not destined to be perfect.

"A lot of people ascribe it to the bust but the band was together about a year after that. John and I started fighting. Irrespective of what you may hear from Stephen and Joe but John and I were sort of the band. We just got very flat and stale. The band wasn't growing, this is from my perspective, I should have quit but I was making too much money. I wasn't very happy. Butler and I didn't get along very much although I've always liked Stephen. I thought musically it was pretty formula. John wanted to stay at home all the time. He had his new wife and he just wanted to write about his new life. I thought his writing was pretty sappy and on a flight back from Denver I told him so. There was a huge fight and then the boys got together and fired me."

Boone made it clear that he would not be the one to tell Yanovsky that he was no longer wanted, but it did not turn out as planned, "I didn't think the solution was to fire Zally. There was problems with Zally, behaviour problems, attitude problems, but I said to them that I didn't think it was the correct solution, but John and Joe voted that was the solution. So I said, "All right John, you call the meeting and you tell him. I'm not going to be the one to tell him."

"So we go over to John's house the next afternoon. Two o'clock, Zally comes in, real ol' Zal, cuttin' up, "What's goin' on?" You know, playing the guitar, a few jokes. Then we sit down, just the four of us sitting around the room - nobody's saying nothing! I look at John, he's just sitting there, Joe's like fidgeting. This was pissing me off because I didn't want to be the messenger, I voted not to do it and now nobody is speaking up when it becomes time to do it! Finally, I said, "Zally, the reason of the meeting is that you're fired." And it was that simple."

Being friends all this time, it was put to Boone that Yanovsky surely must have known what was going to happen, to which he replied, "Well you know, he did suss but nobody would come out and say it. (After he was told) John goes, "Oh blah, blah, blah" and Joe, "Hubba, dubba, dubba" and Zally's going, "Okay fine, I'm outta here," and that was it, that was the whole meeting. Later we had the settlement." Butler describes Yanovsky's reaction, "I'm sure he was hurt and shocked in some ways, he didn't think it was possible that we'd do it."

Next to go was Jacobsen, mainly because the group thought that they could successfully prise Halee away from his secure Columbia job, although Sebastian had still not forgiven Jacobsen for the "Darling Be Home Soon" incident. Butler claims that this was probably the reason and goes on to give his own, "I heard that that was part of John's reasoning. My reasoning was I saw that we could be produced by a guy called Roy Halee directly. He was as sensitive as Jake, in some ways much better than Jake because he had a wider scope of musicality. Jake was a folkie extreme and that was good in a way and served us well to be in the niche. It might not have been so much of his niche if we had branched out more musically. If I was further along in my musical development as I am now, and Zally too, we would have pulled a lot further towards rock and roll. More than the precious little quartet, which it was in some ways."

Sebastian strangely puts his reason for sacking Jacobsen down to Yanovsky, who had already been fired himself! "He was a very valuable member of the team but Zally used to complain a lot, everybody kvetched, but the fact is we made our best records with him. He and Zally had tremendous friction because Zally always wanted the band to be rougher sounding and Erik, for better or worse, understood that this was a medium that was appealing to young girls and you had to play it a little gentle. So I think as time went on and music became a little rougher edged, that Zally, who was always aware of that kind of thing, was probably the first to say, "Turn me up, louder drums!" you know, "Everything more."

Yanovsky only has respect for Jacobsen's latter day work. On Jacobsen's time with the Spoonful Yanovsky remembers, "I disagreed with a lot of Erik's ideas. I wasn't crazy about a lot of the mixes to be honest with you. I thought they were a bit flatter than the band actually was. The band was much better in live performance, I think." Jacobsen was not too bothered as he had other irons in the fire and quite truthfully, he had tired of Mr. and Mrs. Sebastian, "I was fired. John fired me and he fired Zal, more or less at the same time. Well, from my point of view, he got with this girlfriend who was just...it's like the oldest story in the book, the Spinal Tap/Yoko Ono combo and he didn't know what he was doing. He got manipulated and he was too kind of dumb to understand what was going on. It was going heavily and disgustingly big time by then, I mean it was so disgusting by the time we did "Darling Be Home Soon" that he just lost all apparent balls that he had in his work and it all became very soppy. He just retreated from the kind of camaraderie of the situation and interested himself in just public smooching and displays of affection with this woman."

On being asked whether his second wife, not a favourite topic today, was a type of Yoko Ono influence Sebastian replied, “Well I don’t like to talk people down but yeah (laughs) you know, I can see how people get that impression.” Yanovsky claims that Lorey Sebastian, “had no influence over the band at all.” Jacobsen didn’t even have Cavallo on his side as Cavallo wrongly suspected that Jacobsen was having an affair with Cavallo’s wife. At least this time Sebastian did the job of handing out the cards himself as Jacobsen clearly remembers, “John handled it. He took me to lunch and told me that he wanted to try and move on. It was amicable. He said he’d never try to screw me, he would give me the royalties of everything I’d ever worked on and it had been fun and everything. But it was just time to move on to something else, Zally had just been fired and I found the whole thing with Lorey just insufferable, it lost everything for me. It was fun while it lasted but by that time I was tired of it.”

Without any fanfare, Kama Sutra took the title tune of the Coppola film; *You’re A Big Boy Now* backed with “Amy’s Theme”, as the next Spoonful single. It may have been withdrawn, however, as it never reached the top one hundred. It would also be the last single to feature both Yanovsky and Jacobsen. Replacements were easy to come by. In for Jacobsen came Joe Wissert, who was from Koppelman and Rubin’s talented stable and was fresh from working with The Turtles on their *Happy Together* album.

The Turtles had been signed to Koppelman and Rubin (albeit without the group’s knowledge) and have been described in some quarters as the West Coast’s Lovin’ Spoonful. Also on the *Happy Together* album were some of The Turtles’ other hits, all written by Bonner and Gordon, “She’d Rather Be With Me” and “Me About You”. By coincidence, it turned out to be Jerry Yester, who had arranged the strings and horns on The Turtles version of “Me About You”, who came in for Yanovsky in the Spoonful.

During their time with Phil Spector, “We were just his toy,” Yester recalls, The MFQ changed their image somewhat and recorded a strong single for Dunhill Records, the raga influenced “Night Time Girl” (produced by Jack Nitzsche) which only reached number 102, but should have done much better. This was the straw that broke the camel’s back and the group amicably went their separate ways.

Henry Diltz had already dabbled in photography and his first clients were the Spoonful. Here he offers some Spoonful memories, “Well, I was a musician and photography became my hobby. Erik Jacobsen said to me, “If you want to learn how to do it professionally, come to New York”. So for nine months I lived in Zal’s house, right across from John. I went to the studio, on the road, in fact wherever they went I went. Zal was pretty crazy; he called me his, well it alternated between his “prisoner” and his “son”. One day he brought Mama Cass over with Graham Nash and that’s where we met.”

Cyrus Faryar became a session musician and played on the Stone Poney’s first album as well as the superb Fred Neil album *Sessions*. Chip Douglas joined the Gene Clark group (Clark had recently left The Byrds) briefly before being offered the bass playing role in The Turtles. He was in the group long enough to play on the aforementioned million seller, “Happy Together” in early ‘67, before getting the call to produce The Monkees’ hit album *Headquarters*. Jerry Yester also features on *Headquarters,* as he played bass on “Shades Of Grey” and guitar on “No Time” during a session in mid-March 1967, in Hollywood. “It was interesting going down to the studio to see them progressing as a unit,” Yester recalls about the group he almost joined. “They actually got some group spirit.”

Yester was kept on at Dunhill, who hoped to turn him into a star in his own right. His first single was the bizarre "Tweedlee Dum's Drive In" under the pseudonym Gabriel and The Teenage Choir. This was one of Jacobsen's other "irons in the fire" in 1966 as he produced the record under his sarcastically titled production company Sweet Reliable. Even the publisher was Great Honesty Music.

Fortunately Yester's next two solo singles, both produced by Jacobsen also, were released under his own name. A Jacobsen composition "Sound Of Summer Showers" was backed with "Ashes Have Turned", a song co-written with wife Judy, which Yester wishes, "I'd sung about a fifth lower". These were both fine slices of sixties folk rock/pop as was the follow up, "I Can Live Without You"/"Garden Of Imagining". A Spoonful connection comes with this last single as Yester recalls; "Those songs were mixed in the same session as "Summer In The City". Erik had just finished producing it and brought the tapes with him from New York to L.A., because he had time booked with me to do these things. When we finished recording, we just booked mixing time and mixed all of them. It was the first time I heard "Summer In The City" and it was one of those times when it was obvious that I had just heard a number one record."

Publicity on Yester's singles was limited. The second came with a picture sleeve, but Yester did not have the make-up for selling himself, "I did one promotional tour from L.A. to San Francisco in two days, hitting all those tiny radio stations with the guy from Dunhill. But there never was much push on it and I'm not much of a pusher myself." A third single was recorded ("She Moved Through The Fair") but by that time Dunhill were not interested and chose not to release it.

As Yester had arranged and conducted on his solo singles, this was deemed enough by his brother's group, The Association, that he would be a good choice to produce their second album. This was not down to any nepotism on Jim Yester's part as he states, "Well, actually everybody in the band knew him before they met me, because of The MFQ. The Association had a lot of MFQ input. We were all aware of the group and had watched them work at the Troubadour."

Jerry Yester takes up the story; "After The MFQ broke up I did the singles and a girl named Rita Martinson asked me to produce a demo of hers, which I did, then I got a call from The Association, who were on the road in Chicago, and said, "We want you to produce our second album," and I said, "You guys are crazy! You've got a number one record and a hot album and you want me to produce your second album? What about Curt? (Boettcher, who had produced *And Along Comes. The Association*) They said, "Nah, we don't want Curt, we thought about it and we want you to produce our record."

"So they flew me to Chicago to talk about it and they were just absolutely nuts on the road. (There is a story about an American Football game between the Spoonful and The Association that took place on the runway at an airport - the Spoonful won!) I mean, these guys were like kids, throwing water balloons, they were into squirt guns and they all fired on me when I arrived."

After the success of The Association's first album, which included the hits "Along Comes Mary" and "Cherish", the follow up, *Renaissance*, sounded completely different with poor production qualities and weaker vocal arrangements. This was not all down to Jerry Yester though as drummer Ted Bluechel told *Goldmine*, "We were very tired and had just come off the road. Another reason was we only had a very short time to make that album. Jerry mixed it down incredibly fast." As Jim Yester admits, "Yeah, he was a little green, but so were we."

"So, I produced that album and it was just a God awful production as far as the sound was concerned," remembers Jerry Yester. "I liked it musically, but what I learned on that as a first production was - leave the engineer alone, don't go in there and say, "More highs, more lows, more echo," you know. I ruined it for that, as far as I'm concerned. Henry Lewy was a real good engineer and if I had just let him mix it and leave him alone, I think it would have been a hundred percent better."

Yester continued working with The Association for their follow up single but again his commercial ear did not seem to be working, "Well I recorded just two songs. Ruth Ann Friedman came up and played "Windy" for me and I went, "Naahhh," to my sorrow. Also I heard "Never My Love" and I thought, "Yeah, okay" but I was never crazy about it. ("Windy" was number one in the States for four weeks and "Never My Love" reached number two and was once the second most played song in BMI's history!) Then they flew me to New York and I did a version of "Requiem For The Masses" and wrote the mass parts, which I never got any credit for. I loved the version, I thought it was very soulful. It had Jo Allen, who was Jim's wife at the time, singing on it and it was a real kind of passionate singing, real gooseflesh. I wish I had a copy of that. Anyway, right after that finished, Buckley happened."

Indeed, look at the cover of Tim Buckley's awesome second album *Goodbye And Hello* and there is the credit Recording Director - Jerry Yester. Yester's involvement with Buckley stemmed from their mutual association with Herb Cohen and as Yester explains, "Herb wanted to keep it in the family." Yester recalls his first meeting with the gifted artist; "I loved Buckley from the moment I met him. I'd met him maybe a year before at Herb Cohen's house. He came over and auditioned for Herbie on an evening Judy and I were having dinner there. Jim Fielder was playing stand-up bass; a real square looking kid with his hair combed back wearing a blue suit, real straight and naive. (Larry) Beckett (who wrote the lyrics) was there, too, and Buckley's first wife - they were just kids. Well, he was signed to Elektra and Elektra's big producer was Paul Rothchild and I would imagine the reason I did it was Paul was busy with The Doors and Herbie wanted me to do it. Jac Holzman had to come out to California and he talked to me before he decided to go ahead.

"When they decided on me as the producer, then Beckett and Buckley would come to my house, every day for a week and a half and I'd listen to the tunes and we'd talk about them. They had them written and they had the order figured out, which was great. The first thing we did was because Holzman wanted to try out the combination of Buckley and I with a couple of singles. Buckley and Beckett came up later and said, "Okay, we've written these two songs, we've had to write down to the market!" They had a real superior attitude; just a couple of cocky little farts is what they were! (laughs) But they were kind of neat. They were called "Lady Give Me Your Key" and "Once Upon A Time" where the solo was done on a music box and a pipe organ, which took a while to get right. Holzman heard this and he said, "Forget that stuff, let's just go back and do the album and forget about this rock and roll business!"

They have been accusations over the years that Yester over produced *Goodbye And Hello* but this is not fair. Even Buckley himself thought Yester did a good job, as he told *Zig Zag*, "On my second album Jerry Yester and I got together and he did what a producer is supposed to do - not get in the way of the song, and the artists feel for it." *Goodbye And Hello* is a classic album, albeit a bit adolescent and is still the best seller in the Buckley catalogue. The album was recorded in Los Angeles in June 1967 - the same month Yester got the call that would change his plans considerably for the next twelve months.

Yester remembers what went through his mind before he agreed to be a Spoonful, "Very soon after the Buckley album was over, John called. I guess they were all sitting around, Steve, John and Joe. John called and said, "Do you want to join the Spoonful?" and I thought, "Whoa, is that lucky?" It was good timing for just finishing Buckley in a way, but I said, "God, I'm just getting into production, I'm really liking it, I can stay home and I'm not going out on the road," so I said to John, "I've got to think about this." "I hung up and thought for about five minutes. Judy was there and I said to her, "Well I don't know, what do you think about this?" She said, "Well, it's a good opportunity" So, I called John back five minutes later and said, "Okay!"

The Monterey Pop Festival that commenced on June 16th 1967 has gone down in rock history as the pivotal moment when the culture took a new course. Everybody on the scene was there and the festival was the first major American performance for Jimi Hendrix, Janis Joplin and The Who. This could have also been the launch pad for a change of direction for The Lovin' Spoonful, but it was not to be the case. By now their name was mud and even though the organisers of the festival were all friends of the group, there was no way that the Spoonful would be allowed to participate, even though Butler recalls that they were offered the gig.

Indeed, emerging acts like The Jefferson Airplane and The Grateful Dead or debuting groups (including Cyrus Faryar's Group With No Name) were cheered whereas established groups were frowned upon. Fairly square acts, like The Association, were allowed to perform, although they did not receive too much respect as Jim Yester recalls, "We were the guinea pigs. We got the sound set for everybody and the camera angles and everything. We were never in the movie and you never hear anybody say anything about our performance. There was a big split, too, because we were so mom and apple pie and suits and all that. At the time everybody was getting a little hippie orientated and so we were kind of like the establishment."

As the Spoonful were now considered to be part of the establishment, because of the bust, they stayed away. At the festival, Cass Elliot commented that people had even urged her not to talk to Yanovsky to which she yelled, "He's one of my best friends, that's ridiculous." Comedian Lenny Bruce's comment, "Shove that hot lead up my ass and I'll name everybody," fell on deaf ears. Ralph Gleason would go on to write a compassionate piece on the whole affair siding with the Spoonful's predicament which asked, "Do we REALLY want to be selling postcards of the hanging?" All these efforts were too late in the day to prevent the split.

The first journalist to sniff an exclusive regarding Yanovsky's imminent departure from the group was Richard Robinson, who at the time was writing for *Go* magazine. In a "World Exclusive" Robinson tracked down his prey after hearing from a "source close to the Spoonful" that a change was expected. Finding that the rest of the group were away in Long Island rehearsing with Yester, Robinson visited Yanovsky's house in the Village. Running down the list of mailboxes outside the apartment building, Robinson came across "nobody" and rang the corresponding bell. Yanovsky came to the door and Robinson asked him, "Are you leaving?" Yanovsky sarcastically consulted his watch and replied, "Yes, in about five minutes!"

Yanovsky then went on to deny that he was leaving his partners, only for the official announcement of his departure coming at noon the following day. At exactly 12:01pm on Wednesday June 22, 1967, Yanovsky phoned Robinson and lied through his teeth for the next ten minutes. He stated that it was he who had said that he wanted to leave, not the fact that he had been sacked and also; "We are not parting as enemies and there has been no trouble inside the group. We are good friends and I expect we will remain good friends." Adding another layer Yanovsky added, "They just accepted my decision and that was it."

Yanovsky's plans for the future varied from being a slum landlord to a ditch digger but definitely not joining any groups; "Unless maybe if I get a call from The Beatles." Having put his name on the dotted line, Yanovsky still had to come up with the goods as he admitted, "I'm still under contract to Kama Sutra as an individual artist, but I don't have any plans at the moment to cut any records as an individual. I don't have anything special in mind."

Two days after this interview, Yanovsky played his last concert with the Spoonful at The Forest Hills Tennis Stadium in New York in front of over 14,000 people, with support from Judy Collins. Yester watched from the side of the stage and saw what he had to follow. One critic who attended the show, more to see if the pop groups of the day could match their recorded performances, was distant in his praise; "The group itself is not hard to enjoy, even if you are generally unimpressed by rock music. They are, like many of the current combos, careless and flip in their approach to their music. On stage, they fool around a lot, and cater to their followers with little "in" jokes and what seems sometimes like calculated irreverence. They played most of their hits and sounded good from first to last, even though they had some trouble with dead microphones. The performance, incidentally, was the last for one member of the group, Zalman Yanovsky. He has resigned, he said, because he was "getting bored."

The "dead microphones" at Yanovsky's final concert was a reference to Yanovsky devilishly getting the last word in on the people who had sacked him. According to Phil Steinberg; "They did a farewell concert in Forest Hills and Zal sabotaged the concert. 17,000 people and he blew out all the electrics! There was no way to hear the group. A lot of stuff was going on between that group towards the end."

Four days later, in an interview with *Hit Parader* (not with Paulsen, as he had moved on) Yanovsky got nearer the truth in his comments. On being asked what musical ideas had he that conflicted with the Spoonful he replied, "I wanted to get away from the direction they'd been going for the last seven months. It was a little cushy. I don't mind a little cushyness, but...you know." On being pressed, Yanovsky would only state, "I feel that John has been going in another direction. That's all."

It emerged in this interview that Frank Zappa had approached Yanovsky, in the hope that he would join The Mothers Of Invention. Yanovsky's response outlined the probable reason he was asked in the first place, "I was asked and I said no at the present only because I don't want to get involved in a group. I was very pleased they asked me and quite flattered because I really like Frank Zappa. I think he should write a suburban musical and put

PAID ADVERTISEMENT

DO YOU BELIEVE IN MAGIC?

Steve Boone & Zal Yasinski

of the

LOVIN' SPOONFUL

ARE

The last time they were in San Francisco, they set up Will Loughborough for a pot bust in order to get off their arrest.

DEMONSTRATE YOUR DISLIKE

- COMPLAIN TO YOUR DJ ABOUT SPOONFUL ON RADIO
- BURN YOUR SPOONFUL ALBUMS, PICTURES & MEMENTOES
- DON'T BALL THEM
- READ JIM BRODEY'S ROCK COLUMN

WILL YOU PAY FOR A FINK'S TRIP?

This information presented in the public interest by The Defense Fund and Freedom League of the Brotherhood of Smoke.

it on Broadway with Julie Andrews." Yanovsky also refused to call back Andy Warhol who had wanted him to appear in one of his movies.

Ironically, in *KRLA Beat* the headlined 'Zal Quits Spoonful' story shared the front page with an article that made martyrs of Mick Jagger and Keith Richard who had just been busted for possession of marijuana and pep pills. With him, Yanovsky took a lucrative settlement of $25,000. His plans for the future were simple for a young man with money in his pocket; "Get up, go out, come up to the office and see what's happening, sit around and drink, smoke about five packs a day."

In the July 28th edition of the *Los Angeles Free Press* (who had published the full-page paid advertisement "Steve Boone and Zal Yasinski (sic) of the Lovin' Spoonful are finks") included an article, written by the same Jim Brodey, demanding that an upcoming Spoonful concert at the Hollywood Bowl with Simon & Garfunkel should be picketed. The next week's edition then changed tack with an article titled "Why Waste Vitriol on Lovin' Spoonful? Establishment Provides Better Targets" which sided with the group, saying at one point, "The Spoonful were killed in the systematic programme to rid this wet chrome dream country of all that it does not immediately understand. They are casualties. They were gobbled up by the immoral paradox that turns men into jabbering informants, rewards their treachery, and makes the whole process, we are told, indispensable to the workings of Justice."

What was going on? Well, remember these were the same people that said Paul McCartney was dead long after it was obvious he was not. The following edition helped explain the turnaround as it included five letters of support for the Spoonful's plight, pointing out really how far was this from the McCarthy Witch-hunts? Nobody saw any picket lines, pointed out Yanovsky had already left the group and informed that under the "Fink" graffiti on Haight Street it now read, "Did You Ever Have To Make Up Your Mind?" The editor of the *Los Angeles Free Press* then tried to distance his magazine from this furious response by stating that the advert was, "paid for by the person who wound up in jail as a result of this whole mess." This is doubtful as Loughborough was an intelligent man, who could probably spell Zalman's name correctly as well as *his own*!

One man with the insight was comedian Larry Hankin: "I knew Zal the best and hung with him, stayed at his house with his wife for a month or two while he was vilified in *Rolling Stone* mag (sic). People would spit on him when we walked in the Village at one point. I lost some close friends for two years because I stayed with him and still considered him a friend. My reasoning was: everybody needs at least one friend. So I was the designated friend for Zally in the United States (self-deemed). I told him when this blows over or he gets another friend, then I'll think about dumping him, but that point never came. He was young and I was and still am unable to carry a grudge.

"Steve was a passive kind of guy. Deep and smart but quiet and tended to be in the background. Not Zal. He was outspoken and had a laser wit and reaction. I liked him because he was accurate and acerbic. But he was hard to take in long doses. I loved being around him because I could rest and not be The Funny Guy. Plus we loved each other's humour. We'd constantly laugh. Zal's humour was a bit more devastating than mine. Fine with me. He'd get the attention.

"Later he'd rue that trait because he got the full brunt of the public's outrage as well as *Rolling Stone's* and The Committee's outrage also. He stood out, Boone didn't. But the Sandy Love incident was always under the surface, feeding the rage against him and the Spoonful in general in North Beach. No one spoke about it, but in the privacy of rehearsals, I got Hell for even bring his name into conversation anywhere inside The Committee. I too, used the Lenny Analogy, but it fell on deaf satirists ears. Satirists are very unforgiving. Zal and I considered ourselves brothers from an ancient time in another life, brothers from some ancient tribe. Some former connection."

It was at a concert at the Rhode Island Auditorium, supporting Simon & Garfunkel on Aug 4th that *Avatar*, a Boston underground newspaper, tried to interview Boone backstage. Boone was stressed as the other Spoonfuls had not arrived at the Auditorium and Simon & Garfunkel had finished their set ("Never again!" yelled Simon in the earshot of the reporter as the duo left the stage). All the reporter got was a quick quote from Boone talking about Yanovsky's plan, "He's going to record. I told him to take a year off. That's what I'd like to do." To the question: "Is there anything you want to say to the underground press?" Boone, knowing what that meant quipped: "If the sun doesn't come out soon, I'm not going to be able to go sailing."

After an announcement over the sound system that the concert had been cancelled (Sebastian, Butler and Yester had been stopped for speeding by the local police, of course) they arrived just in time to scramble onstage and perform before everybody left. After the concert Boone sat down with the reporter to discuss the bust and its connotations; "It's a big drag. The real drag about it is John, Joe and Jerry are involved. The whole thing has nothing to do with them. I can only go so far or I'll put the guys back in trouble again. This has made me almost crazy. That's my punishment. If you want to print this without calling the office, fine. It's a drag. People have accused me of doing it for the money. Anybody put in the same position would have done it. If no one likes me, that's okay. I don't want you to come out in favour of me. I just want the facts to come out. My mother – she's really straight – said she thought I was wrong but it was the only thing I can do. This front group called the Communication Company keeps taking out adds against the Spoonful. Don't they have anything better to do with their money?"

The new Lovin' Spoonful had retreated to the Sebastian's house on Long Island to rehearse their new member and to write some new songs. Boone remembers more than one occasion where Lorey Sebastian interrupted the group to tell them to keep the noise down! It was during Yester's introduction to the group that Bill Love visited along with his girlfriend and the manager of The Quicksilver Messenger Company, Ron Polte. Polte, described once as a, "evangelist of the new community" in San Francisco was contacted by Dylan's manager, Albert Grossman, to attempt to sort out the problem in a satisfactory manner.

Boone vaguely recalls the events of the secret meeting; "A year after the bust, we flew him to the East Coast when Jerry was first rehearsing with us at John's house out on Long Island. We had this meeting, we paid him a lot of money in cash, a payoff, hired his lawyer and if I'm correct and I'm pretty sure I am, he never served a day except for when he was arrested. He was in jail for a couple of days." Returning to the west coast, Polte and Love thought that they had convinced Boone and Yanovsky to appear at the trial. In the end they both only sent in affidavits, fearing a court subpoena if they stepped foot into San Francisco.

At the time Loughborough spoke of this meeting to *Mojo Navigator*, "I spent some time with Steve in New York a short time ago and he says he's going crazy. I told him that I don't blame him but I don't know whether it did any good. He looks like he's lost thirty pounds. Even now he denies that it was a group action but one of the reasons for it was to save the group. It sounds to me as if he thought the set-up would not result in what happened. They didn't know any better. They didn't really mean any harm – they're just puppies. They had no idea it would lead to all of this - I think they have learned a lesson."

The article continued by stating that the jury convicted Love on two counts, which can bring a sentence of five years to life. Love's sentencing would be on Sep 8th. It also reported that, " Boone said he'd sign an affidavit to the effect that he did co-operate with the DA and this could get Love a new trial. Whether or not Boone will produce the necessary affidavit should be known in the next few days." The article ended; "We present the facts of the case without comment except to caution our readers to be wary, personally, in the company of these musicians. The fate of the Lovin' Spoonful itself depends on how much the public really cares about such things at this point." – Mojo Navigator.

The affidavits the two Spoonful's plus Cavallo produced supposedly stated that the undercover police officer Hampton, had not seen the original grass transaction between the Spoonful's and Loughborough on May 25th and that the alleged transaction between Hampton and Loughborough, on May 27th never took place. Maybe the Spoonful's lawyers had realised they had a naive rookie cop on their hands. Some testimony from the original trial, reprinted in the *Berkley Barb* attests to this theory: "Attorney James White, council for the victimised Bill, asked Officer Hampton during last December's preliminary hearing; "At the time you first met Steve Boone and Zalman Yanovsky, at the time Inspectors Martinovich and Magnani were present, was a cover story advised so that it would appear that you were not a total stranger to Mr. Boone and Mr. Yanovsky?" Hampton, "That is correct." White: "Would you tell me what the cover story was to be, or what was the cover story?" Hampton: "Well, the first instruction was to make sure he didn't tell him I was a Police Officer. "

Later in the cross-examination, Hampton explained, "We didn't go in there with any real story, if need to, they were to say I was interested in the music field and not to give a whole background on me. " The article continued: " The Trial date for the People of the State of California vs. Bill Loughborough is scheduled to be set February 27th, in Superior Court. Bill was arrested last September. Not in the pad of the alleged sale, but at his job. Hampton testified that the cops didn't know Bill's last name. The warrant was issued for "John Doe Bill". The young, undercover cop also swore that he never saw Bill at the Washington St. address where the sale allegedly took place, subsequent to that early morning in May. Did the cops have a problem in identification? Was the case against Bill not sufficiently strong?"

When the case eventually came up before Judge Karesh, Loughborough, mysteriously, did not suffer any further jail time. How this came into being is totally "off the record" but the powerful machinery behind the Spoonful insured the deal. Boone thinks Love did quite well, considering. "The trial, if it ever ended in a conviction, was a non-jail time conviction. He never spent a day in jail after that and he made like $25,000 in the way of a cash payoff." (The only record of this payoff quotes $2,500.)

The addition of Yester was a clean break for the Spoonful. With their troubles seemingly behind them, Butler was pleased to announce a new era for The Lovin' Spoonful to *The Beat* magazine, "Right now we're going through a period of growth. We had gone as far as we could go with the four people we had been working with and now there's a new four people in effect. It looks like we're over the worst part of it; getting the basic show together took a few days, but it's just a matter of grooving with it. Zal is a very distinct kind of personality and it's really, well, he has the ability to turn people on and to make up little games. That's a lot of fun, but it can also be very hectic. Jerry is more easy going and we thought that within a group situation he'd really work out fine, and it's really great. A twenty one gun salute for Jerry Yester."

TRI X PAN FILM
→0A
→1A
→2
→2A
→3
KODAK SAFETY FILM
→4A
→5
→5A
→6
→6A
→7
→7A
→8
KODAK SAFETY FILM
→9A
→10
→10A
→11
→11A
→12
→12A
→13
KODAK SAFETY FILM
→19A
→20
→20A
→14A
→15
→15A
→16
→16A

SHE IS STILL A MYSTERY

Words and Music by JOHN B. SEBASTIAN

THE LOVIN' SPOONFUL

on KAMA SUTRA KA-239

75¢

FAITHFUL VIRTUE
MUSIC CO., INC.
a product of Koppelman-Rubin Associates, Inc.

Distributed by ROBBINS FEIST MILLER The Big 3

CHAPTER 5 – "THE SPOONFUL WERE A COMET"

Within three months, the first Lovin' Spoonful single with their new member and producer was ready for release. The picture sleeve that adorned "She Is Still A Mystery" showed the new Spoonful all well turned out in their suits and ties. But, if you look closely, in the background there is a bare-chested Yanovsky, sulking like a little child whose friends won't let him play with them. Boone laughed on seeing the sleeve years later and said, "I love that picture, I mean it's just so Spoonful too. That's really where we were." Sebastian agrees, but hints that they did not really have any choice in the matter;

"Henry Diltz was the photographer and he was living at Zal's house. Diltz and Jerry had been in a group together; it was all still interwoven. Whether or not we had said, "Okay, Zally's out of the group" er, you know, Zally was still around." On seeing the picture Butler blasted, "He even hung around after the fact, came back and got into projects with Jerry almost as a way to be destructive; "God damn, if I'm out of this I'll be in your hair. You don't choose to get rid of me; I'll choose when to be rid of you!"

As good as "She Is Still A Mystery" is, with its vocal interplay and unforgettable chorus; it comes out sounding like a Turtles record. It seems, even at this early stage sans Yanovsky, that the group started to take itself a little too seriously and the finished product sounds overly commercial. Sebastian remembers "She Is Still A Mystery" and the stimulus for writing the song; "One of Jerry's strengths was being able to read and write music. As a result "She Is Still A Mystery" leans heavily on his orchestral contributions. The subject matter was a cross between my first (second) wife and much warmer recollections of earlier romances. In fact, I was thinking about the twins I'd gone to camp with, who were the subject of "Did You Ever Have To Make Up Your Mind"."

After a brief period out of the spotlight Yanovsky started to be more visible and when he made his first solo public appearance, as a master of ceremonies at a street festival in Hamilton, Ontario, he declared his intentions for a solo career saying, "We've got the right material and I think the first 45 will be a gas!" As the Spoonful's new song slowly crept up the charts during October (it peaked at number 27, their first top twenty miss), Yanovsky was one step behind. Going against what he had said in the interviews he gave after his dismissal, he released his first ever single on the subsidiary to Kama Sutra, Buddah. Buddah had been formed in September by Neil Bogart, who had formerly worked with Cameo-Parkway. Bogart's intention was to make hit singles, whatever the cost.

Jack Nitzsche had arranged on almost all of the Phil Spector Philles records and had worked with Jerry Yester when The MFQ had recorded with Spector. In late 1967, Nitzsche found himself in the Koppelman and Rubin stable of writers and producers although he, "did not relish the experience." Nitzsche had recently produced Garry Bonner's "The Heart Of Juliet Jones (which had a version of "Me About You" on the flip side) and arranged The Turtles' "She'd Rather Be With Me" before producing and arranging the first single for the ex-Spoonful. Yanovsky's solo career could have turned out quite differently if he'd taken what was on offer; "I think I turned down "Quinn The Eskimo" (a.k.a. "Mighty Quinn", a UK No. 1 and US top ten song for Manfred Mann). That's like letting Babe Ruth go, isn't it?"

AS LONG AS YOU'RE HERE

Words and Music by GARRY BONNER and ALAN GORDON

Recorded by **ZALMAN YANOVSKY** on BUDDAH

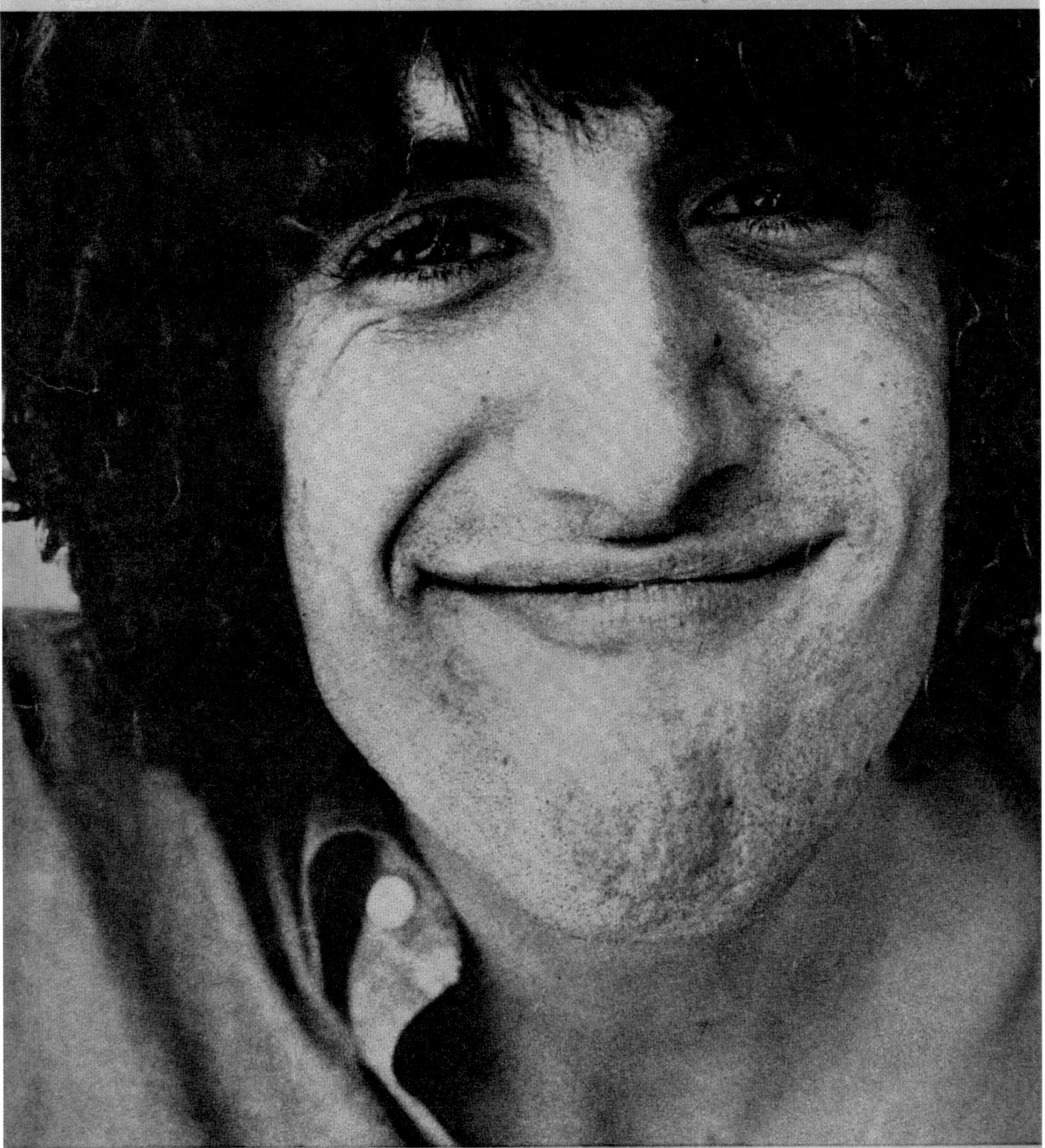

CHARDON MUSIC, INC.
a product of Koppelman-Rubin Associates, Inc.

PRICE 85¢ IN U.S.A.

stributed by

"As Long As You're Here" is another Bonner and Gordon song, although in reality it became the foundation for Yanovsky to go crazy. Joel Vance from Buddah summed up the record, when he wrote a few years later, "Certainly it is 2:09 of compressed lunacy, with the tweety-bird background singers sweetly tweeting, 'Is it a hiiiiit? Is it a miiiiiss?' Well, it was both. Our accountants can tell you with a nostalgic tear that "As Long As You're Here" was Buddah's first chart single." Yanovsky, who remembers "As Long As You're Here" as, "that stupid single - a piece of shit", had strong support from some heavy session musicians including Ry Cooder, Jesse Hill and Mac Rebennack. The flip side was the A side backwards. The label, that stated this person was Zalman Yanovsky and put Zally in brackets in case you forgot who he was from a few months back, was even printed backwards.

To promote the record, Yanovsky made a promotional film with Larry Hankin, who had played the Jew's harp at the opening of the single. Hankin had already made some experimental films, including the improvisational *By The Bay*. This rarely seen promo, (an copy of which appeared on the internet briefly) shot on location in Yanovsky's West 11th Street backyard and at the Fulton Fish Market was only part of Yanovsky's new venture as he had set up his own film production company with his settlement money.

Larry Hankin recalls the making of the promo, "For the shooting of the "As Long As You're Here" video we rented two cars. We carried all our equipment in a Ford Fairlane station wagon – two Arrowflex 16mm cameras, lights, tripod etc. A station wagon has windows all around. We arrived at 7:30a.m. and parked in the middle of an open pier out on the water. Maybe three or four longshoremen were around with a drunk sitting on the pier near where we parked – a pretty empty spot on a sunny morning. We took one camera, locked the car up and went inside the fish market to film Zal holding a huge 80lb. dead tuna like it was a guitar (w/guitar strap and pick) and Zal played it to the guitar riff on the soundtrack we played right there. All the fishmongers and customers laughed. It was really funny, Zal got into it. It was as funny as it sounds.

"When we got back to the dock, all the windows were knocked out of the station wagon and all the camera equipment was gone. About $40,000 worth. There was nobody around that saw anything. Longshoremen just shrugged and walked away. No one said a word. If there was any reaction, it was smirks at "the hippy's" loss. Zal got real determined at that, took out a hundred dollar bill and went over to the drunk still sitting on a piling about fifty feet from the car. Zal said: "I'll give you $100 if you tell me who did it."

"The bum took the $100 and started to say something when a tough longshoreman quickly came over, grabbed the bill from his hand, shoved it back in Zal's hand and said: "You don't wanna do that, mister. For a hundred bucks he'll tell you who did it and tomorrow they'll fish him dead outta the water. You don't want that to happen. Beat it! You've just learnt an expensive lesson." And he stood next to the drunk defiantly. The drunk hung his head. Zal turned, told all of us to get in the cars – which we dutifully did – and we drove silently away. Insurance covered some of the stuff. Zal ponied up the rest out of his pocket. Just another day of shooting America's First Music Video.

"There was another scene in an open field in Central Park. It was just a spoof of the cliché shot – boy and girl lovingly running towards one another in slow motion across a field of grass and flowers. She had on a slight and revealing summer dress and Zal had on the wild satyr's leer on his face. They collide in a slow motion embrace and fall as the camera pans up and you see bras and pants and underwear being thrown towards the sky…the camera pans down again and there's a circle of hippies simply throwing handfuls of clean laundry into the air and Zal and the girl are nowhere around. Cute.

"Years later Zal would complain that we had made the first American music video and nobody recognised it at the time. He wanted to do it just so he didn't have to go to all the TV appearances across the country to promo the single. His idea was to send our music video so he could stay home. Oh, well. Zal was level-headed about fame. And friends. I admired his lack of pretence. Hangers-on couldn't stand Zal's acerbic wit for too long."

Hardly one to keep his attention span going for too long, Yanovsky spent his days (and money) fooling around with a cine camera and his hangers-on. There was an idea behind all the tomfoolery, however, as Yanovsky recalls, "We thought, "This is a good idea," going to various record companies and basically making live action films of people, not necessarily lip synching but doing other things while their record's playing in the background. Needless to say, nothing ever came of it!"

Free from the restrictions of a pop group, Yanovsky showed he had a serious side too. In November alongside Phil Ochs, Yester's now pregnant wife and others, he participated in the New York "War Is Over" march along Fifth Avenue to Washington Square. Yanovsky stuck his neck out as the first "War Is Over" march in L.A. had ended with the police charging the demonstrators and brutally attacking them with clubs. According to Boone, Yanovsky really thought he was going to be a star in his own right, but could not, due to his excesses, "He could have been too, if he hadn't been.... except for booze, I don't think Zally was on anything hard. Not that I know of anyway."

Towards the end of 1967, the new Spoonful's potential magnum opus was finally released, fully a year after their last proper album - quite a long time for the Spoonful. The intense distractions, diverting the group from the music, are seemingly apparent. Looking down the list of composer credits, one can see that this was not to be the usual Sebastian fronted effort. On playing the album, this becomes a lot clearer. With Yanovsky's departure and Yester's arrival, Boone and Butler took their chances and made a case for their more than usual contribution. Even though Sebastian was now in charge of the group, he felt no reason to curtail their enthusiasm. In his heart of hearts, he knew the rest of the group's compositions were not a match for his own.

To the question of whether the group were at each other's throats during the recording of the aptly titled (by Sebastian) *Everything Playing* Sebastian replied, "No, we weren't, we really weren't. What was happening was when Zally left and I no longer had the essential chemistry, I became anxious for these guys that wanted to have the group be this democratic thing. The sixties were a time when a lot of bands wanted to have a democratic process, but couldn't, as they didn't really have the equipment. Creedence Clearwater Revival went through something very similar where John Fogerty was writing most of the tunes and, at a certain point, everybody wanted to write a tune. Fogerty stepped back and said, "Okay, go ahead"...and it was gone."

Sebastian's perceptive choice of using Creedence as an analogy to what happened to the Spoonful rings true when one looks at their corresponding album to the Spoonful's *Everything Playing*: *Mardi Gras*. Memorable songs such as Fogerty's "Someday Never Comes" and "Sweet Hitch-Hiker" overshadow the lesser tracks, written and sung by the rhythm section, to a great extent. The end results of *Everything Playing* were best described by Mark Sebastian who once wrote, "There is a lack of common ground from cut to cut. Sebastian does his thing in fine form on "She Is Still A Mystery" and "Try A Little Bit", with Boone and Butler collaborating ably elsewhere and Yester bringing in new colours, but seldom are they doing it all together."

Boone recalls Sebastian's initial interest in their new member faltering during the recording of the album, "I think he really wanted to see this new incarnation work, with Jerry in it. I think when he first got Jerry there, it was like, "Gee, this is great" because Jerry was involved in the group before I was. But Jerry is twice the musician John is and he is also the consummate arranger, and that scared John. He all of a sudden realised, maybe a couple of months into it, that, "If this becomes successful, maybe I'm not going to be Mr. Key Man anymore, because Jerry is taking control." That *Everything Playing* was a difficult album."

Even after losing his provocateur in Yanovsky, Sebastian still managed to find his replacement's presence intimidating, although for different reasons. Yester noticed this as well. As Sebastian's continuing preoccupation with Lorey that had not been evident when he had worked with the group previously, "John doesn't really like it when someone else gets the spotlight. He didn't mind it with Zally because they were like a two-headed person. But when the women came around, when it became couples, it changed everything. Nobody had ever said, "When you find partners for your life, your relationships are going to change." I mean, who knew that? And John became this devoted husband."

Sebastian remembers that he was more concerned with their new producer and began to notice that he was not the ideal choice almost as soon as they began to record material for the album, "Odd things happened during the course of that record. For one thing we were working with Joe Wissert who was, um, an interesting guy, somewhat enigmatic and kind of hard to know. What it was was a drastic reminder of how much we needed an opinionated producer. It was good when you had something to push against but this fellow was more like, "I don't know, what shall we do?" Although it was what we thought we needed at the time, it made the results a little enigmatic themselves."

The fact that the group had acquired a producer from outside the camp did not help *Everything Playing*. The fact that during the recording of the album Joe Wissert appeared to have suffered a nervous breakdown did not help the album either. Also described by Sebastian as, "kind of vague and hard to stay in touch with," Wissert was destined never to finish the project. Joe Butler; "He was co-operative but he was getting strange. I think he was used to working with people where he was totally in control and we were so used to doing it ourselves that we would just jump ahead. So he felt he wasn't in control. That was one thing. The other thing was he was starting to get strange and wound up being signed to the 'bins' for a while."

With Wissert disappearing halfway through the project, the whole thing got dumped onto Jerry Yester's lap, who was quite eager to impress at this stage. The rhythm section both appreciated Yester's subsequent efforts, if only because nobody else in their entourage was able to create the songs. Steve Boone: "The fact that it came out at all is thanks to Jerry. He had enough concentration and enough smarts to get through it. Everybody else literally threw up their hands and said, "We just don't know how to do it." Joe Butler; "It was Jerry that did it under a tremendous amount of duress. Things were constantly falling apart. It was a really haphazard studio as it had not been finished."

However, Jerry Yester certainly does not want to put this album on his C.V. as he explains, "I certainly don't want to take any credit for it. That's a pretty tacky album in its...God...in its production and its mixing. It's because the original producer wasn't there to finish it. He went a little bonkers and stopped showing up and it turns out, they said, that he was in a mental hospital in Philadelphia or somewhere. So we were on our own. It was Joe's (Wissert) idea to work at Mirasound and originally it was delightful for us. Well, delightful for me anyway."

The complications with the new equipment and Yester's inexperience started from day one after Wissert's disappearance as Yester recalls, "The first problem was, I've got to confess it was my problem and it was from when I first started doing solo singles. I started to do work as an instrumental arranger. I'd been doing a lot of vocal arrangements up to then but I'd always wanted to do instrumental arrangements. I started small with a string quartet and worked up maybe to an octet, then on Buckley's thing I had a little chamber group. Now I was in the Spoonful - I could have an orchestra! So I talked them into doing something that was kind of like "Darling Be Home Soon", that kind of approach."

Sebastian was easily persuaded to go along with Yester, as he saw the album as an opportunity to emulate The Beatles, "It was feeling the effect of the orchestral direction that rock had taken. Everybody had a reaction to *Sgt. Pepper* and I think we were partially reacting to that." As Yester himself admits, "I'm good at talking people into things," but this was to be the downfall of the album, alongside Wissert's original idea of using the brand new sixteen-track console at the Mirasound recording studio in New York. The album would be a milestone for the group as Boone states, "That was the first sixteen-track album that was ever released, and we ended up mixing it ourselves, because the engineer didn't know how to do it."

The fact that he had all these extra tracks at his disposal meant, in Yester's mind, that they all needed to be filled, "Yeah, at first, there's a disease. A producer's disease of, "Oh my God, there's an empty track, what are we going to put on it?" This was no problem when Joe was there because we were not really concerned on what track it was on. All we were concerned with was that did it need anything. A few things were recorded when Joe left, a few overdubs and the mixing - I really wish he had been there for the mixing."

The cover for the album is a childish drawing by Sebastian of the Spoonful surrounded by a bunch of bizarre creatures. The inner sleeve included the classic picture of the group all heaped in a very happy pile, circa "Do You Believe In Magic". The picture of the Spoonful on the back cover of *Everything Playing* showed how much they had changed; gone were the laughing faces, the wrap-around furs, the cowboy boots, the jeans, the look of a unit and most noticeably gone was Zalman Yanovsky. A sophisticated group had emerged and as their image changed, then so did their music.

The second track on the album, the fairly awful "Priscilla Millionaira" is a good example to demonstrate the difficulties that surrounded the recording of the album. Sebastian wrote the song and intended to sing it, but his wish was denied as Yester recalls, "I think John was really pissed off that he didn't end up singing "Priscilla Millionaira"." On the finished cut, it was to be Boone's one and only time where he was allowed to record lead vocals. One time too many, perhaps. As the reviewer for *Crawdaddy* commented, "The singing is really nice, out of tune as it may be."

Boone readily admits that, "Obviously I didn't sing it real good" but in hindsight Sebastian should have really done the job. Even Yanovsky, who was to record the track in the future, made the song listenable. Although Boone recalls that Sebastian asked him to sing the song, Yester's recollection is quite different; "It wasn't his idea for Stephen to do that it was Stephen's idea. John acquiesced but I don't think he wanted to. He loved the song and he wanted to do it and he didn't."

Another song, the stunning Butler/Yester offering "Only Pretty, What A Pity", did not wash too well with Sebastian either as Yester remembers, "When we wanted to do "Only Pretty, What A Pity" live, he said, "I gotta tell you man, I hate that song." When we were doing it, he loved it. He played wonderfully on it, did really well, but I think - this is my own opinion - the more that part of him liked it, the more the other part of him hated it. He probably hated the part of him that liked it and so it surprised me when he said that. I thought, "Whoa, for someone who hated it you did a real good job on it."

Asked to comment on the song, Sebastian replied, rather uninterestedly, ""Only Pretty, What A Pity", I don't have much to do with." That was all that was offered, giving credence to Yester's inner thoughts. Yester also had this to say on the friction between Sebastian and Butler, which provides a window into Sebastian's thought process. "He had problems with Joe. I think he envied Joe because he was independent and able to defend himself physically and vocally wherever he was and how much at ease with women he was. I think there were a lot of things that John envied about him, so he resented Joe's musical contributions a lot."

There is also visual evidence of Sebastian's indifference to "Only Pretty, What A Pity", when on October 15th the group performed the song on the *Ed Sullivan Show*. After a rehearsal earlier in the day, Yester and Butler had spent their moments waiting for airtime getting somewhat intoxicated. When it came to the live mimed performance in the evening, both were somewhat glazed. After being introduced by the strait-laced Sullivan as, "the Lovin' Spoonful combo," the group launched into "She Is Still A Mystery" with Sebastian, adorned by his frilled hippy jacket, looking quite pleased and contented, probably relishing the fact that Yanovsky was not present to upstage him and ridicule his songs this time.

The song went down well and the band went into the flip side. Halfway through "Only Pretty, What A Pity" there is a spoken interlude where in the studio Jeremy Steig mimicked Yester's voice on his flute, with the end result sounding rather bizarre. However, for this mimed performance, Yester pretends to speak the interlude into a hairdryer instead of his microphone. It is quite clear that whilst doing this he is struggling not to wet himself with laughter. Then Butler stops drumming and goes around to the front of his kit and casually drops some cowbells onto the stage, in an attempt to replicate the sound that ends the interlude on the record. After Butler did this the camera caught Sebastian's obvious puzzled expression and if, as the line Yester says came true, 'Mommy said when you were younger, the face you made would stay that way,' then Sebastian would be in a lot of trouble.

"Only Pretty, What A Pity" still manages to be a highlight of the Spoonful catalogue, yet it was another track that suffered due to the confusion that reigned inside Mirasound as Yester admits, "We discovered long after that some of the best background voices were just forgotten. They weren't in there because we forgot to put them in there. I love the song and I love Joe Wissert's mix of it on the single. The mix on the album is okay but I think Joe would have done a better job. I just wish he would have done the album."

The song itself showed Butler's maturity of thought. Analysing empty headed, good-looking high society women, Butler wrote; 'Everyone except the baby, answers for the face they wear. It's the map of your contentment, or the mask of your despair. Only pretty, what a pity.' Sebastian's subsequent lackadaisical approach regarding the album is puzzling, as all of his own songs were of the usual high standard. Beside the two previous singles, the most memorable Sebastian song on *Everything Playing* is "Younger Generation", described in the publicity for the album as "What is sure to be the most talked about track of 1968."

Well it was hardly that, but it would receive some recognition. The song inspired one Los Angeles radio station to record interviews with leading clergymen and university professors for a special symposium on the future of the next generation. In 1970 Sebastian remarked on the song's theme; "It reflected some of the thoughts I was having about the possibility of having a child and it just came to me in the light of some remarks that were being made at the time about the generation gap."

This cliché of a song is a little too precious and the fanciful notion of each generation making the same overblown mistakes as the last did not even come true with Sebastian's first-born. With his tongue firmly planted in his cheek, Sebastian told an audience in the '80s, "This tune is about as far off a mark as I have ever been as a songwriter. The reason is that this song was about the problems that can occur in communication and I guess I anticipated quite differently what the next generation was going to be like. See, my son is now attending an academically difficult school where he is maintaining a B plus average. My wife and I go up there and the teachers say, "Your son is so well motivated, he's so eager." And my wife and I looked at each other saying, "Where did we go wrong?"

"Boredom" is pure Sebastian. Describing his mounting tiredness of the road and the loneliness of a motel room, the song includes the classic line; 'I feel about as local as a fish in a tree.' This was a reference to his surroundings whilst composing the song, as he told Fusion magazine, "I find I can write at home or on the road and with all kinds of inspirations, there's not much of a pattern. I wrote "Boredom" sitting in a motel in Ohio listening to some guy who was playing bagpipes out by the swimming pool."

Words and Music by JOHN B. SEBASTIAN

THE LOVIN' SPOONFUL

on KAMA-SUTRA KA-241

FAITHFUL VIRTUE
MUSIC CO., INC.

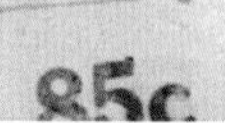

Distributed by

The fact that Sebastian was acquiring power and hangers-on had to become a subject for him to cover in one of his songs. With over emphasis on the banjo, that led to the song being described in one quarter as, "lukewarm C&W", "Money", the third single off the album (and the first not to reach the top forty) hinted at Sebastian's cynical approach to the people surrounding him. Bill who, 'helps me make up my mind' is probably Cavallo, Joe who, 'will pay me back on time,' is probably Joe Stevens, the Spoonful's roadie of the day and Hank who, 'owns a bank' must be Koppelman. The delightful use of a typewriter, played by Sebastian, taking the solo is an admirable reference to the business side of the music business.

"Forever", which continued the sequence of instrumentals, is the only song in the Spoonful catalogue ever to be attributed to Steve Boone singularly. In reality this should not be the case as the man himself readily admits, "I played Jerry this melody that I had. He loved it and he said, "God, that's great, let me arrange it." So I just laid it down on the piano during a recording session and he took it, ran with it and arranged it. Over the years a lot of people have complemented me on that song, so I say, "Well, to tell you the truth..."

With its continuous metronome beat and a near classical theme, quite reminiscent of Brian Wilson's work of the day, the song is the furthest the Spoonful ever went away from "Good Time Music". With no Spoonful member playing on the track, (even the double bass was played by session supremo Richard Davis) the song has no Spoonful identity at all, although it is a pleasant listen. As with Boone's song, Butler's sole lone contribution was a credible piece of work, although Butler admits that Sebastian did help with one word of the lyrics. A realistic touching song, with even a sigh before the song starts (Butler ruins the moment by claiming it was him sighing at yet another take,) "Old Folks" was about an image from Butler's childhood in reference to his grandfather. Although not directly an influence, "Old Folks" is a nod to Simon and Garfunkel's "Voices Of Old People" and "Old Friends/Bookends" with reference to how things change and the sadness of old age.

The closest Sebastian ever got to Atlantic Soul was the impressive and so un-Spoonfuly "Try A Little Bit". Another conversation piece undoubtedly, "Try A Little Bit" is Sebastian's offering to us all, about how we should work at expressing our emotions. 'You might even have to cry a little bit,' could be a reference to an earlier incident. With some brilliant organ work and delightful background vocals by an assembly of female gospel singers the song, excellent though it is, typifies the over the top diversity of the whole album. Fortunately "Try A Little Bit" is the exclusive contribution to the album where all the mixture of styles and instrumental ideas actually blend to a satisfying effect and Aretha Franklin would do her career no harm if she covered it.

"Close Your Eyes" was a Sebastian/Yester composition as the latter remembers, "I showed John the tune and he said, "Oh yeah, I'll write the words for that" and he did. I never really was that crazy about it and that's another song that could have been a whole lot better." This is so true. "Close Your Eyes" is a fantastic song instrumentally, especially when it reveals a depth to the autoharp totally dissimilar to the earlier hits, as well as including some superb guitar parts (probably by Yanovsky). The problem is Yester's awfully strained vocals, "I never sang naturally that high. If only someone had shaken me and said, "Why are you doing that?" It should have been down a fifth. But John wrote it for me to sing - he would throw crumbs."

Indeed this song typifies the album in the way that a truly excellent song can be ruined by inexperience and an overabundance of production work. Most of the group would love to re-record the album today and it is clear to see why. Take out Yester's middle section to "Only Pretty, What A Pity" and you have a classic song. Take out his vocal on "Close Your Eyes", Boone's vocal on "Priscilla Millionaira", (even the whole song) and there is a Spoonful album worthy of anything of the time. But it wasn't to be, what had come naturally before was swallowed by over-ambition here.

A full page advert announced the release of *Everything Playing* stating, "Yes, Virginia, there is a new Lovin' Spoonful album." This was a reference to a famous letter sent by an eight year old girl, Virginia Hanlon to the *New York Sun* in 1897, where she explained her doubts about Santa Claus. The reply that came from the paper ran the headline, 'Yes, Virginia, You Can Believe, For Santa Claus Surely Does Exist.' The Virginia's of the day certainly did not ask for the new Lovin' Spoonful album to be in their Christmas stocking.

Everything Playing was slated by whoever bothered to review it, with one reviewer summing it up adequately by saying, "As a whole it is very disappointing. The spirit doesn't really seem to be there anymore." The attempt at *Sgt. Pepper* came out more like *The White Album*, i.e. good individual moments but no cohesion. The end was in sight.

Meanwhile, Yester and his family had moved into Greenwich Village, on the strength of him now being a salaried member of The Lovin' Spoonful; "I got three hundred bucks a week, which wasn't bad then and they paid all my rent for the house on Long Island. I had to pay rent for the apartment in New York but we lived very well. I mean, it was enough to live on as a member of the Spoonful." Yester never signed any contract, however, "Well, (laughs) I joined the group and Bob Cavallo and I were talking one night out on Long Island and he said, "You know, you've gotta come in and sign some contracts, we gotta get that done. Although I wouldn't blame you if you didn't - I see a lot of tax problems coming up on the horizon." He just kinda like threw that in under the table. So every time he said, "We gotta sign those contracts." I'd say, "Yeah, we gotta do that," and I never did."

Settled into life in Greenwich Village, the Yesters became frequent guests at Chez Yanovsky, "We were always staying up late over at Zally's house watching movies and stuff like that. Then, Zally was being produced by Jack Nitzsche and when Jack was in town we would listen to his tracks. Then Nitzsche saw that it was going to take a long time (to finish a whole album) and he didn't want to spend a lot of time in New York." Whether Yanovsky saw his next move as a way of upsetting the rest of the Spoonful is unlikely, as he and Yester would become very good friends, but Yester replaced Nitzsche in the producer's chair at Bell Sound.

Some of the work had already been done by Nitzsche as Yester recalls, "He did some basic tracks for about four of the tunes, "Last Date" and a few others. Anyway, I was there for most of the basics. Basically it was Zally just working it all out and I'd put a basic drums, bass and guitar - maybe!" The resulting album, *Alive And Well In Argentina*, has Yanovsky trying to break out of his madcap mould, although the album does have its moments of nonsense, alongside some well-chosen covers including "You Talk Too Much", a hit for Joe Jones, Ivory Joe Hunter's song "I Almost Lost My Mind" (popularised by Pat Boone) and Robert Byrd's "Little Bitty Pretty One".

The album opens with, what else, but farmyard noises! This has nothing to do with "Raven In A Cage", a well-produced song with great guitar, full drums and choog-along rhythm. Written by Yanovsky and the Yesters, it is a promising start with Yanovsky's obvious sub-standard singing not marring the song, which ends with, what else, but a fairground organ. Floyd Cramer's instrumental "Last Date" is the highlight of the album. This is where Yanovsky's superb guitar style and Yester's full blown production skills combine to yield perfect music even though Yanovsky forgot the bridge (it was a first take).

The title track was written by Yanovsky and one Rapport-de-Boeuf (a pseudonym for Carl Gottlieb) and a fine dish it is too. It opens with the German national anthem "Deutschlandlied" which is abruptly shut off by some finger picking banjo and rinky-tink piano. The song's references to Adolf Hitler (paper hanger and cleaner) and the ending, which includes recordings from the Nazi rallies, is obviously Yanovsky's attempt to ridicule the Nazi movement. His reasoning is not hard to understand but the message is. At one point in the song you have "Deutschlandlied" coming out of one speaker and the Israeli national anthem "Hatikvah" coming out of the other.

Yanovsky's crack at Sebastian's "Priscilla Millionaira" is far superior to the Spoonful's version. Yester turns the song into a livelier and funkier piece with saxophone, organ and (probably at Yanovsky's insistence) sleigh bells. Yanovsky had a fascination with toads and the Yester's wrote a song about them for him. The name of the production company on this song, Barmpathomph, was inspired by an acid trip Yester took as he embarrassingly explains, "It's a long story. It's a word that came to me in 1965, the day that we moved from New York to L.A. I'd taken some acid the night before and I stayed up all night listening to The Ronettes and The Beach Boys and I was playing piano. I was playing a figure on the piano that sounded like that word, and it became a word for a new kind of music that I'd come onto. That's basically it!"

"Hip Toad" is the album's low point but it is rescued by the epic instrumental "Lt. Schtinckhausen". With seemingly every instrument known to man taking its turn to solo, this experimental instrumental (sounding in some places like the instrumental side of The Beatles' *Yellow Submarine* soundtrack) requires many airings. Unfortunately it loses its way near the end only because of its exhausting insistence with changing instruments and turning the beat around (done by Butler, incidentally, who played on a few other cuts on the album as did Boone, Richard Davis, Bill Keith, Howard Johnson, Gary Illingworth and Danny Cohen). Cohen, who changed his name to Casey Kelly in 1971, remembers Yanovsky was still teasing Butler at the time, "Zal used to ruthlessly poke fun at everybody. One of his favourite jibes was, "Hey Joe, did you bring your stick?" Apparently at one time they would only let Joe play using one stick so he wouldn't be tempted to try any fills or so the story goes according to Zally."

Carl Gottlieb from The Committee wrote the hilarious sleeve notes for the album, describing the people involved and their involvement. For Yester he wrote, "He didn't care what he had to do, as long as he thought it sounded right" and for Koppelman and Rubin there was this sly comment; "They worked together in an unholy alliance - what strange bond existed between them...?" In some ways the album was an attempt to capsize Koppelman & Rubin as Yanovsky readily admits, "It's a piece of fluff but there is some pretty funny stuff on it. I guess Charlie and Don weren't very happy so I feel happy about that (laughs). I think it cost them about 60 grand so I feel good about that - they'll never get that back!" At the time of the album's release Yanovsky penned his own review for the Toronto Daily Star newspaper – a good way round a boycott.

Alive And Well In Argentina could have been a lot worse and over the years it has gained some respect, forcing a re-issue at one point. Sebastian dismisses the entire project by saying, "It was one of those things where you plant the seeds of your own destruction. That album was almost determined to be inaccessible. It's very out, you

know." Yester disagrees, "Zally was totally dedicated to that album. We took a long time doing it, like "Lt. Schtinckhausen" took about twenty straight hours to mix, as we mixed it maybe three times. He was really involved and it wasn't a case of him being bored in the studio, I mean, he was totally alive."

The album was years ahead of its time, before anybody had heard Lord Buckley, The Firesign Theatre, The Bonzo Dog Doo Dah Band or even some of Zappa's material. When it was re-issued in 1971, (with a cover parodying Captain Beefheart's *Strictly Personal*) it was given a glowing review in Sounds; "Despite all the fooling and send-ups it shows Zalman to be a very fine musician when he wants to be. It seems that people today are more receptive and unlikely to dismiss Yanovsky's madcap behaviour as readily as they did in '67." This would be the first review of the album in the UK, as it was never released there first time around. The reissue cover bemused Yanovsky; "They buried it. I think they really hated it. Charlie and Don, at best, couldn't understand it. Then they did a reissue with a new cover - that's how stupid they are. They had a Peter Max cover - I designed how it should be and they did a shitty job for their five grand - but irrespective of that it is a Peter Max cover."

Phil Steinberg reckons the album was only recorded to fulfil the seven-album contract; "We put out a Zal album 'cause Zal needed some money. There were circumstances all around that, which had nothing to do with putting out Zal as an artist. It was just trying to get Zal some bread." The sleeve notes on the re-issue, by Joel Vance, explain what happened, "This record is four years old. When the master tapes were first delivered to Buddah, executives and staff recoiled in horror. But manfully the promo men trudged into AM stations and tried to get it played. This was after all, Zal's first solo effort and Zal had been after all, one of the main men of The Lovin' Spoonful, so maybe.... The consensus of AM station opinion ran something like: "Last month you brought us Captain Beefheart. And now this! Get out!" So we cut the record out of the catalogue. Luckless Zally. He was underground before the term was fashionable."

Yanovsky chose not to tour to support the album, yet on December 9th, the same day Jim Morrison was arrested on-stage in New Haven, Connecticut, the new Spoonful played a more low key gig in New York, at the Fordham University Gym, supported by Richie Havens. The concert was a triumph for the group, as they gave twelve encores to the 4,500 audience packed into the Gym. The reason for the extended show was that John Sebastian Sr. was seeing his son's group for the first time. One review described Yester's befuddlement at the extended set, "After the ninth song, Jerry Yester, the new lead guitarist of the group, ran across the stage slamming his palm on his forehead, looking for whatever instrument to pick up next and telling the audience, "We were kind of caught off guard, 'cause usually this would be the end of the show."

The journalist liked the new quartet and rounded off his review by saying, "With the fluttering eyelashes of their music and the hick put-on of their wit, The Lovin' Spoonful still occupies one of the penthouses of American pop music." 1967 was being left on an up note but with their concert schedule thinning out, the Spoonful began to dissolve as a unit and disperse into separate lives and projects. Sebastian had suggested that the old Strangers drummer Eric Eisner get his girlfriend of the time, Woody Guthrie's daughter Nora, to interpret Eisner's songs. One single came from his suggestion, the amazing "Emily's Illness" on Mercury Records produced and arranged by Jack Lewis and Artie Schroeck. Boone spent much of the winter sailing in the Bahamas and Butler read scripts as he was planning on an acting career.

1968 started out with a stagnant period for the Spoonful, with only sporadic concert opportunities to promote *Everything Playing*. Sebastian became even more distant from the rest of the group and a concert in the Philharmonic Hall at the Lincoln Centre in New York, on February 21st, cemented his despondency with it all. From the ecstatic capacity audience at the Fordham concert only ten weeks previous, barely 1,900 showed up. Unfortunately one of the audience was Zalman Yanovsky. Accompanied for the evening by Eric Clapton (who has gone on record as an admirer of Yanovsky's guitar playing), the presence of these two master guitarists put even more pressure onto the Spoonful, and in particular Yester, to play better than ever. Richard Robinson was in the audience and recalled the experience for some sleeve notes a couple of years later; "Zally sat in the audience, plump in front of me with Eric Clapton next to him. He called up to the stage as Yester frantically placed guitar strings and Butler made unpleasant religious jokes and Sebastian smiled the weary smile of a prophet in his own land."

On being told of Robinson's comments on his remarks at the concert, Butler became angry and yelled, "That shows you what control we don't have, that they actually put something like that on an album cover! It really makes me angry. I'll tell you what it was about; it was a highly topical thing about the Catholic Church and the abortion issue. What I said was, "Listen, if the Pope and the Catholic Church is so intent on women having these babies then let them provide some places for them to be raised and provide education." You know, what the hell were they talking about?"

Butler winces as he recalls this concert, "He was there with Clapton, and it was real embarrassing. None of us were together enough to say, "Zally, come on stage." It was just weird. Also I was so embarrassed. I didn't know what to say and I blew it, I got tongue-tied and the audience didn't understand what I was trying to say. They would shout, "Where's Zally?" and I would say, "He's right over there, you could reach out and whack him!" And suddenly there was an, "Awwww" and they thought I meant to hit him." To the question of was Yanovsky there only to heckle, Butler reluctantly admitted, "Kind of - in his way."

One reviewer of the Philharmonic Hall concert, who had seen the group many times before, noted; "The attendance may have accounted for the somewhat subdued quality of the program. Then, too, the antic first guitarist, Zal Yanovsky, has been replaced by the capable but comparatively quiescent Jerry Yester. It was quality pop music, given a quality performance even though the spirit of the evening rarely cackled with excitement." A few weeks after the concert, Kama Sutra scraped the barrel and released *The Best Of The Lovin' Spoonful Vol.2*, only a year after the first volume. The album only reached the heady heights of No. 156 in America, proving that the top placing of *Everything Playing*, at No. 118, was no glitch - the Spoonful were so out of favour it was beginning to hurt. With the advent of Buddah Records, Bubblegum music had overtaken Good Time Music and would become the biggest artificial and commercial trend for the next two years.

The ingredients for Bubblegum was to sing dreadfully catchy lyrics, have a repetitive bass line and that the people that looked "oh-so-cool" on the cover were not the people playing on the record. The trend really got going when The Monkees were too busy filming their TV show to make it into the recording studio, (or that they just could not play!) Jerry Kasenetz and Jeff Katz started the craze when they founded their company Super K early in '67, which went under Buddah's wing by the end of the year. It was then everything fell into place. Openly and exclusively using session men, the one hit wonders, usually the same people, took Buddah, and Neil Bogart in particular, into the big time. Who can forget: The Ohio Express with "Yummy, Yummy, Yummy" and even "Chewy, Chewy", The 1910 Fruit Company with "Simon Says" and the fact that they even sold you The Brooklyn Bridge.

One significant occasion that illustrated just what had gone wrong was observed by Don Paulsen, who was now working for Richard Gersch Associates, a publicity agency; "After Zal had been kicked out of the Spoonful, I was on the streets of the Village one afternoon taking new publicity photos for The 1910 Fruit Company, of all people. They were a manufactured studio group. I was on the corner of 6th Avenue and West 3rd Street when this taxicab comes along and Zal Yanovsky is waving out of the window shouting, "Hey, Don, how are you doing?" The light changed and this cab kept going and I just kept waving at him. Suddenly a thought came to my mind, it was like I was waving goodbye to the past and Zal was going off somewhere, who knows where, and here was this group I was photographing, who knows how long they were going to last but this was my job now, just to get some good images of this group. The wheel of time turns and the wheel of time hit and ran over Zal, knocked him down in a way. It was a sad moment."

With AOR (Album Orientated Rock) on the rise, the Spoonful seemed to fall in between that and Bubblegum and dropped out of sight. With their audience dwindling away, the lack of interest and camaraderie within the Spoonful is highlighted in an extremely rare soundboard recording of a concert from the 1st of March, which Yester recorded as a memento. On being told what a historical find the tape was, Butler joked, "Historical? It's hysterical!" The, at times quite dreadful, at times quite delightful, rag-bag performance discloses obvious tensions within the group, particularly between Butler and Sebastian. An apparent attempt to edit the tape was abandoned half way, probably on the realisation that the concert was not fit for a commercial release, so all in-between song stage patter can be heard. Sebastian and Boone don't say a word and Yester is only heard moaning about his equipment failures. Butler is the spokesman on-stage (at one point he struggles; "It's nice of you to come down and not watch television" (!) and sometimes his attempts at levity are ignored by the audience, hungry for Yanovsky's crowd pleasing clowning.

Yester is embarrassed by the tape as he, "plays like a lox." Unfortunately he is right, as his guitar playing in particular ruins most of the performance. He is not the only one letting the side down, however, as Boone's subdued bass playing and Butler's at times amateurish drumming do not help either. The rock is Sebastian who plays and sings consistently well throughout the performance, although without any heart. The concert (venue unknown) starts with a pedestrian performance of their old closing number, "Do You Believe In Magic", which is immediately followed by a dreadful "Jug Band Music" where Sebastian gets in a muddle and goes into a verse when it should be the chorus. Audible sniggers from his fellow members occur after this faux pas. One of the highlights of the set, which includes excellent organ playing by Yester, "Try A Little Bit", follows.

The next three songs are all sung by different vocalists than on the records; Sebastian sings, far better than Boone, on "Priscilla Millionaira", Yester ruins "Respoken" and Butler (not Sebastian who sang on the recording) adequately performs "Boredom". "She Is Still A Mystery" is too slow but "Six O'clock" is superb. A couple of hits, "You Didn't Have To Be So Nice" and "Daydream" are confidently handled, as is Boone's singing on his own song, "Butchie's Tune". With Sebastian on harmonica, the song is turned into a C&W number with Boone's nasal drawl blending to a pleasing effect. A superb solo rendition of "Younger Generation" by Sebastian is followed by a few minutes of embarrassing silence as the group come to the front of the stage to perform an acoustic version of "Henry Thomas".

Sounding like an inspired jug band (without the jug, but with evident banjo, slidewhistle and kazoo) the acoustic interlude is the only moment of the concert where the group all seem to be actually enjoying themselves and gel as a unit, something that the audience react to. The silence was worth it as the song is another high point and turns the course of the show which is all uphill from now on, with "Did You Ever Have To Make Up Your Mind" and "Full Measure" being accomplished worthily. Before "Full Measure", Butler entertains by criticising the Grammys for awarding Ed Ames (for the song, "My Cup Runneth Over") over The Beatles and when a hysterical girl relentlessly screams, Butler sings, "I gave my love a cup - to make her shut up!" to appreciative applause from the crowd. Butler came ever so close in telling her to, "Shut the fuck up!" but restrained himself, as some harassed police officers were at the front of the stage.

Problems with instrument failure before "Summer In The City", does not deter from enjoying this garagey alive version of their classic song, which is attacked with twin organs. The set finishes with an explosion from the speakers and the crowd seems to appreciate the performance. The group exit the stage only to quickly return. Sebastian, now tiring with all the screaming, sighs out a, "Gee, kids" which for some strange reason actually shuts them up long enough for the encore. A delightful, dreamy "Darling Be Home Soon" finds the group in their niche but this turns out to be the last song of the evening. The screams and applause fade and this invaluable recording ends.

Butler is quite humbly sorry for the erratic performance, "We were so loose and goofy it was beyond belief, the only thing we didn't lack was courage but the music was, well there's no comparison to the records. I'm sure we were blasé and a lot of other things - being young and silly and not taking our job seriously." Hearing the tape, it becomes quite clear where the future for Sebastian lay and his departure from the group was on the horizon.

In April '68, with the assassination of Martin Luther King on the balcony of a Memphis hotel, The Beatles seemingly falling under the spell of the Maharishi and the musical *Hair* opening on Broadway, nobody bothered to notice that The Lovin' Spoonful were on the verge of splitting up. Jerry Yester recalls the moment when Sebastian announced his future plans, "One day we were rehearsing on a theatre stage on the East Side, where we had been rehearsing for the last month or so. John, I guess, had been talking to Bob Cavallo and said, "Okay, well we had a little meeting up in the balcony..." He then said, "This is it, you guys can go on if you want to but I'm not going to go on any further." So we said, "Okay" and then John left and we sat around and talked and pretty much decided that was it for us too."

Sebastian was happy for The Lovin' Spoonful to carry on without him, as he recalled in a sleeve note once, "It's important that people realise that I didn't have any hard feelings about the group continuing without me. It was completely amicable." Butler has a more grandiose comment to make; "I had told John, "Yeah, you're free after we finish our commitments," which was a pretty gracious thing to do. I know it was stupid to throw it all away but I really did want to be an actor. I was tired of John too."

Bob Cavallo saw his opportunity of managing both a solo Sebastian, as well as the Lovin' Spoonful. He approached Butler with an extravagant offer, "Cavallo said, "Listen I've already had offers for the band without John, just you and Zally would come back. We've had offers - five grand." Butler was missing Yanovsky - until he had a meeting with him, "We even entertained the possibility of having Zally come back on board, although I'll tell you something, we had one meeting with Zally and he was such a f... We just realised afterwards, who wants to be around this? Life is too short, this is horrible. He had all this emotional baggage and I realised we just didn't like each other no more."

The group continued fulfilling their commitments and, out in California, Butler, Boone and Yester went into Sunset Sounds with Chip Douglas to record without their Key Man. "We were working in Disneyland with John," Butler recalls. "We were recording while we were working with him. He knew we were in the studio working on things, we made no bones about it - we were not going to hang up our spurs." Of the two songs recorded in Hollywood, "Never Going Back" came out as the next Lovin' Spoonful single, the first A side without a Sebastian songwriting credit, as it was written by John Stewart, who had left The Kingston Trio the previous year.

An earlier Stewart composition, "Daydream Believer" had been recorded by The Monkees in June '67 (it became their second biggest seller of all time) and produced by Chip Douglas, hence the connection (Douglas had almost beaten Stewart for the vacant role in The Kingston Trio years earlier but was a little too young). The Spoonful's interpretation of "Never Going Back" includes Stewart on guitar, as well as Orville "Red" Rhodes contributing superb pedal steel guitar. Boone swears he played bass but records show Douglas filling the slot.

The single managed to reach number 73 in the US charts before disappearing but deserved a better fate. It is a pleasant enough C&W effort, well produced and sung, with excellent musicianship. It was heard by enough

RENTAL CAR

people to upset Sebastian, as they still call out for it at his solo concerts! The other song recorded without Sebastian is recalled by Butler; “”Baby I Could Be So Good At Loving You”, that the record company was really hot for, never came out, as we really liked “Never Going Back”. We got Fast Eddie (Hoh, from The MFQ) to play on that, it was our big Wall Of Sound song.”

The last Lovin’ Spoonful concert took place on June 20th, 1968 in Richmond, Virginia, where they headlined a bill over The Three Degrees and Tiny Tim. The only thing that anybody remembers about that concert was the ironic incident of all the lights going out. Almost a year to the day he joined the group, Yester’s cheques stopped coming in. Two months later a single emerged bearing the credit “The Lovin’ Spoonful featuring Joe Butler.” Jerry Yester; “It wasn’t a case of me leaving cause Steve wasn’t there either, as far as I know.” Basically, rightly or wrongly, Butler had gone on without his pals and kept the group’s name. Everybody now followed their own separate path, although Yester and Yanovsky, the two who had not been forced together, teamed up for a series of interesting projects.

The first to emerge was Butler with the single, “(Till I) Run With You”, a fine pop song with brass and female backing and yet another from Koppelman and Rubin’s top songwriters Bonner and Gordon, who sang backing vocals on the record. The song would be the only Lovin’ Spoonful single to not ever make the top 100, with the promotion people, Richard Gersch Associates, barely bothering with it.

With Butler assembling a Lovin’ Spoonful album, all the ex-Spoonfuls branched out into other projects and enjoyed having a life, something that had been impossible for the last three years. The one who totally disappeared was Steve Boone; “I met my first wife on the last concert tour we did. At the last show, she went on a date with me and then we moved out to Long Island for the summer. I rented a house out there and basically spent the whole summer partying. I bought a speedboat and we were hanging out, having wild parties all night long. It was a good productive summer though, as we were writing a lot of music. Skip was living close by and there were a lot of musicians I knew coming out there, including The Mamas & The Papas.”

Butler’s summer was spent more productively and by November his album was released. “I wanted to say something.” he said in his first ever interview about the album. “The war was just hideous and it had eaten lives. It was just a dumb war. I had fought within the group, many times, for us to make money (for a cause) or at least make a political stance. I never asked John to write because I knew John was a love song writer. I had started writing but I wasn’t sure and I didn’t want to write a lot of protest stuff that I thought was like Phil Ochs or Bob Dylan, as I didn’t think I could do it any better than them. But finally, when I had a chance and I didn’t have to get a vote on it, I really wanted to make a statement. So I did - maybe too much, maybe I over compensated.”

This was Butler’s passionate statement regarding the album *Revelation: Revolution ‘69*, twenty three years on from the event: Butler was still incensed about an unnecessary, idiotic war that had killed so many of his young countrymen. At the time, noticing that Yanovsky had been able to go on the War Is Over march on his departure from the Spoonful, Butler went over the top in trying to get his message across. November ‘68 was the time of John and Yoko’s *Two Virgins* nude cover and the on stage nudity of *Hair*. So Butler came up with the idea of the arresting cover photo for his album, of a naked girl (with nipples airbrushed out) and Spoonful, running alongside a superimposed lion (that covered their genitalia). This demonstrated to the teenyboppers that this was not the run of the mill Lovin' Spoonful album. The title gave another clue and the track listing, including titles like "The Prophet" and another called "War Games", with a seven minute running time, cemented the fact.

The problems Butler had with the album started before its release, due to continuous management reshuffling at MGM, "The trouble was, I was told one thing and then the president would be fired, and then there would be somebody new there two weeks later. So many of the underlings of the president of MGM were stealing from the artists. The individual offices of the company had separate deals, where they would pirate tape and let certain distributors or certain pressing plants press just for them, under the table. When the MGM board found out about this, they didn't want it known, as they did not want their stock to nose-dive. So they kept these guys on, but they had no power, they were just figureheads.

"That album was not supposed to be called *Revelation: Revolution '69*, it was supposed to be called *Amazing Air* after one of the cuts. It was supposed to be, as I wanted it to be, pressed in absolutely clear vinyl, which was available and could be done. I even wanted the label to be clear but they couldn't do that, so we settled for silver and blue. We wanted it packaged in a plastic sleeve, making it completely clear and call it *Amazing Air*. It went through a lot of titles, *Till I Run With You* was next, so we took the picture running with the lion (initial pressings were titled *Till I Run With You*,) so what happened was we got a mishmash of titles and it became a conglomeration."

Koppelman gave Butler the go ahead to complete an album keeping the Spoonful name. There was a catch, however, "Here's the deal, see, the money for this album came from Koppelman and I could only do songs he published. So I had a limited choice in terms of material. Some of the songs were good, like Bonner and Gordon's." In reality Koppelman was probably just desperate to fulfil the Spoonful contract and release as many Chardon Music (another new publishing venture) songs as possible and get the last drop of product from the Lovin' Spoonful name.

Koppelman openly encouraged the fairly inexperienced Butler to write songs for this solo album (which is what *Revelation: Revolution '69* is) as Butler recalls, "He'd liked "Old Folks", he thought that was good, so he started to see that maybe I was coming into something as a writer. When he'd said he'd liked it, I said, "You like John's songs and you give him colour TV's, give me a colour TV! You tell me you like it, give me a prize - a toaster oven! (laughs)" Out of the ten tracks, there are three apiece from the songwriting teams of Bonner and Gordon and Dino and Sembello and three Butler originals and the semi-hit "Never Going Back", the only song to feature Yester and Boone, tagged on. "Baby I Could Be So Good At Loving You" was left out, and lost forever, as it was published by Third Story Music.

For the project Butler was teamed with producer Bob Finiz (nee Finizio), who would write the music for Butler's songs. Finiz's background had been in Philadelphia, where he sung bass in the white Doo Wop group The Four J's - a million miles away from the material on this album. The orchestral arranger was Richard Rome, who had previously worked with Simon and Garfunkel and with some top session musicians, including Joe Mack on bass (with Butler not playing the drums on all the cuts) all in all *Revelation: Revolution '69* has a smooth folk rock sound, which is only shattered by the sound collage "War Games", the probable sole reason for all the derogatory statements that have surrounded this album continually since its debut.

If Butler had released the album under his own name and without the sound collage, the critics and public alike could have welcomed it as a worthy effort. Instead anyone reviewing or buying the record, due to the fact that it is accredited to be a Lovin' Spoonful album, with featuring Joe Butler in smaller type, must have felt cheated. One British critic summed it up by saying, "My, how the Spoonful have changed. Gone are the days of light pleasant songs, now it's all, "Yeah, man, valid statement, take a trip, do your thing," and I don't like it. The nude lady on the cover is the only worthwhile thing about the LP."

With this dire need to make a political statement, Butler assembled a sound collage with the outline of a soldier's life, from birth to death in the jungles of Vietnam. First we hear the sounds of birth, a quick smack and the heartbeat starts, which acts as a metronome for the whole piece. From the schoolyard, through a marching band, we then hear children, 'pledge our allegiance to the United States of America.' An army recruitment commercial follows and with the words, 'It makes you a man, it teaches you responsibility' ringing in the characters' ears, he is off to war. A couple of gun shots lead to loud machine gun bursts (a tad different to the effects on "Summer In The City") then grenades explode amongst total mayhem. The atom bomb is then detonated and the heartbeat stops. As the piece fades, a slight gust of wind is audible, then side one ends.

It is easily apparent what message is being broadcast here but it is in the wrong place and totally inappropriate to its surroundings. Like any dialogue on a pop record, be it interview material, The Beatles' "Revolution 9" or Art Garfunkel's equally illogical "Voices Of Old People", repeated plays become unbearable. Thank God for the CD and its programming. Today Butler admits his naiveté; "It was a mistake. I was trying to say something but it was not on the right format. The thought was a good one, it was just misplaced. These things come back to haunt you, you can't re-write history and I'm stuck with it. Even down to the point where the beginning sounds like a woman having an orgasm, until you realise it's childbirth, I mean, I wanted to push guilt buttons on people. I was angry about the war and I dedicated a lot of the album to it. "War Games" was just carried too far."

On its own merits, the rest of the album is fine. "Amazing Air" written and featuring Bonner and Gordon is excellent whilst Butler's "The Prophet" is a production extravaganza, but the highest praise goes to "Only Yesterday" which is Butler's best performance to date. "Jug Of Wine", also written by Ralph Dino and John Sembello, had already been a single, sung by Garry Bonner, which Butler's version was based on. Butler upped the tempo a little and added an extra verse without credit. The title song revealed Butler's poetic style of writing. Proud of his statement, the Phil Ochs inspired lyrics were printed on the reverse of the cover, which Butler wrongfully regrets today. Again the sentiments are a touch puerile but at least it is presented in a respectable form with a strong vocal performance; 'And no one dares to ask them what they do there after dark, And the prize they give to men who kill is a statue in the park, Don't let them cut your wings dear ones before you learn to fly, Too soon the game will seem too real and then no one will ask why, I'm scared to start but can't stop my heart, Now I want the Revolution.'

Previously recorded by The Turtles; "Me About You" was radically altered by Butler, who preferred to stay closer to the Bonner demo. Again the infatuation with the war raised its head and Butler added military style drumming to the track, "I did all the voices on "Me About You", which I'm real proud of. I think there were two girl parts but I did like four or five voices on that. See that song The Turtles had already done but they did it so fast. I thought it would be better as a ballad, maybe, but when I look back the military marching was silly." Another Dino and

JOE BUTLER
REVELATION, REVOLUTION '69
KA-264
RECORDS
MGM RECORDS.

Sembello track, "Words", with superb guitar work from none other than Yanovsky, resembling a racing car screaming past by, is another highlight on which to finish the collection.

As a contractual obligation album *Revelation: Revolution '69* turned out to be one of the better works of the sixties (and I will argue the case with anyone). Its flaws are clear but it puts a different perspective on the body of work by the Spoonful and without it, it would be far easier to dismiss the group's contribution. The effort adds a protest dimension so far ignored by the critics.

The news of Sebastian's and in fact the Spoonful's, imminent departure had been kept from the music press. In August, *Go* magazine reported that, "the question of whether John Sebastian will remain with The Lovin' Spoonful is still unresolved." The article did manage an exclusive, however, by saying, "He is definitely writing the music for an upcoming Broadway play, *Jimmy Shine*"

"Working for the play was probably the biggest challenge I've had yet," said Sebastian in 1970. "Because it took away my most familiar territory, the recording studio. The songs had to be worked out for the live performance and not for recordings. Also, writing for Broadway meant that I was trying to deal with a new audience. That's important because a performer should always be trying to broaden his audience. It's too easy to just keep communicating with the same audience all of the time, and communicating with strangers is always a groovy thing if done successfully. For *Jimmy Shine*, though, I had to work with a lot of people I didn't know and didn't always respect."

Jimmy Shine was written by Murray Schisgal, produced by Claire Nichtern and Zev Bufman and starred Dustin Hoffman, coming out in between his early major roles in *The Graduate* and *Midnight Cowboy*. The main character was cut from the same basic cloth as young Benjamin from The Graduate, except that instead of the Beverly Hills mansion, Jimmy lived in a warehouse. The play told of a young man looking for his future and exploring his dreams and fantasies in search of personal growth.

How Sebastian got involved in the play is not known even to him, "They had gotten my name from somewhere and I went up there to talk to them. It was a very funny kind of moment because I was just coming off the Spoonful, and being in a group and coming out of a group is a whole change of mind and attitude and everything. With all those things spinning around my head, I walked into this theatrical office and talked to these people about this play, to immediately discover that they had never heard of the Spoonful. Of course, they don't listen to the radio; they're making plays, right?

"I was suddenly faced with this whole group of people who had no idea what I did, who were kind of reaching out to find who I was and what I did, and it was a very funny moment. In any case, they said, "Well, we'd like to get an example of your work as soon as possible, tomorrow, preferably." Well, it was kind of good for me because it burned me a little bit and it sent me home, where I finished three songs in one evening."

The script helped build Sebastian's internal fire and the fact that it included a character similar to Fred Neil gave him the advantage of insight, "I went home and read the script and it was out of sight. So the combination of being inspired by the script and having that little edge of irritation over the afternoon was great. There's a character in the play who is a modern minstrel type. He's from San Francisco and he has a whole coterie of hangers-on. There's a great opportunity. I saw the character, I said, "Yeah." Because that makes it much more easy, somebody that close."

With Hoffman's hot movie star status, he received a salary of $4,500 a week plus a percentage of the gross and more. This did not leave much money for the music as Sebastian states, "They wanted to have music in it, but they didn't want to spend the money to have music in it. So they were telling me, "This isn't a musical, this is only a show with songs in it." Okay, I got it. Then I'd say, "All right guys, you don't have to give me an orchestra or anything, all I need is a four-piece band." And they'd say, "How about a three-piece band?"

"The people behind the show were very weird in their concepts, almost antique in their portrayal of contemporary things, and getting them to assimilate the music took a long time. I mean, I never expected rock 'n' roll heaven when I first became involved, but it turned out to be a very lonely experience in that hot summer of '68. I never really knew the boundaries I was working within. I never got a full rein."

One of the new songs Sebastian wrote has never been released, "I wrote a tune for the show called "There's A Future In Fish, Mr. Shine", which was my showtune. It was sung by the guy who used to play one of the uncles on the Molly Goldberg radio show." Not all of Sebastian's work was appreciated, one new song "I Had A Dream" was tossed out and another, "She's A Lady" was cut in half because the actor couldn't sing it.

Sebastian did not let the producers' judgements bother him and released "She's A Lady" as his first solo single, shortly after the official statement of his leaving the Spoonful was sent out on October 12th. "I said, "Okay guys, I'm just going to go ahead and make the record my way and make a recording of it." Don Paulsen recalls the origins of the song, "Again it was Lorey. He had bought her a dress in Hawaii, an old fashioned turn of the century kind of dress and I remember it had all these buttons. It was a moment of intimacy between them. John was able to sense and capture a lot of the nuances of a relationship."

Whilst being a favourable song in a live situation, this lush ballad was a little too sickly sweet for the public's taste (it stalled at number 84 in the US, even after legendary New York disc jockey Murray The K played it no less than eight times in a row) and even for Sebastian, who had teamed up again with Paul Rothchild, "Now that track was a little too hasty," Sebastian told Zig Zag four years later. "To this day, Paul Rothchild and I regret the mix on that. Most of the things we've done have stood the test of time to my mind, but that is a particular bane of ours, it's just that little bit too greasy, we could do it better now."

After an apparent hectic three-week rehearsal period and a brief stint in Baltimore, *Jimmy Shine* opened in New York on the 5th of December 1968. Whilst technically not a flop (it survived 161 performances) the play was hardly a hit. One review stated *Jimmy Shine* was, "the baddest bad play possible to conceive." Another said of the play, "It is a mess, and an incredibly hackneyed, shamelessly exploitive, farrago." Sebastian took it all in his stride and began to record tracks with his friends, for his first solo album.

Yester and Yanovsky formed a production company, candidly titled Hairshirt Productions, whose first job was producing for a group that had come from the embers of The Strangers, The Fifth Avenue Band. Yanovsky had always been a big fan of The Strangers as Sebastian recalls, "Zal used to drag me to see The Strangers saying, "Look at this man - third generation R&B. Muddy Waters inspired the Stones and the Stones inspired these cats." It was true too. It was still the Muddy song or the Howlin' Wolf song, but done a la Stones. We thought they were out of sight, and we took them as our little brother band, though they were much better than we were musically. They went back to college though and finished their studies before leaping back into the world of music, drugs and other pleasures."

This theme is continued by Erik Jacobsen who tried to produce The Strangers, "Some of the guys in that band I was with before I was with Cavallo. Peter Gallway, Kenny Altman and also Eric Eisner - they came to me when they were sixteen year old kids and by the time they were eighteen they were just all junked out, the whole band went on junk." The Strangers did release one single, "Land Of Music"/ "I Need Your Love Inside Me" on KR records (yet another Koppelman and Rubin venture,) via Chess in 1966 after Eisner had left the group.

Given another chance, this new band, without Eisner but with Pete Haywood, Jon Lind, Jerry Burnham and Murray Weinstock, began putting down songs with Yester and Yanovsky behind the mixing desk at Sun West Recording Studios in Hollywood. The completed album was rejected by Reprise, who did not like the results, so Jacobsen was given the job of re-recording five of the songs, including the single "Fast Freight"/"One Way Or The Other", at Mirasound in New York.

The eponymous album is a true underground classic; with Gallway's songs in particular being the pick of the good harvest on offer. The easy-going style of the album did not appeal to the record buying public, however, and the group disbanded shortly after. Asked to comment on Yester and Yanovsky's production work for this book, Gallway merely said, "They were good." Sebastian continually promoted the band in an interview with underground magazine *Rat*.

Hairshirt's next venture was to produce the last ever pop album Pat Boone would ever make. Assembling crack session musicians and choosing the songs themselves, the ex-Spoonfuls made sure the album was a *Departure* for Boone. It was recorded for a new company set up by comedian Bill Cosby and his partner Roy Silver, Yanovsky's old manager from the Mugwumps days. Silver was delighted to get away with the name for his label, Tetragrammaton, "The unspoken name of God - look it up," he challenged one reporter. Indeed Tetragrammaton would be known as the company that distributed the *Two Virgins* album by John Lennon and Yoko Ono in November of '68 - hardly a label to include the devoutly religious Pat Boone on its roster.

Taking some tracks that both Yester and Yanovsky loved, including Fred Neil's "I've Got A Secret" and both John Stewart's "July, You're A Woman" and ironically "Never Going Back", alongside a couple of tunes from Tetragrammaton artist Biff Rose and a friend of Pat Boone's Roger Dollarhide, the album is extraordinary mainly for the inclusion of the first ever appearance of Tim Buckley's majestic "Song Of The Siren". Apparently, a year earlier, Judy Henske had mocked a line in the song, 'I am puzzled as the oyster'. This upset Buckley to such an extent that he dropped it from his set, until co-writer Larry Beckett forced him to put it on the *Stairsailor* album in November 1970.

Even then, according to Yester, the song had been too radically changed for its own good, "He did it on The Monkees' show (in December '67) with just a 12-string guitar. He did a straight version of it and it was so beautiful. When I heard Buckley's version on his album, I wanted to spank him. I wanted to call him up and chew him out for doing that to that song and say, "Are you out of your God damned mind? Have fun in your bathroom doing shit like that, but don't put it on a record."

Yester's version with Pat Boone was no better as he admits, "Well, Boone saying, 'Yo ho ho and a bottle of rum,' I thought that was stupid to have left that in there and I'll take the blame for that. But I wonder if I had trouble in producing and arranging that because it was hinting at being close to home?" Yester is still fond of the majority of *Departure* though, "The songs were good and Pat Boone sang really well, which surprised me. I mean we took the work as a lark but that album was a really good album. I found he really outdid himself. Now bear in mind it's Pat Boone but he out Pat Boone'd himself. He took himself way past anywhere else he'd ever been before."

The relationship between the strait-laced Boone and the effervescent Yanovsky was surprisingly good as Yester recalls, "He loved Zally and he liked me a lot. I mean he liked my arranging, we weren't buddies. Zally was like the opposite of him and Boone was really drawn to him. There was this one time in the studio when we had Boone in the dark, so he could hear himself, you know? (laughs) The whole thing was an experiment with Zally and I. I worked with Boone for a while, but he just wasn't getting it and I said, "Zally, take over." Zally comes up, pushes the talkback and says; "I don't know Boone, sing it like you're singing out of your asshole!" There is this long silence, and then you hear, "Hmmm."

Boone's lacklustre attempt at retaliation backfired, as Yester recollects, "One day Boone came into the booth and Judy was sitting at the console. She had long black hair, about the same as Zally. She was reading a magazine and Boone came up behind her and mussed up her hair. She turned around and he was just about shitting himself! "Oh, I am so sorry!" He had touched another man's wife! Oh my God, what a thing!"

The musicians gathered for the project were top notch and included regulars from Elvis's band Jerry Scheff and James Burton plus Clarence White, David Lindley, Ry Cooder, Larry Knechtel and Red Rhodes playing steel, whose frustration in being outplayed by White is a particular memory for Yester. "When we did "Never Going Back", it was like the second session and everybody was familiar with each other and they were just really cooking. So Red was feeling real superior and plays this great solo and looks over at Clarence, and Clarence just blew him away, just did this solo that, I mean, everybody went, "God!"

"We're in the booth and we said, "Let's do another one, you guys want to do another one?" Red shouts, "Yeah!" Now Red's warming his hands and just waiting, like a thoroughbred at the gate, and he gets to his solo and he just goes crazy. Clarence didn't bat and eye, no expression on his face, he just looks over and blew him away again.

We said, "That's really great" leaving Red saying, "No! One more!" You just couldn't get away from Clarence, he was so good, just a phenomenal guy."

The reason why Yanovsky's and Yester's names were not included on *Departure* (although it was still dedicated to, "Zalman's mother, who made this possible,") is a sore point for Yester, "The fact that he went against our wishes and changed the album when we'd finished with it annoyed us. It was just one tune, "Molly". Now we did it and the intention was to do it with an orchestra but Mike Lawford, playing piano, did a wonderful job and it turned out to be so charming in itself we left it. I guess Boone and his manager hired an arranger, which really pissed me off, and went behind our backs and recut it. Roger Dollarhide, who was Boone's gofer, called me and said, "Oh, do you want to hear what we did?" I said, "I don't want to even hear it, fuck you guys!" We got so pissed off that we said, "Take our name off it, we don't want production credit for this!"

The album did not make front-page news and turned out to be Boone's last stab at pop music. His entourage made sure of that, "He was totally hamstrung by his wife," Yester remembers. "When we finished making the album, he showed up at home one night and all of the church elders and his wife were sitting in the living room discussing his career and they said, "That's it for you and showbiz, you'll just be doing church stuff from now on," and that was it. The album never did anything, he didn't push it and he never made a pop album after that. But it was nice to be there for the last one."

Yanovsky had the last laugh, however, as Yester relates, "It was New Year's Eve, and Zally called him up and said, "Hey Boone! We just want to get a feel of the stuff, could you sing your old hits over the phone?" So he said, "Really? You want me to?" "Yeah, yeah I'd really like that." Then Zally holds out the phone and you can hear, 'On a day like today, we passed the time away....' Later, Judy and I put Zally's hair up in curlers. She had just got a Clairol heat curler set for Christmas and Zal ended up looking like this real homely Jewish housewife!"

Whilst recording Pat Boone, Hairshirt were concurrently recording Tim Buckley's immense third album *Happy Sad*. This was to be a different scenario from Buckley's previous album, recorded shortly before Yester joined the Spoonful, however, as Yester recalls, "Zally didn't have a lot to do with it and neither did I. Tim had a band and all the arrangements were done. They had it down the way they wanted and I just helped record it with Bruce Botnick. I just co-ordinated it. They really didn't want a producer, especially his band who were the snottiest bunch of guys I ever run across. I really didn't like them at all. They were scheming to get as much recording money out of the budget as they could. Tim was easily swayed then and I'm afraid he was easily swayed a lot by Lee Underwood, who I think was a horrible influence on him."

The album would turn out to be Buckley's best collection, but one take was almost ruined by a mistake in the studio which Yester turned into a triumph of accidental art, "The surf on "Love From Room 109 At The Islander On Pacific Coast Highway" was because Bruce forgot to put the Dolbys in record. He left them in play which added five times the amount of hiss. Tim had a shrieking fit! He loved the performance. So I had Tim's roadie go over to Tim's place in Malibu and string up two microphones under the dock and record an hour of surf that covered up the hiss!" The Buckley sessions only took a week and on completion, Hairshirt had a blank diary.

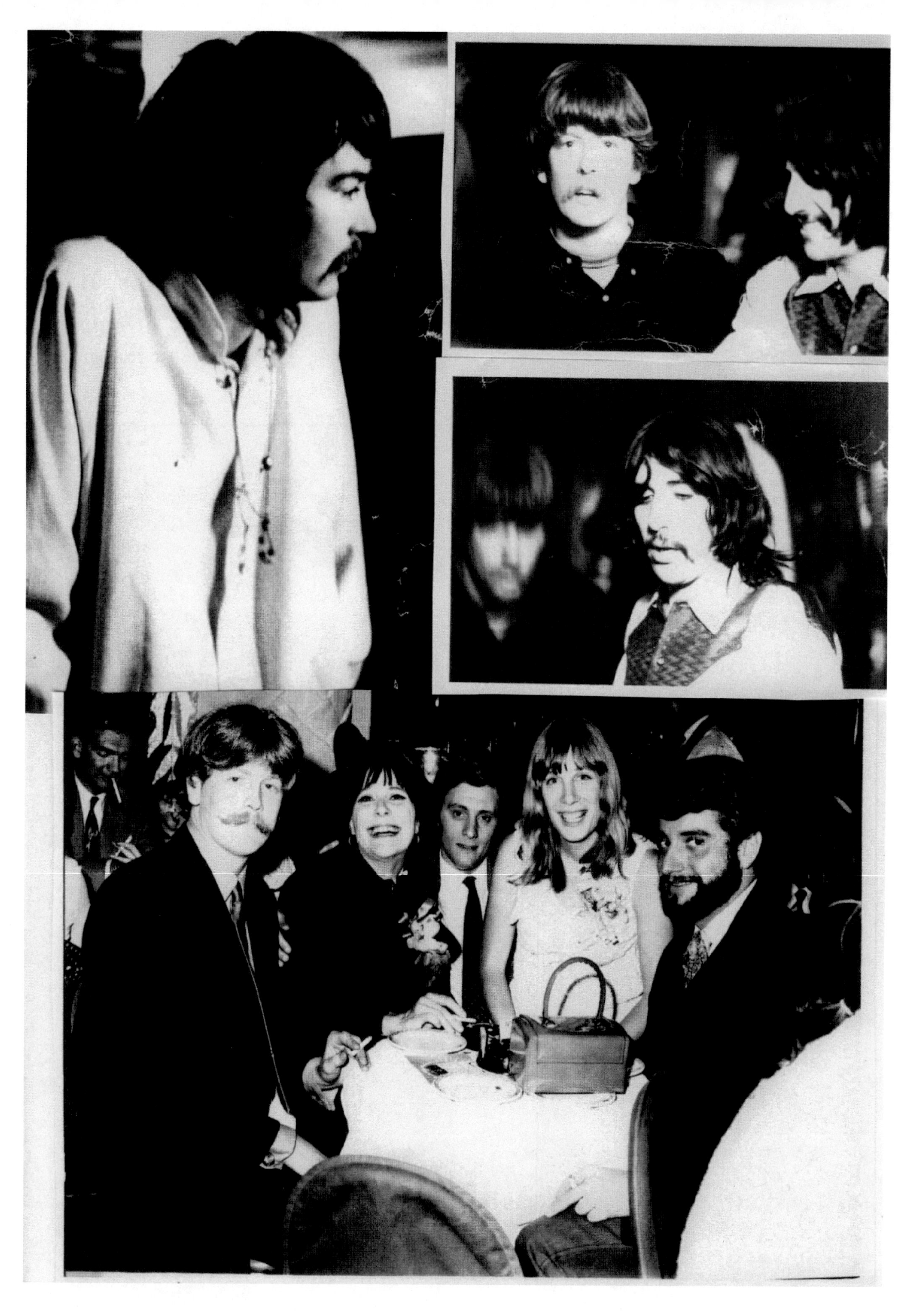

CHAPTER 6 – SIDE TRIPS

Around October 1968, Sebastian started to put down tracks for his solo album. These were recorded at the Elektra Studios in Hollywood as Sebastian had tired of New York and migrated west. Even though he was born there and had an inclination to endure its seediness, things came to a head one night; "New York just got so dirty and so very depressing that I felt I just couldn't make it a base of operations any more. I think what settled it was one particular evening when I just went out to get some milk and I saw three junkies puking, two cats hit me for money and a stoned hooker tagged on to me....and it hit me - I only wanted some milk, but I had to go through all this grimness. It just sapped my energy and patience in the end."

Finding a home in Laurel Canyon, California, Sebastian discovered that most of his musician friends from the Village had drifted over as well, as he said just after his arrival there, "It's really funny, because here I am in Los Angeles - I've been here for about two months - and in that time I have reconnoitred with at least twenty friends from the New York Street. A lot of people are coming out of groups and are kind of looking around, not with the idea of, "Let's all be in a band and be stars," or anything, but just kind of a musical level of communication."

Cass Elliot, fresh from leaving her group, also lived in the canyon and her parties usually ended in sing-alongs around her swimming pool. Guests would get stoned at these "liquid jams" and at one particular gathering, bandless Stephen Stills and David Crosby had harmonised memorably in front of Elliot and Sebastian. Crosby and Stills had recently recorded some demos together and were itching to form a band. Years earlier, when Graham Nash was on an American tour with The Hollies, Elliot had introduced him to Crosby, just as she put Sebastian and Yanovsky together. Their friendship grew too, and one day, late 1968, Nash, Stills and Crosby went out for a drive in the back of Stills' Bentley, smoked some joints and got to know each other. Crosby looked at Stills and said, "Okay, which one of us is gonna steal him?"

Nobody really remembers where Crosby, Stills and Nash first sung together, whether it was in Cass Elliot's kitchen, the Sebastians' house or Joni Mitchell's' living room, but this interview segment from *Hit Parader* seems to answer the question. Talking about people who have left groups and who just want to jam, Sebastian said, "The sessions aren't always in the studio any more. The sessions are in that room over there a lot (he gestures at a small room off his living room). For example, Graham Nash is staying with us now. Graham's from The Hollies. He sings on the top, really high. He knows David Crosby. Because he knows Cass and he knows me, he knows David. So David introduced him to Steve Stills one day over here. He and David had been hanging out and singing together and saying, "Ooooh, what a nice noise!" And David and Stephen had been hanging out together. So all of a sudden yesterday there was a fainter of a trio in there, one of the most incredible vocal sounds I've ever heard. We just sat around while they sang some tunes of Stephen's and some tunes of Graham's and some tunes of David's. It was beautiful and immediately they started saying, "Well, gee, let's make a record. Why not?" There's the kernel of a scene there."

Nash then had to go back to England to fulfil some Hollies' business. Crosby thought he might lose the impetus of the situation, so late in December, Crosby, Stills and Sebastian arrived in London, incognito, to court and steal Nash. One music reporter, D. Boltwood, witnessed a powwow between the four at a trendy London nightclub. The next day Boltwood secured an interview with Sebastian; "I hadn't planned to come to England. But Dave and

Stephen were coming over, so I took the opportunity to take a short holiday. They're staying a while - they're taking a flat with a recording studio in it, and they'll be working with Graham."

Asked if the four will be forming a group, Sebastian erroneously claimed, "I doubt it. Well, I definitely won't be, I don't want to be involved in a group scene anymore and anyway, I'm just starting out on a solo career. I don't know whether the others are going to form a group - I think it's unlikely that they would. Not a regular gigging group - we're all basically in the same position, we're individuals, solo artists."

Sebastian left what would become Crosby, Stills and Nash to get it together in Moscow Road in London, while he returned to America to start his solo career, as he told the counterculture paper *Rat* on his return, "Most of my bookings will be college concerts but right now in order to prepare for that and to get my thing on stage together, I'm working in a small coffee shop in Washington. I went over to England and played in living rooms a lot. I'm going to be just working with my guitar and harmonium and just whatever I can do by myself."

With Crosby, Stills and Nash coming back over to Los Angeles, Nash stayed at Crosby's house over Christmas 1968 and also helped out on the remaining sessions for Sebastian's solo debut. Sebastian had been fairly excited by the project and with some budget at his disposal, he assembled around a dozen musicians and producer Paul Rothchild for the first cut, "Baby Don't Ya Get Crazy"; "For the first session I did I had a big boogying tune, a full out thing. I had Paul Harris from New York playing piano and arranging, on bass was Harvey Brooks and Stephen Stills from New York on guitar. Then I said I wanted some ladies to sing with me and was trying to think of the right ladies when Paul Rothchild said, "Hey, man, I know Ike Turner." So we had The Ikettes singing in the background."

Sebastian also worked on a recut of "She's A Lady"; "It has kind of renaissance overtones. So Paul came up with a lutist who had worked for Elektra. Paul called him up and he said, "Well yes. And can I bring my wife? She plays recorder and viola da gamba. And can I bring my friend so and so? He plays viola d'amour and crumhorn." After about two days of setting it up, here I was in the studio with this marvellous, old, wizened, white-haired lady who plays a big bass recorder and has wind that just doesn't quit! But it was nice because the lutist is married to the recorder player and it really comes through. They're listening for each other. They're trying to tickle each other a bit because they're sitting together in a date. We came out with this lovely warm classical feeling.

"Later that evening, I decided David Crosby should come in and play his out-of-sight rhythm, the best 12-string in the world, David has. David comes in, plays 12-string, Steve Stills comes in, plays a little country guitar and I come in and play what I was playing the first time, so they can hear it and I'm singing it, but we're not recording it. I'm just making it happen again for them. And whammo! Got what we wanted."

Sebastian's first solo appearance of note was on Cass Elliot's TV special in January alongside Joni Mitchell. Sebastian had earlier played on Elliot's current album *Dream A Little Dream Of Me* which also included Cyrus Faryar and Stills. A song Sebastian wrote for Elliot, "The Room Nobody Lives In", appeared here for the first time.

The rest of January '69 was spent in Sag Harbour, Long Island where Sebastian found Crosby, Stills and Nash a house a few doors down from his own. They were, by now, serious about recording an album together. Even though their voices had blended perfectly in an acoustic situation, Stills still wanted a rhythm section. He turned to Sebastian; "Stephen at one point asked me to come in. I'm an amateur drummer, always have been. So, he said, "Look, we don't need a great drummer in this band, we need somebody who can sing along and maybe provide another voice and just kind of keep time, and would you do it?" And I said, "God." The timing was all wrong. I had just recorded this *John B.* album and I was waiting for it to get into the stores, so my judgement call on the thing was, it's too late. I've already committed to this solo thing for a while. The idea seemed like a good one, but I couldn't take it seriously at the time."

Indeed CSN's manager David Geffen has gone on record saying that Sebastian, "didn't think it was worth shit and didn't join." Today, with CSN still playing the larger arenas, Sebastian disagrees, "I saw the opportunity for them to be really big but it just felt like my die was already cast and I had to go with it."

Stills had enjoyed working with Sebastian's rhythm section from his album, so CSN rehearsed drummer Dallas Taylor, bassist Harvey Brooks and even keyboardist Paul Harris at their house. Taylor fitted into the mood perfectly and got the job. In his memoirs, Taylor recalls that it was Lorey Sebastian that had talked her husband out of joining Crosby, Stills and Nash, because she was sleeping with Graham Nash at the time. This story is supported by Erik Jacobsen who recalls, "She took him for everything and just fucking left one day to go off with Graham Nash." Nash, who stayed friends with Sebastian, had a song called "Lady Of The Island" which fitted the bill and he once said that the song was about two women, one being from Long Island. During this period in Sag Harbour Crosby would write his anthem "Almost Cut My Hair" and Nash his guiding "Teach Your Children".

Whatever happened next is unclear but Sebastian (after a couple of nights on a friend's couch) left his wife and went off to live in a VW van in Burbank, California. Taking one dog, Bear, from the menagerie, Sebastian certainly had a change of scene, "I had accumulated all these belongings, and it was wonderful to get away from this atmosphere of possessions that I'd begun to feel very stifled by. My first wife was very concerned with buying things and shopping, so I was reacting against that, I think, and really enjoying having nothing but my fishing-tackle box full of guitar tools, an instrument or two and enough clothes. Not to make it sound too much like roughing it, I was not very far from a place where I could go and make phone calls and do what I had to do."

Twelve people lived on this farm including Cyrus Faryar who had got a gig of renting out the complex of buildings there, including one Volkswagen Camper Van. The situation was glorious, being underneath a mountain in Burbank, surrounded by out of view freeways. It was quite an artistic colony too, as Sebastian informs, "It wasn't a commune in the Life magazine sense of the word. It was a creative community of people who did very separate things. Everybody lived in very separate but close houses."

Amongst the artists, the tie-dyers and the musicians at "Chicken Flats", some fairly heavy drugs were being consumed, "We had a passing junkie now and then," Sebastian recalls. "But primarily it was a grass scene. Psychedelics occasionally. Little acid, a little mescaline, a little THC before we found out it was cow tranquillisers, and were getting totally transcendental." Sebastian also admits that during this period he started to use cocaine, which would lead to a period lacking in creativity. He was rumoured to be writing the score for the film *The Magic Christian*, but nothing ever appeared.

The sessions for what was to be *John B. Sebastian* lasted till May 1969 and with the album now in the can, Sebastian pondered his future plans; "Donovan and I are planning to do some things. Also the Crosby-Stills-Nash bunch. They've just finished their album, and I just finished mine, so we'll probably get together." Around this time, Crosby, Stills and Nash had ventured down to Faryar's farm and played their entire first album to an impressed audience of one. Their next step was to add Neil Young to their set up and rehearsals started up at Peter Tork's old house, that Stills had rented, in L.A.

Sebastian was on the periphery of these sessions and could see the embryonic clashes of egos. There was some fun though as Pete Townshend told *Zig Zag*, "The last time I ever heard a record stoned on pot was *Music From Big Pink*, the night I first met John Sebastian, at Peter Tork's house - so there!" Sebastian then retreated to his tent and agreed to meet the quartet at their second gig - Woodstock.

Nearing the end of his summer long sabbatical, Boone was visited one day by a couple of associates; "I guess about August '68, two friends of mine, Jock McClain and Arma Anden, who were road managers for The Beatles and worked for Nat Weiss (The Beatles' representative in the US since Epstein's death in August '67) came over to my house. They had heard this band The Oxpetals from somebody and they brought a couple of them over, as they wanted to know if I'd take some pictures of the group, because they knew I was into photography at the time. Although I was not interested in producing them then - I was interested in my girlfriend and going water-skiing."

The Oxpetals came to New York from a Bohemian scene in Eden Alley, Virginia Beach, where the local rednecks did not go for their long hair and the heat from the "narcs" was becoming unbearable. The first to branch out from this scene were Emmylou Harris and Juice Newton. Benjamin Herndon (guitar), Bobby Webber (keyboards) and Dan "Ace" Allison (drums) followed the ladies into the big city in 1968 and crashed at Harris's apartment. Knowing they needed management to hit the big time, Herndon audaciously phoned The Beatles' manager. Getting through to Weiss's secretary only to be informed, "We don't make appointments over the phone," being "young and cocky" Herndon replied, "That's okay, we'll be down in an hour!"

Storming the offices and making themselves as disruptive as possible, including throwing paper cups full of water all over the place ("We should have been The Monkees,") the group refused to leave until they had been seen by Weiss. A little flustered, the secretary got Arma Anden to come down to reception to evict her tormentors. Anden asked the group to leave, although Herndon could tell, "that he appreciated our balls." Noting The Oxpetals' name and address and promising to be in touch, Anden actually kept his word and turned up where the group were staying the following day. They played some songs on acoustic guitars for him; he loved them, and set up an audition for The Oxpetals to occur a few weeks later.

Returning to Virginia Beach, the group spent six intense long weeks rehearsing in a relative's suburban house, with the addition of Guy Phillips (lead guitar) and Stephen Pague (bass). Pague had previously been in a group called Full Measure, who played many Spoonful covers in their set. In true romantic fashion, Nat Weiss was to be impressed enough to give the Oxpetals a management contract, though he didn't sign it and only took 2% instead

of the 20% due, "The guy was smart enough and rich enough to be a real shark," recalls Guy Phillips. "But he was a sweetheart."

Weiss set up a showcase for The Oxpetals at the Gaslight in the Village, where Boone saw them and was impressed enough to want to work with the group. By now Boone was married to Patti and they both moved into the city, "When the summer was over, I moved into Manhattan and got an apartment on the West Side. We found it by reading the obituaries on a Sunday morning and went over and gave the super a deposit and got this nice seven-room apartment. Judy Collins lived in my building and Steve Stills was living there. Then that fall, I started getting into a business arrangement with The Oxpetals and I agreed to become their producer. I also met this man named Gene Kiefer.

"He was from Des Moines, Iowa, and was about ten to fifteen years older than me. He had just moved to New York and he was the key to all of this coming together. He had been a political advisor to the Governor of Iowa and he also had his own state-of-the-art colour separation printing company, which was very successful, so he was a pretty wealthy man. He was also involved with the Edgar Cayce Foundation." In the 1920s Edgar Cayce was referred to as the "Sleeping Prophet". Similar to a psychic, Cayce started a foundation called the Association for Research and Enlightenment (A.R.E.), which had its headquarters in Virginia Beach.

Striving for a record contract, The Oxpetals were playing showcases whilst living in the still very humble Albert Hotel, which had been recommended to them by Boone, probably remembering how the hotel made the Spoonful desperate for success. This move backfired as after having his guitar stolen on the second day, Herndon became a bit wary of the place and would spend more time at the Boone's apartment. But Boone always had an open door for the group; "He was not like Mr. Star, recalls Herndon. "He never had an attitude, that's why we loved him so much. In the very beginning, he literally opened his house to The Oxpetals and provided food, showers, I mean, even when we'd come in at three in the morning. He was literally our older brother and he took us under his wing."

Around this time, on a radio interview to promote The Oxpetals, clearly high and speaking at a mile a minute, Boone gave his first public reaction to The Lovin' Spoonful split, "You can look at sports teams and the same thing happens. Like the Jets, they have a great season, beat the biggest team in the NFL in the Super Bowl and the next year, with no success, it falls apart. That's an example. As soon as you make it, it's not so important anymore; it was just making it. So now all these other little things come out that weren't coming out before, like the little friction you had with the drummer, or whatever. Everybody knows how to smile when the photographer is there but as soon as the clicks are over, it's back down with the long faces again."

Boone went on to cite the differences he had had with Sebastian and his frustration at not doing the Coke commercial, in a brief conversation dwelling on the money side of the business. It was a business he was keen to immerse himself back into, however, as with his stack of new material under his arm and Koppelman still willing to fulfil the seven album deal, an agreement was struck for Boone to record his solo album. Even though it must have been obvious that Boone's voice would not be tolerable for a whole album, Boone started recording. "I got the deal on the strength of one song, "If I Stare"," Boone recalls. "Steve Soles and I did the demo for Charlie and Don and they were convinced it was a hit record and they sent me into the studio." None of the recordings would ever see the light of day.

All the Oxpetals played on these recordings, except for Steven Pague, who was draft dodging and in a quandary about whether or not to turn himself in. His decision to report back was assisted by a little puff of Dutch courage, "The day I turned myself into the FBI, I had been smoking hashish with Steve and Patti Boone." For being AWOL, Pague was to spend a harsh four months in a stockade.

The recordings for Boone's proposed album took place at Homestead Sounds on 40th Street in New York on eight track, with Gene Redice, who had previously worked with Spanky & Our Gang, as the engineer. Guy Phillips recalls the sessions; "It was fun, God we had an incredible scene there. When we did overdub vocals, we had a chorus of twenty people, including kids crawling around the floor and dogs howling. Steve had a Shepherd at the time and if you sang it would howl!" Phillips is not diplomatic when he recalls Boone's singing at the sessions, "He was terrible - I loved it! Oh man, you had to give him a whole damn quart of whiskey before he could sing at all and then you'd have to get him quick before he'd pass out! (laughs)."

Boone sounds very discouraged as he recalls his solo album that never was, "There's not that much you can say about it. It was a well-conceived but poorly executed project. I got too many musicians involved and I didn't keep my focus on the project." Only a few songs into the album, the rug was pulled from under Boone's feet, "I got "If I Stare" cut, another song called "Mississippi Belle", which I really liked and another one which I don't even remember and they were coming out real neat. Then one day I came to the studio with my musicians and found out I had been cancelled. They cut me off because I was spending too much money and I couldn't sing. The mistake I made was, rather than talking with the musicians and getting them to give a price, I paid them all union scale and double scale and overtime. The bill went up but it was turning out some good recordings."

Indeed, the one song that has since been unearthed, "If I Stare", is a fine slice of country rock/honky tonk which chugs along fine and includes a catchy signature piece at the end of each verse that stays in the mind forever. Definitely a hit that never was, but Boone had spent more than could be recouped, although he blames Koppelman and Rubin, "I really thought it was not fair because I never had enough of an opportunity. They didn't get a producer involved; they let me go into a studio by myself. It was their responsibility to watch their money, rather than let this twenty odd year old go into the studio. I got so mad, I didn't even call them back." Boone would now focus his attentions on securing The Oxpetals a recording contract, but with money tight they needed supporting.

In the late sixties, with everybody getting into cosmic consciousness with the discovery of LSD, The Oxpetals became aware of the A.R.E. when, tired of the Albert, they rented a house beside a lake in New Jersey, from a Dr. Riley, one of the main components of the A.R.E. and a friend of Kiefer's. Boone recalls how the Hollywood story for the untried group continued; "Kiefer became a fan of the group because they had positiveness in their music. It was the same time that The Moody Blues came out with their cosmical *In Search Of The Lost Chord* and Gene Kiefer was convinced that this was the direction music was going. So Kiefer got involved as the financial backer. He was also a marketing wiz and then I got involved as a producer and we took the demo to Mercury Records.

"Simon Hayes was an English fellow I had met through the Beatle road managers and he was in charge of A&R at Mercury Records. (Hayes was also the business manager of the collective known as The Fool who helped themselves to a hefty slice of The Beatles' Apple pie) Simon, right away, wanted to sign the group. The President was nervous because the company was not doing well at the time. Anyway, the president and this gangster guy, Green, I think his name was, came out to their house at Moose Pack Lake, and heard them play in their living room. They always sounded great in their living room, whenever they went out to a club to play they'd stink, but when you were in their living room, where they were set up, they sounded like a million bucks. They did their set and the President jumped out of his chair, "Sign 'em Simon, these guys are great!"

According to Pague, the group were signed for some forty thousand dollars - not bad for a bunch of kids fresh from the sticks. With his share of the advance, Boone set up a production company called Purple Planet Productions and set to work recording The Oxpetals' self-titled album. Boone became engrossed in their music as he tried to shape the group's sound into something tangible. He openly encouraged the entire group to write songs as Herndon was their only songwriter and Boone wanted to avoid the pitfalls that scenario could open.

Boone's subsequent comparison of The Oxpetals with The Moody Blues' *In Search Of The Lost Chord* period is way off, mainly due to Boone getting nowhere near to Tony Clarke's production skills. Mixed by Skip and Steve Boone and engineer Warren Dewey, the resulting album is mostly an embarrassing affair, whilst showing some signs of potential, especially on the opener, the Charlatanesque "Don't Cry Mother" which has its moments. The single, "Down From The Mountain"/"What Can You Say" ensured the group would remain unknown. "The album is not a representation of the group," recalls Pague, a comment echoed by the rest of The Oxpetals, especially Guy Phillips; "They were interesting songs but we just didn't know much about being in the studio. It was Steve's first production and he didn't know what he was doing either. That's a rotten record I'm telling you."

After a lavish press party (which insured reviews in *Rolling Stone* and *Crawdaddy*) on its release, in the summer of 1970 and some airplay in New York, The Oxpetals' album disappeared into oblivion. After opening for Van Morrison, Traffic and Joe Cocker, Herndon quit the group citing the classic, "personal difficulties." "We were a flash in the pan," he recalls today. "It was almost over before it started." Guy Phillips looks back on the whole venture without any regrets, "Shit, it was a gas! They gave us a lot of money. It was a lot of fun driving around in Limos' in New York when you're twenty-three years old." He sums up The Oxpetals by saying, "We were a good musical group, but as a band on a record, we really sucked!"

Boone did not even put his name to The Oxpetals record and quit before it came out, probably due to Bobby Webber having an affair with his wife. Now down to his last few dollars, Boone had to scuffle for cash, "I was just broke from then on, you know, so I was hustling around trying to make some money, sell some pot there, play a gig here; whatever I could do to make money." Fortunately for Boone, now would be payback time for his best friend, Peter Davey (from the European trip prior to the Spoonful) as Boone explains, "From high school on, we were inseparable buddies. All during the Spoonful, Peter would go on the road with us and I supported him - paid his rent. He was heir to a fortune, a guy who was going to inherit money for the rest of his life, just a zillionaire. My thing was, I said, "Peter, when you get your inheritance, you've gotta buy me a sailboat." So he did! When he got his first money in 1970, right after The Oxpetals' album came out."

The boat became Boone's escape vehicle. His income had all dried up and he had acquired quite a tax problem because of the way the Spoonful got paid - large sums all at once, with long periods with no money. Yester had been warned of this possibility when he joined the group, as he remembers with relief, "The group ran into some serious tax problems when we broke up but I wasn't involved because I wasn't signed." Boone admits he was naive in his spending prowess, "I was more impulsive than the rest and didn't really listen to the little advice we got. It was easy to get a large sum and spend it all with little thought to paying taxes." Because of the speedboats and the continuous rock and roll life-style he carried on living after the Spoonful had split, Boone was in trouble, some $40,000 in trouble, to be exact.

"By the time 1970 rolled around, the IRS came in and slapped a three year old tax bill on me from back in the Spoonful, that I didn't even know was coming. They were taking it all, so I said, "Well hasta luego! I'm outta here, you're never going to see my ass again." I didn't have a chance to pay that money; I didn't have any income as they had seized all my royalties. So my wife and I moved to the Virgin Islands and I bought my sailboat down there. Peter lived up in the hills of St. Thomas and I'd be on my sailboat and we had a good couple of years down there."

On either the 19th or 20th of May, 1969, Sebastian played on a session with Stills, Buddy Miles and Jimi Hendrix (on bass!) at the Record Plant in New York. The jam, "Live And Let Live", formed the funky background for a collage of Timothy Leary quotes from press conferences. Doctor Leary, a proponent of sensory expansion, formulated his "Turn On, Tune In, Drop Out" mantra that caused panic amongst middle America in the mid-sixties. The song became the opener for an album that was to be part of Leary's campaign to run for Governor of California against Ronald Reagan, but by the time the album was released the next year; Leary was in jail for his beliefs.

If Sebastian was seeking a way out from being associated with the Spoonful bust by appearing on the album, his next notable move would forever disassociate himself from a "fink's trip." The milestone for all that was the hippie generation became known as Woodstock. This once in a lifetime event was a moment in rock and cultural history that described the sixties for all its good and bad virtues.

The Woodstock Music And Art Fair began on August 15th, 1969 at Max Yasgur's farm in Bethel, New York. Over 400,000 people turned up, most without buying a ticket, forcing the organisers to declare it a free festival. On the one hand you had the beautiful music: Hendrix, The Who, CSN&Y, Joplin, et al; the joy of being amongst like-minded people and the stimulating drugs but on the other there was the rip-offs, the brown acid, the poor organisation and the mud. With all the rampant drug use, inadequate food and drink and the poor sanitation, the pluses and minuses continued as the festival included three deaths, two births and four miscarriages.

Sebastian's involvement in Woodstock was a pivotal moment in his career, when somehow the strong group leader became somewhat a figure of ridicule. It all started quite innocently, however, after meeting a former roadie for the Spoonful (Walter Gundy) at the Albany airport, who got him into the Incredible String Band's helicopter, Sebastian found himself backstage at what was to be the site of his most significant performance ever, "I came to Woodstock as a member of the audience. I was not intending to play and, in fact, I sort of got drafted as a backstage helper to try and keep the mud out of one of the dressing tents." With his recently learned skill of under the canvas life-style, Sebastian spent the first night of the festival sleeping with the instruments of the Incredible String Band.

After a delayed start, the festival opened with an extended set from Richie Havens followed by Country Joe McDonald followed by rain, lots of rain. Sebastian by now was completely stoned (on THC acquired from a stage security guard) in this backstage musical environment amongst friends and performers; "So I came completely unprepared to play. I had no instruments. I was not particularly conscious of bringing any stage clothes or anything. What I came in was just this Levi suit that I had tie-dyed. And so, when the rain became intense enough that the power was off the stage, Chip Monck came to me and said, "Look, we need somebody to hold them while we sweep the stage, and we know you can do it with an acoustic guitar, so you're elected."

"I said, "Chip, I didn't bring an instrument!" At the time, I mooched a guitar from Timmy Hardin. Actually, Timmy had put this guitar in my hands and he never collected it. This was a Harmony Sovereign, the kind of guitar that you can buy and leave at the gig." Sebastian's hour-long appearance was littered with stoned sermons and moments where he forgets his own lyrics. On his defence, he was out of his mind in front of close to half a million people. "I was a little too anaesthetised to be terrified. I was certainly impressed by the size of the crowd. It was absolutely the most amazing congregation of people I had ever seen. I had no idea - and I mentioned it on stage - that there were so many like-minded people at that time. The youth culture had not really discovered itself before Woodstock."

What he actually said was; "Oh boy! This is really a mindfucker of all times, man. I've never seen anything like this, man." His nowadays common soundbite on his departure; "Wow, just love everybody all around you and clean up a little garbage on your way out and everything's gonna be all right," ensured his association forever with the festival and an unwanted image; "Unfortunately, it created a perception of this kind of stoned-out hippie kind of impression. Not only was it detrimental, but it really wasn't me very much. It was me that day."

Apparently, Sebastian received $1,000 for his impromptu appearance. After his set Sebastian and a member of The Band helped backstage with the acid casualties; "Rick Danko and I went over to the large white tents where Wavy Gravy and the Hog Farmers were cooling out acid casualties. The people were lying on canvas cots and Wavy was walking around in a white outfit. Every kid who came in would go up to Gravy and say, "Here man, please take these and don't let me ever see them again!" Rick and I tried to think of all the soothing songs we could play for the mentally disorientated. It was hard core easy-listening music."

As the muddied field cleared and Jimi Hendrix took to the stage, early on the Monday morning, Sebastian was still helping out; "When Jimi was playing "The Star-Spangled Banner", my brother and I were pushing somebody's car out of the mud and making our exit. Most of the people had gone and it looked like a battlefield out there, like a war had gone on." A few days later Sebastian, alongside CSN&Y, Joan Baez and Joni Mitchell, played at a benefit concert in Big Sur. The concert was documented in the movie *Celebration At Big Sur* memorable only for Stills assaulting a member of the audience. The film provided work for Yanovsky who was in charge of re-recording alongside Peter Pilafian.

Celebrate with:
JOAN BAEZ
CROSBY, STILLS, NASH & YOUNG
JONI MITCHELL
JOHN SEBASTIAN
And Introducing
DOROTHY MORRISON
Everyone did it... for the sheer love of it.

CELEBRATION AT BIG SUR

...it happened one weekend by the sea.

Ted Mann Productions presents a film by Baird Bryant & Johanna Demetrakas
Produced by Carl Gottlieb Color by DE LUXE® **— see it by yourself... or with everyone you know.**

RELEASED BY 20th CENTURY-FOX

GP ALL AGES ADMITTED Parental Guidance Suggested

T H E A T R E

MAT—401

136 lines x 4 columns (544 lines)
4 columns x 9¾ inches

In fact, Yanovsky had found a lot of work behind the scenes. He and Douglas Bush had written the score for the Cinema verite *A Married Couple* for director Allan King in 1969, that was filmed in Toronto. Yanovsky alone scored the Imax documentary *North Of Superior* in 1971 before working for the sound department in a short sequel to *Celebration At Big Sur, One Hand Clapping* in '72.

During the time between finishing and releasing his first solo album, Sebastian continued to appear live and perform as a session player. After a residency at The Bitter End in New York in September '69, a series of concerts at the Fillmore West and Winterland, where Sebastian was to support CSN&Y in early October, were cancelled after the shocking death of Crosby's girlfriend, Christine Gail Hinton - the same day the *Crosby, Stills and Nash* album went gold.

An involvement with The Doors, fresh from Jim Morrison's obscenity trial in Miami, was Sebastian's first musical milestone of the seventies. With Paul Rothchild producing The Doors' fifth album *Morrison Hotel*, he called on Sebastian to play harmonica on the classic track "Roadhouse Blues", after Morrison's attempt was deemed unsuitable. Sebastian put down the now familiar funky harmonica backing and was rewarded with double scale. Not many people know that it is Sebastian on the record, however, as the credit goes to one G. Puglese.

In his memoirs, John Densmore, The Doors' drummer, stated that Paul Rothchild told him that Sebastian used a pseudonym, as he would be embarrassed to be associated with The Doors, probably due to the Miami incident. Sebastian refutes this allegation, "In retrospect, there has been different opinions about how that got started. The Doors thought that I didn't want anybody to know that I was on a Doors record, like (laughs) that's not very complimentary to them. Now I may not have been their most enthusiastic supporter but on the other hand I would have been fine having my name on their album, as it was on many other albums - I enjoy my work as a sideman. The fact was that Paul Rothchild, I think, did not want to tip the hand that the musicians were not always The Doors on those records. He was less reluctant about bass because it was obvious there was no bass player (Lonnie Mack plays bass on "Roadhouse Blues").

"When it came to giving me the credit for the harmonica, he gave it to me as my father's name, before he changed it. It was Puglese, and you see, if my father hadn't changed his name at about twenty three I would have been Giovanni Puglese. So that was a little bit of humour and not wanting to show that it was the same guy from the Spoonful that you had already heard playing harmonica on this record or something like that. I don't really know. But it wasn't what I believe Robbie Krieger (Doors' guitarist) thought, that it was because I didn't want my name on the record."

To corroborate Sebastian's recollection, he performed on-stage with The Doors, as well as Dallas Taylor, at one of their concerts at the Felt Forum in New York on either January 17th or 18th of 1970. These concerts were recorded for The Doors' album *Absolutely Live*, although Sebastian did not appear on the finished work. Years later an outtake featuring Sebastian on "Little Red Rooster" appeared on the *Alive She Cried* album, where you hear Morrison introduce Sebastian onto the stage; "Hey listen, at this time I'd like to introduce a friend of ours, a real talented guy, John Sebastian!"

Even up to early 1970, Sebastian was still talking about his proposed album as if it was still being worked on; "I'm mostly letting it go tune by tune. Each tune I tried to look at pretty much as a separate entity and arrange it as such, rather than the way I customarily would approach an album - which is to go in and go tune for tune with pretty much the same musicians. I tried to pick the people that I'd like to play on a given new tune." Part of Sebastian's stable line up was musician/arranger Paul Harris, who told Melody Maker in May 1970, "I've just finished working with John Sebastian in the States, and that's taken a long time; in fact the album was started over two summers ago." The reason for the delay was a legal one.

The background to the complicated scenario surrounding *John B. Sebastian* was explained by Sebastian to *Fusion*, also in May, "I was originally on Kama Sutra with the Spoonful, and that was an MGM subsidiary. After my first single, Buddah was going to take over Kama Sutra, so MGM bought my contract. Then everything got really weird. My chance to break away came at contract option time and I ended up on Warner Brothers/Reprise."

The complications that had surrounded Butler's solo release and the corporate turmoil at MGM made for a good excuse for Sebastian to slip away: "People there were afraid to make any decisions for fear it would cost them their jobs. They couldn't even appropriate money to design an album cover when it had to be done."

The switch to free himself from the madness at MGM, who had promoted the album in the trades then refused to release it, would logically have enabled Sebastian to release the now over a year old album on Reprise. But MGM would not let go of Sebastian and tied up all the contracts in court for a month before Reprise could release the album.

Enter Mike Curb. Born in Savannah, Georgia on Christmas Eve 1944, Curb first came to prominence when he wrote the motorcycle jingle, "You Meet The Nicest People On A Honda" which was subsequently reworked as The Hondells' hit in 1964, "Little Honda". He then started his own production company, Sidewalk who leased masters to different labels, primarily Tower. He also did the schlock soundtracks for a variety of American International Pictures.

He came to the attention of the Spoonful circle when, in 1967, he put together a bogus Mugwumps group that recorded two Spoonful related singles ("Jug Band Music"/"Bald Headed Lena" on Sidewalk 900 and "Season Of The Witch"/"My Gal" on Sidewalk 909) and a track on the soundtrack for the film *Riot On Sunset Strip*. This was a clear attempt to cash in on the success of the Spoonful and The Mamas & The Papas. Also, in an unrelated incident, in October '69 a Lovin' Spoonful toured the UK (including a concert at the Royal in Tottenham) but this was a bogus group also. After a couple of bars of "Daydream" the impostors then launched into their own set much to the disappointment of the audience.

In 1970 Curb became the president of MGM Records. His first step was to rid the label of any act that, "glorified the use of narcotics", although he missed out Eric Burdon. This is the same man who had soundtracked both *Maryjane* and *Psych-Out* in 1968. He even became the entertainment chairman for Richard Nixon and recorded a song for his presidential campaign, under the moniker The Mike Curb Congregation, that went something like, 'Nixon now, Nixon now, more than ever we need Nixon now!'

So when Sebastian delivered the tapes of his album to Reprise in the fall of 1969, he thought he had escaped the clutches of Mr. Curb. Not so. Curb thought that he owned Sebastian, due to the clause in the Spoonful's contract, as Curb said in 1970, "We picked up John's rights through Kama Sutra. We paid Koppelman-Rubin $750,000 for them, and there was a clause in the contract that said they could replace anybody but Sebastian." Reprise had already been to court to acquire the album and Sebastian. The court ruled that MGM only had Sebastian as a member of the now defunct Lovin' Spoonful and that if Reprise paid MGM the costs of recording the album, some $58,000, they could put out the album.

Curb reckoned that the tapes had been delivered to him, "We had a scheduled March 20th (1970) release date on the album, and when John signed with Reprise, I had no idea he'd go with the same LP we had. I almost had a heart attack when I heard they had the same LP." Two odd occurrences make Curb's statement hard to believe, the first brought up by Bob Cavallo; "Curb offered me a $200,000 a year advance for Sebastian last year. If he already had him, why'd he offer to pay so much for him?" Also, when Reprise released their album in late March 1970, Curb asked *Rolling Stone* for a review copy, stating, "Sure'd love to hear it."

The newly acquired power of Curb's must have gone to his head, as in a fit of pique; he went on to copy the review copy and release the album on MGM with the original sleeve design. The executive vice president of Warner Brothers, Joe Smith, reacted swiftly suing MGM for $10 million in punitive damages and $1 million in actual damages, on charges of piracy, counterfeiting, violating New York civil rights and unfair competition. "We do not sue lightly," Smith said at the time. "When we are wrong and are sued, we back off. When we are right, we sue."

So with the public a little bemused by the fact that there were two new John Sebastian albums, with different covers but the same songs, at least *John B. Sebastian* was available one way or the other, approximately eighteen months after it had been finished. With eleven self-written tracks, albeit with one unnecessary retread solo rendition of "You're A Big Boy Now", the album was as good as a singer-songwriter album can be. The optimistic upbeat material like the twangy country of "Rainbows All Over Your Blues" compared nicely with the moodiness of the descriptive "The Room Nobody Lives In". Apart from the time out throwaway "Fa-Fana Fa" (with Buzzy Linhart sounding like he'd swallowed a gulp of helium) the album is perfection.

Paul Harris's orchestral arrangement on the fairly schmaltzy "I Had A Dream" works perfectly as does his harmonium playing amongst the deep imagery of "How Have You Been", the best track on the album. Paul Rothchild's production is top notch and the collaboration with famous friends peaks with Graham Nash's high harmony on the jokingly philosophical "What She Thinks About".

What with all the confusion, the album still did well in Europe and the States, where it peaked at number 20, spending thirty one weeks on the charts, all without the benefit of a hit single. Saying that, Sebastian had two songs from the album on the multimillion selling *Woodstock* triple album released not long after Sebastian's solo. There were, in all, four singles taken from *John B. Sebastian*, including one on MGM, which never got beyond the promotional stage.

John B. Sebastian could, and should, have done much better and Sebastian has a good reason why it did not kick start his solo career, "What was devastating was to have to stand around for a year, while an album I had made in such a straightforward way, went into litigation and couldn't get on the market. Because this is every bit a fleeting situation as selling fruit. There's only so long that it's fresh, and so you have to get it out then. So, I think it might have done better if it had been released after I'd finished it, rather than a year after that."

To promote *Revelation: Revolution '69*, Kama Sutra used Gersh Enterprises and therefore Don Paulsen; "I did catch up with Joe Butler when I started at the Gersh office. It was sort of like a reunion for me and Joe and I remember taking some publicity pictures and setting up some interviews for him, on that last Spoonful album, but it never really took off." During one such interview to Carol Botwin, that appeared under the headline, "Goodbye To The Lovin' Spoonful", Butler informed, in his best publicity manner, the foundations for the split, "Zally started going crazy first. His attention span makes him flip out quickly. Playing the same songs blew his mind. It wasn't the same as when we were starting out in Greenwich Village together. What used to be fun naturally, we had to start working at."

Butler went on to list other reasons; "It's hard to create new ideas with the same four people...You've heard everybody's story the third time...You become a business enterprise and are busy selling instead of creating." Now married to Leslie (with baby Yancy on the way) Butler's priorities were changing, "Marriage is easier than keeping a group together. At least in marriage there's sex."

Sebastian had already given his first view on the Spoonful split to the counterculture paper *Rat*; "We went through various personality changes. All of us. And personnel changes as well. It was a fantastic experience that was really exciting for two and a half years and then it became boring for a year. I said, "Hey, this is boring." So I left."

Butler knocked all thoughts of The Lovin' Spoonful on the head and tried to forge a career acting. He studied drama with Sharon Chatten of the Actors' Studio and became a charter member of the renowned Circle Theatre Repertory Company. Here he would perform Chekov, Lanford Wilson and experimental material. His first major role was for *Hair*; "To audition for the job I sang that "Revolution" thing and then the ballad "Only Yesterday". Murray Weinstock, who was in The Fifth Avenue Band, played with me and I played the tambourine like a good Hippie. I remember Tommy Smothers was there and he liked that and that's why they took me seriously for Claude, the lead."

Hair had opened at the Biltmore Theatre, New York, after six months off-Broadway in April 1968. The show was the first "rock musical" to play on the "Great White Way". It featured songs about draft-card burning and drugs and also included a controversial nude scene. A year later *Hair* tribes were playing in London, Los Angeles, Copenhagen and elsewhere. Come April '69, its apparent dated nature almost put off Butler's future co-star, folk singer Barry McGuire, from joining the second troupe.

CARMEN CAPALBO and ABE MARGOLIES
present

BARBARA HARRIS   ESTELLE PARSONS   MORT SHUMAN

in

Carmen Capalbo's production
of

BERTOLT BRECHT and KURT WEILL'S

THE RISE AND FALL OF THE CITY OF

mahagonny

featuring
JACK DE LON
DAVE VAN RONK   JOE BUTLER   VAL PRINGLE   DON CRABTREE

English Adaptation by
ARNOLD WEINSTEIN

Musical Director
SAMUEL MATLOVSKY

Original Cast Album on Atlantic Records

Stage Design by ROBIN WAGNER   Costumes by RUTH MORLEY   Lighting by THOMAS SKELTON

Associate Producer
CHARLES ROME SMITH

Associate Conductor THEODORE SAIDENBERG   Production Stage Manager NICK RUSSIYAN

Production Conceived and Directed by
CARMEN CAPALBO

PRESENTED IN ASSOCIATION WITH ATLANTIC RECORDING CORPORATION

ANDERSON THEATRE
66 Second Ave. (4th St.), N.Y. 10003 Phone • OR 4-2350

Ironically his detractor was Sebastian, as McGuire recalled to *Goldmine*, "One morning I was over at Cass Elliot's house, and the phone rang. It was some people from New York looking for me, and they had tracked me down to her house. They said they wanted me to come back and do (a replacement role) a show called Hair. John Sebastian was there and we were sitting out at her swimming pool, and I said, "What's "*Hair*?" He says, "Oh *Hair* is a play about, well, it's kind of about what was happening in the streets of New York a couple of years ago." I said, "Well, I don't want to do something that was happening a couple of years ago. I want to do something happening today."

"Cass is leaning out of the window of the house with the telephone and I said, "Tell him I don't want to do it." She says, "McGuire, why don't you just go back there and see what it's all about?" I flew back and wound up doing *Hair* for the next year." With Butler, or as he was now known, Joseph Campbell Butler as Claude, McGuire as Berger and Heather MacRae as the florist, the new look play impressed the *New York Times* critic, who claimed the new cast better than the original. He singled out Butler, saying of his performance, "Mr. Butler, weaker and more sensitive (than McGuire) has great charm and aplomb."

Butler relished his time on Broadway and enjoyed mingling with a different selection of people, "*Hair* was a really interesting show. My first performances were as part of the tribe doing the big infamous nude scene but when I was Claude, he would be the only one dressed on-stage. I remember one time Salvador Dali came down and was sat in the front row. At the beginning of the show Claude sits there with a flower and all the tribe come up and in slow-motion dance around him. I saw Dali and walked over to him in slow motion and handed him a rose and went back onto the stage in slow motion and sat down again. Of course from then on he invited me to the Plaza where he held court with a mandolier. Andy Warhol's people were there and I would go there with Leslie and just make a whole connection that I never had before."

Butler stayed in the show for the next six months. During his stint he released a solo single on Kama Sutra with the picture sleeve portraying him as Claude from the show. The single was a recut of "Revelation: Revolution '69" about which Butler recalls, "Like a year after, Artie Ripp, God bless him, and I went in and changed one thing. We sang one little lift in two spots and that was it." In reality, there was a completely new vocal but this did not alter the fact that the record is the hardest Spoonful related record to find.

Leaving *Hair*, Butler got a part in the revival of the Kurt Weill and Bertolt Brecht opera, *The Rise And Fall Of The City Of Mahagonny.* Since its premiere in Leipzig in 1930, when the Nazis demonstrated against the collaboration between the Communist and the Jew, *Mahagonny* (spider's web) acquired a mythology amongst 20th century operas. It took cabaret into the opera house and has as many lovers as detractors. In later years, Weill would distance himself from the project.

The first American production was presented by Carmen Capalbo who had previously produced *The Threepenny Opera*. It starred Barbara Harris and Estelle Parsons (*You're A Big Boy Now*) and lower down the credits appeared Sebastian's old Greenwich Village friends Valentine Pringle and Dave Van Ronk, as well as Butler. *Mahagonny* underwent a long and reputedly agonising stretch of rehearsals and previews before it opened, officially, at the off-Broadway Anderson Theatre on April 29, 1970. Apart from the famous "Alabama Song", Weill's score lacked bite or sparkle and the Capalbo production was described as, "Nothing short of a disaster," by the New York Post. There were also problems with the translation. At one point 'money' was rhymed with 'stomach runny!'

Butler liked it; "I played this character Alaska Wolf Joe and there was Jim Mahoney and Jenny the hooker. It was a story about gangsters; it's a parable to Las Vegas and a political piece about total fascism and total anarchy. Interesting piece of music - tough to sing. Val Pringle played Trinidad Moses. We used to have a boxing match in which he kills me but I had to teach him how to punch. He was so bad, we used to go to the gym and work the scene out."

After singing the theme song for an early Alan Alda vehicle, *Jenny*, Butler went back to the theatre to perform in *Soon*, which opened on Broadway just after Christmas, 1970 and closed within a week. The outline of the play was described by the late Peter Allen, who played Henry, to *Goldmine*; "It was supposed to be another *Hair*. It was about this acoustic rock group that's forced to go electric and I played the agent that convinced them. It was terrible, but the cast! There was Barry Bostwick, Joe Butler from The Lovin' Spoonful and Vicki Sue Robinson, who became a disco star. The young lovers, if you can believe it, were Richard Gere and Nell Carter!"

Butler recalls Allen; "Peter and I were friends from being in that cast. We shared a dressing room and he had never done a play and he knew I had done a couple. So there were some things I could work on like I showed him how to put on make-up." Future megastar Gere has since described the time spent doing the play as "Wrist-slitting times in Manhattan." Soon folded faster than its name might imply although, as Butler recalls, "It may have only ran a couple of days but we were there for about two months or so".

Butler then tried to break into films. His only role was as a taxi driver in the film *Born To Win*, notable today only for an early part for Robert De Niro. Starring George Segal and Karen Black *(You're A Big Boy Now)*, the self-indulgent black comedy about heroin addiction had the much more appropriate shooting title of *Scraping Bottom*. Despite an excellent cast, this 1971 United Artists production is rarely seen.

Butler spent all of 1971 in Greenwich Village, renovating an apartment at 105¼ Bank Street. After a couple of tenants had been thrown out, Butler ran into John Lennon and Yoko Ono at his neighbour's (John Cage) house. The Lennons' sublet this apartment off Butler for the next eighteen months and moved in immediately, even before Butler had moved out. Lennon admired the huge thirty foot square bedroom and the fact that there was an emergency exit.

Butler fondly recalls his two weeks with John and Yoko; "He was trying to learn how to type and every morning he would get up and sit very stiffly in the chair and type out the filthiest stuff about him and Yoko - what he was going to do to her. I guess that was the only way he could stick through going through the rigours of learning how to type. I wish I would have saved some of that stuff, 'cause it was hilarious. It was pornographic, but it was funny." Butler recalls that Lennon always told him to keep things relating to the ex-Beatle, as he knew that they would become valuable.

Lennon saw the seedier side of New York for the first time when Butler's previous tenant, paid a visit armed with a handgun. "I had rented my apartment to a bunch of guys and I thought they were on the up and up but the cheque bounced. Then I met some other guy and that cheque bounced. It turned out they were double-teaming me - they were like mini Mafia. Anyway, the Mafia guy was gay and they were renting it out to male hookers, running male hookers out of my apartment! I had made this bed out of two church pews put together and John and Yoko loved it. I don't think they ever changed the mattress, they never knew they were running male hookers out of the God damned place. So Serpico, who was a friend of mine, came down and we went down to kick them out. (Frank Serpico is famous for uncovering mass corruption in the NYC Police Department) When we get there the guy goes on the phone and said, "What am I paying for?" and five minutes later a bunch of cops show up, see Serpico sitting there and they turn white and ran."

Thinking the man and his henchman were friends of Butler's, Lennon let them in only to be held up at gunpoint. Butler: "They started taking stuff out of the apartment and John visibly went to stop them, "Don't take the telly," he says. "I'm watching it." Yoko grabbed John. Later, when Yoko was relating the story, she was shook up about it, she said, "I could have strangled him!" Apparently Lennon thought the whole situation was rather quaint and that it was charming that he had been treated like anyone else. There was a problem, however, as along with Butler's Dali lithograph, the thieves had stolen Lennon's wallet and address book that contained the numbers of (Black Panther) Bobby Seale and Timothy Leary, who had absconded from jail. Fortunately the Lennon's chauffeur had Godfatherly connections and the book was swiftly returned.

The following day the thief was arrested as Butler fondly recalls, "John and I are going over the paper and I said, "Look here is the guy that ripped us off." This guy was busted for having like nine credit cards plus when he gets to the police station he bribes the cops with $28,000 in cash. Then with four or five of them all in one room together, he takes a receipt for the bribery money! So he went up the river for thirteen years and John got his first taste of New York City."

Before leaving the apartment (the Lennons must have loved it as it is pictured on the rear of their *Sometime In New York City* album) Butler remembers he told Lennon that the song he had just recorded, "Happy Xmas (War Is Over)" was a dead ringer to "Stewball" by The Greenbriar Boys, much to Lennon's dismay. On leaving the apartment, Butler migrated West to California and worked as a sound editor making effects for movies as well as a singer on commercials in Hollywood, during 1972/3.

CHAPTER 7 – "APRES LE DELUGE"

Just prior to his performance at Woodstock, Sebastian had met the lady who was to be his new wife; "I met Catherine after six months on the farm. I was living by myself up in the tent, and we met at a sort of a Farm party. We eyed each other for several subsequent parties and got together! We then lived in the tent together. This is a Volkswagen bus tent. It was a beautiful thing to do. We got a large chunk of understanding from living in an eight by eight foot space for a year."

In fact, it was the love from Catherine that rescued a wondering Sebastian from the continuing temptation of heroin and cocaine, as he told *Crawdaddy* in '72, "Ceci pulled me out of a coke rant that could have killed me. I was doing it in a particular infamous, unproductive time so nobody really noticed." The *Crawdaddy* interview is the only one where Sebastian described his drug experiences, although not totally. "See, I'm glad I've tried everything I've tried. Part of it was the mystique. I liked coke better than heroin (laughs). All I learned was: yes, you are like everybody else and it's going to kill you if you don't stop."

Sebastian articulately describes the experience, "The thing is, not too many people like themselves. It's more than just standing around in the living room. It's like taking a piece of pottery with a tiny tiny flaw, and subjecting it to tremendous pressure. Then drawing the conclusion when it breaks that it had a flaw in it. They almost all do! Don't put it in that situation and its fine. There's nothing better to accentuate your neuroses than a good drug habit."

Sebastian stalled when it came to discussing his own cold turkey; "It was easy. Ceci and I were together, we were in love, we'd both been messing around and we said, "Hey. We're going to be in big trouble." This isn't anything I want to talk about in the article. Regardless of how I tell you this story, there will be a certain deliciousness attached to the experience which isn't the case."

April and May of 1970, found Sebastian touring on both coasts of America, where Ralph J. Gleason wrote glowing concert reviews in both *The New York Post* and *Rolling Stone*. After getting married during a trip across America around May of 1970, Sebastian left the farm to play at the Atlanta Pop Festival on the 3rd of July, sharing a bill with Jimi Hendrix, B.B. King and Felix Pappalardi's new group, Mountain. The festival was another chaotic affair, with the local doctors declaring the site a health disaster area due to the, "out of control drug situation." The next day, American Independence Day, a fairly knackered Sebastian was dragged onto the stage at the Woodstock Sound Festival (not THE Woodstock) to play his set, one of 150 in 1970.

This particular performance starts off with Sebastian explaining to the audience, "Everybody seem to have a good time. So I confess, I'm wasted but if you guys send me up a little energy while I'm on, I'll try to get it together." How we know what Sebastian said that day is because Mike Curb had sent an underling to secretly record the concert! Sebastian, to put it mildly, is still furious at this indiscretion. "That was the most unethical thing I have ever experienced; a record company secretly recording me, at a show that I would never have recorded, because, it was in the rain, it was done after I had been at the Atlanta Pop Festival, which inevitably means you stay up all night long waiting to go on, and plod around in the mud. I came to Woodstock because I was told,

"Look, there's a lotta people here in the rain, they've been told you're going to show up." I said, "Okay, I'm still comin'," even though the Pop Festival dragged on a lot longer than I thought. I came up, they did not even have the right amplifier for me, I said, "Hey, this is life, so you go on." But the fact that it was recorded, and then an official label was put on it, without ever any sanction from me, or even hearing the album before it was in the stores, was completely objectionable to me."

Considering Sebastian's condition and the poor equipment, the resulting album oozed with his charisma and is a good performance, representative of his set of the time. Sebastian did not think so and gave out a plea to his fans; "The bad thing about this, is that no one knows it was a bootleg. It's the most shocking piece of music I've ever heard of. I want people to know that the album is not at all representative of my work." He added in a separate interview; "Some unknown shit put that album out but those people fall, because you've got to be honest if you're gonna survive in this life, okay?"

At the time, Sebastian honestly thought that he had rid himself of his former record company, "Mike Curb was holding a Spoonful contract that MGM hadn't seen fit to exercise in three years. I don't see why they wanted to hurt me. If they had pulled this a year ago, I would have been through. If I owed them an album, I gladly would have recorded one with new material. I didn't want to release the same material again."

At the "New York Pop" festival at Downing Stadium, Randall's Island, New York, on July 18th, the gates were crashed and everyone got in free. "community groups" had threatened to call it a free festival, unless they were given some of the proceeds! The festival, which was attended by over 30,000 who had come to see Jimi Hendrix, Steppenwolf, Little Richard and many others, was disrupted when these protesters took over the proceedings and preached to the audience for over four hours.

Sebastian had had enough and just walked out and started his set; "The people didn't want to sit around and listen to all the shit, so I started to play and no one stopped my set. The people who were talking on stage were boring everyone and besides that, they're not even revolutionaries. They're not even radicals. They drive up in daddy's new car and then try to tell people their "revolutionary" ideas."

Whilst still taking the bookings, Sebastian could see that these Woodstock imitation festivals which kept cropping up, were doomed by the infantile "Free Music" movement; "The trouble with a lot of festivals since Woodstock, is that promoters think they can have another Woodstock. It's insane. Woodstock is in the past and besides, it wasn't planned to come off the way it did. It just kinda happened that way. Putting barbed wire around festival grounds is not the way to do it - it's just plain crazy."

After a performance at Shea Stadium for an anti-war festival on the twenty-fifth anniversary of America dropping the atom bomb, Sebastian travelled to the Isle Of Wight for another festival, which would become as ugly as the previous one. The evening before Sebastian was due to perform had been an explosive one, with problems both on and off stage with bands being booed due to sound problems and people without tickets trying to barge their way in.

Sebastian was ignorant of this as he was at his hotel with Jimi Hendrix (a few weeks before Hendrix died), "Jimi and I played acoustic guitars and had a real fine time," Sebastian recalled shortly after. "It was the first time I had really gotten to know and talk to him and I'm glad we had a good time because that's the way I'll remember him." Apparently the pair wrote some songs together, as Sebastian said in 1992, "Jimi said, "I'll be back in New York next week and we'll cut some of this stuff. He was dead before the next week came."

With Catherine in tow, Sebastian arrived backstage to find he was the only performer around and the hostile crowd were ready to explode. Sebastian promptly hit the stage. The ensuing performance was written about under the headline, "The Saviour!" by Barry Plummer in *Disc And Music Echo*: "John B. Sebastian probably saved the Isle Of Wight Festival, 1970, from a complete holocaust of violence, and held the body of the crowd together. A lesser talent, a lesser personality, might have started the day off on the wrong foot, but Sebastian could have played all day and no one would have questioned the absence of the other bands."

After reading the article years later Sebastian said, "It's very nice that somebody documented that because it's true. I remember that I was getting ready to go on and there were tremendous difficulties with sound problems and there were things that weren't finished and I said at a certain point, "Look, I am walking on this stage now and I don't care if this isn't all together. I know crowds and this crowd is not going to wait any longer."

The performance, of over ninety five minutes, gave Sebastian some tremendous positive publicity and endured him to the attending British public from that moment on. Bouncing onto the stage in the same jacket he'd worn at Woodstock, the following set goes down in Spoonful history also, as after performing "Rainbows All Over Your Blues", Sebastian was handed a note. He read it three times before he understood it, then read aloud, "Just ask Zally up on stage." "Zal was in the audience unbeknownst to me," Sebastian recalls. "I didn't even know he was in Europe."

Yanovsky and Yester had both been active in the music world since *Departure*. In 1969, Frank Zappa's subsidiary label to Warner Brothers, Bizarre, created a second outlet called Straight. With his mutual connection through Herb Cohen, Yester managed to secure a contract as a performer alongside wife Judy. Zappa's venture would yield sixteen albums as varied as his own work, with absolutely nothing bordering on straight at all. The first release was Alice Cooper's *Pretties For You* and the second was the extraordinary *Farewell Aldebaran* by Judy Henske and Jerry Yester, produced by Yester and Yanovsky.

The working title for the album had been *Zanzibar* and the cover photo showed the couple with new-born Kate at a burned out house in Topagna Canyon. All the lyrics were written by Henske and the music by Yester, with one notable exception, "Snowblind", which included Yanovsky's name in the credits. "Judy had the words," Yester recalls. "Then one night in the studio, we just started playing it and came up with a live version with (Larry) Beckett playing drums, Zal playing a six string bass, me playing guitar and Judy singing. Then Zal overdubbed a couple of lead guitars and that was the recording that we used on the album."

A fascinating accurate review of *Farewell Aldebaran*, by the late Steve Burgess, that summed up the album intensely, appeared years later in *Dark Star*; "*Aldebaran* is simply one of the most nihilistic, despairing, death-fixated, brutal, beautiful, zomboid and dispirited elpees (sic) you'll ever have to come to terms with. Lady Macbeth's solo album, as it were, since Henske penned the entire morbid lyrics. "Horses On A Stick" likens life to a fool's paradise carousel surrounded by the void; Lullaby conjures up Mervyn Peake's heart of darkness ('The end of the world is a shadowed cowl...listen baby to the night.')

""Three Ravens" dwells on the death of a knight; "Mrs. Connor" (the song is called "One More Time" on the cover but not on the label) is a jazz-lament-poem for a woman who, 'lusts only for the far, dark, deep of grave'; *Rapture* seems to describe death as the ultimate trip, death = ecstasy; "Charity" is about a ghostly clipper, doomed to sail into eternity; and "Farewell Aldebaran" is the converse to The Byrds' "CTA-102", an alien's song to a dead galaxy. Prolonged exposure can only result in psychosis."

The wild and wonderful arrangements on *Farewell Aldebaran* were done at Yester's insistence and became a cause for friction between the Hairshirt team. When asked who actually produced the album Yester replied, "It was Zally and I, but it leaned more toward me. I didn't want to have anybody else's vision on it. I wanted Zally and I to work together but a couple of times Zally wanted to do it a certain way, like on "Rapture", he wanted to do it as a band and I wanted to do it as a piece overdubbed.

"There's basically two ways of recording. One is like a photograph and one is like a painting. The photograph is like a band playing a song and when it's through it's done, basically, except for a little bit here and there. The painting starts from the ground up, layer by layer. I like 'em both. Zally really disagreed on "Rapture" and I stuck to my guns. When it wasn't *Aldebaran*, then Zally and I had no problem at all, we got along really well, our tastes ran along the same lines and we would both bend, give and take a little really well with each other. We worked really well together."

Yester discovered the problems of producing himself for the first time on *Farewell Aldebaran*; "I think I was trying too hard - I don't know what it was. We tried mixing it a few times in L.A., then we thought, "Well, let's go back to New York and use our old engineer that we used on *Alive And Well In Argentina* and maybe that'll work." So we flew to New York and worked all night and didn't get it. I was staying at the Chelsea Hotel and dreamed all night long of mixing *Farewell Aldebaran* and then one by one all the parts were re-done and they were perfect and I woke up and went, "Ahhhh!"

Unfortunately for Yester it really was only a dream; "We got back to L.A. and it still wasn't mixed and I was in the Troubadour bar one night and saw John Boylan. I was talking to him about what we'd just done and he said, "Well listen, maybe what you need is an objective ear. I've got some time booked over at Wally Heider, why don't you come over and I'll engineer it and be the third ear and I'm sure we can get it done. So we did, and mixed it in a couple of hours and that's the version on the album."

The album would be the last collaboration between Yanovsky and Yester, with Yester claiming that his partner had grown tired of living in Hollywood. In any case, Yanovsky had drifted into a new gig as he soon joined the emerging Kris Kristofferson's band as Kristofferson told *Skyline* magazine in 1970, "I met Zal Yanovsky when I was playing the Troubadour in Los Angeles. We played a date together at the new Troubadour in San Francisco, with

Billy Swan on bass. Now Billy had never played bass before, he learnt to play on stage that night! Actually, our whole crew is a pretty weird outfit."

At the time Don Paulsen was the publicity man for Kristofferson and he could see that this new partnership was doomed; "Monument (Kristofferson's label) wanted to showcase Kris in New York and Dick Gersch made a few calls and spoke to Paul Colby and got Kris a gig at the Other End. Colby was smart, he took an option for two more performances, and this first bill was with Carly Simon. Kris needed some back-up musicians but I was very blown away to discover Zal in Kris's band. Somehow Zal was recommended but it was a bad mix. Zal was clowning around on stage too often - it was oil and water. I mean, Kris was an easy-going, good humoured guy but at certain times he had some fairly heavy songs - "Me And Bobby McGee", "For The Good Times" - and at times Zal would solo a little too loud or he would mug to the crowd and ham up a little bit too much." Around this time Kristofferson was called by someone at *Rolling Stone* who tried to get him to fire Yanovsky for past misdemeanours, which only encouraged Kristofferson to keep Yanovsky in the band.

In a case of group unity, Butler went to the show to offer moral support as he had done when Sebastian played his solo gigs in New York. Kristofferson commented on the friction as early as their third booking, the Isle Of Wight Festival, "He and I have these incredible private exchanges on stage, like I'll be singing and when I turn around there he is doing all these rock 'n' roll breaks on guitar, and I say, "Turn it down you son of a bitch!" He just grins and says, "Keep smilin' for the folks boss." Really weird. Zal will stick around as long as the bread, booze and broads last out I think."

At the festival the band were booed off the stage due to sound problems rather than a poor performance. Whilst a hoarse Yanovsky bellows out, "Can you hear?" before the song "Blame It On The Stones", Kristofferson announces, "Hey man, we're going to do this song in spite of anything - except rifle fire!" With Yanovsky laughing, and the crowd hollering, the song still gets finished. A couple of songs later Kristofferson tired of the banging tin cans and left the stage.

Kristofferson spoke about the concert shortly after; "Our spots were nothing to write home about. We had all sorts of problems with the sound equipment and we never had enough rehearsal time. There always seems to be a problem and only now are we starting to get things together. Basically, we are a very new band. We had no rehearsals before our Bitter End gig and virtually none before the festival. But it is starting to happen now. A weird crew we may be but I think it could all work out surprisingly well." When the misunderstanding was rectified, the band played a full set the day after Yanovsky joined up with Sebastian.

On stage at the Isle Of Wight Festival, Sebastian and Yanovsky first played "Blues In The Bottle", alternating lead vocals. After a ragged "Do You Believe In Magic", the pair went into "Boredom", a strange selection, as Yanovsky had not played on the record. Yanovsky then sang lead on "Bald Headed Lena" before the pair finished on, ironically the song that split them apart, "Darling Be Home Soon". Sebastian then re-appeared by himself for two encores, finishing off saying, "You plumb wore my ass out. Be beautiful, take care of yourself...share with your neighbour...smoke a joint for me!"

Backstage, *Zig Zag* magazine's John Tobler tried to interview Yanovsky, but their conversation was broken off when the easily distracted Yanovsky saw somebody across the other side of the tent, where the interview was taking place. "He only gave me half a dozen sentences," Tobler recalls. "He was a wacky fellow."

Yanovsky's mere presence was enough for a different *Zig Zag* journalist; "Yanovsky was ubiquitous, he became a symbol of permanence. He was there on his feet to applaud Joni singing "Woodstock", he was there outside the refreshment tent with a bottle of Teacher's on the table talking to anybody and everybody. He was there all the time, and you felt that if he was there, somewhere, the festival would go on, and that if he went away, it would collapse. Even the fact that a news-sheet referred to him as "Zolly Minovsky" could not diminish the effect of his presence."

A few weeks afterwards, Sebastian explained how happy he was with the performance at the Isle Of Wight, "If I ever want to release a live album, it will be from the set from there. Everything went right; it was great playing with Zally, it was a great festival and a lot of fun." Coming off the island into London, Sebastian recorded an *In Concert* performance for the BBC, as well as performing a chaotic set at a free concert in Hyde Park, where amongst the rain showers, the crowd asked, "Where's Zally?" He impressed the critics again with this performance and also the omnipresent Hell's Angels, with a rip-roaring rendition of "Johnny B Goode", complete with Chuck Berry duckwalk across the stage.

Sebastian spent some of his time in Europe with his father in Rome or staying at the home of Pete Townshend, with whom he struck up a friendship. Townshend even wrote a song about Sebastian, "Mr. Tie-Die". Commenting on Sebastian's on stage apparel, Townshend once informed the press, "Even his underpants are tie-dyed!" Sebastian also spent some time with the Who's drummer and was absorbed by his life-style, as he said at the time, "Last night I sat down after an evening out with Keith Moon, during which we got extremely drunk, and I got an idea. It was a good one and I was sure it was a good song. Trouble is, I can't remember the damned thing now!"

Back in New York, Sebastian hit the TV promotional circuit appearing on the *Dick Cavett, Flip Wilson* and *David Frost Shows.* Frost invited Sebastian on a second time and on this occasion Sebastian Senior and Junior shared the stage. After recollections on how each other took up music, the pair played a beautiful rendition of "Amy's Theme" on harmonicas.

With the acceptance Sebastian was receiving from his audiences, alongside the annoyance of being bootlegged by his former record label, Sebastian, against his better judgement, decided to record some shows for a sanctioned live release. "It did serious damage as far as the, you know, a sequence is precious in an artist's career, a sequence in which you release records. Right after *John B.* I was in the process of beginning *The Four Of Us* and having the live boot come out made me want to put a decent live album out because I was so unhappy with this...with the (Fender) Champ amplifier, I mean, it was just too silly. I didn't even know it existed, you have to understand; it was in the stores. So, I thought that it was entirely appropriate that Mike Curb would end up in politics."

Cheapo-Cheapo Productions Presents Real Live John Sebastian was perhaps overemphasising the fact that this was essentially a solo performance, although Paul Harris played piano on some songs. Played in its entirety, the album is a joy with Sebastian answering calls for his old songs willingly and even digging out "Rooty Toot" at one point. But in essence, here was yet another re-hash of a few familiar tunes ("Blue Suede Shoes", "Goodnight, Irene") and nine tracks that you had already heard the Spoonful do and no really new songs.

A promotional single came out that captured the spirit of the album in snippets which helped lift the album to a peak of number 75, far higher than the MGM album, but really the album was something that could have waited. The MGM version was a better collection of songs and an honest concert, whereas *Real Live* was bits and snippets from four separate shows, two of the venues being Davis College and Chapman College. One reviewer stated, "Instead of concentrating on playing good rock music, John now directs his energies towards being as groovy as he can be."

On the other side of the coin, Sebastian answered his critics, who were saying that he was keeping his feet on firm ground, by releasing *The Four Of Us* no less than four months later. Taking a different stance, Sebastian put together a diary in song form of a trip across America that lasted over sixteen verses and the same number of minutes. Sebastian described the innovative idea for side two of the album, "It's a story about a trip that Catherine and me, and two friends of ours called Bart and Carolina Carpinelli, made across the States, but we took a strange route, going from New York, down to Florida, then across in a sort of a smile shape to Los Angeles.

"The journey took six weeks, and we just waddled along at thirty five miles an hour in our old GMC truck. Along the way, we made several stopovers and they're described in sections of the song. It was during a time that I very definitely needed to take a re-assessment of my life, and Catherine and I had just met and fallen in love and so the trip was serving a real purpose for us...it was a good way of getting to know each other. There was no radio and we were driving eight hours a day, talking to each other all the time...it was a peculiar type of therapy. But the GMC truck was just about dead by the time we wheeled into Los Angeles!"

The first side of *The Four Of Us* was a standard collection of songs including the delightful "Apple Hill", which is a reminiscence about the children's summer camp Sebastian had stayed at in New Hampshire, also the basis for "Did You Ever Have To Make Up Your Mind". "Well, Well, Well" was an extension of the jam "Live And Let Live" that Sebastian had played on with Hendrix and Stills on the Timothy Leary album. "I Don't Want Nobody Else", the other notable song, like most of the album, was about Catherine.

Sebastian rightly stands by the album today, "That was what I wanted to put out right then and there's things that are called bad moves by accountants that aren't called bad moves by the artists and that was the case with this project." Indeed, the album and its lack of success (chart peak, number 93) meant that Reprise started to lose interest in Sebastian. Tellingly, only one review, a good one surprisingly, was located to use in this book, a fact Sebastian addressed in *Crawdaddy*.

"I've been chronically unhappy with albums. With what the final product was. Then I took the bull by the horns, worked by myself for a year, and only the audiences have noticed. Not the rock and roll magazines. I made an album after that (*Cheapo-Cheapo*), I was hitting a peak as a solo performer, and I made an album out of two peak live performances, yet the album went relatively unnoticed. It wasn't the kind of thing that could be played on the air because it was a two hour show. Taken out of context, it was an isolated tune with an audience responding unusually. There wasn't much attention. Same thing on the last album about *The Four Of Us*, yet I was really talking about it for myself. People noticed, but nobody reviewed it!"

With few promotional duties to perform, Sebastian arrived at Heathrow Airport with a heavily pregnant Catherine in early October '71, for a week's holiday in London. A hotel was booked but Keith Moon had other ideas. Moon met the Sebastians at the airport, posing as a chauffeur, in his pink Rolls Royce and insisted that the couple stay at his house in the country. In a case of mild kidnap, Sebastian was then driven to Surrey University, Guildford, for The Who's warm up gig before a major tour. Half way through the set, Sebastian was dragged onto the stage and made to play, using Townshend's tuning harmonica!

During the week, *Zig Zag* managed to interview Sebastian. In an interesting chat, it was clear Sebastian was tiring of the Spoonful questions, but he still managed to have a dig at his old adversary when he was asked whether he would play with Zal again, "No, man, not really. I'll tell you what though; one day Zally came by to see me in New York - "I got it, man," he said. And this was only the second time I'd seen him in two years, "We put the Spoonful back together for a big bang-up tour...thirty cities in twenty days - I mean, you wouldn't mind playing with Joe Butler again for just a few weeks...we could teach him to play drums again." I told him to get lost, or words to that effect, but he wasn't really being serious, he just wanted to see how far I'd go along."

The title for the Sebastian piece in *Zig Zag* was, "A Potted History of Odd-Socks Knox...Alias John Sebastian." This was in reference to an in-joke that had surfaced during the recording of Peter Gallway's latest project, *Ohio Knox*; "Well Peter Gallway's first solo album was conceived in Cyrus Faryar's living room at the Farm, which he converted into a studio. I played a bit on that album, Catherine played tambourine and there were a lot of other Knox's on it too. The Knox family is a very extensive family - the only requirement you need to become a part of it is to think of an original Christian name beginning with an O, then you can join. Peter Gallway is Ohio Knox, I am Orville and Catherine is Orlisa (under which names they did *The Four Of Us* trip - the other two were Oscar and Olive Knox). Keith Moon is Orchestra Knox, John Entwistle is Ox Knox and Pete Townshend is Overall Knox, but the list goes on and on."

The album has Gallway using the same musicians as Sebastian had on *The Four Of Us* and who would subsequently become Sebastian's band - Paul Harris, Ray Neapolitan and Dallas Taylor. Gallway's manager was even Cavallo. Like the Fifth Avenue Band, Ohio Knox met with no commercial success whilst being a fantastic piece of work. A few weeks after the release of "Well, Well, Well" as a single, photographer Roger Kemp left Cornwall to visit America, where John Sebastian saved him from a nasty injury. "I went to America for a holiday at Christmas 1971," Kemp recalls. "I tried to cover the cost by writing and photographing for teen magazines over there. I think it was the promotions girl at Warner Brothers who suggested I interview John Sebastian. I don't drive so I was glad to be driven by anyone. This twenty five year old mentally deranged divorcee drove me - we'd been introduced at a party a week earlier. She fancied me and hoped I'd marry her. When she found out during the interview that I planned to return alone to St. Ives, she went for her car threatening to run over me. John Sebastian realising her intention rugby tackled her and saved my life." This story sounds a bit far-fetched to be true but it is one Sebastian verified to this author.

According to Kemp, Sebastian was a little strapped for cash during his stay, "Another interesting memory is that he was late getting home for the interview. He'd been delayed at a hospital where he'd been donating blood. Apparently it is very expensive in California and Sebastian was having cash flow problems at the time. He had entered an experiment where blood could be exchanged for blood. By donating some of his, his wife could have some and they wouldn't have to pay so much medical fees."

Ben Sebastian was born in early January 1972. Sebastian had already announced his intentions for the future after the birth; "I'm going to take a few days off and stare at it." Sebastian did more than that and would not release an album for another two and a half years.

After the Isle Of Wight Festival, Kristofferson summed up his future plans; "I just want to write some songs, have some laughs and make some music with the guys. It's an incredible life and there's always Zally around to dynamite things up. He's just "Travellin' with the boss," having a good time, and living in the hope of getting a little raise." With no agent, no manager and no ties, Kristofferson had the ideal set-up but he soon tired of the larger than life character.

Inevitably, in March of 1971, after the first night of a ten-day engagement at the Gaslight in the Village, Kristofferson fired Yanovsky, "following a dispute about the music Zal was playing." It got worse for Kristofferson when Yanovsky's replacement could not make the last gig of the run, which ended up with an exhausted Kristofferson offering refunds to the audience, including his heroes Chet Atkins and Floyd Cramer.

Before he was fired, Yanovsky had performed live with Kristofferson and his band on "Lovin' Her Was Easier" for *The Johnny Cash Show*. Don Paulsen sums up Yanovsky's second sacking; "Zal was his own worst enemy in some cases and I was sorry to see that because I think Zal was an incredible guitar player and a wonderful personality. I wasn't surprised that after not that long, Kris decided that Zal had to go." Yanovsky's next move of note was to become an actor in a musical, albeit one with a difference.

By October 1972, the *National Lampoon* magazine had created its own niche in the satirical press market. In a plan to boost the public's awareness of the magazine, two of its writers, Tony Hendra and Sean Kelly, began writing a play based around parodying one of the cultures' sacred cows - Woodstock. The title for this play, *Lemmings*, stemmed from a *New York Times* editorial that blasted those who went to the festival, describing them as lemmings that would march to their deaths in the sea.

There were some easy contemporary targets to parody - Bob Dylan, James Taylor, Crosby, Stills, Nash and Young, not forgetting Joe Cocker! The person who did the best take on Cocker's spasmodic stage manner was John Belushi, who would make his theatrical debut in the show, alongside another future *Saturday Night Live* comedian, Chevy Chase and future Spinal Tap member Christopher Guest. All the cast needed to be fairly accomplished musicians, leading to Yanovsky securing a part in the play (ironically Butler turned down Chase's drumming role).

The show eventually opened at the Village Gate Theatre in New York on January 25, 1973. It ran for 350 performances before closing on November 25 the same year. It's hard to believe Yanovsky played all of these dates. For the play Yanovsky co-wrote the Donovan parody "Nirvana Banana" and performed a Dr. John routine. Yanovsky's role in the play is not clear as the existing reviews all centre on Belushi and Chase. By November 30th *Lemmings* started to tour the country (there is a photo online of Belushi and Yanovsky playing the Omaha Civic Auditorium on this date) and Steve Boone recalls seeing Yanovsky in the show in Baltimore and Washington and remembers him as, "really funny." Yanovsky quit the play shortly before it was recorded for posterity as, according to Boone; "He left in a huff, real unexpected. I think he got pissed off with Chevy Chase." Yanovsky did appear on the next *National Lampoon* record, however, as he can be heard as a crazy Russian introducing segments from the Watergate hearings! The album, *National Lampoon's Missing White House Tapes*, released in 1974, would be the last recording Yanovsky would make, apart from a brief voice-over role (as Barbarian #2) in the 1981 Canadian animated movie *Heavy Metal*.

In the late seventies, with his remaining money from the Spoonful settlement, Yanovsky opened a restaurant in Kingston, Ontario, called Chez Piggy. His credentials for opening a restaurant? "I ate in them," he told *Rolling Stone* in 1985. Situated downtown, near the historic Kingston waterfront (according to a 1984 tourist guide) the renovated Georgian livery stable would become Yanovsky's business interest from then on. When it opened, Yanovsky would cook in front of the diners, but after a few too many occasions where he threw food at them, he retreated behind the scenes. It is believed that he was concurrently working as a director/producer for Canadian Broadcasting (on *Magistrate's Court,* a forerunner of *Judge Judy*) and was the music consultant for the Imax documentary *Hail Columbia* about the space shuttle, during the first couple of years of Chez Piggy's opening.

In another poor career move, Yester turned down the chance to become a staff producer for Elektra in the latter part of 1969. There were two good reasons, however. One was his on/off relationship with president Jac Holzman, the other a very welcome cheque from Warner Brothers for over $4000 that Yester had just received, due to one of the tracks he produced on *Renaissance* turning up on The Association's *Greatest Hits* album, which stayed in the charts for over two years.

Come early 1970 the money was running out and Yester was kicking his heels in L.A. when Sebastian came to town. "I saw John at the Troubadour a couple of years after the Spoonful and he said, "Oh, man, there's so much in my heart I want to talk to you about." Then, unbeknownst to him, I was invited to the same party he was and we sat on a couch for a couple of hours." Yester then shrugged his shoulders to express the lack of communication between the pair, before continuing, "Nothin' really shakin'. I can understand that, though, having those feelings but maybe not being able to express them at the time." On being asked that this stand-off seemed strange as the pair were good friends Yester replied, "We were, but more - it was different after. I mean, those early days in the Village, it just wasn't the same. It was drawing heavily on those days, then, I guess, the bank account was polished off. Even so, I still have nothing but good feelings about John."

Later in the same year Yester managed to gain some production work from the remains of The Turtles but the group would split up before releasing the material. The recordings remained unreleased until the group's resurgence in the '80s when released as *Shell Shock* (and Yester is still waiting for his cheque!) Mark Volman, from The Turtles, recalled the circumstances to John Tobler in the late '70s; "Yester came to us after his bout with the Spoonful, after he had left Koppelman-Rubin. We had just left them too, so it was a mutual GGGHHRRRR!

They were a publishing company that owed us and the Spoonful. We started the last album, *Shell Shock* with Jerry Yester. It was never finished because we said, "That's it."

The next significant production work for Yester came through the Straight connection when he chose to work with a Tim Buckley wannabe, Tim Dawe. The work was only taken due to Yester's hardship as he readily admits, "This is an album I talked Herbie into doing because I needed the money." With some money behind them, Yester and Henske formed a band with John Seiter (ex-Spanky & Our Gang and Turtles) on drums, Ray Brown on bass and Craig Doerge (say "Durgee") on piano. Doerge had played on the Straight album by the GTO's, *Permanent Damage* and alongside Yester on The Association's Russ Giguere solo effort, *Hexagram 16*. Taking their name from Orson Welles's final mutterings in *Citizen Kane*, Rosebud took off slowly at first, with an attempt to record a few demos at a cheap studio almost splitting the group up before they started.

"We booked to do some demos at this place called Protone on Santa Monica Boulevard," Yester recalls. "It had this tacky wall with a window cut out between the booth and the studio but it had no glass, yet the guy still pressed the button and talked to us with the talk-back. I said, "Could you stop doing that? We're sitting right here!" He had this awful equipment, just this awful sounding, buzzing equipment and this piano that looked like the world had thrown up on and Craig says, "I'm supposed to play this?" I said, "Let's just do the best we can and this guy mixed down the thing and we almost broke up. "We sounded so bad. and everything sounded so bad it was like, "What are we kidding ourselves for? This is ridiculous, this is awful, it sucks." So the next day all the members came over and I said, "Look, before we break up and decide that we should get into real estate or something, let's just do an overdub version of "Le Soleil"," which we did in my living room. We ping-pong'd it and played it back until we said, "All right! All right! Burn that old tape!"

Getting the deal they needed from Straight, Rosebud started to record. The first track attempted, "Panama", became the opener for the record but only after some radical reworking as Yester explains, "The song was originally called "What's The Matter With Sam", a horrible song that Judy and I had written. It was the first song that Rosebud ever worked up, so we had some kind of weird sentimental attachment to it. We recorded it on the demo that got us the Warner's deal. In the studio we said, "This song sucks but we can't let this go." So Judy sat down and wrote another lyric for it, which was "Panama" and I changed the music a little bit to fit. We just loved it. "The basic track was done with me playing bass and John Seiter playing African drums. A strange basic track but it was very tight. Then Craig overdubbed a piano and John overdubbed lots of percussion and then I had the idea of having it start with somebody walking down a lonely street into a night club. I had lots of tapes of stereo Troubadour bar left over from Pat Boone's album, that we used in there and you can hear people saying every once in a while, "Get it on, Pat!"

During the sessions bassist David Vaught replaced Brown. The finished album is far more clean and conventional compared with *Farewell Aldebaran* and is the shining moment from any ex-Spoonful. Every track is a winner, from Yester's frail, near hysterical vocals on "Lorelei" through Doerge's deep version of Henske's autobiographical *Western Wisconsin* to the lady herself's vocals (which have been compared to something like a cross between Buffy Sainte-Marie and George Melly) on the harmony filled "Le Soleil". The lyrics for the songs come from Henske again but this time Doerge also contributes, particularly on *Salvation*. The production is Yester's best effort to date and he himself would acknowledge the engineer, Richie Moore.

Typically, with the album in the can, there had to be something to get in the way of it being a success. In this case it was the collapse of Yester's marriage; "Well, what happened was, Judy and I broke up. There's a sad story that goes with it, but Judy went off with Craig. It was a long time in happening and it got kinda crazy at the end. The last gig we played was some place down south of L.A. I knew in my subconscious it was happening and this was the last day, so I said, "Fuck it" and I went to the mission at San Juan Capistrano and I was drinking brandy all day, throwing them down, got real drunk, went back to the club and someone came up and said, "Oh, here's a present" and gave me a bag of cocaine. I got a screwdriver and was shovelling it in and was in wonderful shape to do a performance then. I go on-stage and I looked over at Judy and Craig and I said, "What am I doing here?" I put down my guitar and was gonna make a real dramatic exit, when I tripped on my guitar cord, spun off the stage, turned around three times and I landed in a chair in the front row, facing the group and I just said, "Whoa, I'll just stay and watch the show." And that's how it ended."

With Yester gone, Rosebud was finished, although the manager tried his best to continue as Yester remembers, "The album was really liked by Warner Brothers. Two weeks after Judy and I were officially split up, the manager, who was The Association's manager, Pat Colecchio, tried to keep the four other members together and said, "Why don't we replace Jerry and keep going?" Johnny and David didn't want to, they were real faithful to me. So it died there. A few days later I was walking out of the parking lot at Warner Brothers and Mo Ostin (president of W.B.) pulled up and said, "We loved the album, we're going to give it a big push, this is gonna go all the way." I said, "Judy and I just broke up, Mo." So they just pulled all the push."

Yester went back to Elektra to produce an uninspiring album by the duo Aztec Two-Step, released in June '72, notable only for a brief reunion between Yester and Sebastian, who was in L.A. the day the song "So Easy" was recorded. Yester started a follow up album that was canned when Elektra was taken over in 1973. By then he was busy with another of Herb Cohen's clients, Tom Waits. "Matter of fact, from the first day that he came over to my house, I mean, I just loved him," remembers Yester. "He had called from the little store on the corner, he says, "Where's your house?" I took the phone out onto the porch and said, "Turn around to your left, see that guy on the porch waving at you? That's me, come over here!" He came over and I had my gold baby grand piano and tape recorder set up and said, "Why don't you just play your songs?" He sat down and played. Marlene (Yester's new wife) is in the bathroom washing the tub and looks out and says, "Who is this guy?" and came out and sat down and we just listened to him and said "He's too much, this guy." He's a great talent, the Hoagey Carmichael of our time."

Yester produced Waits's debut album, the superb *Closing Time*, which included the now familiar songs "Martha", "Ol '55" and "I Hope That I Don't Fall In Love With You". Although a great album, Waits does not appreciate the recording. In 1976 the singer, composer, actor told John Platt of his differences with Yester, "We were pulling against each other on the first album. If he had his way he would have made it a more folk-based album, and I wanted to hear upright bass and muted trumpet. I was just a kid in the studio. Jerry had been round the block, he knew what to do, and at the same time had his own specific ideas. He got very emotionally involved with the whole project, and I was just overwhelmed to be recording at all."

The next project of note for Yester was some arrangements for a version of Prokofiev's *Peter And The Wolf* narrated by Rob Reiner. "It was yet another remake," Yester recalls. "It was actually a project that was Zally's idea and (producer) Carl Gottlieb was around when Zally had the idea and I guess they were going to do it together and then Carl decided to go on without Zally and called him up and said, "Well, do you want to do it, Zally?" And

Zally said, "I can't do it now." So he went ahead and I think Zally told him to go fuck himself or something. He doesn't like Carl anymore. Carl became such a jerk on that album, I mean I really used to like him a lot but it just soured me and the album was a nightmare. It was a monumental project to try and remain faithful to Prokofiev; my favourite music is his first violin concerto. There are some parts of it that I really like a lot, other parts, you know, not good." The album would mark the end of a prolific period for Yester and he would spend the next few years sporadically producing and recording (notably on the Spanky & Our Gang's last album, *Change* and Tina Turner's country album, *Turn The Country On*) whilst bringing up his family, with daughter Lena arriving in December '75.

Boone's idyllic life-style cruising around the Caribbean lasted for a good two years before tragedy struck. In 1972, having broken up from his first wife, Boone was visiting Long Island when he received a disturbing message from the Islands. "I got a phone call - "Peter's dead." Boone's childhood buddy had become over interested in heroin (a drug Boone claims he never touched!) and had died of an overdose whilst living on Boone's sailboat. "It was ugly, man," Boone recalls. "The cops were on me like stink on shit. They thought I was bringing heroin in. So, at that point, I got out of the St. Thomas Harbour and moved the boat to a remote part of the island and started living a kind of vagabond life, not really in the mainstream. I stayed away."

Here the devastated and disconsolate Boone fell into a lucrative new and illegal business venture; "I got hooked up with some guys who owned sailboats too. They were sailing out to those islands off South America on dive charters and they'd come back with, like, 200 pounds of real good Colombian marijuana. They (the locals) were giving it to them! This was the first time it was ever being done, nobody had ever heard of sailing it back. At that time it was all coming from Mexico. "So a friend of mine pulled into the harbour one day and said, "Steve, come here, look at this." I said, "Man, that's the best high quality stuff, where'd you get it?" He'd made fifty thousand bucks in addition to his dive charter. So I got to know the circle of people that were doing this, it was all marijuana smuggling, none of the cocaine smuggling, no guns and it was pretty exciting. All the people that were doing it were either returning Vietnam vets or they were college educated, middle-class people. There were no low-lifes."

Boone met percussionist Trudy Morgal in late 1973, not telling her his surname for six months, keeping up the anonymity he was enjoying. The pair opened the wildly popular Grass Shack Club (which was a real grass shack) although this was soon shut down due to the obvious potential fire hazard. Close friend Guy Phillips from The Oxpetals visited Boone and looks back fondly at this period, "We lived on Steve's sailboat out in the Caribbean together and formed a kinda funky R&B band. We used to sail around for a few days and play for a few days in a thatched roofed shack. We would play there and sail around the rest of the time - we were kind of drop-outs in the early '70s."

Boone and Morgal then left the Islands, around the middle of 1974, to live in Baltimore, where Morgal had previously played in a band. The fact that Baltimore is a huge harbour near the head of Chesapeake Bay was no coincidence as Boone explains, "I would help them get it (the marijuana) into the country. I would go and meet them at a dock with a truck, unload and take the truck and drive it up to New England. Sometimes I would set-up deals where I could sell, oh, a hundred pounds here or a hundred pounds there. So I started to make some pretty good money."

Boone was now stuck in Baltimore as his boat had gone down near Venezuela. A trio to whom Boone had sold half-share of the boat to, had attempted to sail the unseaworthy vessel across a rough stretch of the Caribbean in a vain attempt to score the easy money. "I knew what they were going to try and do," Boone recalls. "They didn't make it and they all - I don't know what happened to them - they disappeared. They knew the risk they were getting into." In Baltimore Boone and Morgal formed a mainly cover band, Blanche. On a trip to a studio to record, Boone flipped when he discovered that the state of the art studio was due to be scrapped. For once in his life, the normally subdued Boone sprang into action and secured a lease and long term contract from the owners, International Telecom. Boone then bought the studio and relocated it on a 135-foot houseboat in Baltimore's inner harbour, calling it the Blue Seas Studio.

Desperate for clients, Boone phoned Cavallo and on the promise of supplying special long segments of time, Cavallo sent down one of his new clients to record their fourth album. This group was the re-formed Little Feat and their lead singer was Lowell George, a man who needed time to compose as Boone recalls, "He would be alone in the studio for hours at a time, with his rhythm machine and some instruments and listen all day long for ideas. Then he would call the band in and they played what Lowell told them." The resulting album, *Feats Don't Fail Me Now*, also included Emmylou Harris who would record at Blue Seas, as would a few other notables as the ever-present Guy Phillips recalls, "We did work with Emmylou Harris, Sonny Terry, which is the favourite thing I've done, half of *Pressure Drop* with Robert Palmer and a guy from Earth, Wind & Fire." Add to the list Bonnie Raitt, Ricky Skaggs and The Seldom Scene and the future was looking bright for Boone. Boone would choose this successful moment in his life to try and bring his old friends together to record at his flourishing studio.

On a trip to New York in November 1974, Boone gave an interview to the *Village Voice*, where he hinted at the possibility of a Lovin' Spoonful reunion. Apparently both Yanovsky and Butler were interested in the opportunity. The interview soon made the headlines in England, "Spoonful Re-form: LP, Tour," stated the *New Musical Express*, but it was not properly discussed as Boone now admits, "It was really only musings, rather than any definite plans that we had made at the time." In any case Boone had more than enough work for the next three years, playing in his band (and occasionally with friend Scott Cunningham and his Blues Band) and a lot more as he remembers, "I did some commercials as a writer and some production work with new bands starting out in Baltimore, helping them do their demos and getting them through the first stages of getting contacts."

Leaving Hollywood behind, Butler then appeared on the scene; "With Steve and Skip we formed a company called Stunning Incorporated and we had Bunky Horack, this very talented guy who had won jazz and arranging awards, with us. The only reason he suffered me was he couldn't play drums, he couldn't sing and he wasn't a lyricist. So I wrote stuff like, 'Here's to Pittsburgh, here's to Channel two, here's to things we all get down to.' Or, 'You can get it all right, set yourself up, you can stay up all night, here's to Pittsburgh!' Fucking jingles - whatever." Still on the scene, Guy Phillips remembers Butler being a healthy asset to their work, "The stuff we did was radio and TV commercials - movie themes, local bank ads. We used Butler on the commercials. He was a good singer for that stuff, he could really sing over himself very well. He did a lot of vocal overdubs and some of the speaking parts, though mostly they used DJ's."

Butler recalls how well Boone's venture of discovering local talent was going, "Steve was good at that, he had a good networking thing, although I don't think he was making any money because it was Baltimore. Cavallo threw

him some work but I don't think he got on with Maurice White (of Earth, Wind & Fire). Something happened and Maurice didn't want to record there."

The lull in recording bookings would become quite significant when on Christmas Day, 1977, the barge sunk under very dubious circumstances. Speculation that a rival studio had a hand in the skulduggery has never been disproved as Boone recalls, "Nobody really knows. It is an interesting story because it was an old wooden barge that had been converted to a houseboat. It was never again going to take to the sea, so they only corked it about a foot above the waterline and for the remaining three feet up until the deck level, it was not corked.

"But they had these two massive pumps. If one failed the other would still be able to cope with any amount of bilge leakage. Now we really don't know why it happened, I was out of town, but one pump went out earlier in the day, it was Christmas night, so they had no way of getting a repair man in and apparently sometime after three in the morning of the 26th, the second pump went out."

The authorities presumed it was an insurance fiddle until they were informed that the barge was not insured! "Interesting stories abound," Boone states. "One was that it had been sabotaged by either a competitor of ours or the owner of the barge we were leasing it from. In a local bar a girlfriend of ours overheard some guys bragging that they had sunk the Blue Seas Studio, but the conclusion was that the sinking was of an undetermined cause. We managed to salvage everything, except for the grand piano, and paid off our bank loans." Gone forever were a large amount of tapes including some Spoonful outtakes, Lowell George demos and Little Feat live recordings. Boone had to start all over again.

In February of 1972, Sebastian released a new single as a protest against the nuclear explosion that had occurred near Amchitka Island the previous November. The single was a revelation for Sebastian, as he said at the time to *Crawdaddy*, "Give Us A Break" is the beginning of a new time for me. For one thing I produced it myself. It was a step up because it was doing something out of a growing self-confidence, rather than doing it because you knew you could. I was always produced by somebody else. I was always afraid to be the ears on both sides of the glass at once, and thought it would be impossible. As it turns out I'm working with an engineer (Fritz Richmond, from The Jim Kweskin Jug Band) who makes it possible. He's a musician and a very sensitive guy about making records."

The single is quite rare these days as a result of its lack of promotion, a fact that still riles Sebastian, "It was one of those Warner Brothers' oddities. I wrote the song, it was topical but I think they were nervous about the idea. That was one of those cases of a record company having say over an artist and I can't make people put things out."

After a relatively quiet 1972, with Sebastian still playing solo, he felt the urge to put together a band again at the beginning of '73; "My first answer had been to call up Ry Cooder and Jim Keltner and a few people like that. The first people I tried to do this with actually were Paul Harris, Dallas Taylor and Kenny Altman because at that point soloing had more or less exhausted itself, as far as the possibilities ahead were concerned. The potential was there and we started to make *The Four Of Us* which I wanted to be a band album. I wanted to find the right combination and then move on but everyone in the group was horrified, as had become the tradition among musicians."

With Taylor and Harris leaving to play on the Ohio Knox album, then joining up in Manassas with Stephen Stills, Chris Hillman and others and Altman venturing to New York to star in a movie, Sebastian used up the time without a band wisely, almost forming a supergroup in the process. With Rothchild producing The Everly Brothers attempted resurgence album for their new label, RCA, Sebastian gave the pair a song inspired by his life with Catherine which became the title for the album; *Stories We Could Tell*. The song was even recorded in Sebastian's living room and is the highlight of a mediocre album. The brothers were soon to go their separate ways and Phil Everly has since described the sessions as, "hell on earth."

Afterwards, Sebastian started to sing with Phil Everly and the pair lined up a few gigs. They tried to assemble a band without much success. One person they tried to get was Lowell George who shared the same manager as Sebastian, Bob Cavallo. George once told *Zig Zag*; "John played me a cassette of him and Phil, and Phil had this beautiful high voice and John had a contralto, and I had a tenor that fit right in the middle. It was a nice vocal blend. But in fact, money was the prime motivation for that little scene and I don't think I could have handled it. Money moves me but I don't think I could have handled it." Other names touted in the rock press included Ry Cooder and Kenny Altman.

In the end, Ry Cooder became horrified about the project, Altman didn't want the gig and Everly had second thoughts and abandoned the whole thing. A stranded Sebastian went back on the road but the critics were tiring of him, with a typical review of the time running the headline, "Nothing New From Sebastian." Undeterred, Sebastian put together a new band with Ray Neapolitan on bass, Ronnie Koss on guitar and teenager Kelly Shanahan on drums. This line-up (with Jerry McEwen coming in for Koss) was observed as, "providing perhaps Sebastian's best backup ever," by a *Rolling Stone* critic. With this impetus, Sebastian and his new band began to record a new album.

Sebastian became his own spin-doctor when the sessions started, as he told *Sounds*, "We've got half an album recorded. It's been going for about three months and it's going beautifully. We've almost recorded an album's worth of material and it's a luxury I've never had before. In fact it's the happiest time of my life." In reality the sessions collapsed and Sebastian realised he needed to make a few calls to his former partners, whom he had sacked seven years earlier.

A more honest Sebastian reflected on what really went on behind the scenes; "You might construe that the album took a long time to record but that isn't strictly so. What happened was, after I got six tunes down I cancelled out because I was producing the album and I didn't like the way it was sounding. I threw the album away at that point and called up my old friend Erik Jacobsen, suggesting that there might be something worth getting into together. Two weeks later he called back agreeing with the idea and suddenly it became very business-like."

Jacobsen's reasoning for joining the project were purely financial and his apathy towards the material is quite clearly illustrated; "John was still working with Cavallo at the time and I was doing nothing and they said, "Well, we'll give you some money." It's kind of listenable. We brought Zally in, who was already starting to be unable to tune his guitar. We couldn't use anything - he couldn't play."

The resulting album was titled *Tarzana Kid* as Sebastian and family had moved to Tarzana when young Ben started to walk and suddenly living on a cliff did not seem to be a good idea. The album only had two new Sebastian compositions alongside oft heard songs including "Singing The Blues," "Sitting In Limbo" and two more re-recordings from the Spoonful catalogue. Even two songs recorded for the project but which remained unreleased were covers (Eric Von Schmidt's "Catch It While You Can" and Jimmy Cliff's "Johnny Too Bad"). All in all there was not too much for the contemporary critics to get excited about and as a unit they slaughtered *Tarzana Kid*.

Bob Cavallo, who was now overseeing Orleans, Weather Report and Earth, Wind & Fire, gave a rare, illuminating interview just after the release of the album, where he put the figures to Sebastian's lack of creativity, "John wrote a hundred songs in three years and then twenty five the next four. His interest just levelled off." This was noticed primarily in England where the mood was summed up by Charles Shaar Murray when he wrote, "When a man with the spark of rock and roll genius in him produces such a washed-out snivelling couldn't-give-a-shit-man excuse for an album, then we are all in trouble."

In America also, the critics could not get interested with Ken Emerson writing in *Rolling Stone*, "Almost everything is so familiar that the album is incapable of making much of an impression." With all this said and with the assistance of hindsight, the critics were maybe a little too harsh. True, there is a lot of casual dross on the album but the two brand new songs would be appreciated in the years to come as they were amongst the last drops from such a talented writer. "Friends Again" with backing vocals from The Pointer Sisters and ex-Charlatan Richard Olsen on clarinet, was a dramatically wrong assessment of the relations between the two Everly Brothers. But with incorrect presumptions aside, the good time groove is evident here, as is Sebastian's fading optimism.

The highlight of Sebastian's solo career to date, however, is "Face Of Appalachia" which came from a tape Lowell George sent Sebastian where he had hummed a melody alongside a series of chords, "Writing with Lowell was great fun," Sebastian recalls. "I really enjoyed that and was really sorry that we couldn't have done a little bit more of that. We had just hit a thing, and we came to each other with the same tune one week. It was quite shocking to have really come up with just about the same tune, within a week period we had both wrote it. Not the lyrics or anything, but the melody was just about the same."

This beautiful, smoky, lazy portrayal of pastoral America was the one track Sebastian seemingly had an interest in, "I knew very early on that it was never going to be a single, but it was nonetheless something I wanted so much to get out and to have it done right, that I cut it five times before I was satisfied." The effort was to no avail and the album failed to crack the charts on both sides of the Atlantic. Sebastian honestly addressed the critics' evaluation shortly after the release of *Tarzana Kid* saying, "The dry period I had wasn't in terms of not writing, it was just that I wasn't writing anything good. And my impulse when I'm not writing good things is not to release anything, which has not been the particular style of a lot of characters in the last couple of years."

The end of 1974 and the first part of 1975 had Sebastian returning to his safe living by performing solo and playing on sessions, notably on Keith Moon's solo album and on Bonnie Raitt's *Home Plate*. Then, just when he was drifting towards obscurity he was number one again - totally out of the blue!

On September 9th, 1975 a new situation comedy appeared on ABC-TV called *Welcome Back Kotter* about a teacher (Gabe Kaplan) returning to his old high school to teach its rowdiest pupils (including John Travolta). Prior to the airing, the producer for the series, Alan Sacks, was talking to his agent, David Bendett, about the need for a theme tune resembling a Lovin' Spoonful type of song. Bendett happened to be Sebastian's agent too and put his clients together.

Sebastian was sent a ten page synopsis and got to work but found the only thing that rhymed with Kotter was otter. After scrapping one attempt, Sebastian came up with "Welcome Back", a song that would pay for his entire mortgage. As the show picked up success, demand for the sixty-second theme tune to be released became so great that in February of 1976, it was extended and released as a single backed with another Spoonful re-recording, "Warm Baby".

By May the song was number one and a revitalised Sebastian, with a new session band behind him, appeared on the hottest show in America to promote the record. With Raquel Welch hosting, Sebastian appeared on *Saturday Night Live* in front of his biggest audience since Woodstock and promptly fell apart, having to start the song three times - on live TV. Today he claims that the poor PA system did him no favours but when he came to perform the harmonica solo towards the end of the song, John Belushi, in full tie dye straight from his *Lemmings* days, bounced on-stage and held up the harmonica for Sebastian much to everyone's delight. Unfortunately, both Sebastian's biggest audiences saw him goof up, something he is constantly reminded of in interviews.

"Welcome Back", reminiscent of "Daydream" in places with its warmth and structure, is hardly a classic Sebastian tune. During an interview for *Goldmine*, William Ruhlman described the song as a toss-off, which brought this constructive response from Sebastian, "It was written very much doing a job, which is you read a story that somebody's trying to put across, and you are musically accompanying that story. The job isn't always about writing about what I thought this morning. I'm proud of all the good stuff I've done and "Welcome Back" is, would you believe, the biggest record I've ever had. This may comment to some degree on the power of television but I can't slight the fact that this show and the song went together very well. So, anyway, that's why I don't go along with the fact that it was a toss-off."

With success, Sebastian was able to form a new band with Richard Bell on keyboards, David Hungate on bass and Jeff Porcaro on drums. Porcaro was second choice for Sebastian as another soon to be famous drummer, Stan Lynch of Tom Petty & The Heartbreakers, turned the job down, as Sebastian remembers, "I actually recorded a few tunes with Tom going back to the very beginning of his career. It was so early that Stan the drummer was considering going out with me for the summer until Tom had enough of the album to record."

On the verge of tossing Sebastian away, Reprise realised they had a hit on their hands, "Reprise had just about written me off, when they called and said I had a monster hit. They were damn near ready to let me out of the last record I owed them, just to get me out of their hair. Now, they had the second biggest single of that year on their hands and they didn't eat crow gracefully either. They simply took the money that came from the single and put no money into publicising the accompanying album. While the song was very lucrative for me, my future was far from secure. I had a son now."

The album, strangely enough named after the hit single, appeared in April with Sebastian answering the critics with ten self-written songs (except "One Step Forward, Two Steps Back", written with John Charles Lewis) albeit with two Spoonful re-treads. The co-producer was Steve Barri, better known for his production work with the Grass Roots and on TV shows including *Happy Days* and the theme from *S.W.A.T.* and who was once in a duo with P.F. Sloan called The Fantastic Baggys.

Between them, Barri and Sebastian produced a nothing more than pleasant commercial sound, unique in Sebastian's career. Of the songs, "A Song A Day In Nashville", sounding more like Randy Travis singing than Sebastian, returns to an old theme enjoyed elsewhere, "Let This Be Our Time To Get Along" is the best of the ballads aplenty on offer here but the highlight of *Welcome Back* is "I Needed Her Most When I Told Her To Go", Sebastian's mature love song.

The mainstream success was short lived with the album peaking at number 79 and the follow up single, the over-cute Cantina-style "Hideaway" just scraping the top 100. Sebastian and family would now move to Woodstock, a place introduced to Sebastian by Albert Grossman and Bob Dylan and one which had an existing musical community. It was also near the East Coast college circuit where Sebastian realised his future lie.

On 20th November, 1976 at the Memorial Auditorium in Sacramento, California, Sebastian was reunited on stage with one of his mentors, Fred Neil, at the request of Governor Jerry Brown for the "California Celebrates The Whales Day". This appearance, one of the last times Neil would perform, was soon followed by a series of concerts on the East Coast. To ensure his attendance, Neil needed a guard in case he disappeared due to his nervousness and an old trusted friend came in to do this job, Joe Marra;

"They called me to do the concert and at first I thought these guys are crazy! They asked me to do a benefit, but for what! They said, "Whales," I said, "But we are going to eat the whales!" I thought about it as it did give me a chance to get to Fred Neil. He was so elusive. We did two shows at the Playhouse in Coconut Grove with John Sebastian and Peter Childs and I baby-sat Fred. Basically I was on top of this Fred for days. I wouldn't let him go to the bathroom, I didn't let him do anything, I made sure he was there. Anyway, in the end, they gave me a T shirt, it was great!"

Sebastian's last public performance with Fred Neil turned out to be in Japan of all places at the event, "Japan Celebrates The Whale And Dolphin". Along with another one hundred fourteen American musicians and environmentalists, notably Jackson Browne and J.D. Souther, Sebastian played alongside Fred Neil and the Rolling Coconut Revue to a less than ecstatic audience in April of 1977.

Sebastian had already left his record company through the back door, surprising as he had just enjoyed a number one record, "At that particular point in time, Warner Brothers had kind of gone Alice Cooper crazy. They were enjoying their new found modernness and considered me a thing of the past. It was very hard to get people's ear over there at that particular point in time." Annoyed at the treatment from his former company, alongside the realisation that his music was not at the forefront of the public's interest, Sebastian laid low for a while and, "waited for Disco to fade." For the rest of the '70s and the entire '80s, Sebastian would continue to make a living out of his musical talents in a wide variety of ways.

Immediately after his relocation, Sebastian became part of the ongoing musical community that existed in Woodstock, where a lot of his contemporaries from the Greenwich Village days had gone to graze. Sebastian soon became involved in the second Mud Acres album, playing and singing on a collection of folk songs old and new. The Mud Acres project had started in the early '70s in Artie Traum's kitchen, when on the promise of a record deal he put together a bunch of friends (including brother Happy, Maria Muldaur, John Herald, Jim Rooney and others) and recorded an album at a small studio in Ft. Edward, New York. The result was called *Mud Acres* after Artie's front yard and sub-titled *Music Among Friends* and became one of the Rounder label's early hits in the folk field.

Five years later, almost to the day, on January 13th 1977, most of the cast assembled again to repeat the process. With the growing community, a lot more musicians became involved with *Woodstock Mountains - More Music From Mud Acres* including Eric Andersen, Paul Butterfield, Rory Block and Sebastian as well as Catherine, who documented the sessions with her camera. For two days and nights the musicians bonded at the Bearsville Studios, set amongst the snow swept mountains of Woodstock and produced over thirty songs, fifteen of which appeared on the final album.

Sebastian is all over the album, playing harmonica here, guitar there, singing back up and even playing bass on one cut. He was singled out in the sleeve notes by Happy Traum who thanked him, "for extra help and enthusiasm." Sebastian's harmonica duet with Paul Butterfield on "Amazing Grace" is beautiful but his only lead vocal, on the traditional "Morning Blues", is the highlight of the album. Sebastian really seemed to be in his element amongst this type of arrangement and had high hopes for the album at the time, "I'm looking forward to seeing how the album *Woodstock Mountains* does. I think it may be a secret smash, because it's the best morning record of the season - it's a great record to play in the morning when you first wake up. There aren't too many albums like that."

The album was popular enough for the nucleus to form a touring group that took the songs on the road, alas, without Sebastian. A third album followed the following year but Sebastian's involvement was minimal, as he was busy at the time playing benefit concerts for environmental causes.

Sebastian had also moved into new arenas; "I did four cartoons. *Rome-O And Julie-Eight, The Devil & Daniel Mouse, Intergalactic Thanksgiving* and *Easter Fever* were the four titles, which was lovely fun. I started off, more or less, just doing songs for them, and ended up actually helping the animators in several different cases showing them how a given character might play an instrument or what the body language of a bass player is, and how it differs from a guitarist and how a lead guitarist differs from a rhythm guitarist in the way he handles his instrument. In fact working with three fingers, I still had most of the characters playing chords and the finger positions were right!"

Sebastian would now concentrate on being a troubadour on stage for the rest of the decade. He knocked any ideas of playing with a band on the head for a while as he had helped design a guitar, made by Lucien Barnes, that had a solid body with built in special effects and synthesiser components, which made it sound like Sebastian was playing two instruments at once. He started to become a nostalgia act probably before he realised it, as in the summer of 1979, Sebastian performed at a shabby "Ten Years On" revisit of Woodstock, alongside surviving acts Country Joe McDonald and Canned Heat. Even though most of the paltry 17,000 audience at the concert held, after much site changing, at Parr Meadows in New York State, were too young to know who he was, Sebastian performed one of his finest sets.

Trying to escape from all the nostalgia, Sebastian performed new material, some of which he has still, criminally, not committed to record. His passion for the environment came out at the concert when he introduced one of these songs "Link In The Chain", "Now one of the best parts of the last festival that I recall was that a lot of people were coming on and taking some chances, trying some new tunes. So I don't wanna just sit here and give you a re-hash because frankly, to tell you the truth, the last ten years as far as I'm concerned were a large yawn. The fact is we should be devoting our energies, not to thinking about ten years ago, or the ten years since, but to get the atomic power plant out of Shoreham Long Island and doing some constructive work along those lines!"

To the howls and whoops of the audience Sebastian launched into the song which comments on the barbarity of whale hunting and the madness of nuclear power. Recorded at a time when songs of this fashion were not fashionable, the song could so easily have been a hit due to its ultra-catchy chorus and intention. Another new song, finished two days before the festival, was "about some feelings I've had lately". Thoughtfully reflecting on his age and time left, Sebastian seemed disillusioned when he sang; 'I'm looking for something better out of this world, 'cause I know that these magic moments won't re-occur. I don't know what's in store, but I'm looking for something more.'

The song, "Looking For Something Better" was Sebastian's unreleased gem for many years until the concert recording was officially released in 1996. These new tunes had been written for another attempt at Broadway, a musical interpretation of the E.B. White story *Charlotte's Web*. This project would take up a huge chunk of Sebastian's time but the man relishes a musical challenge and became engrossed in the idea; "I was called by a producer named Jarrod Redfield, and he wanted me to write music and lyrics for *Charlotte's Web* which was a property that he owned, and I said, "Wonderful!" I did the songs, and he was enthusiastic enough to say, "Look you should be doing the adaptation so that you get to make the song holes as well as the songs, you get to make the places for the songs." So, that was a good year's project. I locked up and did an eighty five page adaptation."

People still wanted to hear the Spoonful songs (as well as "Welcome Back") at his solo concerts and the past caught up with Sebastian in early 1980 when The Lovin' Spoonful reformed.

CHAPTER 8 – MORE THAN ONE TRICK

The project that would reunite the original line-up of The Lovin' Spoonful for the first time since 1967 was Paul Simon's self-indulgent movie *One Trick Pony*. Simon had previously acted in Woody Allen's *Annie Hall* and had looked ill at ease, though managing to get away with it. Unfortunately his appeal as a leading man was minimal. *One Trick Pony* was haphazardly assembled during a power struggle between Simon and his former record company. With this firmly in his mind, Simon used the film as propaganda for his own side.

Simon even went as far as to cast Rip Torn as the diabolical record executive, Walter Fox, playing what was an obvious impression of Walter Yetnikoff, Simon's enemy. In the film, Simon gets his "fantasy revenge" on Yetnikoff when Jonah Levin, the faded rock star portrayed by Simon, seduces Fox's wife. Whilst being one of the few films to accurately portray the true rock and roll life-style, *One Trick Pony* is flawed by the central character's performance.

The Lovin' Spoonful's involvement centres on a tacky "Salute To The Sixties" segment where Simon makes sure that the audience knows how low this sort of concert would be and that he was selling his soul to be a part of it. For this scene, Simon assembled a selection of what he thought were one hit wonders (what a one trick pony really is) for a kitschy sixties reunion concert. Even though they had had more top ten hits in the sixties than Simon & Garfunkel, the Spoonful, alongside Sam & Dave and Tiny Tim (who ironically played at the last Spoonful concert in 1968) were chosen for the project.

Joe Butler was keen in doing the film initially, as he had been out of the business since his return from the West Coast. Trying to make his way in construction, a recently divorced Butler was also learning the Method as well as driving a cab around the streets of New York City at the time he got the call from Sebastian. Immediately he was suspicious; "Paul Simon wanted the group. I believe what happened was John and his manager tried to sell him but Simon was not interested, he really wanted the group. Richie Chiaro was managing John at the time but John called anyway and said, "Look, I think we should really do this thing, it would be nice to just do it the one time."

With an easily convinced Boone on board, Sebastian took charge as he recalled to *Goldmine*, "I rehearsed Joe and Steve for three days up at my house and then we all went to the Concord Hotel where Paul was filming. He wanted his character in the film to have this reunion concert, so he said he needed three or four bands from that period that would reunite, so we got drafted. So, I rehearsed the rhythm section and added Zally at the last moment and it was absolutely great."

The following sugary version of how Yanovsky got involved was told in the one-sided sleeve notes that accompanied Rhino Records' *Anthology* package in 1990; "John rang up Zal saying, "Okay, you heard the last offer, which was for like millions of dollars. Now Paul's calling, and he wants us for four days, and we'll get $400 a day." "You know, that sounds more like us," said Zal. "I thought so too," said John. And they did it." Yanovsky only spent around five hours rehearsing with the group, "That's the right amount" he quipped later. Unfortunately it showed.

Since the split of the Spoonful, Sebastian had hardly seen Yanovsky up until a short time before the *One Trick Pony* filming. Sebastian had invested a lot of time and energy talking things through with his old friend, sometimes arguing long into the night, in an attempt to get his relationship with Yanovsky back onto an even keel. With this virtually achieved, Sebastian became, and still is, a self-appointed press officer for Yanovsky. The reunion was anything but "absolutely great", and Yanovsky seemingly still wanted to spoil the party as Butler recalls, "He insisted that he never sang on anything! (laughs) After you say, "Zally, come on," no, he maintains it and he's serious and he starts getting angry and I'm left singing my half of the background part. He only came in on the last day - what bullshit!"

Sebastian recalled in 1984 that the Spoonful played an extended set during the filming, "We blew them away! Simon felt out of it. We did about ten tracks and they had a sixteen track recorder there but they only taped one song and all they did was have close ups of me." What does exist from the reunion is a goose pimple inducing performance, albeit tarnished by Yanovsky, of "Do You Believe In Magic". After a brief glimpse of the Spoonful surrounding Simon backstage during Sam & Dave's one trick, "Soul Man", the group are announced and appear out of the darkness with their backs to the audience on a huge revolving forty five record. Bounding towards their places on the stage, the ensuing years are evident when you notice that Butler's full head of hair has turned completely silver. Yanovsky looks like an extra from the film *Deliverance* with a full beard and lumberjack shirt, whilst Sebastian appears strangely different due to his use of contact lenses. It is only Boone, with his hair thinning a little that looks the same as before. Just as in *What's Up, Tiger Lily*, Boone barely appears in the finished cut.

With a quick "one, two" from Sebastian, with his autoharp at the ready, The Lovin' Spoonful launch into their first hit remarkably tightly, until it becomes evident that Yanovsky really isn't singing the famous back-up parts. Come the guitar solo and he completely loses it, taking his hands off the guitar, shrugging his shoulders and yelling something inaudible towards the audience. Most of this is obstructed by a brief cut away shot of Simon backstage, grimacing as Tiny Tim rehearses his moment. All too briefly the Spoonful finish and close the curtain. There was talk of carrying on but the personal conflicts between them would make any attempt impossible.

Whilst keeping up the good time publicity ("We used to be crazy," Butler told *Rolling Stone*. "Now we even rehearse."), Butler was internally the most dissatisfied with the performance, "Well we didn't do it one time, we did our five easy pieces you know! I didn't get to sing anything! Christ, in the meantime I had done three Broadway leads and an opera for fucking Christ's sake! When we did our show that was like half an-hour/thirty five minutes I didn't get to sing one lead. Well, what the fuck was that about? So really I had a right as an artist to insist, "Wait a minute, John, I'm your drummer but I'm also...let's get a drummer in here and I want you guys to learn the song "Hair", I want you to do it good for the audience. I'll be your second banana but I'm not going to do it from behind a set of drums. I want to get out and do the song from *Hair*, when none of you guys were around and they stand up and clap, I want to do that one!" The final ignominy for Butler came when the closing credits for the film rolled, claiming him as Zoe Butler.

One Trick Pony premiered on October 1st, 1980. By then the Spoonful had gone back to their separate camps and another decade would be wasted before their flag would be unfurled again. To dismiss an entire decade would seem outrageous after what had gone on before but in reality nothing memorable came out of the Spoonful camp during the 1980s. Musically and professionally, everybody either trod water, re-lived the past or in Butler and Yanovsky's case, disappeared off the face of the earth. It was left to Sebastian to produce the odd product of note but even he would struggle for recognition from now on.

Come the start of the decade, with the drug habits of America changing to more heavyweight matter, the heat was definitely on Boone; "By the time 1980 came around, it was starting to get heavy. I got down to South America and they didn't want to load marijuana, they wanted to put cocaine on board. Then they wanted me to bring guns down." Boone had been lucky up to the start of the new decade but a totally unrelated incident would finally put a stop to his smuggling ways; "It's a long and complicated story. My first wife had hooked up with these guys that were supplying the stuff in South America and rented a house for them in Chesapeake Bay, and a boat got busted. They had abandoned their boat full of marijuana on a sand bar in Maryland and the coast guard found it. Not only did they abandon it; they left their passports in it and a book with my phone number in it.

"I wasn't involved in this at all but they had names - this was the Feds - they knew I was involved even though they didn't have any proof. By 1981 the investigation was getting real close but our side of the unit, my crew, myself, the guy I worked for, we were all solid. We didn't think they could get us because they didn't have the evidence; but then they got my ex-wife to testify. She had been involved in one deal where she had baby-sat a house for us while we were waiting to use it, so she had details and once they got her to talk....The same thing happened to me in the Spoonful days, you know, it's like the unwilling fink, but she had no choice. They threatened her with taking the baby away and she was a user at the time. She was using the hard stuff too and she couldn't make good choices, so as a result we all coped a plea."

Boone was lucky not to have to spend time behind bars as he readily admits, "The Judge really, knock on wood, was the nicest guy in the world. I guess he saw the people involved were not hardened gangsters. I only had to do thirty days in what they call work release, and then five years of probation and pay a fine." Boone, whilst realising his good fortune, did pay a penalty but can still see the funny side, "That's the real drag. I'm a convicted felon now. That means I can't vote, I can't have a pilot's license - I was a pilot, I had to surrender that. I can't own handguns, I can't run for President, not that that's stopped anyone else."

The probation period forced Boone to go back to what he could do best - making music. His friend, Scott Cunningham, opened a blues joint called The Parrot Club in the 1800 Block on Maryland Avenue, where Boone would play as he recalls, "By 1981 I was playing in The Scott Cunningham Blues Band all the time, two or three nights a week. We were the most popular blues band in Baltimore, everybody loved it and we had a record deal coming up. Then we went up to New York about 1983 and he showcased at JP's on the East Side, got tight and choked big time. So he retreated back to Baltimore and started a car dealership and blues became a part time thing." This period in Boone's musical career was documented on a rare recording: *Blues Take You Over.* "We made an album which Scott financed himself - although I loaned him some money. It's a nice blues album but it was mastered a little poorly and some of the performances aren't up to par but I'm not embarrassed by it. I'll play it for anybody."

The music gave Boone's life some purpose, "All throughout the '80s, when I was doing my probation, I restored old houses and played in a blues band. That's the reason that I play bass as well as I do now, playing with musicians like Dave Carrero the guitar player and a couple of the most fabulous drummers I've ever played with -

it got me back into it." In April 1982, Boone played at a memorable benefit show for WCVT Radio in Baltimore alongside David Cawkwell of The Accused and Bobby Hird and John Tracey from Crack The Sky, but outside of his local area Boone had been confined to the "Where Are They Now?" file with Butler and Yanovsky.

The Modern Folk Quartet had re-formed in its original incarnation in the late '70s, when Yester came up with an arrangement for a song he had written with Larry Beckett called "Brooklyn Girl". The piece screamed out for The MFQ, so Yester brought the band together again and out of this a second phase started for the group. They toured for most of 1977 with Dave Guard and took bookings at clubs up and down the California coast, as well as on cruise ships. Sometimes Henry Diltz would be on a photographic assignment and couldn't make it to a show so the others needed a replacement and who better than a now solo Jim Yester;

"I was doing a solo show in '78 in places like the Ice House in Pasadena and The MFQ had kind of reformed about that time and Henry had to go back East, so they asked me to learn his parts. It was good fun and when Henry came back they asked me to stay and do a five part. So Henry did his part and then I went to either unison with Jerry or occasionally we'd put in a fifth part." These gigs lasted up till January of 1979, when they all branched out again. Yester would then join his brother Jim in The Association. This was for the second time as he had had a brief stint in the early '70s after original member Brian Cole had overdosed and died, as Ted Bluechel revealed to *Goldmine*, "Brian was an extremely intelligent guy, but he built psychological walls around him to protect himself, and he began using drugs to shield himself. He got real sick one night and died of a China White OD. Smack and cocaine brought him down."

On September 26, 1980, all the surviving members of The Association re-formed for a cable TV special concert and would continue together up until the present day, with at least two original members remaining. For Independence Day 1981, they brought in Jerry Yester for some arranging work which led to one of Yester's personal favourite musical memories - conducting the Philadelphia Orchestra; "What an experience, whew! It was the most terrifying thing I've ever done in my life and not something I'd do again but for the privilege of standing in front of an orchestra, that close, and hearing them playing something I'd written, is a wonderful thing."

The next year Yester saw his old partner again; "I went and saw Zal in 1982, which was the last time I really saw him, when I drove across country with Beckett. We drove up to Kingston and stayed with Zally overnight and it was great." A couple of years later Canadian TV viewers got to see Yanovsky for the first time in years too. One of these viewers, John Morton, recalls what he saw, "In 1984 there was a documentary on the Canadian Rock scene narrated by Donald Sutherland called *Hearts Of Gold*. It showed John and Zal together being interviewed for the program., where one subject was sales, Yanovsky; "I think it was less – they shipped a lot more – I think you could buy your way on the charts. I won't mention the two guys or anything cause they may see this film and break my legs!"

They did a duet of "Did You Ever Have To Make Up Your Mind" and afterwards John said that a lot of his writing came from running conversations he and Zal had. During this time Zal was constantly smoking cigarettes and after John explained his writing techniques, Zal asks, "Great, now when are you going to give me a cheque

AMERICAN-MADE
WORLD-PLAYED
334
HEAVY
ACOUSTIC – BRONZE WD
MADE IN U.S.A.
Vinci - Quarius Strings
.014 .018 .027 .039 .049 .059
I can honestly say that these are the finest strings available
John Sebastian
VINCI - QUARIUS STRINGS
P.O. Box 196 • Brooklyn, New York 11223
P.O. Box 113 • Farmingdale, New York 11735

for all those millions in royalties?" Whereby John jokingly pretends to punch Zally. Zal ends by saying, "It was fun in The Lovin' Spoonful; all the drugs, money and girls you could handle."

Yester had joined The Association even though he dreaded having to sing their massive hit "Cherish". Things were running smoothly until Jim Yester got itchy feet due to the uncertainty of bookings and family commitments in 1983; "It had lost a great deal of clout. Actually, we got back together, I think, a little too soon. Sixties revivals hadn't really started to happen then." Leaving The Association himself a short time afterwards, Jerry Yester's name then appeared infrequently as an arranger for Tom Waits, America or The Manhattan Transfer but in reality he was scuffling.

The third coming of the Modern Folk Quartet (cum-Quintet) came in 1984 when Yester relocated to Hawaii to live near Faryar and Douglas. They got around to recording an album this time for John Stewart's label Homecoming - that even got released in England on the appropriate Off Beat label. *Moonlight Serenade* is a collection of pop standards given the MFQ touch but the eventual release of "Brooklyn Girl" is the highlight here. This and the Scott Cunningham album would be the only album projects by any former Spoonful in the entire 1980s.

In 1979, Sebastian's only lasting piece of work was for a terrible teenage flick about roller-skating. *Skatetown USA* is known only today as the debut movie for Patrick Swayze, who was pictured on the rear jacket as was Sebastian, in dungarees, wearing roller skates, much to his horror fifteen years later; "I was roller skating a lot in L.A. during that time, just for fun and I had written a song called "Roller Girl" for Alan Sacks, who was trying to produce a show about roller derbies and I had written this song as a joke, (sings) 'Mama said find a sober girl and I'm in love with a roller girl, fastest thing on skates!'

"Then this roller derby movie came along so there was this general call for songs about roller skating and I said, "Whoa, I've got one," so it was included in the movie. But you say there is a picture of me on skates on the cover, oh no!" (laughs). The song's only piece of interest was that it reunited Sebastian with Joe Wissert. Since disappearing from the *Everything Playing* sessions, Wissert had gone on to make a name for himself producing artists including Boz Scaggs, Helen Reddy and Earth Wind & Fire.

The new decade started terribly for Sebastian as his father died in 1980 at the age of 66. In between the deaths of two of his other earlier influences, Tim Hardin in 1980 of a heroin overdose and Lightnin' Hopkins in 1982, Sebastian endured another period of being out of fashion. His only work of note was for another soundtrack album for the television movie *Kent State* which was about the four days in 1970 that ended in tragic confrontation at Kent State University, also the inspiration for Crosby, Nash and Young's "Ohio". One side of the soundtrack (produced by Jack Lewis) had a supergroup of session musicians (including Garth Hudson, Richard Manuel, Howie Epstein and James Burton) backing either Grace Slick, Richie Havens or Sebastian on original material. Sebastian's contribution, "Don't Hide Your Light", is easily forgettable.

Also during this period, in July 1981, Sebastian made a brief return to England to play at the Cambridge Folk Festival as well as the Dominion Theatre in London. Optimistically the promoters had advertised two performances but when ticket sales were not forthcoming, Sebastian performed only one. With Elvis Costello looking on from near the front, Sebastian was spurred on by the small gathering and performed well, even playing "Summer In The City" and "Do You Believe In Magic" for his dwindling British audience.

1982 was notable as Sebastian got his first ever work as a producer, working with Rory Block on her fifth album *High Heeled Blues* for Rounder Records. Rory Block is the daughter of Alan Block, who owned a sandal shop in Greenwich Village which became a hangout in the early sixties for the local musicians as well as the touring ones, including Mississippi John Hurt and Doc Watson. It was at one of these gatherings that Sebastian first heard the young Rory play the guitar and was swept away by her understanding of the blues;

"I had been coaxing Rory for a number of years to make an album exploiting some of the talents she hadn't been able to use on her more R&B flavoured albums. I'd always felt that one of her tremendous strong suits was her guitar playing, the way she remembers blues, the incredible exactness with which she plays and also her strength as a ragtime guitarist, which very few people know. When she finally decided to make that kind of an album, she called me up to say, "Would you produce it?" And I did."

Even though the credits read that Sebastian was the co-producer, he claims that he solely produced Block's album. Rounder Records got upset with Sebastian for overspending on the album and in a possible coincidence, he has never produced any other albums since. Another new venture that would continue from this point on was making musical instruction tapes for Happy Traum's company, Homespun. The first was a six-tape set, explaining the rudiments of playing the blues harmonica, performed with the help of Paul Butterfield.

Another tragic death of one of Sebastian's early friends occurred in April of 1983, when Felix Pappalardi was shot dead in New York City by his wife, Gail Collins. Months later, also in the city, Sebastian was roundly booed off the stage at Radio City Music Hall, when he was poorly matched with comedian Rodney Dangerfield. These events did not sway Sebastian, as he was to reach a new popularity on the live circuit after a chance meeting with a new band.

One night Sebastian and Yanovsky went to see the group NRBQ (New Rhythm & Blues Quartet) play a gig in Woodstock, just like they both had gone to see The Strangers in the early days. Sebastian and NRBQ then met up at a benefit in New Paltz, New York and it turned out that the group were huge Spoonful fans and could play all the hits, which they did that night. This would become a bit of a trend and Sebastian now had his most proficient band ever behind him.

The reviews became much more upbeat, as this one taken from *Goldmine* in November '83 shows, "If The Lovin' Spoonful can't be reunited, then NRBQ must be the next best thing. NRBQ must have studied their Spoonful records, as they put down note-for-note versions of each chestnut. Even the ballad "Darling Be Home Soon" worked. "Summer In The City" was awkward without the needed car horns of the record, but the spirit was there. After two rousing closers by all involved the good time music of the '60s once again gave way to the realities of the streets of Manhattan 1983."

GLC IN ASSOCIATION WITH THE TUC PRESENTS

TOLPUDDLE MARTYRS

1834 150TH ANNIVERSARY 1984

FREE FESTIVAL

FEATURING PAUL BUTTERFIELD THE SPINNERS

JOHN SEBASTIAN ALAN PRICE

CHRISTY MOORE

PLUS SPECIAL SURPRISE GUESTS

PLUS JAZZ · FOLK · THEATRE

BRASS BANDS · KIDS EVENTS

EXHIBITIONS · BEER TENT

HOW TO GET THERE: BUSES 19·39·44·45·49·137·170
BRITISH RAIL:
BATTERSEA PARK · QUEENSTOWN ROAD · BATTERSEA

Keep GLC
Working for the Arts in London

SUNDAY 29 JULY NOON-10PM

BATTERSEA PARK SW11

Another band who were big fans of the Spoonful were the emerging REM. When they had debuted in New York, Michael Stipe announced to the audience, "Since we're here in New York City, we're The Lovin' Spoonful and this is our song!" In July of '84 they selected Sebastian and Roger McGuinn as their Rock Influences for an MTV special. For the encore at REM's concert at the Capital Theatre in Passaic, New Jersey, McGuinn came on to perform "So You Want To Be A Rock 'N' Roll Star" with the band followed swiftly by Sebastian who sang on a ragged version of "Do You Believe In Magic". Sebastian addressed the performance in the special when he said, "There are common bonds that exist between the Spoonful and REM; being young, being sloppy and wanting to do it great!" A few days later Bill Berry of REM described the performance of "Do You Believe In Magic" as, "the high point of my career so far."

With some satisfaction coming from live performances; Sebastian was still making some poor choices in the soundtrack field. He wrote and performed, with songwriter Phil Galdston, the music for *The Jerk Too*, an awful sequel to the Steve Martin movie. All was not well when Sebastian came back to England to play the Cambridge Folk Festival again, as well as a benefit gig for the GLC in London, when it became noticeable that his singing voice had become somewhat strained, something he failed to hide this from the audiences.

The September 12th, 1985 edition of *Rolling Stone* magazine carried a large "Where Are They Now?" feature on "The Music Greats Of The '60s & '70's". Ironically, the cover star was Prince, one of Bob Cavallo's new artists. The Lovin' Spoonful were featured and Yanovsky, in a rare interview, used the opportunity to bury any thoughts of a further reunion. Also in the piece, alongside a few reminiscences, Butler touched upon the difficulty the group had had in tracking down their money from the Spoonful days and mentioned that they hired a lawyer to trace it, who had given up after six months.

The whole confusing legal mess of Kama Sutra/Buddah/Faithful Virtue/MGM and Koppelman & Rubin started in 1968 when Kama Sutra was sold to a company called Viewlex. This was only done due to the friction between Artie Ripp and Hy Mizrahi as the third partner, Phil Steinberg, reveals, "The Viewlex deal was put together for only one reason. We'd never have done anything like that. The deal was put together so that Hy could be bought out of the company - that's the only reason. In fact, we had fist fights in the office every day. Those two got into a big...they just didn't like each other."

A lot of thought went into who Kama Sutra would offer themselves to and it seemed, at first, that they had made a good choice. Phil Steinberg; "So we sat down and picked out about four or five companies that we would speak to about purchasing our company and Viewlex seemed the right size, they had the right products and they were going to buy Bell Sound. They were also buying pressing plants and they had pre-established contracts before the oil embargo which meant that their oil was that much cheaper, therefore they could buy vinyl much cheaper. It was a company that we could go to and really get involved with." With Mizrahi out of the picture, four new partners were brought in to share the new remaining third. These were Neil Bogart, Marty Traw, Cecile Holmes and the accountant at MGM when the Kama Sutra deal had gone through, Art Kass. An early compilation from 1970, *The Very Best Of The Lovin' Spoonful*, exhibited the take-over as it bore the slogan, "Buddah Records, a leisure time subsidiary of Viewlex Inc."

Steve Boone takes up the story; "In 1968, MGM sold its distribution rights to a company called Commonwealth United which was a big business conglomerate and they went bankrupt less than a year later. In the process of dissolving, all the assets including the Lovin' Spoonful's publishing and record contract, were sold back to Charles Koppelman again. Well you can raise your eyebrows on that one because that sounded very suspicious all along. Koppelman kept the publishing on the choice songs, the hits, and sold the rest back to Buddah, then Buddah became the new licensee of the product."

So, the Spoonful's copyright was now out of their hands. This happened to a host of sixties acts whose owner had gone into liquidation, the most notable being The Small Faces. Erik Jacobsen's publishing company was swallowed up too as Boone says: "Faithful Virtue was intact until Commonwealth United went bust and then when the sell-out of the assets happened, Faithful Virtue got dissolved. Charles Koppelman kept twelve, I think, of the strongest songs and made many deals. Then Koppelman sold the publishing to Fred Beinstock - which is Hudson Bay Music."

When Erik Jacobsen was asked about the fall of Faithful Virtue he was reluctant to talk on the subject; "Koppelman and Rubin stole the whole thing from me. I don't know, it's a long story, man." Jacobsen was more forthcoming on a later occasion; "Basically we were one more stone they stepped on - pushed into the mud on their way up. I mean, I still don't get a God damned dime on my producers' royalties. I've got a big project coming up that I'm hoping to pitch to Charlie and when I get him in a room I'm gonna say, "Hey! You son of a bitch, give me my fucking royalties back, you stole the whole God damned thing!" The only consolation is: he lost it." On being informed that Koppelman bought the rights back shortly thereafter Jacobsen said, "Did he buy it all back? That son of a bitch. Well, I love Charlie, he helped me get in the business, so I don't hold any ill thoughts of him, but that fucker. Between he and Cavallo they fucked me good time, man. I mean I'd be sitting here a multimillionaire if it weren't for my partners.

"Cavallo didn't know what end was up. As a manager he was good. When we first made money and he got us with some guy in the stock market, we put all our profits in the stock market and two years later our broker was arrested and we lost all our money. All the money in my big payoff; it took that whole huge amount of money that time which, I think, was $300,000 of which the tax was $150,000. I put the whole $300,000 in the stock market in safe places, which Cavallo helped me set up and six months later I sold my remaining stocks for $150,000 and wrote the cheque to the government and that was it Charlie, my entire thing gone."

In September 1973, Bogart quit Buddah and started Casablanca Records in California, eventually hitting it big with Kiss, Donna Summer and The Village People. Artie Ripp and Phil Steinberg had already departed, as Steinberg recalls, "There was an autonomy clause in this thing between Artie Ripp and myself. If either one of us left the arrangement the autonomy would be broken down and reverted to Viewlex on all of our companies. Artie took up an artist, Billy Joel, and he was on the run and he wanted to break out and our autonomy was broken. At that point they wanted to re-negotiate, they wanted a triumvirate of three presidents, myself, Neil Bogart and Art Kass and I reneged on that." With the other business partners taking the money and running, Art Kass was the only one left.

In 1976 Viewlex went bankrupt. Art Kass bought back Buddah with $2.7 million in mostly borrowed money, including $25,000 from Bogart. Kass kept borrowing money until, in 1978, at around $10 million in debt, he was summoned to the bank. "I needed money immediately and I had one last phone call," recalls Kass. "There was nobody else I could even ask for that sum of money. I called Morris (Levy) and he came straight down to the bank. Right there and then he signed a note for $250,000." As Levy told Dorothy Wade and Justin Picardie, "They call this office the clinic. Labels get sick, they come here for treatment and they get better. We cut their overheads, their mega payment plans, and nurse them. It is practical business applied to creative business."

Levy helped dissuade Kass's major creditors (including CBS, where Koppelman had worked) to delay bankrupting him and took Buddah under his wing, sharing in the success when Sutra, as Buddah became known, signed rap group the Disco 3 in 1984 who later became famous as the Fat Boys. Meanwhile, the Spoonful were still not getting paid and with the CD revolution approaching even their master tapes had disappeared. Phil Steinberg remembers that they were at Bell Sound until the collapse of Viewlex and have not been seen since.

Boone and Butler made a new attempt at tracing their money to be met with even more obstacles from what Levy had done to their material. With numerous shoddy repackages springing out from all corners, The Lovin' Spoonful's work was bandied around with as much respect as all the Bubblegum act's material. To this day, one company, Highland Music, can use Spoonful material in whatever way they like with no recrimination. Erik Jacobsen sums up the feelings of those who had been had, "I can't see the people selling a Lovin' Spoonful record, after I put the group together and produced the records and every other fucking thing - and I don't get a dime? That is not right."

In 1985 Sebastian put together an impressive group of musicians to record one of his songs as a closer to a syndicated television special. Wittily entitled *Deja View*, the special was based on the idea of making contemporary videos for some of the old '60s songs (using celebrities from acting and music) that were never given the visual treatment. So, there was Terri Garr in "She's Not There", Harry Dean Stanton in "A Whiter Shade Of Pale" as well as original Hollie Graham Nash in "Bus Stop" and Brian Wilson in "Don't Worry Baby".

Sebastian's video of an original song, the nostalgic "You And Me Go Way Back", was a contrast to the others on the special as it featured a group performing, albeit in lip-synchronisation. But what a group! The roll call was Sebastian, Roger McGuinn from The Byrds, Richard Manuel from The Band, Felix Cavaliere from The (Young) Rascals, Al Anderson from NRBQ and Ronnie Spector from The Ronettes.

Sadly, the first time most of the new Spoonful fans bought a Spoonful related record on its release, it was a single taken from a children's film *The Care Bears Movie*. Hardly the 'magic of rock and roll'! The single and the two other songs on the soundtrack, however, did show that Sebastian had a knack for work in the children's field. Bootlegs of his work for another kiddies cartoon, *Strawberry Shortcake*, performed with NRBQ, cement the fact.

1986 had Sebastian on a mammoth tour of the States, opening for Arlo Guthrie. He also played many gigs with NRBQ and when at Levering Hall at John Hopkins University in Baltimore, a Spoonful reunion of sorts occurred when, "on the spur of the moment," Boone and Butler encored with Sebastian and the band. The spark of excitement from this performance was enough to make the rhythm section repeat the process the following night in Washington.

Mark Sebastian

Nothing more came of this brief reunion, although not for want of trying by a peripheral person from the Spoonful story - Mark Sebastian. Wanting the group to record one of his songs, he picked up the phone; "Zally just totally...I don't know, he didn't shut me down, actually. The way I pitched it to him was I wanted to try to do a track where I employ all these guys, somehow, on a song that would be appropriate. Zally kind of said, "Well, we'll cross that bridge when we come to it." He didn't say, "Get fucked and die," which is always nice." Although all the members recall Mark's efforts, none took him seriously enough.

A TV special recorded in the summer of 1986 showed the frustration of being a Spoonful fan to the uppermost. The show, hosted by Bill Graham, was a celebration concert held twenty years to the day of the opening of his Fillmore club in San Francisco. Highlights of the seven-hour concert, including Fillmore stalwarts such as Joe Cocker, Joan Baez, John Lee Hooker, Carlos Santana and Paul Butterfield were screened as *A Night At The Fillmore*. Sebastian and Boone reformed for the special and played with NRBQ, who played the Spoonful songs far tighter than the Spoonful ever did. Two ironical features occur before the Spoonful section of the show in relation to it being Boone's first concert in San Francisco since the bust. The first was Howard Hesseman's appearance (he being a member of The Committee) and the second being a perfect eulogy about the Spoonful from Bill Graham (even though he banned the group from his club). Looking painfully thin and gaunt, Boone, alongside Sebastian, first performed an acoustic section before being joined by NRBQ for a final assault on the collection of young and old hippies in the audience.

The main topic of interest in their segment though is the quality of Sebastian's singing. Two songs were shown on the special, "Summer In The City" and "Do You Believe In Magic" (as Sebastian picks up his autoharp he said, "Yes, it's here. It's out of mothballs!") Both songs, spine tingling moments that they are, are ruined by Sebastian's deteriorating vocals. At times it looks like the veins in Sebastian's neck are going to pop out as he croaks and sputters his way through the Spoonful classics. This has always been a sticky conversation point with Sebastian, exhibited here when it was mentioned that he had had an operation on his throat, right? "No, not right!" Sebastian shot back. "I'm not sure exactly what this refers to. I did have to stop touring and it was because of vocal problems but I went into the hospital for a pneumonia variation which shows up on your face in the form of a large blotch and so that was why I had to stop. There were several gigs that I had to cancel simply because I was hooked up to tubes!"

Sebastian's vocal problems filtered throughout the musical community and were even mentioned in the national press. Reports came through that Sebastian was leaving the stage early, after talking for most of the time in any case. At one concert he was even dubbed, "A man called hoarse". In a separate interview occasion, with Pete Fornatale on New York radio in the '90s he was less disingenuous, "To this day I can say that it was partially physical and it was partially psychological. It's a very complex beast. The voice is an amazing tool; it's something that can get away from you if you have to sing the same fifteen tunes for a good twenty years. Especially to play them correctly, you have to play them in the key they were written in. For myself, yeah, I don't think my voice is what it was when I was twenty, I don't think it will ever be. I worked for twenty years fairly unnoticed and during that time my voice sounded great. Having the problems was the first piece of publicity I've gotten in fifteen years!"

This was not enough for Butler. Already annoyed that he was not asked to participate in the Fillmore show (a subject Boone dodges and something he once fast forwarded through when it was being shown in Butler's presence), Butler takes the performance as an excuse to launch into a tirade at his former collaborator; "John never called me to do it. Well I'm glad, he sang like a piece of shit! It was disgusting. He ripped his voice apart. You can't do that to your voice, that was crazy. Madness, you can't force it. I had reached out to John on a number of occasions to do something once in a while, not to be a regular thing and John was so icy to it and then he goes ahead and does this little thing, doesn't think to include me."

Now into his flow, Butler brings up what he thought of the way Sebastian used the Spoonful's name and music for in the ensuing years, "What would happen was everything that came to the group went to Bendett. He was the only one in business, so everything was totally taken by him. Every gig. I read half these encyclopaedia things and it's his tale that he's telling and it mostly plays down our contributions and, in some places, negates them completely. It's so heavy handed. It could only come out of some kind of real abnormal need for approval. When we get on stage we are like a family. Well, that word never came up, that word we. It just didn't exist. It's like; "You little prick, when I think of the things we did and what we did for each other."

The Fillmore show was also one of the last with NRBQ. From live tapes of their performances together, it is clear that the group were mocking Sebastian, something Boone noticed too, "I'll tell you what I think, this is a personal observation but I think that the old saying "familiarity breeds contempt"...I think they became too familiar with John and as a result they didn't give him enough respect. Now maybe that's not a fair word, I'm sure that they respected him very much but I would notice when I would be around all of them and John that they would almost treat him in an offhand manner. I don't think they gave John enough latitude to really direct them, they were too strong a band with their own identity."

With a sequel to *The Care Bears Movie*, *Care Bears In Wonderland*, featuring songs by Sebastian on release in 1987, he was noticeable enough for Disney to back a children's television special around one of his most famous songs. Unfortunately, *What A Day For A Daydream*, turned into a disappointment for Sebastian, "It was a Disney project that was put out by the Disney Channel. It was a mismatch as they used a kind of Vegas-y director who was used to doing things like pageants. I don't know why they paired me with this fellow. He does what he does very well, don't get me wrong but his oeuvre is somewhat more polished than whatever it is that I do." The closing years of the '80s found Sebastian on the comedy circuit opening for acts like Jay Leno, Steve Martin, Billy Crystal and Robin Williams, a link that led to Sebastian writing the music for Williams's HBO special. The August edition of *Life* magazine in 1989 carried a cover article on the 20th anniversary of the Woodstock festival including a "Where Are They Now?" segment. In it Sebastian mentioned that he enjoyed these anniversaries as his fee went up and announced to the world he had written a screenplay on his time with The Lovin' Spoonful.

The fourth coming of The MFQ came in the late '80s when Henry Diltz met up with a Japanese photographer who was a friend of a promoter in Tokyo, Hiroshi Asada. Asada had made a name for himself in Japan by bringing over offbeat American acts to the Eastern Shore. Sebastian had even been booked to play in Tokyo in 1988 but he pulled out due to his throat problems to be replaced at short notice by Peter Gallway. Asada secured the necessary money from Yosh Nagato, "Tokyo's Living Encyclopaedia of American Pop" as he has been described, and The Modern Folk Quintet toured Japan in December 1988.

To their surprise the group discovered their albums were revered in Japan and even more unnerving was the appearance of a copy group who played only MFQ songs as Jim Yester remembers, "The first night in Tokyo, our manager took us out to a restaurant and we walked in the door and here's The MFQ, a Japanese MFQ! They're called Kent and they were doing MFQ material, note for note and it was really good. They're not as good singers but they're real precise. They had all the parts down." Nagato recorded the real MFQ on the tour, resulting in a live album released by his own Village Green label, a division of Pony Canyon Records. Nagato even went as far as to get the first two MFQ albums reissued on CD and encouraged the group to record a new album.

Now with their own studio out on Hawaii, The MFQ nestled down and recorded *Bamboo Saloon* which was released in Japan early into the new decade. By the time the MFQ went over for another tour of Japan in April, 1990 one of the singles from the CD, their interpretation of "Sister Golden Hair" was in the local charts. Later on "Keeping The Dream Alive" also charted. The opening track from *Bamboo Saloon*, however, was the song that rang a chord with this author. The MFQ's affectionate look back to their bygone days in Greenwich Village, "Whatever Happened To The Lovin' Spoonful", became the stimulus for attempting this book and in the summer of 1990 I made contact with Sebastian and began a venture that would endure (off and on) throughout the next few years.

GOOD TIME MUSIC.

for fans of

Price: £1-u.k.
$3-u.s.
includes P&P

IN THIS ISSUE:
SPOONFUL ON VIDEO
JOHN NEW L.P. SHOCK
WHATS ON C.D.
1966 INTERVIEW AND MORE..

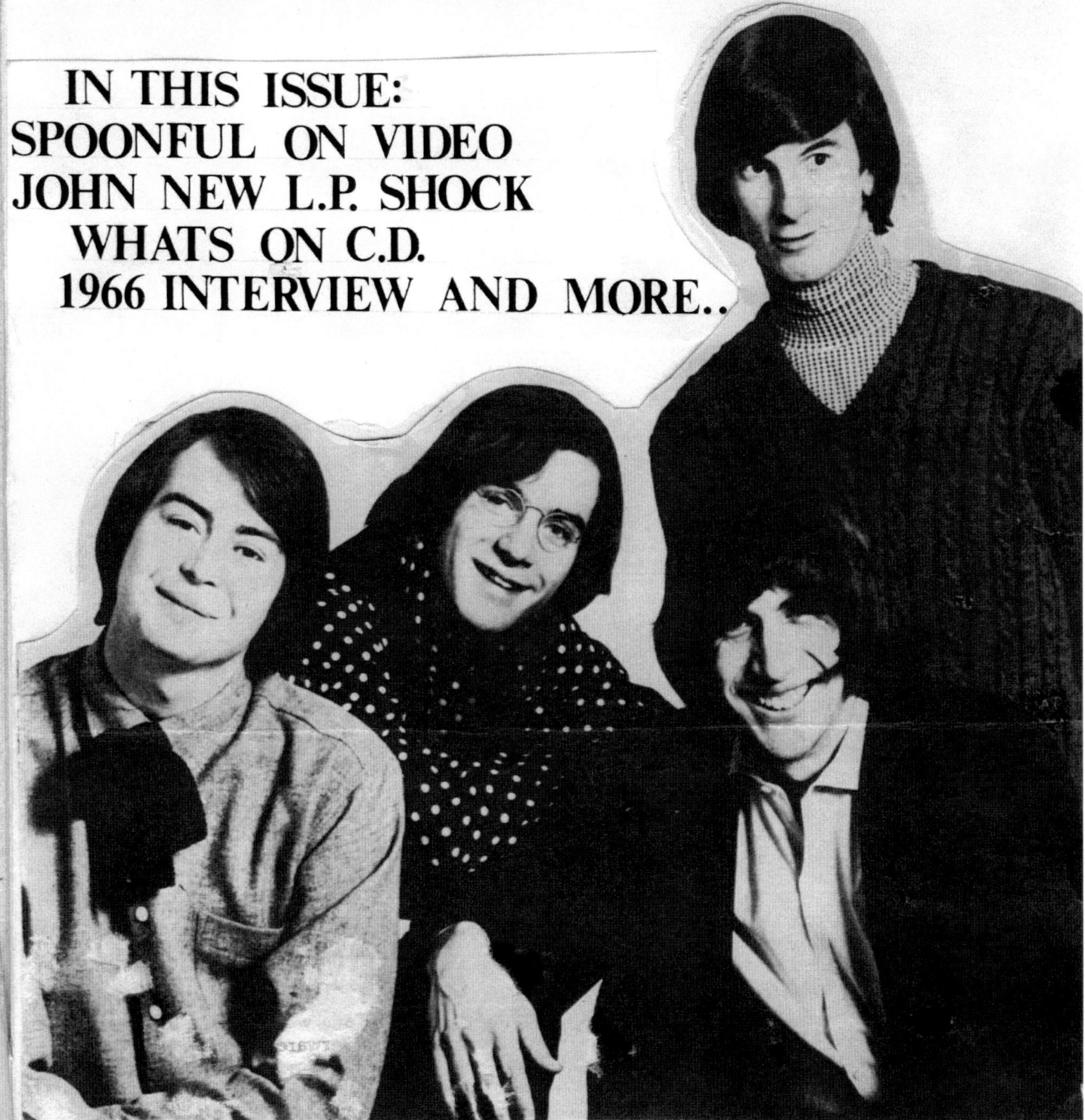

CHAPTER 9 – BRINGING IT ALL BACK HOME

To be honest, my initial chats with Sebastian were a little too gushing on my part. To his credit Sebastian was friendly, co-operative and patient but also distant and vague. He would willingly garnish some of the stories I knew but would rarely add anything new. Although he did want to see a Spoonful biography, he seemed not to want everything to be told. In March '91, with the impetus of Sebastian's input, I put together a Lovin' Spoonful fanzine, *Good Time Music*, in an attempt to gather material for such a book.

After several conversations, Sebastian put me in touch with Boone and Butler and they were duly sent fanzines. The first to react was Boone. One of the first things Boone mentioned to me was that he was in the process of putting together a new Lovin' Spoonful with Butler and Mark Sebastian. I remember not expressing too much enthusiasm about this line up and after finding out about Sebastian's and Yanovsky's reluctance to join, I suggested Boone calling Yester. Boone said that he had phoned Yester a year previous (when Yester was enjoying some success in Japan) and that he was not too keen as he had settled on Hawaii. Through speaking to Henry Diltz, I knew that Yester had recently recorded a good in parts solo album, only available in Japan *Just Like The Big Time...Only Smaller*, and had moved inland to Portland, Oregon. Boone agreed that it may be worth giving Yester another shot and that was where we left it. Butler soon made contact and struck me as a passionate supporter of the Spoonful name, who wanted things to be done right and was looking forward to playing the drums again.

The main reason for all the activity was that Boone and Butler had finally made a settlement on the Spoonful money after six long years of trying. "We chased a villain out of the business back into his palatial estate in Great Lake, Long Island," Butler boasted in an obvious reference to Art Kass. Hardly a great deal but after somewhere in-between either a $29,000 to a $47,000 plus incidentals payment to Boone, Butler and Sebastian, from summer 1991 onwards (with no back pay), the Spoonful would receive their royalties.

Yanovsky, much to his apparent disgust, got nothing, although he had already received a payment on leaving the group. "Stephen and Joe and I had a falling out," stated Yanovsky. "They were finally renegotiating for past royalties and they were going to split the money four ways and at the last moment they decided not to. John was a really nice guy, we certainly made our peace and gave me a portion of his money and I got an eighth or something like that." The impetus for the reunion, like so many, was not entirely a musical one as Boone explains, "Throughout the '70s and the '80s the record company was not squaring up with us on the royalties and so we felt that if we were going to go out on the road and work and increase the sales of the catalogue and they're still not paying us, it's almost like working for nothing. This summer we finally resolved our long-standing dispute. There are new owners of the record catalogue (Essex Entertainment) and they appear to be fair and honest."

The first record of the next event comes from a letter dated 29th, September 1991 from Boone; "Speaking with you on the phone was very interesting and in fact, your information about Jerry Yester was very helpful in convincing me to pursue getting in touch with him, and since he is now part of the team I thank you very much." The letter goes on to say; "On the subject of The Lovin' Spoonful, Jerry's brother Jim will be joining us as the

MAR-17-1992 11:49 FROM OBER,KALER,et al TO 13055229161 P.02

Scott Johnson
Ober,Kaler,Grimes&Shriver
120 East Baltimore Street
Baltimore,Maryland 21202-1643

Dear Scott:

Thank you for your incredibly presumptuous letter.Yes,I know you represent Joe Butler and Steve Boone,and now by default,Jerry Yester.

But do you represent or can you speak for the Lovin' Spoonful?-Believe me Scott,this isn't the one that's gonna get your name on the letterhead.Let me fill you in on a little history.

The Lovin'Spoonful were four guys-me,Zal Yanovsky,and eventually the guys you represent.We earned our reputation by playing our own instruments in a day when studio substitutes were the norm for bands.I felt then as I do now,that anything less than that was foreign to the spirit of the band and dishonest to the public.Joe and Steve's "many efforts over the years"consisted of trying to convince me to do it without Zally-the guy who provided our onstage whammy!And during that time,Steve lost his bass,Joe didn't even own drums.I know because I fronted the money,found him a kit(which he hasn't paid me back for)and still had to listen to vague ideas of regained stardom and not once the simple,responsible idea of getting together to see how we might sound.

Are you suprised that I didn't think highly of this? So now they go back to Zally to try to get him to do it without me.He laughed in their faces.Now they got mad and when the opportunity came,they cut Zal out of a measily royalty statement that morally should be his.The irony here is that if they'd just not been so greedy and politically stupid,I could have had Zal at least at a rehearsal within a month.

During the course of the Lovin' Spoonful,we all had equal chances to create and contribute.When I left the band they had every opportunity to pick up the flag.Have you ever heard "Revalation/Revolution?"Have you even seen the cover?The reason for your clients obscurity was not lack of opportunity.The songs they will be trading on were written mostly by me.

So now these guys want to be in show business.And Americas' appetite for nostalgia is great and these guys are hungry.And when they tire of the unscrupulous promoters that will hire them,they can go back to contracting and carpentry and leave a spoiled reputation for a band that had the Beatles as fans.And do you know Scott,who will be asked to explain this,before and after? The calls won't be coming to Scott Johnson,representative of Joe Butler and Steve Boone.Be glad.

Yours truly,

John Sebastian

John Sebastian

TOTAL P.03

fourth member and we are set to begin rehearsing this weekend, Oct 5. There is still the possibility that John Sebastian's brother Mark will be joining us as a fifth member although that is still unsettled. I wish I could report that John and Zal were involved, but that will not be the case at this time, although the door will never be shut entirely."

Sebastian made his feelings on the reunion known when he wrote the following letter to Scott Johnson the Spoonful's new attorney from the firm Ober, Kaler, Grimes & Shriver, after Johnson had written to Sebastian saying, "As you know, this firm represents Steve Boone and Joe Butler in connection with their reorganisation of the Lovin' Spoonful. Steve and Joe have both informed me of their many efforts over the years and recently to interest you in re-joining the group, and of your consistent position that you do not have an interest in doing so. This is to inform you that our clients are proceeding to reorganise the Lovin' Spoonful, with rehearsals to commence in New York on or about October 1, 1991. You are once again invited to re-join the group at that time, and your participation would be most welcome. Nevertheless, unless you inform us in writing to the contrary by September 13, 1991, it will be deemed that you have declined to take part in the reformed Lovin' Spoonful, and our clients will proceed on that basis. Yours truly, E. Scott Johnson." Now sit back and read Sebastian's reply;

"Dear Scott: Thank you for your incredibly presumptuous letter. Yes, I know you represent Joe Butler and Steve Boone, and now, by default, Jerry Yester. But do you represent or can you speak for the Lovin' Spoonful? Believe me Scott, this isn't the one that's gonna get your name on the letterhead. Let me fill you in on a little history.

"The Lovin' Spoonful were four guys – me, Zal Yanovsky, and eventually the guys you represent. We earned our reputation by playing our own instruments in a day when studio substitutes were the norm for bands. I felt then as I do now, anything less than that was foreign to the spirit of the band and dishonest to the public. Joe and Steve's "many efforts over the years" consisted of trying to convince me to do it without Zally – the guy who provided our onstage whammy! And during that time, Steve lost his bass, Joe didn't even own drums. I know because I fronted the money, found him a kit (which he hasn't paid me back for) and still had to listen to vague ideas of regained stardom and not once the simple, responsible idea of getting together to see how we might sound.

"Are you surprised that I didn't think highly of this? So now they go back to Zally to try and get him to do it without me. He laughed in their faces. Now they got mad and when the opportunity came, they cut Zal out of a measly royalty statement that morally should be his. The irony here is that if they'd just not been so greedy and politically stupid, I could have had Zal at least at a rehearsal within a month. During the course of the Lovin' Spoonful, we all had equal chances to create and contribute. When I left the band they had every opportunity to pick up the flag. Have you ever heard "Revelation/Revolution"? Have you ever seen the cover? The reason for your client's obscurity was not lack of opportunity. The songs they will be trading on were written mostly by me. So now these guys want to be in show business. And America's appetite for nostalgia is great and these guys are hungry. And when they tire of the unscrupulous promoters that will hire them, they can go back to contracting and carpentry and leave a spoiled reputation for a band that had the Beatles as fans. And do you know Scott, who will be asked to explain this, before and after? The calls won't be coming to Scott Johnson, representative of Joe Butler and Steve Boone. Be glad. Yours truly, John Sebastian."

Sebastian's response was quite understandable when you consider that the group was built around the talents of himself, Yanovsky and even Jacobsen.

I kept up with the group's progress until in late November, my friend Andy Tillett and I went to join them in Stephentown, upstate New York, for an unforgettable weekend. A couple of days before we visited the Berkshire Forum, a sort of meeting place for Communists with propaganda plastered on every wall, the last ever Spoonful reunion took place as Sebastian, fresh from a recording session with John Mellencamp, had gone to see his old group to discuss the future. Sebastian, Boone, Butler and Yester sat around a table together for the first time since 1967. The atmosphere was a little too tense and Sebastian left shortly afterwards.

A few months later Yester spoke of when he told Sebastian and Yanovsky of his intentions to join the band, prior to this meeting, "When I decided to get back together with Joe and Steve, I called John first and told him I was doing it. I told him I wanted him to find out from me before he found out from somebody else. At first he was convinced I was calling him up to talk him into it. He said, "I've gotta tell you right off, man, I'm not in..." I said, "John whoa, whoa, I'm calling up to say I'm doing it, I'm not trying to talk you into it. I have no doubt that you're not interested at all." Then we started talking, the pressure was off and so he said, "Well, man, if anyone has a right to, you were there, man."

"So we talked a little bit and it seemed a little tense and when I saw him in Stephentown he said he thought I was tense, so God knows, I mean I don't think I was. Then I called Zally and told him I was doing it and he said, "Why do you want to work with those guys?" Well, he was upset with them because of the split of royalties and stuff. Then I said, "Well do you want to know the real reason? I can use the work right now, babe, that's the first reason, also because I've got some business to finish up from the first time through. I didn't like the way it ended up and I look forward to doing it right, you know. Besides, I owe you twenty five hundred bucks and I'll be able to pay you back." He said, "Do it!" He added, "If you ever get close to Kingston, give me a buzz and we'll meet at some neutral place."

Boone had picked us up at the bus station and even though I had seen him on the *Fillmore* TV special only a few weeks previous, he had put on a few pounds since and we might have missed him in a crowded room. Arriving at the Berkshire Forum, Butler was unrecognisable with silver hair and beard and I mistook him for a road manager! Jerry Yester still had a full head of red hair and the same moustache as on the cover of *Everything Playing*. Jim Yester looked tanned and fit and not too dissimilar from his old album covers either.

Butler took the role as the host, with Jerry Yester a little cautious and brother Jim witty and warm. Boone somehow seemed like an old friend. After a meal, they all let off steam playing table tennis and before I knew it they were then behind their instruments ready to run through one of the sets they had been rehearsing for the past six weeks. This was an important moment for me. Could they still cut it all these years later? After about a verse of "Do You Believe In Magic", with Butler on vocals, I knew that the reunion had some potential. The entire band played well and the fact that Sebastian was not present did not seem to matter in the slightest.

I reviewed the set for the second issue of *Good Time Music*, highlights of which follow and all this time later I still stand by my original comments; "To hear these tunes sung by a different member of the Spoonful than on the records would alarm most purists but Joe cares a lot for these songs and delivers them thoughtfully, especially on the slower numbers. As the group had been playing solidly for about six weeks they were as tight (in more ways than one) as can be and the songs are played almost exactly the same as the original versions.

Even after all this time, ideas are brought up in an attempt to improve the performance. Before "Younger Girl" Joe suggests that maybe he should not drum on the tune. After some consideration it is decided that this idea is not a good one due to it differing from the recorded track. A new song, written by Jerry's youngest daughter Lena, "Rocks On The River" follows, which changes the mood. This tune is on par with Jerry's greatest moments in Rosebud. "Nashville Cats", sung by Jim is next, which I thought was out of place after such a hot new number. Back to Jerry for "Didn't Want To Have To Do It" in which a superb new guitar solo has been added that adds to the song, although the harmonies were not up to scratch.

Everybody then comes out front for the acoustic part of the show. A bluegrass number, "See Saw" opens this section which is a Jerry composition that is simply delightful. A brief tune from Jim, probably titled "Why Did You Leave Me At The Airport?" is hilarious as is "Henry Thomas", only this time it is Steve who gets the laughs as he blows himself as red as a beetroot on what looks like an air pump during this tune.

Steve then holds his own now, as its back onto the electric instruments for his first and only vocal on his original composition, "If I Stare". I have never heard him sing before (this was before I was aware that he had sung "Priscilla Millionaira") but I can't understand why. Even though Joe calls him "The Lonesome Cowboy" he's no Johnny Cash but this song was a lot stronger than I expected. "If I Stare" has a habit of staying in my head and was my favourite song performed that night after "Rocks On The River".

A fairly pedestrian "She Is Still A Mystery" follows where Joe sings the lead. Something was wrong at the time and the song just fell apart. Jerry, who is the musical director, made the band go through the ending a few times until a satisfactory version was performed. Even though this was done, this song is probably the worst they played that night, strange as three of the four had played on the original.

"Daydream", sung adequately by Jerry, is followed by a rousing rendition of "You Didn't Have To Be So Nice" with all the right sounds coming to the fore including good harmonic work. This tune will get you shouting for more as will "Summer In The City" which ends the set. This is probably my favourite Lovin' Spoonful song ever and I was not disappointed with this version, which had Joe trying his damnedest to break all his drums. At the end we were left with the sound of an explosion from the amps.

Now I was choking it up. I never thought that I would ever see these guys perform, especially to an audience of two! If the group are half as good as they were that night you shouldn't miss them. Don't judge a book by its cover and get ready to be impressed."

⑨ The Lovin' Spoonful at the Berkshire Forum 24/11/91.

Jim Yester

Joe Butler

Jerry Yester

Steve Boone

⑥

ALL PICS

Later that night, Boone put me in front of his video recorder to interview me to discover why I wanted to write a book on the Spoonful. Turning the tables a little, I started to interview him and not before too long, Butler joined in. During this interview they both described the previous few weeks and their hopes for the future. Steve Boone: "Two months ago, when we spoke at the beginning of this rehearsal, I didn't know what to think. If I had to say a hundred was my maximum expectation number, I'd have to say this is ninety nine. I really do mean that too. I think things go in cycles and it just seems, whether it is serendipity or what but our cycle is coming around right now. (An *Ed Sullivan* retrospective had just been released, featuring live Spoonful material). Not only did this come together in a very nice fashion with the four of us gelling really good but it seems people are interested in the Spoonful again, more so than they have been in many years."

Butler then described his personal reasons for wishing to redress the balance regarding the lack of regard for the Spoonful's name since the '60s; "We found out, Steve and I, that it's not what you've done and what you were, it's what the media says you did. It doesn't just sit there; you have to defend it. That's why we want to play, we want to defend a little turf, you know. It's being pecked away!"

On a separate occasion Butler elaborated; "Unfortunately what's happened with The Lovin' Spoonful, I don't want to say it's a fallen flag but it sure has been stuck on the side-lines and John has only used it to carry himself. He's never really championed the Spoonful as much as he wanted it to champion him. I always thought what you done is there, no one can take it away from you but that's not true. Who you were and what you were is what television today says you were then. Guys that we thought couldn't shine our shoes, musically, became legends because they worked the legend. They kept the press up, the tall tales going and pretty soon people would start believing this. We did none of it, we thought it was tacky, we thought it was classless."

Sebastian agrees with Butler on one part of his argument; "One side of it that I really do regret is the fact that so many bands, that I don't think were nearly as good, are viewed today as the founding fathers of rock. People have forgotten the contribution that the Spoonful made as a quartet at a time when there were not really self-contained bands in America. I think it is a tragic mistake. Just for the information of it all not so that I get things to hang on my wall but so that people understand the transitions that jug band music, blues and rock and roll made and the hybrid that happened on Bleecker and MacDougal. It's unfortunate that because it didn't have the splashiness of Jim Morrison taking his pants down or somebody dying that people don't know this."

The joint interview with Butler and Boone made clear that Mark Sebastian was not going to join. On bringing up his name Butler angrily leapt from his chair and threw something into the fireplace before saying, "He kept on coming on like he wanted to get involved!" Boone took over, sensing Butler's annoyance; "He just couldn't make a commitment. At one point I said to him, "Now's the time." We had just reached our settlement and he didn't make a commitment and I said, "Well we've got to go on." As it turned out, this line-up couldn't have been better. I mean for more than just the musical reasons, we get along great. Mark is ten years younger than we are. The four of us are all within a couple of years of each other. I think, personally, organically speaking, it's a great combo."

Butler followed with; "Also it's stronger for us. The industry kept telling us the thing to do was to replicate John's voice. That's what they told us and that's why we pulled towards Mark. We always felt that was a weak-kneed position, to put a ringer in but people kept telling us that's what we should do." In a letter Mark Sebastian told me that he decided to continue working on his current projects, rather than join the Spoonful. Mark is an actor; he has been in *Cheers* and is a member of the Second City Troupe, as well as a singer of his own compositions. One person the pair thought could do the job was the former lead singer of Dr. Hook, Dennis Locorriere. He politely turned them down. I once asked Locorriere to comment on the proposal and he seemed flabbergasted that I knew, mentioning only that the approach was, "kind of unofficial." The interview with Boone and Butler was hurriedly finished on mention of the bust.

We left the Spoonful camp and I alone went on to visit Sebastian in Woodstock. He did not want anybody else to come, although he never really explained why. I had seen him in concert when I was seventeen, so there was no time-warp shock this time. I don't know what I expected but a subdued Sebastian only gave me an afternoon and added little to what we had discussed before. During our discussions it became clear that he was not happy with the reunion. The same day as our interview, the new Spoonful were playing their first concerts since 1967 in Kitchener, Ontario, Canada and they were given a good reception with Boone describing the two shows as, "A real good spiritual lift."

Their next gig occurred in Athens, Greece - of all places - as part of a televised nostalgia concert, on New Year's Eve, 1991 alongside a host of '50s and '60s stars including Davy Jones, Dion, The Mamas & The Papas, The Shirelles, The Comets and Herman's Hermits. The Spoonful's appearance was a disaster. On live television the group had to stand and wait as Jerry Yester suffered a midi-system failure. An argument occurred afterwards and to rub salt into the wounds Boone's bass guitar was stolen. The future was already starting to look bleak when I went to Boca Raton, Florida to see the group's first US show in March, 1992.

The Spoonful were now a five piece with the inclusion of young session drummer, John Marrella, which enabled Butler to come out front and to take some of the pressure off Jerry Yester. From Chicago, Marrella had played with Head East who had been road-managed by the new Spoonful road manager, Ron Lemen and it was through this connection that Marrella got the Spoonful gig. Marrella had only played with the group the night before and even they were still struggling with "She Is Still A Mystery", when I arrived towards the end of the rehearsal.

During the soundcheck this new Spoonful were terrific and lying on a lush green lawn in a huge amphitheatre under a blazing sun, with The Lovin' Spoonful playing "Summer In The City" with hardly anyone else around, is a cherished moment. My enjoyment was short lived. During the two shows there was only an occasional spark of excitement. The group were playing to a funfair audience with loads of noisy kids milling around in front of the stage. To make matters worse, half way through the set an idiot in a mouse costume came on stage to wave at everybody. I was crestfallen. Watching a video of the concert with the group the next day was an uncomfortable experience.

Signed to Pipeline Management, Boone and Butler had also spent a huge amount of money to sign up with publicity company Myers Media. In return all they got was an amateurish press kit and brief articles in US publications *Goldmine* and the New York Daily News, that would have been published anyway. An advert appeared in *Pollstar*, announcing "They're back and they're hot!" Unfortunately it also announced that one of the Spoonful's hits was called "Rain On The *Road*". Now it seemed they were being pushed into being a nostalgia act, whether they liked it or not.

Love from The Lovin' Spoonful
10TH
ANNUAL
meet me downtown
BOCA RATON
MARCH 6·7·8, 1992

MAGIC

JUG BAND

YOUNGER GIRL

CATS

DIDN'T WANA HAVTA

MAKEUP YOUR MIND

SEE-SAW

CIRCUS

HENRY

MYSTERY

DAY DREAM

SO NICE

SUMMER

The group had a surprising ally in Sebastian (who was always happy that the Spoonful split before having to hit this type of circuit), when I told him of my disappointment, "That is unfortunate, Simon. This is the way it goes for pop musicians. I think it's a very difficult choice because the gigs that you are offered seek to further the stereotype and I mean all I can tell you is I've been in their shoes. I don't envy the spot but I've been there! (laughs) I've said, "What the hell am I doing here?" a couple of times."

At his home in Florida after the show, Boone showed me a copy of Sebastian's screenplay which turned out to be Sebastian's interpretation of the Spoonful saga, hardly conforming with this book at all. A more self-satisfying, unrealistic and plainly embarrassing version would have been impossible. In his version Sebastian, and to a lesser extent Yanovsky, did everything, with the others dragging him down. Joe Butler is not a great fan of Sebastian these days and the main reason is Sebastian's dismissal of his contribution; "We slowly dwindled in one's eye to where in the scenario, John became Pinocchio, conqueror of the whale and Steve was a staircase and I was a window!"

During our interview, Sebastian had skirted around the issue of his screenplay but did mention that it was a, "slightly sensationalised version." Boone's copy of the screenplay was littered with yellow "post it" notes that pointed out inaccuracies and exaggerations. Off the record he was most upset with some of Sebastian's exaggerations but on tape he was less harsh, "It was dreadful. I mean it gives you some insight into where his thinking process has got to. It's too bad. That's probably why he hasn't had any hit songs; his thinking process has just gone down the tubes. I don't know why."

Even though I had the time, I couldn't finish reading the screenplay as it was too painful and toe curling. I did flip to the end to discover Sebastian describing his triumphant entrance onto the stage at Woodstock, which in reality was his penultimate mass success. Boone also performed for me a re-enactment of his last conversation with Yanovsky where his old buddy angrily hung up when Boone had told him of his intentions to go on the road as the Spoonful.

Hearing the first Spoonful demo, the aptly titled "Unfinished Business", gave me hope that the new Spoonful could still cut it in the studio. Returning to England armed with more interview material I realised a book was more possible than ever. I got to speak to Yanovsky but the mere mention of The Lovin' Spoonful had him scrambling and I too got the same treatment as Boone. Sebastian gives his explanation for Yanovsky's actions; "Steve and Joe made a couple of mistakes along the way to what I thought was a fairly constructive idea of getting back together. They made a couple of tactical errors with Zally and so it's too bad, they missed the boat. They didn't see the long run. They thought they were in a bind, they thought they were in a corner. I knew better but I couldn't make any promises and that's what Joe wanted."

Butler was incensed at Sebastian's attitude. The group were now struggling to get prestigious gigs simply because Sebastian was not in the line-up, yet he still remained tight-lipped, "Even now I don't call people up and tell them John can't sing. I wouldn't do that. What am I going to do, put my hand up his back and move his mouth? Maybe he deserves that but it's not my style."

It was all too clear that the new Spoonful were struggling to hold an audience's interest. The new front man, Butler, was not used to the role and his embarrassing in-between song patter went above the heads of their new audience. I can also remember trying to talk Butler out of wearing a doctor's outfit and performing a little skit before "Jug Band Music", which would have only made matters worse. There was also the problem of Yester stalling proceedings due to his numerable instrument changes.

This last problem was resolved by the addition of another new member, as Boone wrote in a letter from June '92, "I know this seems at odds with the original concept of The Lovin' Spoonful but we must remember that times have changed and in the nineties I think our ability to stay at work will depend a lot on our ability to entertain the audiences that we will be working for. It will also enable the four "members" of the group to be up front all the time as a focus."

Keyboardist David Jayco started in the Spoonful on June 21st at Schiller Park, Illinois in the middle of a meagre 16 date US summer tour. The press was now starting to critique the new Spoonful and taking it all in, the split was right down the middle. Some would describe the group as "sans Sebastian" or "bogus" with one even writing, "Even more criminal, The Lovin' Spoonful will play without John Sebastian." On the positive side there were quotes ranging from, "pedigree of its own" to the slightly over the top, "The group is just as good, or actually better, than they ever were."

The strength of the Spoonful's back catalogue and the reasoning behind all the passion shown by people outside the group (myself included) was soon demonstrated to them in a bizarre way. Since 1912, the followers of baseball team the Boston Red Sox had endured cornball organ music between the action until a Monday night in July '92 when someone decided to play a record. What did they choose? None other than "Summer In The City".

Sebastian had spent the first part of the '90s making forays into different employment away from singing. These jobs were mentioned in a 1991 letter from his manager David Bendett, who listed; "John recently completed a thirteen week television series called *The Golden Age Of Rock 'N' Roll* which he hosted. John is the host of a syndicated radio show called Rock Stars in which he interviews people such as Paul Simon, George Harrison, Gregg Allman, Chrissie Hynde etc." The letter went on to say that Sebastian puts his "special stamp" on a host of commercials as well as saying that he still performed live, "when the proper occasions present themselves."

Sebastian's most visible performance of '92 came on the crass, yet unbelievably popular US sitcom, *Married With Children*. Alongside a host of old rock 'n' rollers, Sebastian acted his way through a painful couple of scenes, then joined his contemporaries who all sung a parody of "We Are The World"; 'We are the old, we have arthritis.' The embarrassing performance did not bother Sebastian, who was just glad of all the attention, "That was just for fun. They started out with a bunch of Hollywood guys and it really sounded disappointing. I was about to turn it down when they got Richie Havens, Spencer Davis and Robbie Krieger, so it turned out to be a bunch of old friends and it was lovely fun for a week in Los Angeles being treated like Duke Ellington. You have to do that every now and then."

I had not spoken to Sebastian for some time when in February '93, out of the blue, an advert appeared in *Billboard* promoting a new John Sebastian album. After a request for an interview, I only had to wait a day before Sebastian was on the phone. Firstly he explained the background to the release; "The way it came about was that I have an old friend, Stefan Grossman (who refused an interview for this book) who has been working for some time at Shanachie, producing some of the traditional material that they put out. As they began to make forays into the pop music world, they gave a listen to my record and said they would like to put it out."

In reality *Tar Beach* was really a collection of songs that had started life as early as 1977. Unfortunately Sebastian followed the path of Crosby, Stills and Nash's later recordings and produced a polished pop sound with overpowering drums, which detracts from some of the great songs on offer. The book-ends to the twelve songs were the highlights, giving you hope for what was to come and leaving you believing he still had it in him.

Sebastian had hawked the song "Tar Beach" around with him throughout the '80s and he had horrified his die-hard fans by using a drum machine when he performed the song live. About escaping from the bustle of the city and seeking solace on the rooftops, "Tar Beach" had all the hallmarks of a Sebastian classic with plenty of hooks and an unforgettable chorus. Talking before the album's release, Butler found time to offer his opinion on the song, ""Tar Beach" is a good song. I wouldn't put it down, only there is one line that I hate, 'It's right here in the middle of the madness.' I just hate that; it's not street talk. John has slowly moved himself from the street and lost his handle on the lingo. I like "Smokey Don't Go", that's the one I sang on." Indeed, Sebastian's tribute to The Miracles, complete with Motown riffs, includes a reunion of sorts, albeit from the mid '80s, between Butler and Sebastian as the former recalls, "It was in the city and John asked me if I could work on something and I said, "Sure." But I had to pick it up in the studio. I would like to have had some time with the song." On the album Butler is inaudible.

All twelve songs were written by Sebastian, with help from Levon Helm from The Band on the rare duet "Someone's Standing In Your Door" and on four songs by one Phil Galdston. Galdston had jointly won the American Song Festival grand prize in 1975 for the song "Why Don't We Live Together?" and had become friendly with Sebastian helping out on some of his children's projects. He co-produced *Tar Beach* alongside Sebastian.

There are no real loose links in the collection. The deep and personal "Freezin' From The Inside Out" and "Don't You Run With Him" cannot be compared to any happy-go-lucky love songs as, for once, there are none on offer. Sebastian grows up on this album (omitting to mention the slush that is "Try'na Keep The Balls In the Air") and the maturity is matched by his ability to hide his vocal problems although one critic did say, "His modest voice suffers some minor but noticeable mid-range dropout, which leads to the occasional strained moment."

In one of the few interviews he did at the time of release, Sebastian spoke of the background to a couple of the songs, ""Bless 'Em All" is a theme song for a dark, urban Nixon-era political thriller movie made on the cheap about five years ago. "Try'na Keep The Balls In The Air" was a tune that I wrote for James Burrows. He is the director and writer for several good American TV shows like *Cheers* and *Taxi* and he was trying to do a series about a kind of Yuppie woman executive type who was fighting the modern problem of a career and family. The series, I think, eventually didn't fly."

The closing number has Sebastian displaying the dark side of nostalgia, as opposed to the lighter "You And Me Go Way Back". The song, "Night Owl Café", superbly illustrates visions of a trip back to the site of his earliest success as well as snapshots from that moment in time and expresses the sadness that it all had to end, alongside the fact that the place has now fallen away even more. With poor promotion (the press release was packed with errors), little airplay or reviews, the compact disc, Sebastian's first, slipped away unnoticed. This was a tragic shame as the album as a whole is up there with *John B. Sebastian*.

By early '93 The Lovin' Spoonful suffered a setback when Jim Yester left the band. Even as far back as the concert in Boca Raton, Jim seemed to have something on his mind and was a completely different character to the one Andy Tillett and I had met in Stephentown. The very same day that Jerry Yester moved inland to Arkansas to be near his brother, Jim moved to Atlantic City. Jim then formally quit The MFQ. Jerry Yester informed me of the news in a letter from March '93; "Jim has left the group to join The Four Preps. We did our first gig without him in February. He's been replaced by an old friend of mine named Randy Chance. Randy and I go back to 1972 in Chicago where I met him while I was teaching a course in performance at Columbia College there. He's one of the best guitarists I've ever known. Also, we have a new keyboard player. My daughter Lena! We're all excited about the new line-up. We're recording demos in L.A. starting March 22 and things are definitely looking up."

Having a woman on board was going totally against the grain of Spoonful lore and Butler, quite rightfully, objected. He soon relented, as the options were limited. Lena's first performance with the group was on a TV show in Holland followed by a brief tour of Germany with Suzi Quatro (!). I went out to see the group play in Florida in June, '93. By then Randy Chance had already been sacked, with the group deciding not to replace him.

It was still an outdoor family audience they were playing to but the Spoonful were starting to click and this was to be a far better performance than the one I had seen over a year ago. The front three were singing and playing well, Yester had started to play the autoharp and this gave a sort of authentic look and sound to the group. I particularly remember looking around to see who was performing the accurate, blistering guitar solo in *Do You Believe In Magic* to find that it was none other than Lena Yester. This very shy, quiet, intelligent student (she was only seventeen) had no stage presence but was an accomplished guitarist and keyboard player who enhanced the overall sound.

In fact it was Lena who was the most consistently impressive when I got to hear the demos that the group had recorded in California. Her "Modern Music" and "My Little Heaven", although totally out of place as a Spoonful demo, showed what a talent the group had. Jerry Yester's tracks sounded like follow-ups to his solo album and also seemed to be in the wrong setting. With Boone not even contributing it was left to Butler to write the best song on the demo. "Freeboy" proves that Butler still had the force within him, with the help of Yester's musical skill whose arrangement is brilliant and their collaboration is clearly the highlight of a very "Wilson Phillips" sounding tape. The material is too far removed from the Spoonful of old and in some ways I hope it never reaches the outside world.

The rest of 1993 and 1994 for the Spoonful was spent on the oldie's circuit in the States, sometimes playing alongside The Association, Micky Dolenz or headlining over a ragbag of one-hit wonders. Sebastian was also hitting the concert trail as he had now gone full circle and formed the J-Band with friends James Wormworth,

MYERS OF KESWIC

Fritz Richmond and Jimmy Vivino, the guitarist from *Late Night with Conan O'Brien* show. This was Sebastian's foray into jug band music and I guess a worthy attempt to hide his vocals.

Joe Marra went to see the J-Band at a New York performance in September '93 and reported, "I was at the Lone Star Roadhouse a couple of months ago. He didn't have half the voice he had. John can't sing." Boone had also seen Sebastian in concert around this period. Along with his wife, Susan and Butler's first wife, Lesley, Boone sneaked out of his show in Florida when Sebastian had attempted a Spoonful medley. To make matters worse Sebastian saw them leaving. One song on the *Conan O'Brien* show swiftly followed by an appearance on the *Prairie Home Companion* radio show in April '94, however, showed the potential of the ensemble when Sebastian did not have to sing for too long. Richmond's jug and washboard techniques, Wormworth's brush work, Vivino's slide guitar and Sebastian's kazoo playing added an individual and unusual authentic touch and in the days of MTV Unplugged the future was looking rosier again.

Sebastian received some mainstream notoriety in 1994 as he managed to play at Woodstock 2, twenty five years on from his notorious performance. Teamed up with Fritz Richmond on jug, Sebastian gasped his way through an unfortunately broadcasted version of "Daydream" to a bemused younger generation. Sebastian enjoyed the experience, "I was with CSN for a minute and I also did my set with the jug band on the other stage. It was the first thing on Sunday morning while the Gospel thing was going on the big stage, while people were waking up. It was really kinda cool."

There was to be a smaller festival on the site of the original Woodstock, organised by Billy Driscoll, which went ahead even though only 2,000 tickets were sold. It was interesting to compare Sebastian with the other old timers who managed to perform at Woodstock 2. Whilst a scaled up version of The Band were faultless, CSN and Bob Dylan showed that Sebastian was not the only one who had suffered after all the ensuing years on the road. Sebastian, in one of his biggest ironical exercises, also appeared in an amusing television commercial for Pepsi to commemorate the festival, sending himself up when he asked Country Joe McDonald, "Joe, do you remember when we did this twenty five years ago?" "No," replied McDonald.

A reunion of The Lovin' Spoonful almost occurred early on in 1995. The reason was unfortunately due only to the appearance of 'Summer In The City" in the film *Die Hard: With A Vengeance*, the sequel to the sequel of the Bruce Willis vehicle. Initially the producers of the film had wanted the original line up to re-record their biggest hit. Mark Sebastian knew one of the producers and cut the proposed deal, on the assumption he could get his brother into the recording studio. John Sebastian expressed an interest in the idea, but only if Jacobsen produced and, surprisingly, if it include Butler on vocals. John Sebastian and Butler even discussed the project over the phone.

Fortunately, Sebastian then had a change of heart, "There was a moment when they were asking me specifically if I'd like to re-record it and I expressed some reluctance because, you know, and don't you just hate those Jerry Lee Lewis recuts that don't have the fire? I just didn't want to get into it." In the end, after turning down a new version by Isaac Hayes, the producers opted to use the original Spoonful version to open their movie. "Summer In The City" was even re-issued as a single to coincide with the film's release but, like the film, it was a disaster and didn't chart at all.

The Spoonful's repertoire was now in the hands of RCA/BMG and a spokesman for the company admitted that they failed to cash in on the single, even with the video making it onto MTV. They did release a two on one CD of the *Do You Believe In Magic* and *Hums Of The Lovin' Spoonful* albums but with poor sleeve notes (albeit with the addition of some stunning Don Paulsen photos, something he couldn't manage for this book) there was nothing new. They even admitted they couldn't get a hold of the master tapes.

The Spoonful had played some dates in Japan in '95 alongside Chubby Checker of "The Twist" fame. Checker introduced the group to his management company and the Spoonful soon left Pipeline Management, whose head, Gordon Singer, was leaving the business anyway. This new deal would lead to a lot of new bookings for the group who were now at least adding several new songs to their set, as well as a few covers.

After many cancellations, Sebastian finally made it over to the UK for a week of shows in November '95. Without managing to bring over the entire J-Band, Sebastian was accompanied for the shows by the "essence" of the group, Fritz Richmond. After gigs in Dublin and Cambridge, the pair arrived for a poorly sold concert at the Astoria Theatre in London, where the promoters closed the balconies and put seats out in an attempt to fill the venue. I went to the sound check only to find a tense Sebastian not acknowledge my presence. He had recently been sent an early draft of this book, which may have been a reason. I found out later that he had recently approached a journalist to help with his autobiography.

Sebastian sparked up for the performance, although he was addressing me when he referred to the new Spoonful as "a cruise version of The Lovin' Spoonful". The concert was quite a triumph, with Sebastian managing to sing fairly well throughout. Unexpected reprises of "Pow" and even "Summer In The City" were refreshing as were new songs including "Just Don't Stop 'Till You All Worn Out". Sebastian and I spoke briefly after the show but there was no chance of any further interview. In contrast Fritz Richmond was very forthcoming on a host of topics and expressed his enthusiasm for his role in the band.

Unfortunately the poor attendances continued throughout the rest of the tour with Mike King of CMP Promotions noting that, "By the last date he'd had enough." CMP made a loss on the tour but still hold some hope of bringing over the complete J-Band one day. In reality the shows were poorly promoted and while he was in the country Sebastian only appeared on Greater London Radio and VH1. On the plus side, the gigs inspired fan John Knox to start a Sebastian fanzine, *The Red Eye Express*, which includes contributions from Fritz Richmond amongst other interesting Sebastian related features. Sebastian also had his parents bedtime story *JB's Harmonica* published by Harcourt Brace as a children's book with illustrations by Garth Williams, Sebastian's godfather.

1996 started on a sour note when Mark Sebastian filed a lawsuit against the Spoonful's current publishing company, Hudson Bay Music, over him not being paid the correct scale for his contribution to "Summer In The City". Indirectly Mark was suing his own brother as well as Steve Boone. In a pre-trial hearing, John Sebastian gave a deposition that totally slammed the Spoonful's former management and record company. During the hearing tempers were lost and at one point Mark Sebastian even asked a lawyer to step outside during an argument! The case cost both Boone and John Sebastian several thousand dollars. Fortunately, in the end the matter was settled out of court and John Sebastian's deposition remains unpublished.

Things became worse for Boone when his mother passed away. Both Sebastian and Yanovsky telephoned Boone offering their condolences and the sad event sparked off a civil exchange between Boone and Yanovsky, which carried on afterwards. Yanovsky was becoming more visible, when it was announced that he had been nominated for the Canadian Music Hall Of Fame alongside David Clayton-Thomas, John Kay, Domenic Troiano and old friend Denny Doherty, with a special achievement award going to Ronnie Hawkins.

According to Yanovsky's friend, publisher Bob Hilderley, Yanovsky was reluctant to accept the nomination at first but soon relented and became quite flattered to be remembered and regarded so highly by the Canadian music fraternity. On a different note, Yanovsky had just received his first press in years as ownership of a plaster cast of his genitalia (along with others including Hendrix and Eddie Brigati from The Rascals) had been awarded to Cynthia "Plaster Caster" Albritton, who had sued Herb Cohen for the return of her plaster moulds.

On March 9th, 1996, Yanovsky, with current wife, Rose Richardson, former wife Jackie and daughter Zoe attended the award ceremony. Each of the inductees received a tribute in person and a video review of their career. Yanovsky, at his own request, was introduced by Sebastian. Author John Einarson, who was at the ceremony as a guest of John Kay, reports on the occasion, "John gave a warm speech highlighting their early years before and during the Spoonful and Zal's importance to the group. The video presentation on Zal was about ten minutes long and included some rare recording studio footage, circa 1966"

Sebastian walked to the stage with a bemused look as the backing music was "For What It's Worth" by The Buffalo Springfield. His delightful brief speech was broadcast, "Zally would be the first to say that he was one quarter of a band but in all honesty, Zal was more than a quarter of that band. On stage Zal was our greatest asset, our unmeasurable quantity – he was our fire and our humour. We relied on his intuition, on his sense of spontaneity and his fear of being predictable." After the video presentation an emotional Yanovsky appeared on stage with Sebastian for the first time since *One Trick Pony* and gave him a long hug, before saying, "Stay here John. " Yanovsky then starts to pretend to read the autocue, "Zal has always been gracious...no really, thank you." He then continued, "For me this is sort of like a real step back because I've not been doing music really for almost 25 years." Then somebody in the audience says something inaudible and Yanovsky quickly reacts with, "But there's always tomorrow. In any case it's really kind of awkward, sort of cheating that I'm here but now that I'm here, er, I really feel, I guess I really do share this with you (Sebastian). I think I'm really choked up. Thanks a lot." The pair quickly leave the stage with an arm around the shoulders of the other.

Einarson continues, "At the end of the formal ceremonies, the inductees and their introducers (who included Michelle Phillips and Robbie Robertson) joined a stage band of top musicians for a musical presentation, each taking a turn for two songs. John and Zal donned guitars for "Jug Band Music" and "Did You Ever Have To Make Up Your Mind" and, although a little rusty, they were obviously having a ball on stage. (The night before Sebastian, Yanovsky and others including members of The Band had played a secret gig nearby). At the end everyone joined Ronnie Hawkins for a rousing version of "Bo Diddley", with Sebastian on harmonica. On the Sunday show (a televised special) the six were brought up on stage for a brief tribute and were shown video clips from the evening before. The whole weekend was a marvellous experience."

Yanovsky took it all in his usual stride and his attitude to all the publicity shows his current concerns as when he was asked about the Canadian Hall Of Fame and his award he replied, "I didn't know there was one. They asked who I would like to be my inductor, so I said I'd call John Sebastian and that was cool. He came up and we played - that was fun. You have to give an acceptance speech - it was a big dinner, you've seen them on TV a million times. So for two weeks I was on every major TV show, out of the woodwork they were crawling. Then I just said, "Listen I've been here for fucking twenty years, fuck you!" more or less but it was great for business as it was the slow time of the year and I wore restaurant T-shirts on television! Anyway, they gave me a plastic thing with my face on it. It sits on my mail, it's cute."

One of the many requests for his time came, unbelievably, from Koppelman as Yanovsky recalls, "I just got inducted to the Canadian Hall Of Fame and I got a note from some flunky at EMI saying, "Please come to the EMI suite, Charles wants to see you." That fucking cocksucker he owes me a quarter of a million dollars he can go and fuck himself, thank you very much. I'm sure he didn't relay the message. I was tempted to go. I always called those guys Koppeltheif and Robber." With the idea that Yanovsky may be more receptive in helping out with this book, Karl Baker (fresh from briefly re-uniting The Magicians) approached him and managed to secure an interview for July at Chez Piggy. By his own admission Yanovsky's attention span is pretty short and Karl failed to gather much new information. After a night reading an early manuscript of this book, Yanovsky only gave another audience of forty five minutes before Karl gave up, shook hands and went on his way. Yanovsky had already given a much more expansive interview to *Goldmine* magazine and seemed not to relish adding anything to this book.

KINGSTON, ONTARIO
10 A.M. IN AUGUST
Aerial view of Kingston's downtown waterfront with the modern marina depicted in the foreground.

KINGSTON, ONTARIO
À 10 H, AU MOIS D'AOÛT
Vue aérienne de la berge du centre-ville de Kingston, affichant sa marina moderne à l'avant-plan.

So what does Simon say?!?
Zal

Photo: Larry Zarysky
Published by Photo Decor Ltd.
P.O. Box 522, Gananoque, Ontario K7G 2V1
Printed in Canada

Canada 90

Chez Piggy Restaurant
68-R PRINCESS ST.
KINGSTON, ONTARIO
(613) 549-7673
Rose Richardson Zal Yanovsky

CHEZ PIGGY
RESTAURANT

WHAT HAS MADE US
KINGSTON'S FAVOURITE
FOR OVER 17 YEARS?
COZY, FRIENDLY
SURROUNDINGS
AN EAT-IN GARDEN
FRESH INNOVATIVE DISHES
& VINTAGE WINE.

AND NOW THERE ARE EVEN
MORE REASONS...
INCREDIBLE BREAD
& ASTONISHING DESSERTS
DAILY FROM OUR VERY OWN
BAKERY & TAKE OUT,
PAN CHANCHO.

Two days after the Canadian Music Hall Of Fame dinner, Sebastian released the long time in coming J-Band album entitled *I Want My Roots*. The ensemble effort, including guests Paul Rishell, Annie Raines and Rory Block, has Sebastian contributing vocals to only five of the fourteen songs on offer but nonetheless it is a delightful current day interpretation of jug band music. *I Want My Roots* is a joyful, dare I say it, good time music album, with all the right musical ingredients. As Jim Lee correctly stated in his review in *Dirty Linen*, "The music is folky, funky and rocky in a delightful acoustic way. Equally important to the jugband sound is acoustic blues, and there are some fine examples to be found here. Though Sebastian gets top billing, his fellow J-Band members are of equal importance to this project."

After finally putting down a studio version of his concert opener "Mobile Line", Sebastian sings, with Jimmy Vivino, the title tune, which refers to the intention for the album; 'I want my roots, I might need them back someday.' A song from Sebastian's set in the early '70s follows. "Goin' To German", a Gus Cannon number, is more than adequately sung by Paul Rishell. In April '95, Sebastian and Richmond had performed at "Gus Cannon Day" in Memphis where a new headstone was unveiled by the grave of Cannon. Richmond gave a eulogy from the heart before joining Sebastian to perform Cannon's "Viola Lee Blues" playing the jug that had belonged to Cannon.

The only other new Sebastian songs on *I Want My Roots*, alongside well-chosen covers of early country blues and jug band material are "Just Don't Stop 'Till You're All Worn Out", inspired by meeting Dizzy Gillespie, still playing shortly before his death, the self-describing "Ain't Nowhere To Hobo Anymore" and "Rain, Hey, Rain", Sebastian and Vivino's attempt at an original blues.

The icing on the cake for this CD is the addition of an original member of The 3 J's Jug Band (with Sleepy John Estes and Jab Jones), eighty five year-old mandolin player James "Yank" Rachell. Discovering his existence from a mutual friend, The J-Band travelled to Indianapolis to record with the master. The three songs recorded with Rachell are delightful musical moments, interspersed with Rachell's stories from his life, "which left us all like kids at bedtime, begging for just one more story," said Sebastian in the sleeve notes.

The overall sound of the album alongside the polished performances of the ensemble makes for a positive musical future for Sebastian. More of this kind of stuff will keep his fans happy, as John Knox said in his review of *I Want My Roots*, "The album is about John going back to his influences, back to basics. John has laid it on the line with this album. No catchy TV tunes here, this is where John comes from musically; this is where John is happiest. This is John Sebastian at his very best!" Amen.

EPILOGUE

In mid '96 all the members of the Spoonful were sent an early manuscript of this book to give them the chance to respond to any matters of concern. Their reaction or lack of it put me off publishing. Sebastian, Yanovsky and Yester failed to respond. I heard through Boone that Yanovsky had hated it and Yester, "got mad and quit reading." Boone and his wife seemed unimpressed whilst only having nit-picking comments to make. Nobody had any problem with the facts, just that it all came across rather negative as a whole ("Where's the jokes?" was Yanovsky's initial response.) On the positive side, Karl Baker spent several hours with Butler going over the manuscript and he was really helpful with ironing out details and setting the record straight. Boone promised to redress the balance by writing a foreword and sending more material about his time after the Spoonful but this never happened.

My last contact with Boone came in September of 1996. There had recently been a Spoonful meeting where it was announced that Lena Yester was leaving the band. Boone too was getting bored of just playing the hits; "Everybody got a little addicted to the paycheques but I think if we don't take control of our destiny we'll end up like John's letter (to Scott Johnson) said we would." Boone wanted to be more selective in their concert schedule and raise their price. According to John Marrella, Boone had also announced that he would leave the group at the end of the year. He and Susan had started a couple of businesses locally and Boone thought his time would be better spent concentrating on those.

Boone also had thoughts of a reunion of all five original members to benefit a charity, whilst also helping to promote their back catalogue (Yanovsky was interested in making money and not embarrassing himself, Sebastian, being consistent, just wanted them to play together to see how they would sound) and thought that this book would be a politically dangerous thing that would put his idea in jeopardy. Although this wasn't personal; "I don't think you're upsetting any apple carts any more than anybody else would in the circumstances."

Come April of '97 the Spoonful were still together but Marrella had had enough of playing second fiddle and quit the band. He sent me a harrowing 18 page hand-written confidential letter describing how poorly he thought the Spoonful and their set-up had treated him in his five years with them. I, too, had become a little tired of it all and decided not to publish this book. I had lost all interest and had moved on. In New York for a couple of weeks with Andy Tillett again, we met up with Butler one morning in the Village. Whilst it was nice to see him, we both got a little tired of the Spoonful bickering and at times had nothing to say.

But things were still happening. The Spoonful had just started an internet site informing their fans of where they were playing and what they were doing and in July came interviews with both Sebastian and Boone in the US magazine *Discoveries*. Whilst Sebastian's interview was one of his most interesting, helped by being asked intelligent questions by John DeAngelis, Boone's was a little more spin doctorish with him sounding not at all like the man I knew. Whilst Boone promised a new Spoonful album yet again, Sebastian talked of his attempts to get Yanovsky involved with his Jug Band.

Then Lo and behold, in September, Yanovsky agreed to a three-date tour with the J-Band in Denmark of all places. (Between them Greece and Denmark have seen the entire Spoonful perform in recent years.) Reports on the tour were non-existent although a few pictures did appear on the Internet. According to Sebastian, Yanovsky would have followed him and Fritz Richmond to the UK but this coincided with the Saratoga Horse Races. This five date mini-tour of the essence of the J-Band came at the same time of Lady Diana's death and before the final show at the Jazz Cafe in London, Richmond and his wife walked the short distance from their hotel to view the flowers laid down at Kensington Palace.

The London show on September 7th started with a solo Sebastian playing his adapted tribute to Diana, "She's A Lady", which was spoilt by an overzealous photographer. When the show got going, Sebastian's mood was superb and he and Richmond performed a wonderful fresh show, even venturing into the audience at one point. At this show Sebastian would play material by Lightnin' Hopkins and Mississippi John Hurt as well as a tribute to the recently deceased Yank Rachell. He also chose more songs that suited his vocal range and less Spoonful material, which didn't detract from the audiences' enjoyment. With a CD to sell, Sebastian would talk and sign autographs for anyone who stayed on.

With less gigs to play, Boone started playing under the pseudonym of Flasher in a group called Forq. He had touted the idea of the Spoonful playing these songs under the name Spoonlight but was fortunately vetoed. The other members in this Abba looking ensemble remain unidentified but a spy tells me the girls are Lena Beckett nee Yester and her sister Hannah whilst the other guy is Mike Arturi, the new Spoonful drummer. They can be seen and heard on their own Internet site (www.forq.com). Go there if you must.

The Rock Family Trees programme on BBC television finally got around to including the Spoonful, whose story was retold alongside that of The Mamas & The Papas and The Blues Project on September 4th 1998. Whilst it was welcome to see a record of all of this, the Spoonful segment was a rather tamed down version of events with Butler and Boone more restricted by the cameras than the others, leaving Yanovsky to star with his mischievous wit. Also memorable is Butler's vacant expression during the credits. The accompanying book strangely included one Annabelle Yonge as a member of The Sellouts in the Spoonful Family Tree. I knew her as I had sent her a photo of the Spoonful for the programme. Speaking to Pete Frame who researches and draws the Trees, he said he'd put the BBC producer in for a laugh and that I, "was probably the only person who would ever notice."

In late '98, out of the blue, there appeared the first and probably only ever Spoonful bootleg. What was basically a CD compilation of Spoonful TV appearances and a Sebastian live show, was livened up by the addition of a recording supposedly taken from the recording session of *Do You Believe In Magic* - takes 17 to 25. The tape had turned up years earlier on a bizarre mix of sound collages and spoken world material sent by a fan. Then I had dismissed the Spoonful section as a hoax, as the in-between song chatter was not the group in my mind. However, Karl Baker took the recording and slowed it down a notch and I am now 95% sure it is the Spoonful or at least Sebastian and some friends. The origin of this fascinating tape recording is unknown.

More old material came out of the woodwork when Varèse Sarabande released material recorded by the members of The Mamas & The Papas before their fame. Given the task of writing the sleevenotes, Richard Campbell went further than most, locating members of The Smoothies, The Halifax Three, James Hendricks and even Roy Silver (whom I had told the world had died in some sleevenotes for a Big Three reissue). As well as locating some unreleased material by The New Journeymen, the album *Before They Were The Mamas & The Papas...The Magic Circle* contained some of the demos from Erik Jacobsen's collection including the version of "Tom Dooley" with Yester, Diltz, Elliot and Hendricks and "Oh Suzanna (The Banjo Song)" with Yanovsky singing lead.

The Vice President of Varèse Sarabande, Cary Mansfield, persuaded Jacobsen to send him tapes of what else he had in his garage - hopefully for some future release but at the very least preserving these recordings before they got lost forever. These include six mixes of "Warm Baby" sung by Sebastian from before the Spoonful, D & Z's (Doherty and Yanovsky) "I Got The Word" and "Do The Slurp", two mixes of "Fun" by The Mugwumps as well as some unreleased Big Three and MFQ recordings. One thing that almost came to light, but has still to appear is Jacobsen's pre-Kama Sutra tape of the Spoonful live at the Night Owl which, according to press reports includes versions of unreleased covers such as "My Baby Left Me", "Route 66" and Tim Hardin's "You Say You Love Me". Sebastian had expressed a wish for the company to release his next project but instead Varèse Sarabande became the company to release the first Lovin' Spoonful album since 1969.

The Lovin' Spoonful Live At The Hotel Seville was a CD I approached with caution. After spending hundreds of pounds to see the group only a few years earlier, here I was in Tower Records debating with myself whether or not to buy the over-priced import. Part of me was dreading what it would be like as I'd heard the group was now doing gigs like Amway conventions and I really thought they had lost all musical integrity. How wrong I was. *Live At The Hotel Seville* is much better than any fan of the Spoonful could have hoped for. Fortunately this was an unplugged show the group had recorded whilst in Yester's neck of the woods during some recording work. Everyone is on top form (in the end only Marrella left the group) and Mike Arturi seems a welcome addition, having a little more feel for the songs.

Having endured the power drums and synthesiser of earlier concerts, here was the Spoonful similar to when Andy Tillett and I had first seen them when they performed their acoustic interlude. The relaxed setting allowed the group to shine and the in-between song chatter, with Boone jokingly chastising the audience for not recognising them from their old album covers and the like going down a storm. The group decided to keep their new material for another day, although the set does end with the Yester favourite "Don't You Just Know It" made famous by Huey Piano Smith and the Clowns. Highlights of the album include great versions of "Never Goin' Back", "Six O'clock" and even an acoustic "Summer In The City" but the high spot is the reworking of "Didn't Want To Have To Do It" which almost surpasses the original.

Not to be outdone, Sebastian then came up with a new J-Band album *Chasin' Gus' Ghost* on Hollywood Records. Keeping the same musicians from the previous album with the welcome addition of the re-emerging Geoff Muldaur singing on "Minglewood Blues" and "Jug Band Music" (not the Spoonful song) the album is another gem. Alas, Sebastian sings only on the pedestrian "My Passing Fantasy", "Stealin'" and a retread of "One Step Forward" from the *Welcome Back* album, with the fact coming to light that the song's co-writer, JC Lewis, is in fact

Sebastian's cousin. The album is a continuation of *I Want My Roots* with the pleasing country blues and jug band sounds of the sharp musicians being rounded off by the original master.

Tagged on at the end of the album, from a live recording recorded shortly before his death in April of '97, Yank Rachell blows everybody off the stage when he performs three songs with the J-Band. After his introduction, "I'd dance myself but I can't walk," they all get down to a rousing "Laundromat Blues" followed by a definitive "Tap That Thing" ending with "My Baby Left Town". A great way to end a great album and long may the J-Band run. Sebastian has found his ideal place alongside these talented musicians.

Next came the event that would reunite the original quartet of The Lovin' Spoonful and on a smaller note allow this book to come out guilt free. In late '99 Butler called Karl Baker to inform him that the Spoonful had been nominated for the Rock & Roll Hall of Fame. This typically American idea has a panel of record executives, musicians and journalists who select several musicians into its fraternity every year, the only restriction being that your first recording is over 25 years old. The Byrds had got in back in 1991 but the Spoonful had to wait another nine years (whilst their record label got its act together) before their turn.

The music journals started talking about the group again and Sebastian and Yanovsky were interviewed several times before the proceedings. Sebastian talked up the other members of the group, pointing out Boone's musical prowess and Butler's role in being the motivator within the group before rightfully pointing out there were many living legends much older than he who deserved inclusion. Yanovsky was as playful as ever putting over his story with a few little digs at Butler. In one such interview he aptly claimed, "I always call those things the 'Hollow Fame' award."

Not wanting to be outdone, the newly revived Buddah Records released yet another Greatest Hits package. However, this would be different to much of what had gone before. The company claimed that they had found the original master tapes of the Spoonful's recordings and even posted a picture of the tape boxes on their website. These tapes were remastered under the supervision of Sebastian by the ubiquitous Bob Irwin. With unseen Henry Diltz and Don Paulsen photos and liner notes from the knowledgeable Ben Edmonds (whom I had recently helped with a Fred Neil article for Mojo) the package was an impressive one. Although in expert Karl Baker's opinion the improvement in the sound is not all that revelatory at last the Spoonful were being treated right by their label.

Butler told Baker that all the original line up of the Spoonful would attend the function and that for the two songs they would perform, agreed on "Did You Ever Have To Make Up Your Mind?" and "Do You Believe In Magic". They would meet up the night before for a rehearsal before the 15th annual induction ceremony on March 6th at the Waldorf Astoria Hotel in New York City, which was to be televised by VH1. The other inductees in what was called "The Class of 2000" were Eric Clapton, Bonnie Raitt, Earth, Wind & Fire, The Moonglows and James Taylor.

After inductions by the likes of Paul Simon, Paul McCartney, Ray Charles and Robbie Robertson, The Lovin' Spoonful were inducted, sadly, by John Mellencamp. Mellencamp did his best to describe what the Spoonful meant to him growing up, stating that they produced, "music you could fuck to and dance to at the same time." Mellencamp ended his speech saying, "Great music, at its best, makes the listener believe that the magic's in the music and the music is about them. So congratulations to The Lovin' Spoonful for FINALLY getting inducted to the Hall Of Fame." Before the group appeared a video tribute was shown which unearthed some largely unseen footage including the group playing all the wrong instruments on a TV appearance and a brief glimpse of Yanovsky's "As Long As You're Here" promo.

Walking up the steps to collect their awards the Spoonful came. This was the first time in twenty years that they had been seen together and they all looked in good shape (albeit with a few pounds added due to their current affluence) and not too dissimilar from their *One Trick Pony* appearance. First up the steps came a proud Sebastian in a smart white jacket who shook hands with Mellencamp, then followed a casual Yanovsky in a brown suit still sporting the beard he has worn since the early seventies. Next up came a beaming Joe Butler resplendent in a tuxedo and bow tie who exuberantly waved to the audience. Lastly came a very anxious looking Steve Boone dressed as Butler but without the tie.

Arriving at the podium the group all looked nervous and after taking their bows were looking away from each other, as it was clear nobody wanted to speak first. After Yanovsky suggested they all talk at once, Butler proposed Yanovsky, who in a nod to his current life started with, "First there's a message from the Chef – he wanted to know who ordered the kosher meal?" Then in a classic spin doctor moment, he totally changes the tone from when he was interviewed by Karl Baker, "But other than that, I'd like to thank Bob Cavallo, our ex-manager, Erik Jacobsen, our producer. Really the other guys I played with. I had three wonderful years – I don't remember much but what I do was really pretty good. I want to especially thank John for being a real mensch and for keeping the music in the music business. Like all the inductees tonight, it's all about the music and thank you all very much." Just as he was to step back, Yanovsky added, "And we're glad we're getting the award first.," in a nod to long-running ceremonies.

Boone was next; "Hi. I'd like to thank all of you but really, I love these guys, man, they're my bandmates. They've been my whole adult life – what an experience. Of course I definitely like to thank Bob, Erik, Rich, Danny, Charlie, Don, the whole Kama Sutra crew at 1650 – Artie, Hy, Phil but I'm going to leave that to John and Joe because their memories are a lot better than mine. But there is one person I really do have to thank personally, without him I wouldn't be up here tonight – he's a guitar player- he founded a fabulous ground-breaking group known as Autosalvage. He's also my brother Skip, out on Long Island. Thank you very much and to anybody who's ever encouraged me to go for it, thank you too. This is for you." As he finished, Boone got a pat on the back from Yanovsky who cheered, "Great speech!"

Butler then attempted a joke in reference to Mellencamp's speech: "Hey John, do we have to do all that screwing and dancing at the same time or can we get separate times?" Fortunately he quickly moved on; " I'd like to thank the two people I love the most; my wife Kim who's here and my daughter Yancy Butler, who can't be here as she's working on her show *Witchblade*. I'd like to thank John Sebastian, I wouldn't be here if it wasn't for him." Butler then carries on thanking Boone and Yanovsky, who now can't even look at Butler, "This is the gang I always wanted to run with. I always wanted to be accepted and be one of you – be one of the music makers. This means the world to me, thanks."

Lastly came Sebastian, who started on a playful note; "Well I think it's important that the Lovin' Spoonful start out by thanking a group of men who did something at a time before it was really easy to do – that's being a roadie. This goes back to the days before they had those nice rolling cases, you know. I'd like to thank Al Mamlet, Walter Gundy, Rich Chiaro, Fudge, Charlie Boone and Roscoe Herring. Thank you guys for carrying us a really long way. After getting little response from the people in the industry who made up the audience, Sebastian thanked Erik Jacobsen and Bob Cavallo for their help and guidance before emotionally saying, "I'd also like to thank our Jewish Angel, Cass Elliot," (Yanovsky, standing behind Sebastian exclaims, "Absolutely") and the group and audience start applauding which affected Sebastian who shakily continued, "Because I probably wouldn't have met Zally without Cass – thank you."

Managing to carry on Sebastian, the only member of the band to have a written speech said, "I'd like to thank Fritz Richmond for coming up with our name and for being my jug player to this day. I'd like to thank Mississippi John Hurt for his wonderful song; the great jug band men; Gus Cannon, Yank Rachell – it's a long list – I'm not gonna do the whole list but we owe all of these men an awful lot. We'd like to thank Henry Goldrich at Manny's and I know we still owe him money. I'm sure we owe him money, obviously. I'd like to thank Erik Jacobsen for his beautiful crafting of those ships of sound that travelled out into the airwaves and were strong like Scandinavian ships are supposed to be." Heckling from the back, Yanovsky shouts, "Turn up the guitar!" to Butler's amusement.

Unperturbed Sebastian carried on; "I'd like to thank my brother Mark for his contribution to "Summer In The City" – it was our biggest single and probably wouldn't have been the same without his chorus. We'd like to thank Bob Cavallo for managing the unmanageable, at a time when there just wasn't even a clue. All of us would like to thank the various record companies including RCA, BMG, Rhino and the new Buddah . We'd like to thank Lieber and Stoller, Trio gang and our good luck BMI team.

"Personally, a couple of things I couldn't omit would be a thanks to a guy who opened the studio door to me when I was a kid, fellow by the name of Paul Rothchild (voice croaks) who I miss and while I'm at it I want to thank some people who gave me my first jobs; Harry Belafonte, Jay Berliner, who taught me the charts, and I'd also like to thank my Mom and Dad because the music is in me and for your encouragement and partnership in modern times. Thank you Jimmy Vivino, the J –Band, NRBQ, Phil Goldstein, Yank Rachell, Johnnie Johnson, Dave Bendett, my manager for 25 years; picked me up when I couldn't get arrested and we'd like to thank Al Stein for getting us all out from that trouble, Nick Gordon thanks a million and my partner, my girl, Catherine.

"You were there for me after that first rush of fame and we've been together for over 30 years and it was really you and our sons Benson and Charlie, who did really have to say darling be home soon. Thank you." As Sebastian stepped from the podium he and Yanovsky hugged one another then Yanovsky spontaneously extended his arm to beckon Butler into a genuine moment and before you knew it there was a Spoonful scrum in the middle of the stage and their bond was shown to all. Of course this didn't last long as Yanovsky jokingly tried to kiss everyone and they all fell about laughing. They then moved over to where their instruments were set up before starting with "Did You Ever Have To Make Up Your Mind".

It quickly became evident that the group had barely rehearsed (only an hour according to Yanovsky) and that Sebastian's croakey voice isn't up to performing the song anymore. They all make a hash of it, however, not helped by a bass drum pedal malfunction for Butler who laughs at the end of the tune. Then the autoharp comes out of the mothballs for the last ever performance of "Do You Believe In Magic" It didn't go well. The New York Post claimed that they played, "off-key and out of tempo," however the Hall Of Fame website were kinder saying the performance was played in a "enthusiastic, if loose manner." But under the surface the magic was still there. The look on everyone's faces was enough for me. Even though Boone looked as nervous as he used to on the Ed Sullivan Show, they were all having a ball and probably didn't even care how it all sounded to the outside world. Yanovsky even made a mess of his solo, which made Sebastian laugh, yet it was the glances between everyone that made it all worthwhile. Butler played his drums well and provided neat backing vocals. Yanovsky tried to sing along with Sebastian to try and help him through the ordeal even incorporating Mellencamp's speech at one point; 'and we'll go dancing and fucking at the same time.' As the song came to a close Yanovsky walked up to the microphone to announce their next reunion - "See you in another 30 years!"

It took a few views but their performance does produce the chills. Maybe because I got to know most of them in the time between and know how genuinely proud they would have been (Although I'm sure Sebastian took it at face value) but I'm pleased they reformed for one last time whilst they were all alive and well. The time for a reunion proper had evidently long gone but their charm and singular casual stage presence were still there. The only thing that hangs in the mind is the sorrow that they didn't perform together earlier, when Sebastian's voice was still in good shape. Their performance isn't going to make any young kid go out and buy a Lovin' Spoonful record - they will still have to go out of their way like I did.

The obligatory jam session at the end of the ceremony was pretty run of the mill. Most of the inductees acted bored but Butler did his best to liven things up by enthusiastically banging his tambourine at the side of the stage. Boone chose not to appear. Sebastian looked at home with all the people around and produced a great harmonica solo during James Taylor's "How Sweet It Is". At one point during "Route 66" Butler tried to dance with Natalie Cole at the front of the stage which frightened her away, much to Clapton's amusement. Near the end the orchestrater Paul Shaffer points to Yanovsky to solo which he performed well before ignoring Shaffer and nodding to his old friend Clapton to follow suit.

At the following press conference when asked how it felt to be nominated, after being ignored for so many years Yanovsky joked, "We thought Pete Rose would get into the Baseball Hall of Fame first." (Non US readers this is like Hansie Cronje getting an award for cricket.) A few days after the ceremony Butler gave the reporter from the Metro Guide Cable Show (a local New York cable TV channel) a tour of the Spoonful's village haunts. The enjoyable and entertaining half-hour broadcast included the amusing highlight of Joe Butler greeting the guy behind the counter at Bleecker Bob's saying; "Hi, I'm Joe Butler from The Lovin' Spoonful – I've just been indicted into the Hall Of Fame." Ensconced in a small room after the ceremony for a private Spoonful party, where wives and friends mixed with Jacobsen, Cavallo, Dan Moriarty and others from the Spoonful gang, Yanovsky reverted to his normal self. He bitched about the choice of wine on offer, then looking around at all his old colleagues, raised his hand and asked loudly, "Who all here got fired!". Asked a while later about any further reunions, Yanovsky rightly claimed, "I'd say we'll never get together again. Maybe in the next life."

Sadly these words were to prove prophetic when on Friday 13th of December, 2002, Zalman Yanovsky died at his home of congestive heart failure. Tragically, he was only 57. The news came totally out of the blue. Whilst his love of the horses, parties and food and drink had all been evident, I do recall Yanovsky chastising Karl Baker at the start of their interview, for not coming down and watching him play 2nd base in a local softball match the previous evening. In 2004, Larry Hankin remembered his last meeting with his brother in arms; "I saw him for a couple of hours maybe two or three years ago at a friend's house – he seemed the same as always. A little heavier, thicker, but the same Zally; sharp and funny and extremely sociable." Personally speaking, I totally regret not making a pilgrimage myself to Chez Piggy. I'm sure I would have been up for a hard time as Yanovsky had "sped read" an early draft of this book and was not impressed. Though, saying that, the only time I briefly spoke to him on the phone he had been civil and honest.

His shattered friends on the board of the Kingston Literacy Society decided to inaugurate the "Zalman Yanovsky Volunteer Service To Literacy Award" in his honour. This yearly award still honours the local teaching volunteers who embody the spirit of giving. It turned out that alongside his various charity functions at Chez Piggy, a humble Yanovsky, without actually telling his fellow board members, was a regular visitor to Rideau Heights School where he tutored several students. At the time of his death, Yanovsky and wife Rose had also been writing a follow-up to their excellent and useful *Chez Piggy Cookbook* that had come out in 1998 to some acclaim. My copy is stamped with the award of "Winner of the 1999 Cuisine Canada Cookbook Award." Daughter Zoe helped finish this and the *Pan Chancho Cookbook* (named after the bakery the Yanovsky's opened in 1994) was published in 2006. The previous year Rose Richardson had passed away also, sadly followed by Yanovsky's first wife Jackie Burroughs in 2010. Poor Zoe.

The tragic news came in the middle of the most exciting time in years to be a Spoonful fan, as their albums were being re-released on CD in remastered form with the addition of unreleased material. This would be the first time the Spoonful tapes would be remastered properly (by Bob Irwin and Rob Santos at Sundazed) and initially the results sounded cold and flat to me, a view Erik Jacobsen agrees with. However, after a few plays, I found my ears tuned in a little better and now love these versions. Of course, the addition of bonus tracks had this Spoonful geek salivating. On the debut appeared the only unreleased song from the original group, Yanovsky's raucous take on "Alley Oop", which is no masterpiece but a welcome addition to the cannon. I had been told by everyone that the song had been recorded for the Elektra *What's Shakin'* album, so its appearance was a surprise. This was followed by a demo version of "Younger Girl" (with a glockenspiel backing), alternate versions of "Blues In The Bottle"(with totally different lyrics) and "Wild About My Lovin'" plus a stunning instrumental backing track of "Other Side Of This Life".

Daydream's extra delights are an early run through (take six, in fact) of the title tune, where lyrics and arrangements where yet to be finalised. A demo version of "Didn't Want To Have To Do It" is interesting to compare to other demo recordings of this song; Alan Lorber was an arranger in the 60's who'd helped out on the original "Do You Believe In Magic" demo. He also was heavily involved in the Mugwumps recordings. In 2007, Lorber released *Here's A Song (You Might Have Missed)* a compilation CD of his private recordings. Alongside music from Anthony Newly and even Chevy Chase were two amazing versions of "Didn't Want To Have To Do It" sung by Cass Elliot backed by Yanovsky and Sebastian, probably recorded just before the Spoonful came into being.

Other extras are an alternate version of "Fishin' Blues" (which may have come from *Tiger Lily)* and an instrumental of "Jug Band Music" with Yanovsky's fuzzy guitar a delight. Why the Frankenstein remix of "Night Owl Blues" appeared on the wrong album is not known but to hear the original intention of the instrumental sadly failed to live up to the hype. A few years later, to celebrate "Record Store Day" in 2011, Sundazed paired this version with "Alley Oop", adding a retro-style cover for a collectible vinyl 45. The company has also released vinyl versions of the first three albums.

For *Hums* the bonus material consisted of "Darlin' Companion" as a solo demo and an alternate vocal and mix version, a "Rain On The Roof" instrumental, "4 Eyes" in an alternate vocal/extended version with Boone's fuzzy bass out front, a terrific "Full Measure" instrumental, as well as an even madder version of "Voodoo In My Basement" in instrumental form. On the rear sleeve appeared a nice tribute from Peter Buck of REM and sleevenotes from the superb drummer from The Smithereens, Dennis Diken (I witnessed the first UK tours of both these bands). The well ran dry when it came to *Everything Playing* as only single mixes (by Joe Wissert) of "She Is Still A Mystery", "Only Pretty, What A Pity" and "Try A Little Bit" are included. The incomplete sleevenotes were a frustration also, though the reissue does include a unique picture on the rear cover which shows where the future lay - just look at Sebastian's face in contrast to the others'.

These remastered versions were later combined into a box set "Original Album Classics" in 2012, one of a series of budget reissues. This box set includes Butler's *Revelation: Revolution '69* but sadly not the soundtracks. Here the extras were just as slim, with a welcome addition of Butler's rerecording and the original 45 mix of the title song and a single mix of "Me About You". Whether any more recordings from the vaults will appear is unknown, although there are other tapes out there but I'm not allowed to say who has them.

A poorly produced DVD featuring the Spoonful is still available. Titled *Do You Believe In Magic* in the UK and *Summer In The City* in the US, it features Sebastian discussing the history of the group and their songs. This and the footage of the group from US TV shows including *The Ed Sullivan Show* and *Hollywood Palace* and others were welcome but the fake dubbing of audience noise and the views of a so called expert were annoying. Instead of the notorious performance of "Darling Be Home Soon", the producers included an excellent version from a solo Sebastian show circa '73, which was the only new performance on the DVD. The DVD is only an hour long but the extras have Sebastian and Dennis Doherty paying tribute to Yanovsky plus the bonus of a brief (one minute, come on) interview with the man himself . The major UK magazines have now all incorporated a Spoonful feature into their archives – Peter Doggett and myself wrote one for *Record Collector* in 1992, then the best one appeared in *Mojo* in July 2002, featuring an interview with Jacobsen (you've got to interview Jake) and Don Paulsen photos and *Uncut* published a solid piece in August 2011.

Whilst keeping up a regular concert schedule, the new millennium found Sebastian keeping up his interesting projects. In 2004 he played George Farmer in the film *Messengers.* The same year he appeared in the documentary *John Lennon's Jukebox.* This delightful road movie-type trip around the theme of Lennon's recently discovered portable record player (with his 60's handwritten track listing on its lid) and currently visiting the musicians whose records he'd chosen. Sebastian is shown in his back garden to be delighted that the Spoonful appear and went on to tell his Beatle stories. One new one was that during the *Let It Be* sessions, The Beatles had attempted to record "Daydream". These days, thanks to *You Tube,* we can all hear the band start up the tune, with Harrison seemingly particularly keen, helping out by calling out the chords, before it all crashes and burns with Lennon exclaiming, "Damn tunesmiths!" Further proof of the Spoonful's influence on The Beatles, also out in the cloud, is a picture of McCartney from late '66 leaving a doorway clutching a copy of *Hums*.

Sebastian and the same Dave Grisman from the Even Dozen Jug Band days, released *Satisfied* in December 2007. A delightful offering, recorded live in the studio, from these two veterans was welcome indeed. Evidently needing a Jewish accomplice again at his side, the pair gel with Grisman's sublime mandolin playing and Sebastian's improving vocals failing to mar re-treads of lesser known Spoonful classics ("It's Not Time Now" and "Coconut Grove") which fit in perfectly amongst Mississippi John Hurt tunes and other Country Blues material. The album happened concurrently with a filmed documentation of a reunion of the Jug Band fraternity (including Bob Weir, Erik Darling, Geoff Muldaur and Maria Muldaur) and the history of Jug Band Music in Mark Kwait's *Chasin' Gus' Ghost*, with Sebastian featured owning up to how it more than helped with his Spoonful classics.

A CD document concert recording of all of this, *Jug Band Extravaganza* appeared some time later in 2010, shortly followed up by Kwait's next documentary, *Vagabondo,* which Kwait produced with the help of Mark Sebastian. The subject was none other than Fred Neil's old partner and marathon-talker, Vince Martin, (frustratingly the film has only been shown in the States and is not yet on DVD). At the time of writing Vince has left the Village and lives with family in Las Vegas. A Fred Neil book and documentary from Peter Neff is in the works. Meanwhile, the lifetime achievement awards were still coming for Sebastian. In June '08, he was honoured by the Songwriters Hall Of Fame at a lavish ceremony awards show in New York City. Accompanied personally for the evening by Catherine and musically by Steve Boone - the two Spoonfuls performed "Lovin' You" and "You Didn't Have To Be So Nice" together on stage. This time they left it for somebody else to ruin "Do You Believe In Magic" with a youngster from The Naked Brothers taking the vocals and murdering the song. Scary footage appeared online of Sebastian patiently dealing with forceful, demanding autograph hunters after this show.

One significant appearance for Sebastian came at Sting's Rainforest benefit at Carnegie Hall in 2010, where he played alongside Elton John and his band's rendition of "Summer In The City". The Eels were performing this song as an encore around this time, also. In 2012 another of Sebastian's old projects was resurrected by Gary Cohen, a long time Spoonful fan who wrote to me after this book's initial run; "I have run a large theatre in New Jersey for the past 25 years. Two years ago I wrote, and we presented, a children's musical based on JB'S HARMONICA, John's book. This was done with John's blessings, in fact, we recorded the "harmonica" solos in Woodstock with John playing.

"As a side note it is interesting that I could not sell this show to any of the theatrical licensing companies --- a testament to the lack of respect for John's music. I had initially approached John about a full-scale adult musical about his life, using his music, and he told me that his life was too normal for such a venture. I then became friends with his wife Catherine, and have exhibited her photographic images at a number of art shows in Lambertville, NJ, and have also screened the documentary CHASIN' GUS' GHOST at a local boutique movie theatre, and John came and talked." Indeed Catherine Sebastian has an amazing website full of her artistic photographs and some of John and his musician friends, including some awesome pictures of Fred Neil. Coincidently, Lorey Sebastian went on to a very successful career as an on-set movie photographer, being the photographer of choice for the Coen Brothers films and many more.

Sebastian was again honoured in 2012, when he received the Silver Eagle Patriot Award. Like his father did before him, Ben Sebastian performs under an alias, Ben Vita and has released a couple of albums with some input from Father John, who is now a Grandfather. In 2014, a box set of Sebastian's 70s studio albums was released with a cherry on top – the inclusion of Sebastian's *In Concert* performance from the BBC archives which had not been seen in its entirety since 1970. Sebastian keeps up a superb website, which at the time of writing has a healthy concert schedule. Whilst Sebastian has kept his word and is still yet to perform with the touring Spoonful , a rare reunion came on October 13th, 2011. Henry Diltz's rock photography business, The Morrison Hotel Gallery, celebrated its tenth anniversary with a party in New York. The MFQ performed a brief set with the highlight being a guest appearance of John Sebastian on "Good Time Music" – this being the first time Sebastian and Yester have appeared in public together since the sixties.

Yester has been kept busy in these recent times, as he has a studio at his house in Arkansas, Willow Sound, where he has recorded amongst many others; Eric Bibb, Dave Guard's daughter Catherine Guard and the dulcimer music of Dennis Lee. A group consisting of Jerry, brother Jim and daughters Hannah and Lena formed The Yesters and released a self-titled album in 2009, finding a home for "LA Riverbed" from an earlier Spoonful demo (just like when Boone's "If I Stare" came out on *Forq Chops).* Another interesting tune was "Elegy For Jeff Buckley", whom Yester had seen perform and had been amazed by, written with Larry Beckett.

Jerry also added to his cannon with the impressive *Sentimental Journey,* a collection of standards spiced with the recent Dylan song "Make You Feel My Love", a retread of "Mrs. Conner" and new Beckett/Yester composition "The Minutes". Alongside his Spoonful commitments, Yester has stayed with the MFQ, who have enjoyed several Japanese tours (playing warm-ups in California) as recently as 2011. For the encore of a Jerry Yester solo gig in Jan 2013 in Altadena, California, the four members of the MFQ ambled onstage and after a lengthy discourse performed a delightful version of "Hanalei Moon". A new live Spoonful CD to sell at their concerts, recorded at the Lyric Theatre, Harrison, was another Willow Sound production. Recorded by Scott Hoffman and the first recording of the group with new guitarist, Phil Smith, the souvenir includes the usual hits as well as Butler's quality "Me A Man". The accolades were coming in for Boone and Butler, also, as The Lovin' Spoonful got voted into the Vocal Group Hall Of Fame in 2008 (where they performed sans Sebastian) and the pair made it into the Long Island Music Hall Of Fame in 2012.

As early as 2004 it was announced on the Spoonful's website that Butler was penning his memoirs, although nothing has yet appeared. Butler had a tortuous emotional start to the 2000's, with daughter Yancy arrested in January 2003, after a fight at her uncle's Hauppauge NY, home with her father. Yancy was charged with criminal contempt for violating an order of protection and two counts of harassment. Later in November, she was arrested again on a disorderly intoxication charge. Yancy was suffering a prescription pill addiction which she has subsequently fought in a rehabilitation facility. The father and daughter combo had previously enjoyed acting together in one of Yancy's many TV series *Witchblade,* where Joe had played her father, Arnold Buck. Things didn't get any better for Butler at his Greenwich Village home where a nearby hotel's noise violation had him protesting to the authorities.

Butler has also performed at *Hair* reunions and on occasion he sings with some of the other members from the early casts, in tribute shows that benefit the Doctors Without Borders charity (hopefully they skip the nude scene). Butler also dusted off his political chops, prior to Obama's first election victory, recording the song "Save America" with Even Steven Levee for a download. Another promised venture of a one-man show, which sounds promising, is yet to happen.

Steve Boone's autobiography was published in August, 2014, some six months after this book's first appearance. Typical, you wait 50 years for a Spoonful book.... The revelations for this train spotter author were few on the Spoonful front but his drug smuggling stories are gripping. The book deserves to be thought of in the vein of the more worldly interesting rock biographies like Mark Everett of the Eel's as well as Dylan and Neil Young's offerings. Boone's delightful turn of phrase and skill in writing puts this effort in the shade and one selfishly hopes his efforts will spur the others into a similar effort. It's a given that you, the reader, would have read Boone's book before this one but without any presumption, I'd like to think my research was at least a rough guideline for Boone's superior effort. I was glad I didn't get a mention after the treatment John Marrella got, although I should point out that he had already left the group when he wrote to me. I know I became a pain in Steve's butt whilst researching my book and I'd like to apologise for that here. Steve was always cordial towards me; he and Susan even let me stay at their home and it is a huge regret to me that I am no longer in touch.

In fact, looking back, I had spent more social time with Boone than with any other member of the group. He told me at the time that one day he wanted to write his memoirs, so it was always difficult to get him in front of my tape recorder, even though he helped me to buy a microphone. Loads of Steve's stories from the book came flooding back to me (the Ferrari, Mandy's Smith's mum etc.) on reading *Hotter Than A Match Head,* as I'd heard them in the car, or in a bar or at a memorable visit to his swimming club. His wife at the time, Susan, who was a tremendous help to me (although she always seemed to want to control everything) would keep me away from Steve with her demands. The longest time we spent in front of a tape recorder was when Boone's car was boxed in at my hotel. That was the night he tried to copy my well-practised trick of opening a beer bottle on the side of the sink. His effort comically sent glass and beer everywhere. I also remember that I spent one day stuck at a Fort Lauderdale dockside bar waiting to interview Steve – which wasn't totally bad thinking about it – who never showed, as he had been reigned in. Although none of this is my business but Boone's referencing to Susan in his book reinforced my concerns from that time, as she was never as chilled as Steve, to put it one way.

Boone had mentioned previously (in the sleevenotes for the reissues in reference to "Bald Headed Lena") that his wife was named Lena and when I first read that I was a little stunned . Lena had become an impressive bodybuilder since her Spoonful days and was now unrecognisable to me. Their relative age difference and the fact Lena is Jerry's daughter don't seem to have affected the Spoonful outwardly in any way, which is healthy. Thinking back to the time I briefly knew them both, I can see their connection. As a sidebar, I'll always remember Lena's deft way of getting stuff out of the minibar without paying! Boone's heavy admission of his addiction to heroin had been evident in his appearance with Sebastian at the Fillmore. The book stemmed from a superb Blue Seas article in Baltimore magazine by Tony Moss, who co-wrote Boone's book also and who should be commended for a fine job.

Reading Boone's autobiography on the same day as the tragic death of Robin Williams, made me think that we are all so lucky that the principals in this book are mainly still with us (touch wood). Obviously people are missing (Fritz Richmond sadly passed in 2005) just look at the credits page in this book, but in the main the periphery around the Spoonful are getting ready for the chair on the porch. Robert Cavallo retired in January 2012 from his position as chairman of the Disney Music Group, fortunately. He and Jon Lind from the Fifth Avenue Band (who'd moved behind the scenes) were responsible for Miley Cyrus in later years so we can all be thankful. Don Rubin seems to have retired but not Mr. Koppelman!

Charles Koppelman appeared on NBC's *The Apprentice; Martha Stewart* in 2005 as Stewart's right hand man (an American Nick Hewer, I guess, British fans). He also continues to head the boards of many companies and there is no sign that age is going to stop him His latest move in 2014 was when he was appointed chairman for Medient Studios Inc. . His Wikipedia page has the strange by-line warning that it has been written by a "major contributor with a close connection with its subject"! Erik Jacobsen, who after the Spoonful produced Norman Greenbaum's smash hit "Spirit In The Sky" as well as all the Chris Isaak hits, has been seen in the Phil Ochs documentary *There But For A Fortune* in 2011 and heard in a 2005 Radio 2 documentary on Tim Hardin that also featured Sebastian. He is still producing, however, recording *Full Mental Nudity* with Brian Elliot in 2014. One contemporary artist, Jonathan Wilson on his superb album *Fanfare* from 2014, raided Jacobsen's masterwork (Sopwith Camel's reunion album *The Miraculous Hump Returns From The Moon)* for a tremendous, if similar sounding "Fazon". His memoirs would be amazing. Also, it should be mentioned, you could count on one hand the amount of groups from the sixties still together in their original line up and one of them is The Modern Folk Quartet. Even Autosalvage reformed in 2013 to play at the SXSW festival. Sadly, Skip Boone is in poor health and couldn't make it but the rest of the group played well, with Sam Page in for Boone plus the addition of Mark Davenport and Banana from The Youngbloods.

As I said at the beginning, 2015 will be the 50th Anniversary of The Lovin' Spoonful and I know Sebastian and Boone still meet up and write songs together, so who knows what they have in store regarding a celebration? My advice to commemorate the occasion would be to wait for a rainy day, then venture onto YouTube and type in Lovin' Spoonful. Put on some headphones, then start with the electric, priceless only real live concert performances from *The Big TNT Show,* then take in the *Ed Sullivan* footage, ("Only Pretty, What A Pity" has recently surfaced) check out the delightful "Rain On The Roof" promo, the backstage Toronto footage etc. Before you'll know it a whole afternoon will have passed and you will have remembered what a superb group The Lovin' Spoonful were.

So kudos must go to John Benson Sebastian, Joseph Campbell Butler, John Stephen Boone, Jerome Alan Yester and Zalman Yanovsky. Rest In Peace, Zal. And as Steve Boone beat me to my clichéd ending, I'll use an old one in reference to the future for these fine musicians; "As long as they all enjoy themselves and continue their good living that would be fine, like Sebastian says, "I'm checking off the list of things I want to do before the big nap."

TECP-98904-
TO KAM LOVE FROM
Steve Boone
THE BAND
ORIGINAL
The
Lovin' Spoonful

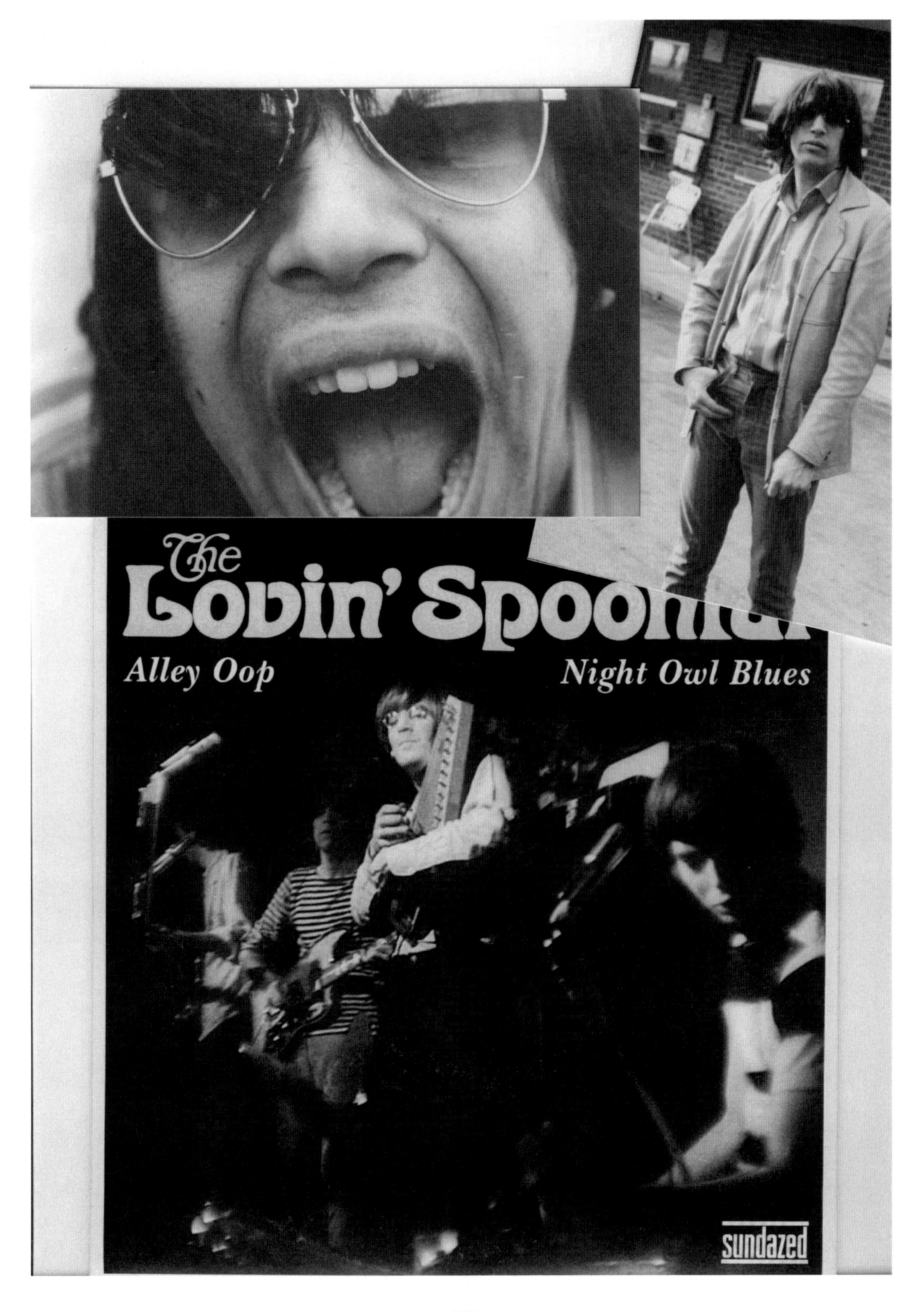
The
Lovin' Spoonful
Alley Oop
Night Owl Blues
sundazed

ACKNOWLEDGMENTS

In the age of the photocopier, I was able to gather a lot of material on the Spoonful from cuttings people sent to me from all over the world. Some stuff I tried to get permission to use but failed. Some stuff I got permission for and used. Some stuff was integral to the work and I just had to use it for the good of the project. If your work falls into that last category I apologise and will willingly add a credit to any further editions. The writers/editors of the magazines/books that fall into the second category are Jeff Tamarkin and William Ruhlmann from *Goldmine*, John Tobler and Pete Frame from *Zig Zag,* Paul Williams from *Crawdaddy*, Don Paulsen from *Hit Parader*, Dorothy Wade and Justine Picardie from *Music Man*, Mike Plumbley, Vic King and Pete Turner from *Isle Of Wight Rock*, Jud Cost from *Cream Puff War* and Peter Doggett from *Record Collector*. I thank these people for their kind permission to quote from their pioneering work.

For the interviews that I travelled across the Atlantic for, or just picked up the phone, I thank; Steve Boone, Joe Butler, John Sebastian, Jerry Yester, Erik Jacobsen, Henry Diltz, John Marrella, Jim Yester, Mark Sebastian, Skip Boone, Larry Hankin, Joe Marra, Sarah Koppelman, Vince Martin, Chip Douglas, Peter Eden, Nik Venet, Tim Rose, Howard Solomon, Don Paulsen, Sid Griffin, Stephen Pague, Benjamin Herndon, Guy Phillips, Davy Jones, Eric Burdon, Fritz Richmond and Phil Steinberg. Zalman Yanovsky was interviewed for this book by Karl Baker. I also briefly spoke to the following people who helped corroborate information; Camilla McGuinn, John Phillips, John Densmore, Scott McKenzie, Elaine "Spanky" McFarlane and Dennis Locorriere. Thanks also to all the secretaries and journalists who helped make these interviews possible. I should mention here that I did contact the following, who all refused to be interviewed; Charles Koppelman, Don Rubin, Bob Cavallo, Stefan Grossman, Fred Neil and Joe Boyd.

Others who helped beyond the call of duty are; Teri Adams, Jim Bradt, Ken Clayburgh, Andrew Darlington, John Einarson, Brian Hogg, Scott Johnson, Andrew Matherson, Craig Morrison, John Morton, Akihide Nakamura, Graham Ritchie, Colin Escott, Derek Barker, Bob Irwin, Catherine Sebastian, Kim Butler, David Terralavoro, Lena Boone, Chrystal Klabunde, Jon Storey, Ian Anderson, David Houseden, Chrissie Oakes, Graham Pedder, Colin Davey, Robert Steinberg, Joe Foster, Colin Larkin, Mike King, Jim Seal, Rick Williams, Tish Woodman, John Knox, Richard J. Sewell, Richard Campbell, Gary Cohen, Terry Delaney and David Hinckley.

Special thanks must go to the people whom without their encouragement and efforts, this book would never have got as far as it has. Thanks to Brian Seaton who has been the lifeblood of the project, always sparing time for the cause. Thanks to Susan B. Peterson for all her initial work, going out of her way to assist me with photo research, typing up interviews and for encouraging me to go back to school. Thanks to Mike Plumbley for seeing the project home with his expert skills and enthusiasm. Thanks to John Tobler for his help in editing. Thanks also to my main correspondents who, regardless of the cost, kept sending material and support; Debbie Grinell, Kathi Kennedy-Guido and Steve Harvey. Most appreciation has to go to Karl Baker for all his research, his encouraging phone calls, putting The Magicians back together, getting Zal on board and thanks also to Jackie for putting up with us both during a freezing week in New York. God bless to the spirits of Bill Hicks, Sam Kinison, Charles Bukowski and Jeff Buckley. Also, a tip of the hat to Marc Maron @ WTF for inspiration.

Thanks also to the people around me who didn't think I was mad to be doing such a thing. Cheers to good friend Andy Tillett for being someone I could depend on for honesty, encouragement and for paying for his round. Cheers to Paul and Lisa Schofield, as well as Richie, for their hospitality and kindness in putting up with Andy and me during our frequent stays in New York. Cheers also to Brother Richard, Andy Hayes, and more recently Scott Sargent, Steve Smith, Mark Keane and Jim Harris. This book is dedicated to my parents June and Richmond - thanks for all that you do for me and for getting me out of the holes I dig for myself. Right! Who fancies helping out on a biog of Tim Hardin?

Photo Captions and Credits:

I have tried to use material that you can't access with a quick google check, although I imagine that some of it is out there somewhere. It was a major frustration that I couldn't convince Don Paulsen to provide any of his amazing photos for this book, however, a lot of them (and some rare shots from the "Daydream" recording sessions and Zal with The Mamas & The Papas) have turned up at the internet site Getty Images and I recommend you check that out. Cover design by Andy Morten for Pepperbox; photo © Henry Diltz. All photos and memorabilia are from the authors collection unless stated.

Page 6 – Artwork from Spoonful tour programme.

Page 10 – The classic line-up circa 1966. L-R Zal Yanovsky, John Sebastian, Steve Boone and Joe Butler. (Courtesy Joe Butler) Autographed in the 60's for Joe's future wife Kim Ablondi, whom Butler married in 1982.

Page 28 – Early Studio Portrait of Joe Butler circa 1961/2. (Courtesy Joe Butler)

Page 30 – The Kingsmen pictured without Steve Boone and Sonny Botari. Top; L-R Skip Boone, King Charles, Seth Conners, Jan Buchner, Joe Butler and Clay Sonier. The Kingsmen's Business Card (Courtesy Joe Butler and Skip Boone)

Page 33 – Butler in front of The Sellouts bass drum circa 1964. As this book was going to press, the contract releasing Butler from The Sellouts appeared on eBay from the estate of Herb Cohen. Signed on the 11th March, 1965, the deal entitled Cohen to a half percent of the recently named Lovin' Spoonful's first "twelve sides" and is counter signed by Bob Cavallo. I'm sure Cohen would have ensured he got his money, Yester once told me he had grenades in the boot of his car, so this deal probably made Cohen rich enough to start his music labels. (Courtesy Joe Butler)

Page 41 – L-R Fritz Richmond, Joe Butler and Joe Marra taken at the Night Owl circa 1966. (Courtesy Joe Butler)

Page 50 – "Song Hits" the Spoonful's first cover, from the agreement with Don Paulsen. (Courtesy Joe Butler)

Page 52 – Spoonful promo picture. Picture taken outside strip club were they were playing. Notice the classy painting of the woman's legs that would spread on opening the doors.

Page 56 – Flyer for "The Tribute to Sparkle Plenty" concert with still from "What's Up Tiger Lily".

Page 58 – Songsheet for "You Didn't Have To Be So Nice".

Page 61 – Magazine advert for the first album.

Page 66 – Flyer from The Supremes Tour. (Courtesy Joe Butler)

Page 68 – Lobbycard from "The Big TNT Show".

Page 69 – Still of Sebastian with his autoharp from "The Big TNT Show".

Page 72 – UK Songsheet for "Daydream".

Page 76 – Bell Sounds acetates for "Bald Headed Lena" and "Full Measure".

Page 83 – The original contract for the Marquee performance signed by Cavallo, who got 50% of the Door.

Page 86 – "Hit Parader" cover.

Page 88 – The flyer for the notorious gig in San Francisco. A Lobbycard for "What's Up Tiger Lily". The two concert snapshots circa 1966 (with Cavallo standing behind the drums) (Courtesy Bun E Carlos). Butler and Boone with (I think) Henry Lewy. (Courtesy Joe Butler)

Page 97 – Songsheet for "Rain On The Roof".

Page 101 – Songsheet for "Nashville Cats".

Page 104 – Promo photo from TV appearance. Butler crowns Sebastian with some flowers. Looks like it wasn't always Yanovsky winding up John.

Page 111 – Street Hand-out from the Communication Co. "Beat The Heat". (Courtesy Paul Williams)

Page 113 – Press Hand-out from the Communication Co. (Courtesy Paul Williams)

Page 116 – Songsheet for "Six O'clock". Artwork by John Sebastian.

Page 119 – UK Songsheet for "Darling Be Home Soon".

Page 131 – The full page advert printed in The Berkeley Barb. "The Lovin' Spoonful Are Finks".

Page 135 – Bell Sounds acetates for "Six O'clock" and "Money". The latter has an extended fade.

Page 136 – Proofsheet from notorious 5 Spoonful's photo session. (Courtesy Jerry Yester) photo © Henry Diltz.

Page 137 – Songsheet for "She Is Still A Mystery".

Page 139 – Songsheet for "As Long As You're Here".

Page 146 – Songsheet for "Money".

Page 150 – Various snapshots 1966/7. The interviewer is Tim Hudson. (Courtesy Steve Boone)

Page 155 – Various snapshots 1966/7. (Courtesy Steve Boone)

Page 159 – The picture sleeve of "Revelation Revolution '69" with Butler in his "Hair" costume. (Courtesy Karl Baker)

Page 165 & 166 – From a letter to the author from Jerry Yester, helpfully dated March 6, 1970 (!); "The pictures of Zal and Jackie, and Judy and I are from Zal's house in Toronto, in Sept. '68. Judy and I were on our way to California, and stopped to visit them on the way. We stayed a couple of days, and Zal and I discussed possible future "Hairshirt Productions" projects. The black and white shots of Joe, Zal and Me were taken at Joe's apartment on Bank St. in the Village, in early '68. Joe threw a party, and Zal and I brought a tape of some of the stuff from his album in progress. I remember that we liked Joe's sound system, and frequently brought freshly mixed tunes over to check them out. There's also a shot of Judy and I, as well as Rich Chiaro (Spoonful Assistant Manager) and John Forsha (Spoonful Road Manager and Judy's former accompanist). The other lady's name is Susan, I think, but can't remember anything else about her." That picture was taken at the Cococabana Club in New York 1969. L-R Jerry Yester, Judy Henske, Rich Chiaro, Susan and John Forsha. (Courtesy Jerry Yester)

Page 171 – Top Autosalvage circa 1967. L-R; (I think)Tom Danaher, Skip Boone, Darius Davenport and Rick Turner. (Courtesy Skip Boone) Middle; The Magicians reunited in the late 90's L-R; Garry Bonner, Allan "Jake" Jacobs, John Townley, the late Alan Gordon and producer at the time Peter Gallway. (Courtesy Karl Baker) Bottom; The Oxpetals circa 1968; Benjamin Herndon, Bobby Webber, Dan "Ace" Allison, Guy "Yug" Phillips and Stephen Pague. Don't know who's who, unfortunately. (Courtesy Steve Boone)

Page 177 – Pressbook for "Celebration At Big Sur".

Page 182 – Joe Butler in a performance of "Hair" at the Biltmore Theatre 1969, playbill for Mahagonny. (Courtesy Joe Butler)

Pages 194 & 195 – John Sebastian at his Laurel Canyon home circa 1971. (Courtesy Roger Kemp)

Page 196 – L-R Zalman Yanovsky, John Belushi, Rhonda Coullet and either Bob Hoban or Tony Scheuren. Picture found on internet. (unknown photographer)

Page 202 – Promo photo of Joe Butler circa early 70's. Quality tash! (Courtesy Joe Butler)

Page 214 – A Vinci Quarius Guitar String Package endorsed by John circa mid 70's. John at the Cambridge Folk Festival 1981. (Courtesy Ian A Anderson @ Folk Roots) John at Battersea (Courtesy Me)

Page 217 – The programme for John's Battersea Park outdoor gig in 1984. The author (when he had hair) with John after the show. (Courtesy Andy Hayes)

Page 221 – Promo Photo of Mark Sebastian circa mid-80's. (Courtesy Mark Sebastian)

Page 225 – Cover of Author's fanzine "Good Time Music".

Pages 227 & 228 – Original faxed copy of John's letter to Scott Johnson and indirectly, the others 1992.

Pages 232 & 233 – Snapshots from the Spoonful's first ever performance in front of people (me and Andy).

Page 236 – The Programme for the Spoonful's first gig back on US soil 1992, promo photo with Lena and John.

Page 237 – Set List from the same concert.

Page 242 – Snapshots from my times researching the book in the early 1990s. Top Left; Joe Marra and Joe Butler in a Greenwich Village bar before setting out in Marra's car for a memorable tour of the hotspots. Top Right; John Marrella after a drinks session/interview. Middle Left; Florida gig with Lena (she was way at the back). Middle Right; Steve and his wife at the time Susan B Peterson. Bottom Left; The late Don Paulsen at his home in Long Island. Great guy. Bottom Right; Joe and my old mate Andy Tillett in the Village outside the English Shop.

Page 244 – John Sebastian promo photo from "Tar Beach" Pressbook. Flyer for Astoria Show and photo of John and Fritz from the soundcheck. (Courtesy Brian Seaton)

Page 247 – Postcard from Zal before he read an early draft of this book – "So what does Simon say?" Zal's Business Card and menu from "Chez Piggy". Pictured with Zal is Karl Baker before their interview for this book. (Courtesy Karl Baker)

Page 262 – Japanese Box Set Booklet, probably the only one in the world signed by the 5 Spoonful's. Zal added "original" plus autographs obtained during rehearsals for the last Ed Sullivan performance, where everybody got drunk – check the footage! (Courtesy Karl Baker) Photo of the 5 Spoonfuls © Henry Diltz.

Page 263 – Snapshots of Zal circa '66/7 (Courtesy Steve Boone) with the 45 cover of "Alley Oop".

Page 269 – Picture of a merry Zal and Steve found on Tumblr. (Unknown photographer)

LETTER SENT TO THE SPOONFUL IN THE EARLY 90'S:

Dear Mr. Sebastian, Mr. Yanovsky, Mr. Butler and Mr. Boone,

I have wanted to write to you for a long time and finally decided to go ahead and do it. I'm a little nervous, never having written a letter like this before, but I finally decided to go ahead and try!

I thought the sixties was a neat time; you grew up fast, because there was so much to deal with that the generations before us didn't have; there were all kinds of moral decisions to make and lots of things to think about, the Vietnam War taught a lot about social consciousness and the sufferings of other people (when my brother went to fight, I was so worried about him; then I found myself thinking about the other young men there and the worries and the heartbreak their families were going through; the overwhelming relief when he came back, tinged with the sadness of those who didn't); I had a lot of fun then too; always something going on, stuff to do, different ideas to explore etc. My generation has many more choices than those before us. It's funny how the actions of those who came previously affect those who came later.

The music of the sixties was rich and full; it was a turbulent time, and this was reflected in the type of music that covered a wide range of sentiments and ideas. So much was said in the music that spoke out on the war, personal freedom, racism, the search for what was wanted in our lives, our relationships with the people we live with, our ideas, values and goals. Most of it had a message – it wanted you to think and to question and not to settle back into the complacency of our parents' and grandparents' lives. When the sixties came, everything that had existed until that decade was blown sky high and it seemed as though the pieces rained down on us through the music that we listened to.

Except for The Lovin' Spoonful. You fellows stepped out into a world of chaos and confusion and gave us music to listen to that was just plain enjoyable. When everyone else was protesting, questioning and criticising, you came underneath us to lift us out of it and give us some air to breathe that didn't smother us with controversy, but instead was warm and friendly, and so very refreshing. You brought a lot of smiles to me and a recognition of things that I always knew existed, but hadn't quite grasped.

I was very young (a child) in the 1960s when my big brother, Stephen, first introduced me to your music. It captured my interest, it was diverse – each new song that came out was different than the one before and there was something new to be discovered in each one. There were the playful tongue-in-cheek lyrics of *Did You Ever Have To Make Up Your Mind*? Lazy *Daydream*, the loving (and so pretty) *Darling Be Home Soon,* and enjoyable ones like *Do You Believe In Magic?* And *You Didn't Have To Be So Nice.* *Coconut Grove* is one of the most sensuously mellow songs I've ever heard; I love it. *Nashville Cats* was appealing to me because I spent many summers of my early teenage years in Nashville and I knew exactly what you were talking about. (There is no culture quite like the Nashville culture!)

Summer In The City almost needs no comment; to this day the volume goes up when that one comes on; it is one of the classics in Rock history. It was put together so well; the heaviness at the beginning, leading into the song that crashes down on you, just like the heat of the summer, the blaring of automobile horns, where you can just see the packed city streets with the sweltering heat enveloping them; the relief at night from the heat, when it cools down and people begin to wake up, and live.

I stumbled across you on television a couple of times. I got a kick out of watching you perform – you seemed to be having such a good time! It was fun watching Zal Yanovsky. I was a serious kid and watching him made me laugh. He looked like he was having a good time and the smile on Zally's face would reach all the way up into his eyes and they, too, were smiling and laughing! Just watching him made me feel good and happy!

The pleasure has lasted all these years, even though so much has changed since then. I have accepted the responsibilities of adulthood (along with my husband). Like all people I have rejoiced, suffered, been disappointed, been fulfilled, had my dreams and made endeavours with my life; but the appeal of your music is one of the things that, in a changing world, has remained constant. It has always made me feel so warm and comfortable.

I have enjoyed writing this letter and I hope it brings all of you cheer in reading it. Never forget that your music did wonderful things to people; I for one wanted to express my appreciation to you.

Sincerely,

Letitia (Tish) Woodman.

Made in the USA
Monee, IL
01 October 2024